When the first volume of ⟨barcode⟩ S0-AAA-335 Western philosophy began to appear, critics unanimously hailed
it with superlative praises and realized then the great promise
it predicted. Now that the series has progressed to this present volume there is no doubt any longer that it will be the
standard history of philosophy for many years to come. As
each new volume comes from Father Copleston's pen, it is
increasingly apparent that this series is a remarkable accomplishment due in no small measure to his continued thor-
oughness in presentation and dispassionate objectivity of exposition. A lucid readable style coupled with great erudition
and scholarship has produced an unequaled achievement of
which the critics have said:

"This magnificent effort to probe man's quest for reality
. . . states many of the problems which still face us."

The Commonweal

". . . meticulous scholarship, synthetic power, balance of
emphasis, and breath of appreciation. The style is clear,
flexible, and interesting. . . ."

Avery Dulles, S.J.

"Here is a continuation of the same objective, progressive,
critical scholarship that marked the first volume producing
a skillful, discerning analysis of the interplay of philosophical
currents in Christian thought over eleven centuries."

America

"There can be no doubt that this is the best text of the
history of philosophy now available in English."

The Historical Bulletin

A History of Philosophy

VOLUME 6

Modern Philosophy

PART I

The French Enlightenment to Kant

by Frederick Copleston, S.J.

IMAGE BOOKS
A Division of Doubleday & Company, Inc.
Garden City, New York

Image Books Edition
by special arrangement with The Newman Press
Image Books Edition published September 1964

DE LICENTIA SUPERIORUM ORDINIS:
John Coventry, S.J., *Praep. Prov. Angliae*

NIHIL OBSTAT:
J. L. Russell, S.J., *Censor Deputatus*

IMPRIMATUR:
✠ Franciscus, *Archiepiscopus Birmingamiensis*

Birmingamiae, die 27 Februarii 1959

CONTENTS

PART IV

KANT

PREFACE

It was my original intention to cover the philosophy of the seventeenth and eighteenth centuries in one volume, *Descartes to Kant*. But this did not prove to be possible. And I have divided the material between three volumes. Volume 4, *Descartes to Leibniz*, treats of the great rationalist systems on the Continent, while in Volume 5, *Hobbes to Hume*, I have outlined the development of British philosophical thought up to and including the Scottish philosophy of common sense. In the present volume I consider the French and German Enlightenments, the rise of the philosophy of history, and the system of Kant.

However, though three volumes have been devoted to the philosophy of the seventeenth and eighteenth centuries, my original plan has been preserved to the extent that there is a common introductory chapter and a common Concluding Review. The former will be found, of course, at the beginning of the fourth volume. And the introductory remarks which relate to the subject-matter of the present volume will not be repeated here. As for the Concluding Review, it forms the final chapter of Volume 6, PART II. In it I have attempted to discuss, not only from the historical but also from a more philosophical point of view, the nature, importance and value of the various styles of philosophizing in the seventeenth and eighteenth centuries. Thus the fourth, fifth and sixth volumes of this *History of Philosophy* form a trilogy.

PART I

THE FRENCH ENLIGHTENMENT

Chapter One

THE FRENCH ENLIGHTENMENT (1)

Introductory remarks – The scepticism of Bayle – Fontenelle – Montesquieu and his study of law – Maupertuis – Voltaire and deism – Vauvenargues – Condillac and the human mind – Helvétius on Man.

1. There is perhaps a natural tendency in many minds to think of the French Enlightenment primarily in terms of destructive criticism and of an outspoken hostility towards Christianity, or at any rate towards the Catholic Church. If we exclude Rousseau, the best-known name among the French philosophers of the eighteenth century is probably that of Voltaire. And this name conjures up in the mind the picture of a brilliant and witty literary man who was never tired of denouncing the Church as an enemy of reason and a friend of intolerance. Further, if one knows anything about the materialism of writers such as La Mettrie and d'Holbach, one may be inclined to regard the Enlightenment in France as an anti-religious movement which passed from the deism of Voltaire and of Diderot in his earlier years to the atheism of d'Holbach and the crudely materialistic outlook of a Cabanis. Given this interpretation of the Enlightenment, one's evaluation of it will depend very largely upon one's religious convictions or lack of them. One man will regard eighteenth-century French philosophy as a movement which progressed ever further into impiety and which bore its fruit in the profanation of the cathedral of Notre Dame at the Revolution. Another man will regard it as a progressive liberation of mind from religious superstition and from ecclesiastical tyranny.

Again, the impression is not uncommon that the French philosophers of the eighteenth century were all enemies of the existing political system and that they prepared the way for the Revolution. Given this political interpretation, different evaluations of the work of the philosophers are obviously possible. One may regard them as irresponsible fomenters of revolution whose writings had practical effect in the Jacobin terror. Or one may regard them as representing a stage in an inevitable social-political development, as helping to initiate, that is to say, the stage of bourgeois democracy, which was fated in its turn to be replaced by the rule of the proletariat.

Both interpretations of the French Enlightenment, the interpretation in terms of an attitude towards religious institutions and towards religion itself and the interpretation in terms of an attitude towards political systems and towards political and social developments, have, of course, their foundations in fact. They are not perhaps equally well founded. On the one hand, though some philosophers certainly disliked the *ancien régime*, it would be a great mistake to regard all the typical philosophers of the Enlightenment as conscious fomenters of revolution. Voltaire, for example, though he desired certain reforms, was not really concerned with the promotion of democracy. He was concerned with freedom of expression for himself and his friends; but he could hardly be called a democrat. Benevolent despotism, especially if the benevolence was directed towards *les philosophes*, was more to his taste than popular rule. It was certainly not his intention to promote a revolution on the part of what he regarded as 'the rabble'. On the other hand, it is true that all the philosophers who are regarded as typical representatives of the French Enlightenment were opposed, in varying degrees, to the domination of the Church. Many of them were opposed to Christianity, and some at least were dogmatic atheists, strongly opposed to all religion, which they regarded as the product of ignorance and fear, as the enemy of intellectual progress and as prejudicial to true morality.

But though both the interpretation in terms of an attitude towards religion and also, though to a lesser extent, the interpretation in terms of political convictions have foundations in fact, it would give a thoroughly inadequate picture of eighteenth-century French philosophy, were one to describe it as a prolonged attack on throne and altar. Obviously, attacks on the Catholic Church, on revealed religion and, in certain cases, on religion in any form, were made in the name of reason. But the exercise of reason meant much more to the philosophers of the French Enlightenment than simply destructive criticism in the religious sphere. Destructive criticism was, so to speak, the negative side of the Enlightenment. The positive aspect consisted in the attempt to understand the world and especially man himself in his psychological, moral and social life.

By saying this I do not intend to minimize the philosophers' views on religious topics or to dismiss them as unimportant. To anyone, indeed, who shares the religious convictions of the present writer their attitude can hardly be a matter of indifference. But, quite apart from one's own beliefs, the attitude of *les philosophes* towards religion was clearly of cultural significance and importance. For it expresses a marked change from the outlook of the mediaeval culture, and it represents a different cultural stage. At the same time we have to remember that what we are witnessing is the growth and extension of the scientific outlook. The eighteenth-century French philosophers believed strongly in progress, that is, in the extension of the scientific outlook from physics to psychology, morality and man's social life. If they tended to reject revealed religion and sometimes all religion, this was partly due to their conviction that religion, either revealed religion in particular or religion in general, is an enemy of intellectual progress and of the unimpeded and clear use of reason. I certainly do not mean to imply that they were right in thinking this. There is no inherent incompatibility between religion and science. But my point is that if we dwell too exclusively on their destructive criticism in the religious sphere, we tend to lose sight of the philosopher's positive aims. And then we get only a one-sided view of the picture.

The French philosophers of the eighteenth century were considerably influenced by English thought, especially by Locke and Newton. Generally speaking, they were in agreement with the former's empiricism. The exercise of reason in philosophy did not mean for them the construction of great systems deduced from innate ideas or self-evident first principles. And in this sense they turned their backs on the speculative metaphysics of the preceding century. This is not to say that they had no concern at all with synthesis and were purely analytic thinkers in the sense of giving their attention to different particular problems and questions without any attempt to synthesize their various conclusions. But they were convinced that the right way of approach is to go to the phenomena themselves and by observation to learn their laws and causes. We can then go on to synthesize, forming universal principles and seeing particular facts in the light of universal truths. In other words, it came to be understood that it is a mistake to suppose that there is one ideal method, the deductive method of mathematics, which is applicable in all branches of study. Buffon, for example, saw this clearly; and his ideas had some influence on the mind of Diderot.

This empiricist approach to knowledge led in some cases, as in that of d'Alembert, to a position which can be described as positivistic. Metaphysics, if one means by this the study of transphenomenal reality, is the sphere of the unknowable. We cannot have certain knowledge in this field, and it is waste of time to look for it. The only sense in which we can have a rational metaphysics is by synthesizing the results of the empirical sciences. And in empirical science itself we are not concerned with 'essences' but with phenomena. In one sense, of course, we can talk about essences, but these are simply what Locke called 'nominal' essences. The word is not being used in a metaphysical sense.

It would, indeed, be a serious error were one to say that all the philosophers of the French Englightenment were 'positivists'. Voltaire, for example, thought that we can prove the existence of God. So did Maupertuis. But we can discern an obvious approximation to positivism in certain thinkers of the period. And so we can say that the philosophy of the eighteenth century helped to prepare the way for the positivism of the following century.

At the same time this interpretation of the French Enlightenment is one-sided: it is in a sense too philosophical. To illustrate what I mean, I take the example of Condillac. This philosopher was much influenced by Locke. And he set out to apply Locke's empiricism, as he understood it, to man's psychical faculties and operations, trying to show how they can all be explained in terms of 'transformed sensations'. Now, Condillac himself was not exactly what we would call a positivist. But it is doubtless possible to interpret his *Treatise on Sensations* as a move in the direction of positivism, as a stage in its development. It is also possible, however, to interpret it simply as a stage in the development of psychology. And psychology, considered in itself, is not necessarily connected with philosophical positivism.

Again, several philosophers of the French Enlightenment reflected on the connections between man's psychical life and its physiological conditions. And in certain cases, as in that of Cabanis, this resulted in the statement of a crude materialism. One may be tempted, therefore, to interpret the whole investigation in terms of this result. At the same time it is possible to regard the dogmatic materialism of certain philosophers as a temporary aberration in the course of the development of a valuable line of study. In other words, if one looks on the psychological studies of the eighteenth-century philosophers as tentative experiments in the early stages of the development of this line of research, one may be inclined to attach less weight to exaggerations and crudities than if one restricts one's mental horizon simply to the French Enlightenment considered in itself. Of course, when one is concerned, as in these chapters, with the thought of a particular period and of a particular group of men, one has to draw attention to these exaggerations and crudities. But it is as well to keep at the back of one's mind an over-all picture and to remind oneself that these features belong to a certain stage in a line of development which stretches forward into the future and which is capable of supplying at a later date criticism and correction of earlier aberrations.

In general, therefore, we may look on the philosophy of the French Enlightenment as an attempt to develop what Hume called 'the science of man'. True, this description does not fit all the facts. We find, for example, cosmological theories. But it draws attention to the interest of eighteenth-century philosophers in doing for human psychical and social life what Newton had done for the physical universe. And in endeavouring to accomplish this aim they adopted an approach which was inspired by the empiricism of Locke rather than by the speculative systems of the preceding century.

It is worth noting also that the philosophers of the French Enlightenment, like a number of English moralists, endeavoured to separate ethics from metaphysics and theology. Their moral ideas certainly differed considerably, ranging, for instance, from the ethical idealism of Diderot to the low-grade utilitarianism of La Mettrie. But they were more or less at one in attempting to set morality on its own feet, so to speak. This is really the significance of Bayle's assertion that a State composed of atheists was quite possible and of La Mettrie's addition that it was not only possible but desirable. It would, however, be incorrect to say that all *les philosophes* agreed with this point of view. In Voltaire's opinion, for instance, if God did not exist, it would be necessary to invent Him, precisely for the moral welfare of society. But, generally speaking, the philosophy of the Enlightenment included a separation of ethics from metaphysical and theological considerations. Whether this separation is tenable or not, is, of course, open to dispute.

Finally we may remind ourselves that eighteenth-century philosophy in France, as in England, was mainly the work of men who were not professors of philosophy in universities and who frequently had extra-philosophical interests. Hume in England was an historian as well as a philosopher. Voltaire in France wrote dramas. Maupertuis went on an expedition to the Arctic with a view to making a contribution towards determining the shape of the earth at its extremities by exact measurements of a degree of latitude. D'Alembert was an eminent mathematician. Montesquieu and Voltaire were of some importance in the development of historiography. La Mettrie was a doctor. In the eighteenth century we are still in the time when some knowledge of philosophical ideas was regarded as a cultural requirement and when philosophy had not yet become an academic preserve. Further, there is still a close connection between philosophy and the sciences, a connection which has, indeed, been a fairly general characteristic of French philosophical thought.

2. Among the French writers who prepared the way for the Enlightenment in France the most influential was probably Pierre Bayle (1647–1706), author of the famous *Dictionnaire historique et critique* (1695–7). Brought up as a Protestant, Bayle became a Catholic for a time, returning

afterwards to Protestantism. In spite, however, of his adherence to the Reformed Church it was his conviction that the Catholics had no monopoly of intolerance. And during his residence at Rotterdam, where he lived from 1680 onwards, he advocated toleration and attacked the Calvinist theologian Jurieu for his intolerant attitude.

In Bayle's opinion, the current theological controversies were confused and pointless. Take, for example, the controversy about the relations between grace and free will. Thomists, Jansenists and Calvinists are all united in hostility towards Molinism. And there is really no fundamental difference between them. Yet the Thomists protest that they are not Jansenists, and the latter repudiate Calvinism, while the Calvinists denounce the others. As for the Molinists, they have recourse to sophistical arguments in their endeavour to show that the doctrine of St. Augustine was different from that of the Jansenists. In general, human beings are only too prone to believe that there are differences where there are no differences and that there are indissoluble connections between different positions when there are no such connections. So many controversies depend for their life and vigour on prejudice and lack of clear judgment.

More important, however, than Bayle's views about current controversy in dogmatic theology were his views about metaphysics and philosophical or natural theology. The human reason, he thought, is better adapted for the detection of errors than for the discovery of positive truth, and this is especially the case with regard to metaphysics. It is, indeed, commonly recognized that a philosopher has the right to criticize any particular proof of God's existence, provided that he does not deny that God's existence can be proved in some way. But in point of fact all the proofs which have ever been offered have been subjected to destructive criticism. Again, nobody has ever solved the problem of evil. Nor is this surprising. For it is not possible to achieve any rational reconciliation of the evil in the world with the affirmation of an infinite, omniscient and omnipotent God. The Manichaeans, with their dualistic philosophy, gave a much better explanation of evil than any explanation proposed by the orthodox. At the same time the metaphysical hypothesis

of the Manichaeans was absurd. As for the immortality of
the soul, no evident proof of it has been forthcoming.

Bayle did not say that the doctrines of God's existence and
of immortality are false. Rather did he place faith outside the
sphere of reason. This statement needs, however, a qualification. For Bayle did not simply say that religious truths are
incapable of rational proof, though they do not contradict
reason. His position was rather that these truths contain
much that is repugnant to reason. There is therefore all the
more merit, he suggested, whether sincerely or not, in accepting revelation. In any case, if the truths of religion pertain
to the sphere of the non-rational, there is no point in in-
dulging in theological argument and controversy. Toleration
should take the place of controversy.

It is to be noted that Bayle separated not only religion and
reason but also religion and morality. That is to say, he insisted that it is a great mistake to suppose that religious
convictions and motives are necessary for leading a moral
life. Non-religious motives can be just as efficacious, or even
stronger, than religious motives. And it would be quite possible to have a moral society which consisted of people who
did not believe in immortality, or, indeed, in God. After all,
says Bayle in his article on the Sadducees in the *Dictionnaire*,
the Sadducees, who did not believe in any resurrection, were
better than the Pharisees, who did. Experience of life does
not suggest that there is any indissoluble connection between belief and practice. We thus come to the concept of
the autonomous moral human being who stands in no need
of religious belief in order to lead a virtuous life.

Subsequent writers of the French Enlightenment, Diderot,
for example, made ample use of Bayle's *Dictionnaire*. The
work was also not without some influence on the German
Aufklärung. In 1767 Frederick the Great wrote to Voltaire
that Bayle had begun the battle, that a number of English
philosophers had followed in his wake, and that Voltaire was
destined to finish the fight.

3. Bernard le Bovier de Fontenelle (1657–1757) is perhaps best known as a popularizer of scientific ideas. He
started his literary career with, among other productions, an
unsuccessful play. But he soon perceived that contemporary
society would welcome clear and intelligible accounts of the

new physics. And his attempt to fulfil this need met with such success that he became secretary of the *Académie des Sciences*. In general he was a defender of the Cartesian physics; and in his *Entretiens sur la pluralité des mondes* (1686) he popularized Cartesian astronomical theories. He was not, indeed, blind to the importance of Newton, and in 1727 he published a *Eulogy of Newton*. But he defended Descartes' theory of vortices in his *Théorie des tourbillons cartésiens* (1752) and attacked Newton's principle of gravitation which seemed to him to involve postulating an occult entity. Manuscript notes which were found in his study after his death make it clear that in the latter part of his life his mind was moving definitely towards empiricism. All our ideas are reducible in the long run to the data of sense-experience.

Besides helping to spread the knowledge of scientific ideas in eighteenth-century France, Fontenelle also contributed, in a somewhat indirect way, to the growth of scepticism in regard to religious truths. He published, for instance, small works on *The Origin of Fables* and on *The History of Oracles*. In the first of these he rejected the view that myths or fables are due, not to the intelligence, but to the play of the imaginative faculty. Greek myths, for instance, originated in the desire to explain phenomena; they were the product of intelligence, even if the imagination played a part in elaborating them. The intellect of man in earlier epochs was not essentially different from the intellect of modern man. Both primitive and modern man try to explain phenomena, to reduce the unknown to the known. The difference between them is this. In earlier times positive knowledge was scanty, and the mind was forced to have recourse to mythological explanations. In the modern world, however, positive knowledge has grown to such an extent that scientific explanation is taking the place of mythological explanation. The implication of this view is obvious enough, though it is not explicitly stated by Fontenelle.

In his writing on oracles Fontenelle maintained that there was no cogent reason for saying either that the pagan oracles were due to the activity of demons or that the oracles were reduced to silence by the coming of Christ. The argument in favour of the power and divinity of Christ which consists in saying that the pagan oracles were silenced lacks, therefore, any historical foundation. The particular points at issue can hardly be said to possess great importance. But the implication seems to be that Christian apologists are accustomed to have recourse to worthless arguments.

Fontenelle was not, however, an atheist. His idea was that God manifests Himself in the law-governed system of Nature, not in history, where human passion and caprice reign. In other words, God for Fontenelle was not the God of any historic religion, revealing Himself in history and giving rise to dogmatic systems, but the God of Nature, revealed in the scientific conception of the world. There were, indeed, atheists among the eighteenth-century French philosophers; but deism, or, as Voltaire called it, theism, was rather more common, even though atheism was found more frequently among the French than among their English contemporaries.

4. It has already been remarked that the philosophers of the French Enlightenment endeavoured to understand man's social and political life. One of the most important works in this field was Montesquieu's treatise on law. Charles de Sécondat (1689–1755), Baron de la Brède et de Montesquieu, was an enthusiast for liberty and an enemy of despotism. In 1721 he published *Lettres persanes*, which were a satire on the political and ecclesiastical conditions in France. From 1728 to 1729 he was in England, where he conceived a great admiration for certain features of the English political system. In 1734 he published *Considérations sur les causes de la grandeur et de la décadence des Romains*. Finally in 1748 there appeared his work on law, *De l'esprit des lois*, which was the fruit of some seventeen years' labour.

In his work on law Montesquieu undertakes a comparative study of society, law and government. His factual knowledge was not, indeed, sufficiently accurate and extensive for an enterprise conceived on so vast a scale; but the enterprise itself, a comparative sociological survey, was of importance. True, Montesquieu had had certain predecessors. Aristotle in particular had initiated the compilation of studies of a great number of Greek constitutions. But Montesquieu's project must be seen in the light of contemporary philosophy. He was applying in the field of politics and law the inductive empirical approach which was applied by other philosophers in other fields.

It was not, however, Montesquieu's aim simply to describe social, political and legal phenomena, to register and describe a large number of particular facts. He wished to understand the facts, to use the comparative survey of phenomena as the basis for a systematic study of the principles of historical development. 'I first of all examined men, and I came to the belief that in this infinite diversity of laws and customs they were not guided solely by their whims. I formulated principles, and I saw particular cases fitting these principles as of themselves, the histories of all nations being only the consequences (of these principles) and every special law being bound to another law or depending on another more general law.'[1] Thus Montesquieu approached his subject, not simply in the spirit of a positivistic sociologist, but rather as a philosopher of history.

Looked at under one of its aspects, Montesquieu's theory of society, government and law consists of generalizations, often over-hasty generalizations, from historical data. The different systems of positive law in different political societies are relative to a variety of factors; to the character of the people, to the nature and principles of the forms of government, to climate and economic conditions, and so on. The totality of these relations forms 'the spirit of laws'. And it is this spirit which Montesquieu undertakes to examine.

Montesquieu speaks first of the relation of laws to government. He divided government into three kinds, 'republican, monarchical and despotic'.[2] A republic can be either a democracy, when the body of the people possess the supreme power, or an aristocracy, when only a part of the people possess supreme power. In a monarchy the prince governs in accordance with certain fundamental laws, and there are generally 'intermediate powers'. In a despotic State there are no such fundamental laws and no 'depositary' of law. 'Hence it is that religion has generally so much influence in these countries, because it forms a kind of permanent depositary, and if this cannot be said of religion, it may be said of the customs which are respected instead of laws.'[3] The principle of republican government is civic virtue; that of monarchical government is honour; and that of despotism is fear. Given these forms of government and their principles, certain types of legal systems will probably prevail. 'There is this difference between the nature and form of government; its nature is that by which it is constituted, and its principle that by which it is made to act. The one is its particular structure, and the other is the human passions which set it in motion. Now, laws ought to be no less relative to the principle than to the nature of each government.'[4]

Now, I have described Montesquieu's theory as though it were meant to be simply an empirical generalization. And one of the obvious objections against it, when so interpreted, is that his classification is traditional and artificial and that it is quite inadequate as a description of the historical data. But it is important to note that Montesquieu is speaking of ideal types of government. Behind, for example, all actual despotisms we can discern an ideal type of despotic government. But it by no means follows that any given despotism will faithfully embody this ideal or pure type, either in its structure or in its 'principle'. We cannot legitimately conclude from the theory of types that in any given republic the operative principle is civic virtue or that in any given despotism the operative principle of behaviour is fear. At the same time, in so far as a given form of government fails to embody its ideal type, it is spoken of as being imperfect. 'Such are the principles of the three governments: which does not mean that in a certain republic people are virtuous, but that they ought to be. This does not prove that in a certain monarchy people have a sense of honour, and that in a particular despotic State people have a sense of fear, but that they ought to have it. Without these qualities a government will be imperfect.'[5] Montesquieu can say, therefore, that under a given form of government a certain system of laws ought to be found rather than that it *is* found. The enlightened legislator will see to it that the laws correspond to the type of political society; but they do not do so necessarily.

Analogous statements can be made about the relation of laws to climatic and economic conditions. Climate, for instance, helps to form the character and passions of a people. The character of the English differs from that of the Sicilians. And laws 'should be adapted in such a manner to the people for whom they are framed as to render it very unlikely for those of one nation to be proper for another'.[6] Montesquieu does not say that climate and economic conditions determine systems of laws in such a way that no intelligent control is possible. They do, indeed, exercise a powerful influence on forms of government and on systems of law; but this influence is not equivalent to that of a determining fate. The wise legislator will adapt law to the climatic and economic conditions. But this may mean, for example, that in certain circumstances he will have to react consciously to the adverse effects of climate on character and behaviour. Man is not simply the plaything of infra-human conditions and factors.

We may perhaps distinguish two important ideas in Montesquieu's theory. There is first the idea of systems of law as the result of a complex of empirical factors. Here we have a generalization from historical data, a generalization which can be used as an hypothesis in a further interpretation of man's social and political life. Secondly, there is the idea of operative ideals in human societies. That is to say, Montesquieu's theory of types, though narrow enough as it stands, might perhaps be taken as meaning that each political society is the imperfect embodiment of an ideal which has been an implicit formative factor in its development and towards which it is tending or from which it is departing. The task of the wise legislator will be to discern the nature of this operative ideal and to adapt legislation to its progressive realization. If interpreted in this way, the theory of types appears as something more than a mere relic of Greek classifications of constitutions. One can say that Montesquieu is trying to express a genuine historical insight with the aid of somewhat antiquated categories.

If, however, we state Montesquieu's theory in this way, we imply that he is concerned simply with an understanding of historical data and that he is content with relativism. Systems of law are the results of different complexes of empirical factors. In each system we can see an operative ideal at work. But there is no absolute standard with reference to which the philosopher can compare and evaluate different political and legal systems.

This interpretation, however, would be misleading on two counts. In the first place Montesquieu admitted immutable laws of justice. God, the creator and preserver of the world, has established laws or rules which govern the physical world.[7] And 'man, as a physical being, is, like other bodies, governed by invariable laws'.[8] As an intelligent or rational being, however, he is subject to laws which he is capable of transgressing. Some of these are of his own making; but others are not dependent on him. 'We must therefore acknowledge relations of justice antecedent to the positive law by which they are established.'[9] 'To say that there is nothing just or unjust but what is commanded or forbidden by positive laws is the same as saying that before the describing of a circle all the radii were not equal.'[10] Assuming the idea of a state of nature, Montesquieu remarks that prior to all positive laws there are 'those of nature, so called because they derive their force entirely from our frame and being'.[11] And in order to know these laws we must consider man as he was before the establishment of society. 'The laws received in such a state would be those of nature.'[12] Whether this idea fits in well with the other aspects of Montesquieu's theory may be disputable. But there is no doubt that he maintained the existence of a natural moral law which is antecedent to all positive laws established by political society. We can say, if we wish, that his treatise on law looks forward to a purely empirical and inductive treatment of political and legal institutions and that his theory of natural law was a hang-over from earlier philosophers of law. But this theory is none the less a real element in his thought.

In the second place Montesquieu was an enthusiast for liberty and not simply a detached observer of historical phenomena. Thus in the eleventh and twelfth books of De l'esprit des lois he sets out to analyse the conditions of political liberty; and as he disliked despotism, the implication is that a liberal constitution is the best. His analysis may take the form of giving a meaning to the word liberty as used in a political context and then examining the conditions under which it can be secured and maintained. And, theoretically speaking, this could be done by a political philosopher who had no liking for political liberty or who was indifferent towards it. But in his analysis Montesquieu had one eye on the English constitution, which he admired, and the other on the French political system, which he disliked. His discussion of political liberty is thus not simply an abstract analysis, at least so far as its spirit and motive are concerned. For he was inquiring how the French system could be so amended as to permit of and to retain liberty.

Political liberty, says Montesquieu, does not consist in unrestrained freedom but 'only in the power of doing what we ought to will and in not being constrained to do what we ought not to will'.[13] 'Liberty is a right of doing whatever the laws permit.'[14] In a free society no citizen is prevented from acting in a manner permitted by law, and no citizen is forced to act in one particular manner when the law allows him to follow his own inclination. This description of liberty is perhaps not very enlightening; but Montesquieu goes on to insist that political liberty involves the separation of powers. That is to say, the legislative, executive and judicial powers must not be vested in one man or one particular group of men. They must be separated or independent of one another in such a way that they can act as checks on one another and constitute a safeguard against despotism and the tyrannical abuse of power.

This statement of the condition of political liberty is arrived at, as Montesquieu explicitly says, by examination of the English constitution. In different States there have been and are different operative ideals. The ideal or end of Rome was increase of dominion, of the Jewish State the preservation and increase of religion, of China public tranquillity. But there is one nation, England, which has political liberty for the direct end of its constitution. Accordingly, 'to discover political liberty in a constitution no great labour is required. If we are capable of seeing where it exists, why should we go any further in search of it?'[15]

It has been said by some writers that Montesquieu saw the English constitution through the eyes of political theorists such as Harrington and Locke and that when he talked about the separation of powers as the signal mark of the English constitution he failed to understand that the Revolution of 1688 had finally settled the supremacy of Parliament. In other words, a man who relied simply on observation of the English constitution would not have fixed on the so-called separation of powers as its chief characteristic. But even if Montesquieu saw and interpreted the English constitution in the light of a theory about it, and even if the phrase 'separation of powers' was not an adequate description of the concrete situation, it seems clear that the phrase drew attention to real features of the situation. The judges did not, of course, constitute a 'power' in the sense that the legislative did; but at the same time they were not subject in the exercise of their functions to the capricious control of the monarch or his ministers. It may be said, with truth, that what Montesquieu admired in the English constitution was the result of a long process of development rather than of the application of an abstract theory about the 'separation of powers'. But he was not so hypnotized by a phrase that, having interpreted the English constitution as a separation of powers, he then demanded that it should be slavishly copied in his own country. 'How should I have such a design, I who think that the very excess of reason is not always desirable, and that men almost always accommodate themselves better to the mean than to extremes?'[16] Montesquieu desired a reform of the French political system, and observation of the English constitution suggested to him ways in which it might be reformed without a violent and drastic revolution.

Montesquieu's ideas about the balancing of powers exercised an influence both in America and in France, as in the case of the 1791 French Declaration of the Rights of Man and of Citizens. In later times, however, more emphasis has been laid on his pioneer work in the empirical and comparative study of political societies and of the connections between forms of government, legal systems and other conditioning factors.

5. In the section on Fontenelle attention was drawn to his defence of Cartesian physical theories. The displacement of Descartes by Newton can be illustrated by the activity of Pierre Louis Moreau de Maupertuis (1698–1759), who attacked the Cartesian theory of vortices and defended Newton's theory of gravitation. Indeed, his championship of Newton's theories contributed to his being elected a Fellow of the Royal Society. In 1736 he headed an expedition to Lapland which, as was mentioned in the first section of this chapter, he had undertaken, at the wish of King Louis XV, to make some exact measurements of a degree of latitude with a view to determining the shape of the earth. The results of these observations, published in 1738, confirmed

Newton's theory that the surface of the earth is flattened towards the Poles.

In some respects Maupertuis's philosophical ideas were empiricist, and even positivist. In 1750, when acting, on the invitation of Frederick the Great, as president of the Prussian Academy at Berlin, he published an *Essay on Cosmology*. In this work he speaks, for example, of the concept of force which originates in our experience of resistance in the physical overcoming of obstacles. 'The word *force* in its proper sense expresses a certain feeling which we experience when we wish to move a body which was at rest or to change or stop the movement of a body which was in motion. The perception which we then experience is so constantly accompanied by a change in the rest or movement of the body that we are unable to prevent ourselves from believing that it is the cause of this change. When, therefore, we see some change taking place in the rest or movement of a body, we do not fail to say that it is the effect of some force. And if we have no feeling of any effort made by us to contribute to this change, and if we only see some other bodies to which we can attribute this phenomenon, we place the *force* in them, as though it belonged to them.'[17] In its origin the idea of force is only 'a feeling of our soul',[18] and, as such, it cannot belong to the bodies to which we attribute it. There is, however, no harm in speaking about a moving force being present in bodies, provided that we remember that it is 'only a word invented to supply for our (lack of) knowledge, and that it signifies only a result of phenomena'.[19] In other words, we should not allow ourselves to be misled by our use of the word *force* into thinking that there is an occult entity corresponding to it. Force is measured 'only by its apparent effects'. In physical science we remain in the realm of phenomena. And the fundamental concepts of mechanics can be interpreted in terms of sensation. Indeed, Maupertuis believed that the impression of necessary connection in mathematical and mechanical principles can also be explained in empiricist terms, for instance by association and custom.

At the same time, however, Maupertuis proposed a teleological conception of natural laws. The fundamental principle in mechanics is the principle 'of the least quantity of action'.[20] This principle states that 'when some change takes place in Nature, the quantity of action employed for this change is always the least possible. It is from this principle that we deduce the laws of motion.'[21] In other words, Nature always employs the least possible amount of force or energy which is required to achieve her purpose. This law of the least possible quantity of action had already been employed by Fermat, the mathematician, in his study of optics; but Maupertuis gave it a universal application. Samuel König, a disciple of Leibniz, argued that the latter had anticipated Maupertuis in the statement of this law; and the French philosopher tried to refute the truth of this assertion. But the question of priority need not concern us here. The point is that Maupertuis felt himself entitled to argue that the teleological system of Nature shows it to be the work of an all-wise Creator. According to him, Descartes' principle of the conservation of energy seems to withdraw the world from the government of the Deity. 'But our principle, more conformable to the idea which we ought to have of things, leaves the world in continual need of the power of the Creator, and it is a necessary consequence of the wisest employment of this power.'[22]

In the 1756 edition of his *Works* Maupertuis included a *Système de la Nature*, a Latin version of which had already been published under the pseudonym of Baumann with the date 1751. In this essay he denied the sharp Cartesian distinction between thought and extension. At bottom, says Maupertuis,[23] the reluctance which one feels to attribute intelligence to matter arises simply out of the fact that one always assumes that this intelligence must be like ours. In reality there is an infinity of degrees of intelligence, ranging from vague sensation to clear intellectual processes. And each entity possesses some degree of it. Maupertuis thus proposed a form of hylozoism, according to which even the lowest material things possess some degree of life and sensibility.

On the strength of this doctrine Maupertuis has sometimes been classed with the crude materialists of the French Enlightenment who will be mentioned later. But the philosopher objected to Diderot's interpretation of his theory as being equivalent to materialism and as doing away with the basis of any valid argument for the existence of God. In his *Reply to the Objections of M. Diderot* which he appended to the 1756 edition of the *Système de la Nature* Maupertuis observes that when Diderot wishes to substitute for the attribution to purely material things of elementary perceptions an attribution to them of sensation analogous to touch, he is simply playing with words. For sensation is a form of perception. And elementary perceptions are not the same as the clear and distinct perceptions which we enjoy. There is no real difference between what 'Baumann' says and what Diderot wishes him to say. Obviously, these observations do not settle the question, whether Maupertuis is a materialist or not. But this is in any case a difficult question to answer. The philosopher appears to have maintained that higher degrees of 'perception' proceed from combinations of atoms or particles which enjoy elementary perception, but which are physical points rather than metaphysical points like Leibniz's monads. And it is certainly arguable that this is a materialist position. At the same time one must bear in mind the fact that for Maupertuis not only qualities but also extension are phenomena, psychic representations. And Brunet has even maintained[24] that in certain of its aspects his philosophy resembles Berkeley's immaterialist doctrine. The truth of the matter seems to be that though Maupertuis's writings contributed to the growth of materialism, his position is too equivocal to warrant our classing him without qualification with the materialistic philosophers of the French Enlightenment. As for Diderot's interpretation, Maupertuis evidently suspected that he had his tongue in his cheek when he spoke of the 'terrible' consequences of Baumann's hypothesis, and that he merely wished to advertise these consequences while verbally rejecting them.

6. We have seen that both Fontenelle and Maupertuis believed that the cosmic system manifests the existence of God. Montesquieu also believed in God. So did Voltaire. His name is associated with his violent and mocking attacks not only on the Catholic Church as an institution and on the shortcomings of ecclesiastics but also on Christian doctrines. But this does not alter the fact that he was no atheist.

François Marie Arouet (1694–1778), who later changed his name and styled himself M. de Voltaire, studied as a boy at the Jesuit College of Louis-le-Grand at Paris. After two visits to the Bastille he went to England in 1726 and remained there until 1729. It was during this sojourn in England that he made acquaintance with the writings of Locke and Newton and developed that admiration for the comparative freedom of English life which is evident in his *Philosophical Letters*.[25] Elsewhere Voltaire remarks that Newton, Locke and Clarke would have been persecuted in France, imprisoned at Rome, burned at Lisbon. This zeal for toleration did not, however, prevent him from expressing lively satisfaction when in 1761 he heard it reported that three priests had been burned at Lisbon by the anti-clerical government.

In 1734 Voltaire went to Cirey, and there he wrote his *Treatise on Metaphysics*, which he thought it more prudent not to publish. His *Philosophy of Newton* appeared in 1738. Voltaire took most of his philosophical ideas from thinkers such as Bayle, Locke and Newton; and he was undoubtedly successful in presenting these ideas in lucid and witty writings and in making them intelligible to French society. But he was not a profound philosopher. Though influenced by Locke, he was not in the same class as a philosopher. And though he wrote on Newton, he was not himself a mathematical physicist.

In 1750 Voltaire went to Berlin at the invitation of Frederick the Great, and in 1752 he composed his satire on Maupertuis, *Doctor Akakia*. This satire was displeasing to Frederick; and as the relations between the philosopher and his royal patron were becoming strained, Voltaire left Berlin in 1753 and went to reside near Geneva. His important *Essai sur les mœurs* appeared in 1756.

Voltaire acquired a property at Ferney in 1758. *Candide* appeared in 1759, the *Treatise on Tolerance* in 1763, the *Philosophical Dictionary* in 1764, *The Ignorant Philosopher* in 1766, a work on Bolingbroke in 1767, the *Profession of Faith of Theists* in 1768. In 1778 Voltaire went to Paris for the first performance of his play *Irène*. He received a tremendous ovation in the capital; but he died at Paris not long after the performance.

In the Beuchot edition of 1829–34 Voltaire's complete works comprise some seventy volumes. He was philosopher, dramatist, poet, historian and novelist. As a man, he certainly had some good points. He had a strong dose of common sense; and his call for a reform in the administration of justice, together with his efforts, even if inspired by very mixed motives, to bring certain miscarriages of justice to public attention, show a certain amount of humane feeling. But, in general, his character was not particularly admirable. He was vain, revengeful, cynical and intellectually unscrupulous. His attacks on Maupertuis, Rousseau and others do him little credit. But nothing, of course, that we may say about his defects of character can alter the fact that he sums up brilliantly in his writings the spirit of the French Enlightenment.

In his work on the elements of the Newtonian philosophy Voltaire maintains that Cartesianism leads straight to Spinozism. 'I have known many people whom Cartesianism has led to admit no other God than the immensity of things, and, on the contrary, I have seen no Newtonian who was not a theist in the strictest sense.'[26] 'The whole philosophy of Newton leads necessarily to the knowledge of a Supreme Being who has created everything and arranged everything freely.'[27] If there is a vacuum, matter must be finite. And if it is finite, it is contingent and dependent. Moreover, attraction and motion are not essential qualities of matter. Hence they must have been implanted by God.

In his *Treatise on Metaphysics* Voltaire offers two lines of argument for God's existence. The first is a proof from final causality. The world is compared to a watch; and Voltaire maintains that just as when one sees a watch, the hands of which mark the time, one concludes that it has been made by someone for the purpose of marking the time, so must one conclude from observation of Nature that it has been made by an intelligent Creator. The second argument is an argument from contingency on the lines laid down by Locke and Clarke. Later on, however, Voltaire left aside this second argument and confined himself to the first. At the end of the article on atheism in his *Philosophical Dictionary* he remarks that 'geometers who are not philosophers have rejected final causes, but true philosophers admit them. And, as a well-known author has said, a catechist announces God to infants whereas Newton demonstrates Him for the wise.' And in the article on Nature he argues that no mere assemblage could account for the universal harmony or system. 'They call me Nature, but I am all art.'

But though Voltaire maintained to the end his belief in

the existence of God, there was a change in his view of the relation of the world to God. At first he shared more or less the cosmic optimism of Leibniz and Pope. Thus in his work on Newton he speaks of the atheist who denies God because of the evil in the world and then remarks that the terms *good* and *well-being* are equivocal. 'That which is bad in relation to you is good in the general system.'[28] Again, are we to abandon the conclusion about God's existence to which reason leads us because wolves devour sheep and because spiders catch flies? 'Do you not see, on the contrary, that these continual generations constantly devoured and constantly reproduced, enter into the plan of the universe?'[29]

The problem of evil was, however, brought vividly to Voltaire's attention by the disastrous earthquake at Lisbon in 1755. And he expressed his reactions to this event in his poem on the disaster at Lisbon and in *Candide*. In the poem he appears to reaffirm the divine liberty; but in his later writings he makes creation necessary. God is the first or supreme cause, existing eternally. But the notion of a cause without an effect is absurd. Therefore the world must proceed eternally from God. It is not, indeed, a part of God, and it is contingent in the sense that it depends on Him for its existence. But creation is eternal and necessary. And as evil is inseparable from the world, it too is necessary. It depends, therefore, on God; but God did not choose to bring it about. We could hold God responsible for evil only if He created freely.

To turn to man. In the *Philosophie de Newton*[30] Voltaire remarks that several people who knew Locke had assured him that Newton once admitted to Locke that our knowledge of Nature is not great enough to allow us to state that it is impossible for God to add the gift of thinking to an extended thing. And it seems sufficiently clear that Voltaire considered the theory of the soul as an immaterial substantial being to be an unnecessary hypothesis. In the article on Soul in the *Philosophical Dictionary* he argues that terms such as 'spiritual soul' are simply words which cover our ignorance. The Greeks made a distinction between the sensitive and the intellectual soul. But the first certainly does not exist; 'it is nothing but the motion of your organs'. And reason can find no better proof for the existence of the higher soul than it can find for the existence of the lower soul. 'It is only by faith that thou canst know it.' Voltaire does not say here in so many words that there is no such thing as a spiritual and immortal soul. But his view is made sufficiently clear elsewhere.

As for human liberty in a psychological sense, Voltaire changed his mind. In the *Treatise on Metaphysics*[31] he defended the reality of liberty by an appeal to the immediate testimony of consciousness which resists all theoretical objections. In his *Philosophie de Newton*,[32] however, he makes a distinction. In certain trivial matters, when I have no motive inclining me to act in one way rather than in another, I may be said to have liberty of indifference. For example, if I have a choice of turning to the left or to the right, and if I have no inclination to do the one and no aversion towards the other, the choice is the result of my own volition. Obviously, liberty of 'indifference' is here taken in a very literal sense. In all other cases when we are free we have the freedom which is called spontaneity; 'that is to say, when we have motives, our will is determined by them. And these motives are always the final result of the understanding or of instinct.'[33] Here liberty is admitted in name. But after having made this distinction Voltaire proceeds to say that 'everything has its cause; therefore your will has one. One cannot will, therefore, except as a consequence of the last idea that one has received. . . . This is why the wise Locke does not venture to pronounce the name *liberty*; a free will does not appear to him to be anything but a chimaera. He knows no other liberty than the power to do what one wills.'[34] In fine, 'we must admit that one can hardly reply to the objections against liberty except by a vague eloquence; a sad theme about which the wise man fears even to think. There is only one consoling reflection, namely that whatever system one embraces, by whatever fatalism one believes our actions to be determined, one will always act as though one were free.'[35] In the next chapter Voltaire proposes a series of objections against liberty of indifference.

In his article on Liberty in the *Philosophical Dictionary* Voltaire says roundly that liberty of indifference is 'a word without sense, invented by people who scarcely had any themselves'. What one wills is determined by motive; but one may be free to act or not to act, in the sense that it may or may not be in one's power to perform the action that one wills to perform. 'Your will is not free, but your actions are; you are free to act when you have the power to act.' In *The Ignorant Philosopher*[36] Voltaire maintains that the idea of a free will is absurd; for a free will would be a will without sufficient motive, and it would fall outside the course of Nature. It would be very odd if 'one little animal, five feet tall', were an exception to the universal reign of law. It would act by chance, and there is no chance. 'We have invented this word to express the known effect of any unknown cause.' As for the consciousness or feeling of freedom, this is quite compatible with determinism in our volition. It shows no more than that one can *do* as one pleases when one has the power to perform the action willed.

This assertion of determinism does not mean that Voltaire discarded the idea of the moral law. He expressed his agreement with Locke about the absence of any innate moral principles. But we are so fashioned by God that in the course of time we come to see the necessity of justice. True, Voltaire was accustomed to draw attention to the variability of moral convictions. Thus, in the *Treatise on Metaphysics*,[37] he remarks that what in one region is called virtue is called vice in another, and that moral rules are as variable as languages and fashions. At the same time 'there are natural laws with respect to which human beings in all parts of the world must agree'.[38] God has endowed man with certain inalienable feelings which are eternal bonds and give rise to the fundamental laws of human society. The content of the fundamental law seems to be very restricted and to consist mainly in not injuring others and in pursuing what is pleasurable to oneself provided that this does not involve wanton injury to one's neighbour. None the less, just as Voltaire always maintained a deistic (or, as he called it, a theistic) position, so he never surrendered completely to relativism in morals. Profound religious feeling of the type to be found in Pascal was certainly not a characteristic of Voltaire; nor was lofty moral idealism. But just as he rejected atheism, so did he reject extreme ethical relativism.

We have said that Voltaire came to adopt a determinist position in regard to human liberty in a psychological sense.

At the same time he was a resolute defender of political liberty. Like Locke, he believed in a doctrine of human rights which should be respected by the State; and, like Montesquieu, he admired the conditions of freedom prevailing in England. But it is necessary to understand what he meant by political liberty. First and foremost he had liberty of thought and expression in mind. In other words, he was primarily concerned with liberty for *les philosophes*, at least when they agreed with Voltaire. He was not a democrat in the sense of wishing to promote popular rule. True, he advocated toleration, which he thought to be necessary for scientific and economic progress; and he disliked tyrannical despotism. But he mocked at Rousseau's ideas about equality, and his ideal was that of a benevolent monarchy, enlightened by the influence of the philosophers. He mistrusted dreamers and idealists; and his correspondence shows that in his opinion the rabble, as he pleasingly called the people, would always remain a rabble. Better conditions of freedom and toleration and better standards of judicial procedure could quite well be secured under the French monarchy, provided that the power of the Church was broken and philosophical enlightenment substituted for Christian dogma and superstition. Voltaire certainly never thought that salvation could come from the people or from violent insurrection. Although, therefore, his writings helped to prepare the ground for the Revolution, it would be a great mistake to picture Voltaire as looking forward to or as consciously intending to promote the Revolution in the form which it was actually to take. His enemy was not the monarchy, but rather the clergy. He was not interested in liberalizing the constitution in the sense of advocating Montesquieu's 'separation of powers'. In fact one can even say that he was interested in increasing the power of the monarchy, in the sense that he wished it to be free of clerical influence.

These remarks are not to be taken as implying that Voltaire was an enemy of progress. On the contrary, he was one of the most influential disseminators of the idea of progress. But the term meant for him the reign of reason, intellectual, scientific and economic progress, rather than political progress, if one understands by this a transition to democracy or popular rule. For in his opinion it was the enlightened monarchic ruler who was most likely to promote progress in science, literature and toleration of ideas.

In spite of the fact that Montesquieu's theories have been treated in this chapter, I propose to reserve Voltaire's opinions on history for the chapter on the rise of the philosophy of history.

7. When one thinks of the period known as the Enlightenment or Age of Reason, one naturally tends to think of an exaltation of cool and critical intelligence. Yet it was Hume, one of the greatest figures of the Enlightenment, who said that reason is and ought to be the slave of the passions and who found the basis of moral life in feeling. And in France Voltaire, whom one naturally pictures as the very embodiment of critical, and somewhat superficial, intelligence, declared that without the passions there would be no human progress. For the passions are a motivating force in man; they are the wheels which make the machines go.[39] Similarly, we are told by Vauvenargues that 'our passions are not distinct from ourselves; some of them are the whole foundation and the whole substance of our soul'.[40] Man's true nature is to be found in the passions rather than in the reason.

Luc de Clapiers, Marquis of Vauvenargues, was born in 1715. From 1733 he was an army officer and took part in several campaigns until his health broke down. He spent the last two years of his life at Paris, where he was a friend of Voltaire and where he died in 1747. In the year preceding his death he published his *Introduction to the Knowledge of the Human Mind*, followed by *Critical Reflections on Some Poets*. Maxims and other pieces were added to subsequent (posthumous) editions.

The first book of Vauvenargues's work is devoted to the mind (*esprit*). 'The object of this first Book is to make known by definitions and reflections founded on experience, all those different qualities of men which are comprised under the name of mind. Those who seek for the physical causes of these same qualities might perhaps be able to speak of them with less uncertainty if in this work one succeeded in developing the effects of which they study the principles.'[41] Vauvenargues did not agree with those who tended to stress the equality of all minds. In his work he discusses briefly a number of qualities which are normally mutually exclusive and which give rise to different types of minds. He also stresses the concept of the genius, in whom we find a combination of normally independent qualities. 'I believe that there is no genius without activity. I believe that genius depends in great part on our passions. I believe that it arises from the meeting of many different qualities, and from the secret agreements of our inclinations with our (mental) lights. When one of these necessary conditions is wanting, there is no genius, or it is only imperfect. . . . It is the necessity of this meeting of mutually independent qualities which is apparently the cause of the fact that genius is always so rare.'[42]

In the second book Vauvenargues treats of the passions which, 'as Mr. Locke says',[43] are all founded on pleasure and pain. These last are to be referred respectively to perfection and imperfection. That is, man is naturally attached to his being, and if his being were in no way imperfect but developed itself always without hindrance or imperfection, he would feel nothing but pleasure. As it is, we experience both pleasure and pain; and 'it is from the experience of these two contraries that we derive the idea of good and evil'.[44] The passions (at least those which come 'by the organ of reflection' and are not merely immediate impressions of sense) are founded on 'the love of being or of the perfection of being, or on the feeling of our imperfection'.[45] For example, there are people in whom the feeling of their imperfection is more vivid than the feeling of perfection, of capacity, of power. We then find passions such as anxiety, melancholy and so on. Great passions arise from the union of these two feelings, that of our power and that of our imperfection and weakness. For 'the feeling of our miseries impels us to go out of ourselves, and the feeling of our resources encourages us to do so and carries us thereto in hope'.[46]

In the third book Vauvenargues treats of moral good and evil. We have seen that the idea of good and evil are founded on experiences of pleasure and pain. But different people find pleasure and pain in different things. Their ideas of good and evil are therefore different. This, however, is not what is meant by moral good and evil. 'In order that something should be regarded as a good by the whole of society, it must tend to the advantage of the whole of society. And in order that something should be regarded as an evil, it must tend to the ruin of society. Here we have the great characteristic of moral good and evil.'[47] Men, being imperfect, are not self-sufficient; society is necessary for them. And social life involves fusing one's particular interest with the general interest. 'This is the foundation of all morality.'[48] But pursuit of the common good involves sacrifice, and it is not everyone who is spontaneously ready to make such sacrifices. Hence the necessity of law.

As for virtue and vice, 'preference for the general interest before one's personal interest is the only definition which is worthy of virtue and which fixes the idea of it. On the contrary, the mercenary sacrifice of the public happiness to one's own interest is the eternal mark of vice.'[49] Mandeville may hold that private vices are public benefits, and that commerce would not flourish without avarice and vanity. But though this is true in a sense, it must also be admitted that the good which is produced by vice is always mixed with great evils. And if these are held in check and subordinated to the public good, it is reason and virtue which do so.

Vauvenargues proposes, therefore, a utilitarian interpretation of morality. But just as in the first book he makes much of the concept of genius, so in the third he devotes a special discussion to greatness of soul. 'Greatness of soul is a sublime instinct which impels men to that which is great, of whatever nature it may be, but which turns them towards good or evil according to their passions, their lights, their education, their fortune, etc.'[50] Greatness of soul is thus morally indifferent in itself. When united with vice, it is dangerous to society (Vauvenargues mentions Cataline); but it is still greatness of soul. 'Where there is greatness, we feel it in spite of ourselves. The glory of conquerors has always been attacked; the people have always suffered from it, and they have always respected it.'[51] It is not surprising that Nietzsche, with his conception of the higher man standing 'beyond good and evil', felt sympathy with Vauvenargues. But the latter was not, of course, concerned to deny what he had already said about the social character of morality. He was drawing attention to the complexity of human nature and character. 'There are vices which do not exclude great qualities, and consequently there are great qualities which

stand apart from virtue. I recognize this truth with sorrow.
. . . (But) those who wish men to be altogether good or
altogether evil do not know nature. In men all is mixed;
everything there is limited; and even vice has its limits.'[52]

In Vauvenargues's *Maxims* we can find a number of say-
ings which obviously recall Pascal. 'Reason does not know the
interests of the heart.'[53] 'Great thoughts come from the
heart.'[54] We find too that insistence on the fundamental role
of the passions to which attention has already been drawn.
'We owe perhaps to the passions the greatest advantages of
the spirit.'[55] 'The passions have taught reason to man. In the
infancy of all peoples, as in that of individuals, feeling has
always preceded reflection and has been its first master.'[56]
It is perhaps worth while mentioning this point as one may
easily think of the Age of Reason as a period in which feeling
and passion were habitually depreciated in favour of the
coldly analytic reason.

It would not be quite correct to say that Vauvenargues was
not a systematic writer on the ground that his writings consist more of aphorisms than of developed discussions. For in
his work on the knowledge of the human mind there is a
more or less systematic arrangement of his thoughts. But he
acknowledged in his preliminary discourses that circumstances
had not permitted him to fulfil his original plan. In any case
Vauvenargues was more concerned with distinguishing and
describing different qualities of mind and different passions
than with investigating the causes, as he put it, of psychical
phenomena. For a study of the way in which mental operations and functions are derived from a primitive foundation
we have to turn to Condillac.

8. Étienne Bonnot de Condillac (1715–80) was first destined for the priesthood and entered the seminary of Saint-
Sulpice. But he left the seminary in 1740 and took to philosophy. From 1758 to 1767 he was tutor to the son of the Duke
of Parma.

Condillac's first publication was an *Essay on the Origin of
Human Knowledge* (*Essai sur l'origine des connaissances humaines*, 1746), which bears the clear imprint of Locke's empiricism. This is not to say that Condillac simply reproduced
the doctrine of the English philosopher. But he was in agreement with the latter's general principles that we must reduce

complex to simple ideas and that we must assign to simple
ideas an empirical or experiential origin.

In discussing the development of our mental life Condillac
laid great stress on the part played by language. Ideas become fixed, as it were, only by being associated with a sign
or word. When I look at the grass, for example, I have a sensation of green; a simple idea of green is transmitted to me
by sense. But this isolated experience, which can, of course,
be repeated indefinitely, becomes an object of reflection and
can enter into combination with other ideas only by being
linked with a sign or symbol, the word *green*. The fundamental material of knowledge is thus the association of an
idea with a sign; and it is in virtue of this association that we
are able to develop a complex intellectual life in accordance
with our growing experience of the world and with our needs
and purposes. True, language, that is to say ordinary language, is defective in the sense that we do not find in it that
perfect correspondence between the sign and the signified
which we find in mathematical language. None the less, we
are intelligent beings, beings capable of reflection, because we
possess the gift of language.

In his *Treatise on Systems* (*Traité des Systèmes*, 1749)
Condillac subjects to adverse criticism the 'spirit of systems'
as manifested in the philosophies of thinkers such as Descartes, Malebranche, Spinoza and Leibniz. The great rationalist philosophers tried to construct systems by proceeding
from first principles and definitions. This is especially true
of Spinoza. But the so-called geometrical system is useless
for developing a real knowledge of the world. A philosopher
may imagine that his definitions express an apprehension of
essences; but in reality they are arbitrary. That is to say, they
are arbitrary unless they are intended to state merely the
senses in which certain words are used as a matter of fact.
And if they are merely dictionary definitions, so to speak,
they cannot do the job which they are supposed to do in the
philosophical systems.

This does not mean, of course, that Condillac condemns
all efforts to systematize knowledge. To subject to adverse
criticism the spirit of systems, the attempt to develop a philosophy from reason alone in an *a priori* manner, is not to
condemn synthesis. A system in the acceptable meaning of

the word is an orderly disposition of the parts of a science so that the relations between them are clearly exhibited. There will certainly be principles. But principles will mean here known phenomena. Thus Newton constructed a system by using the known phenomena of gravitation as a principle and by then explaining phenomena such as the movements of the planets and the tides in the light of this principle.

We find similar ideas in Condillac's *Logic*, which appeared posthumously in 1780. The great metaphysicians of the seventeenth century followed a synthetic method, borrowed from geometry and proceeding by way of deduction from definitions. And this method, as we have seen, cannot give us real knowledge of Nature. The analytic method, however, remains always in the sphere of the given. We start from a confused given and analyse it into its distinct parts: we can recompose the whole in a systematic way. This is the natural method, the method which the mind naturally follows when we wish to develop our knowledge. How, for example, do we come to know a landscape or countryside? First we have a confused impression of it, and then we gradually arrive at a distinct knowledge of its various component features and come to see how these features together make up the whole. In developing a theory of method we are not called upon to elaborate an *a priori* notion of an ideal method; we should study how the mind actually works when it develops its knowledge. It will then be found that there is no one ideal and fixed method. The order in which we ought to study things depends on our need and purpose. And if we wish to study Nature, to acquire a real knowledge of things, we must remain within the sphere of the given, within the phenomenal order which is ultimately given to us in sense-experience.

Condillac is best known for his *Treatise on Sensations* (*Traité des sensations*, 1754). Locke had distinguished between ideas of sensation and ideas of reflection, admitting two founts of ideas, sensation and reflection or introspection. And in his early work on the origin of human knowledge Condillac had more or less assumed Locke's position. But in the *Treatise on Sensations* he made a clear break with Locke's theory of the dual origin of ideas. There is only one origin or fount, namely sensation.

In Condillac's opinion Locke gave only inadequate treat-

ment to ideas of reflection, that is to say, to psychical phenomena. He analysed complex ideas, such as those of substance, into simple ideas; but he simply assumed the mental
operations of comparing, judging, willing, and so on. There is
room, therefore, for an advance on Locke. It has to be shown
how these mental operations and functions are reducible in
the long run to sensations. They cannot, of course, be all
termed sensations; but they are 'transformed sensations'.
That is to say, the whole edifice of the psychical life is built
out of sensation. To show that this is the case is the task
which Condillac sets himself in his *Treatise on Sensations*.

To make his point Condillac asks his readers to imagine a
statue which is gradually endowed with the senses, beginning
with the sense of smell. And he tries to show how the whole
of man's mental life can be explained on the hypothesis that
it arises out of sensations. The analogy of the statue is, indeed, somewhat artificial. But what Condillac wishes his
readers to do is to imagine themselves bereft of all knowledge
and to reconstruct with him their mental operations from
the basis of elementary sensations. His approach to the problem of the origin of our ideas was stimulated by the data
provided by the experiences of persons born blind who under-
went successful operations for cataract at the hands of Cheselden, the London surgeon, and by Diderot's study of the
psychology of the deaf and dumb. In the *Treatise on Sensations*,[57] he speaks at some length of the data provided by
one of Cheselden's operations.

One of the chief features of this treatise is the way in
which Condillac tries to show how each sense, taken separately, can generate all the faculties. Let us take, for example,
a man (represented by the statue) whose range of knowledge is limited to the sense of smell. 'If we give the statue a
rose to smell, to us it is a statue smelling a rose, to itself it
is smell of rose.'[58] That is to say, the man will have no idea
of matter or of external things or of his own body. For his
own consciousness he will be nothing but a sensation of smell.
Now, suppose that the man only has this one sensation, the
smell of a rose. This is 'attention'. And when the rose is
taken away, an impression remains, stronger or weaker according as the attention was more or less lively or vivid. Here
we have the dawn of memory. Attention to past sensation is

memory, which is nothing but a mode of feeling. Then let us suppose that the man, after having repeatedly smelt the scents of roses and pinks, smells a rose. His passive attention is divided between the memories of the smells of roses and pinks. Then we have comparison, which consists in attending to two ideas at the same time. And 'when there is comparison there is judgment. . . . A judgment is only the perception of a relation between two ideas which are compared.'[59] Again, if the man, having a present disagreeable sensation of smell, recalls a past pleasant sensation, we have imagination. For memory and imagination do not differ in kind. Again, the man can form ideas, particular and abstract. Some smells are pleasant, others unpleasant. If the man contracts the habit of separating the ideas of satisfaction and dissatisfaction from their several particular modifications, he will possess abstract ideas. Similarly, he can form ideas of number when he recalls several distinct successive sensations.

Now, every sensation of smell is either agreeable or disagreeable. And if the man who now experiences a disagreeable sensation recalls a past agreeable sensation, he feels the need of re-attaining that happier state. This gives rise to desire. For 'desire is nothing else than the action of these faculties when directed on the things of which we feel the need'.[60] And a desire which expels all others, or at least becomes dominant, is a passion. We thus arrive at the passions of love and hate. 'The statue loves a pleasant smell which it has or wishes to have. It hates an unpleasant smell which pains it.'[61] Further, if the statue remembers that the desire which it now experiences has been at other times followed by satisfaction, it thinks that it can fulfil its desire. It is then said to will. 'For by *will* we understand an absolute desire; that is, we think the thing desired is in our power.'[62]

Condillac thus endeavours to show that all mental operations can be derived from the sensation of smelling. Obviously, if we consider our faculties and operations simply as transformed sensations of smell, their range is extremely limited. And we can say the same of the consciousness of self in a man who is limited to the sense of smell. 'Its (the statue's) "I" is only the collection of the sensations which it experiences, and those which memory recalls to it.'[63] None the less, 'with one sense alone the understanding has as many faculties as with the five joined together'.[64] ('Understanding' is simply the name for all the cognitive faculties taken together.)

Hearing, taste and sight are then considered. But Condillac maintained that though the combination of smell, hearing, taste and sight multiplies the objects of a man's attention, desires and pleasures, it does not produce a judgment of externality. The statue will 'still see only itself. . . . It has no suspicion that it owes its modifications to outside causes. . . . It does not even know that it has a body.'[65] In other words, it is the sense of touch which is ultimately responsible for the judgment of externality. In his account of this matter Condillac's ideas varied somewhat. In the first edition of the *Treatise on Sensations* he made the knowledge of externality independent of movement. But in the second edition he admitted that the notion of externality does not arise independently of movement. In any case, however, it is touch which is primarily responsible for this notion. When a child moves its hand along parts of its body, 'it will feel itself in all parts of the body'.[66] 'But if it touches a foreign body, the "I" which feels itself modified in the hand does not feel itself modified in the foreign body. The "I" does not receive the response from the foreign body which it receives from the hand. The statue, therefore, judges these modes to be altogether outside it.'[67] And when touch is joined to other senses, the man gradually discovers his own several sense-organs and judges that sensations of smell, hearing, and so on are caused by external objects. For example, by touching a rose and making it approach or recede from the face, a man can come to form judgments about the organ of smell and about the external cause of his sensations of smell. Similarly, it is only by combination with touch that the eye learns how to see distance, size and movement. We have become so accustomed to judging size, shape, distance and situation by sight that we are naturally inclined to think that these judgments are due simply to sight. But this is not the case.

It is perhaps worth while drawing attention in passing to a change of view on Condillac's part between the publication of his *Essay on the Origin of Human Knowledge* and his *Treatise on Sensations*. In the first work he seems to maintain that the link between idea and sign or symbol is necessary for intelligence. But in the second work this point of view is modified. When treating, for example, of the man who is limited to the sense of smell he admits that this man can have some idea of number. He can have the ideas of one and one and one. But, according to Condillac, 'memory does not distinctly grasp four units at once. Beyond three it presents only an indefinite multitude. . . . It is the art of ciphering which has taught us to enlarge our point of view.'[68] Thus in the *Treatise* Condillac maintains that intelligence and the use of ideas precedes language, though language is necessary for the development of our mental life beyond a rudimentary stage.

The upshot of the *Treatise* is that 'in the natural order all knowledge arises from sensations'.[69] All man's mental operations, even those which are generally reckoned his higher mental activities, can be explained as 'transformed sensations'. Thus Condillac was convinced that he had made a definite advance on the position of Locke. The latter had thought that the faculties of the soul are innate qualities; he had not suspected that they might have their origin in sensation itself. It might perhaps be objected that Condillac's statement is not quite accurate. For did not Locke suggest that it had not been shown to be impossible for God to confer on matter the faculty of thinking? But in point of fact Locke was concerned with analysing and tracing back to their empirical grounds the ideas about which our faculties are employed; he did not do the same thing for the faculties or psychical functions themselves.

Now, in his *Essay concerning Human Understanding*,[70] Locke had maintained that the will is determined by 'an uneasiness of the mind for want of some absent good'. It is uneasiness or disquiet which 'determines the will to the successive voluntary actions, whereof the greatest part of our lives is made up, and by which we are conducted through different courses to different ends'.[71] Condillac developed and extended the range of this idea. Thus in the *Extrait raisonné*, which he added to later editions of the *Treatise on Sensations*, he maintains that 'uneasiness (*inquiétude*) is the first principle which gives us the habits of touching, seeing, hearing, feeling, tasting, comparing, judging, reflecting, desiring, loving, fearing, hoping, wishing, and that, in a word,

it is through uneasiness that all habits of mind and body are
born'. All psychical phenomena, therefore, depend on uneasiness, which is not so much anticipation of a good as uneasiness or disquietude under certain conditions. Thus one
can say perhaps that Condillac gives a 'voluntaristic' foundation to the whole process by which man's mental life is developed. Attention must be explained with reference to felt
need; and memory is directed by appetite and desire rather
than by a mere mechanical association of ideas. In his *Traité
des animaux*[72] he makes it clear that in his opinion the order of our ideas depends ultimately on need or interest. This
is obviously a fruitful theory. It was to bear fruit later on in
the voluntaristic interpretation of man's intellectual life
which is found, for example, in Schopenhauer.

Condillac's theory of the mind, of mental operations as
transformed sensations, appears at first sight to indicate a
materialistic position. And this impression is increased by his
habit of speaking of the 'faculties' of the soul as being derived from sensation, which may be taken to imply that the
human soul itself is material. Moreover, does he not suggest
that man is nothing but the sum of his acquirements? 'In
giving it (the statue) successively new modes of being and
new senses we saw it form desires, learn from experience to
regulate and satisfy them, and pass from needs to needs, from
cognitions to cognitions, from pleasures to pleasures. The
statue is therefore nothing but the sum of all it has acquired.
May not this be the same with men?'[73] Man may be the
sum of his acquirements; and they are transformed sensations.

It can hardly be denied, I think, that Condillac's theory
helped to promote a materialistic outlook, in that it exercised
an influence on the materialists. But Condillac was not himself a materialist. In the first place he was not a materialist
in the sense of one who holds that there are only bodies and
their modifications. For not only did he affirm the existence
of God as supreme cause but he also maintained the theory
of an immaterial, spiritual soul. He did not intend to reduce
the soul to a bundle of sensations. Rather did he presuppose
the soul as a simple centre of unity and then attempt to reconstruct its activity on the basis of the hypothesis that all
psychical phenomena are ultimately derivable from sensations. Whether his reductive analysis and his acceptance of a

spiritual soul in man fit well together is, of course, disputable. But in any case it is inaccurate to describe Condillac as a materialist.

In the second place Condillac left it an open question whether there are any extended things at all. As we have seen, he said at first that touch assures us of externality. But he soon realized that an account of the way in which the idea of externality arises is not the same thing as a proof that there are extended things. If we wish to say that sounds, tastes, odours and colours do not exist in objects we must also say that extension does not exist in them. Perhaps objects are extended, sonorous, tasty, odiferous and coloured; perhaps they are not. 'I maintain neither the one opinion nor the other, and I am waiting for someone to prove that they are what they appear to us to be, or that they are something else.'[74] It may be objected that if there is no extension, there are no objects. But this is untrue. 'All that we could reasonably infer would be that objects are existences which occasion sensations in us, and that they have properties about which we can have no certain knowledge.'[75] So far, therefore, from being a dogmatic materialist, Condillac leaves the door open for an immaterialist hypothesis, though he does not affirm this hypothesis.

It may be added that Condillac did not admit that his account of man's mental life involved sheer determinism. He appended to the *Treatise on Sensations* a dissertation on freedom, in which he discusses this point.

9. Condillac's attempt to show that all psychical phenomena are transformed sensations was continued by Claude Adrien Helvétius (1715–71) in his work *On the Mind* (*De l'esprit*, 1758). Helvétius came of a medical family whose original name, Schweizer, had been latinized. For a time he held the post of Farmer-General, but the opposition which his book on the mind aroused made it impossible for him to occupy posts in the royal service. So, apart from visits to England and to Berlin, he lived quietly on his estates. His book on man (*De l'homme, de ses facultés et de son éducation*) was published posthumously in 1772.

Helvétius reduces to sensation or sense-perception all the powers of the human understanding. It has been commonly held that man possesses faculties which transcend the level of sense. But this is a false theory. Take judgment, for example. To judge is to perceive similarities and dissimilarities between individual ideas. If I judge that red is different from yellow, what I am doing is to perceive that the colour called 'red' affects my eyes differently from the way in which they are affected by the colour called 'yellow'. To judge, therefore, is simply to perceive.

This process of reductive analysis is applied also to man's ethical life. Self-love is the universal basis of human conduct, and self-love is directed to the acquisition of pleasure. 'Men love themselves: they all desire to be happy, and think their happiness would be complete if they were invested with a degree of power sufficient to procure them every sort of pleasure. The love of power, therefore, takes its rise from the love of pleasure.'[76] All phenomena such as the love of power are secondary; they are simply transformations of the fundamental love of pleasure. 'Corporeal sensibility is therefore the sole mover of man.'[77] Even virtues such as liberality and benevolence can be reduced to self-love, that is, to the love of pleasure. 'What is a benevolent man? One in whom a spectacle of misery produces a painful sensation.'[78] In the long run the benevolent man endeavours to relieve human unhappiness and misery simply because they cause in him painful sensations.

On the basis of this crude reductive psychology Helvétius erects a utilitarian theory of morality. In different societies men hold different moral opinions and attach different meanings to words such as *good* and *virtue*. And it is this fact, namely that different people attach different meanings to the same ethical terms, which causes so much confusion in discussion. Before we indulge in discussions about ethics, we ought, therefore, first to settle the meanings of words. And, 'the words once defined, a question is resolved almost as soon as proposed'.[79] But will not these definitions be arbitrary? Not, says Helvétius, if the work is performed by a free people. 'England is perhaps the only country in Europe from which the universe can expect and obtain this benefaction.'[80] If freedom of thought is presupposed, the common sense of mankind will find expression in agreement as to the proper meanings of ethical terms. 'True virtue is reputed such in all ages and all countries. The name of virtue should be given

to such actions only as are useful to the public and conformable to the general interest.'[81] Although, therefore, self-
interest is the fundamental and universal motive of conduct,
public interest or utility is the norm of morality. And Helvétius tries to show how service of the common interest is
psychologically possible. For example, if a child is taught to
put itself in the place of the miserable and unfortunate, it
will feel painful sensations, and self-love will stimulate a desire to relieve misery. In the course of time the force of
association will set up a habit of benevolent impulses and conduct. Even if, therefore, self-love lies at the basis of all conduct, altruism is psychologically possible.

These considerations suggest that education is all-important in forming habits of conduct. Helvétius is one of the
chief pioneers and promoters of utilitarian moral theory; but
a special characteristic of his writings is his insistence on the
power of education. 'Education can do all' and 'education
makes us what we are'.[82] But the institution of a good system
of education meets with serious obstacles. In the first place
there is the clergy, and in the second place there is the fact
that most governments are very imperfect or bad. We cannot
have a good system of education until the power of the clergy
has been broken and until a truly good system of government, with a corresponding good system of legislation, has
been realized. The first and sole principle of morality is 'the
public good is the supreme law'.[83] But few governments conduct themselves according to this law. Yet 'every important
reformation in the moral part of education supposes one in
the laws and form of government'.[84]

In the light of these ideas Helvétius inveighs against political despotism. Thus in the preface to his work *On Man* he
speaks of the despotism to which France has been subjected,
and adds that 'it is the characteristic of despotic power to
extinguish both genius and virtue'.[85] Again, when speaking of
the too unequal distribution of the national wealth, he remarks that 'for men to flatter themselves with this equal distribution among a people subject to arbitrary power is a
folly'.[86] It is only in a free country that a gradual and more
equitable redistribution of the national wealth can take place.
We can say, therefore, that Helvétius was much more of a
political reformer than was Voltaire; he was much more con-

cerned than the latter with the overthrow of despotism and with the welfare of the people. This is one reason why he can be cited by left-wing writers as one of their predecessors.

Helvétius is tireless in attacking not only the clergy, particularly the Catholic priesthood, but also revealed or 'mysterious' religion, which he regards as detrimental to the interests of society. True, when speaking of the accusation of impiety, he protests that he has not denied any Christian dogma. But it is quite evident from his writings that he does not seriously intend to accept anything but a form of natural religion or deism. And the content of this religion is interpreted in function of morality rather than in function of any theological beliefs. 'The will of God, just and good, is that the children of the earth should be happy and enjoy every pleasure compatible with the public welfare. Such is the true worship, that which philosophy should reveal to the world.'[87] Again, 'morality founded on true principles is the only true natural religion'.[88]

It can hardly be claimed that Helvétius was a profound philosopher. His reduction of all psychical functions to sensation is crude, and in ethics he gives no thorough analysis or defence of his basic ideas. These shortcomings were evident to some of the other thinkers of the French Enlightenment. Diderot, for example, objected to Helvétius's levelling-down tendency and to his explanation of all moral impulses in terms of veiled egotism. None the less, in his reductive analysis, in his insistence on intellectual enlightenment and on the power of education, and in his attacks on Church and State Helvétius represents some important aspects of eighteenth-century French philosophy, even if it is an exaggeration to speak of him as the typical thinker of the period.

Chapter Two

THE FRENCH ENLIGHTENMENT (2)

The Encyclopaedia; *Diderot and d'Alembert – Material-*
ism; La Mettrie, d'Holbach and Cabanis – Natural his-
tory; Buffon, Robinet and Bonnet – The dynamism of
Boscovich – The Physiocrats; Quesnay and Turgot –
Final remarks.

1. The great literary repository of the ideas and ideals of
the French Enlightenment was the *Encylopédie, ou Diction-*
naire raisonné des arts et des métiers. Suggested by a French
translation of Chambers's *Cyclopaedia* or *Dictionary,* the
Encyclopaedia was edited by Diderot and d'Alembert. The
first volume was published in 1751, the second in the following year. The government then attempted to stop the work on
the ground that it was prejudicial to the royal authority and
to religion. However, by 1757 seven volumes had appeared.
In 1758 d'Alembert retired from the editorship, and the
French Government endeavoured to prevent the continuation
of the project. But Diderot was eventually permitted to proceed with the printing, provided that no further volume was
published until the whole work was complete. And in 1765
the final ten volumes (8–17) appeared, together with the
fourth volume of plates, the first of which had been published in 1762. Subsequently other volumes of plates appeared, while a supplement in five volumes and indices in
two volumes were printed at Amsterdam. The complete first
edition of the *Encyclopaedia* (1751–80) consisted of thirty-
five volumes. There were several foreign editions.

Quite apart from any controversy concerning the views expressed in the articles, the *Encyclopaedia,* as its editors freely
acknowledged, left much to be desired. The articles varied
greatly in standard and merit, and editorial supervision and
co-ordination were lacking. In other words, we cannot expect
to find in this work the conciseness, the concentration on

clear and precise factual information, the systematic co-
ordination and arrangement which are to be found in modern
encyclopaedias. But in spite of all its defects the *Encyclopaedia* was a work of great importance. For its aim was not
only to provide factual information for readers and to serve
as a useful work of reference but also to guide and mould
opinion. This is, of course, the reason why its publication
aroused so much opposition. For it was the enemy both of
the Church and of the existing political system. A certain
amount of prudence was, indeed, observed in the writing
of the articles; but the general attitude of the collaborators
was perfectly clear. It was a large-scale manifesto by free-
thinkers and rationalists; and its importance consists in its
ideological aspect rather than in any permanent value as an
encyclopaedia in the modern sense of the term.

Diderot and d'Alembert obtained collaborators who were
of one mind when there was question, for example, of attacking the Church and revealed religion, but who differed considerably among themselves in other respects. Thus some articles were contributed by Voltaire, the deist, though when
he thought that prudence rendered such conduct advisable,
he did not hesitate to state, quite falsely, that he had had no
connection with the *Encyclopaedia*. Another contributor, however, was the outspoken materialist d'Holbach, while the association of Helvétius with the work did nothing to com-
mend it to the ecclesiastical authorities. The contributors
included also Montesquieu and the economist Turgot.

D'Holbach will be considered in the section on materialism, while the ideas of Turgot will be discussed at the end of
this chapter. In the present section I propose to confine myself to Diderot and d'Alembert.

(i) Denis Diderot (1713–84) was, like Voltaire, a pupil
of the Jesuit College of Louis-le-Grand. Again like Voltaire, he
came under the influence of English thought, and he translated several English works into French. Among them was the
Essai sur le mérite et la vertu (1745), in which he added
notes of his own to his translation of Shaftesbury's *Inquiry
concerning Virtue and Merit*. And, as we have already seen,
the idea of the *Encyclopaedia*, his life's work, was suggested
to him by Chambers's *Cyclopaedia*. In 1746 he published
Pensées philosophiques at the Hague and in 1749, at London,

his *Lettre sur les aveugles à l'usage de ceux qui voient*. The views to which he gave expression earned him a few months' imprisonment at Vincennes, after which he devoted himself to the task of producing the *Encyclopaedia*. In 1754 there appeared at London his *Pensées sur l'interprétation de la nature*. A number of essays, such as the *Entretien entre d'Alembert et Diderot* and *Le rêve de d'Alembert* were not published during his lifetime. Diderot was by no means a rich man, and at one time he was in very difficult financial straits. But the Empress Catherine of Russia came to his assistance; and in 1773 he went to St. Petersburg, where he passed some months, partaking in frequent philosophical discussions with his benefactress. He was a noted conversationalist.

Diderot had no fixed system of philosophy. His thought was always on the move. We cannot say, for example, that he was a deist, an atheist or a pantheist; for his position changed. At the time when he wrote the *Pensées philosophiques* he was, indeed, a deist; and in the following year (1747) he wrote an essay on the sufficiency of natural religion, though it was not published until 1770. The historical religions, such as Judaism and Christianity, are mutually exclusive and intolerant. They are the creation of superstition. They began at certain periods in history, and they will all perish. But the historical religions all presuppose natural religion, which alone has always existed, which unites rather than separates men from one another, and which rests on the testimony which God has inscribed within us rather than on testimony provided by superstitious human beings. At a later stage of his development, however, Diderot abandoned deism for atheism and called on men to free themselves from the yoke of religion. Deism had cut off a dozen heads from the Hydra of religion; but from the one head which it had spared all the others would grow again. The only remedy is to make a clean sweep of all superstition. Yet Diderot later proposed a form of naturalistic pantheism. All parts of Nature ultimately form one individual, the Whole or All.

Similarly, the fluid character of his thought makes it impossible to state simply and unequivocally that Diderot was or was not a materialist. In his article on Locke in the *Encyclopaedia* he referred to the English philosopher's suggestion that it might not be impossible for God to confer on matter the capacity for thinking, and he evidently considered that thought developed out of sensibility. In the *Entretien entre d'Alembert et Diderot*, written in 1769, he gave clearer expression to a materialistic interpretation of man. Men and animals are really of the same nature, though their organizations differ. Differences in cognitive power and intelligence are simply the results of different physical organizations. And similar ideas appear in the *Rêve de d'Alembert* where it is implied that all psychological phenomena are reducible to physiological bases, and that the sense of freedom is illusory. Diderot was certainly influenced by Condillac's theory of the role of sensation in man's psychical life; but he came to criticize Condillac's sensationalism on the ground that the latter's analysis did not go far enough. We have to look beyond sensation to its physiological basis. And it is significant that Diderot assisted d'Holbach in the composition of his *Système de la nature* (1770), which was an outspoken exposition of materialism, even if the influence of d'Holbach on the development of his thought should not be exaggerated. At the same time we can find in Diderot a tendency to pan-psychism. He had a considerable admiration for Leibniz, whom he praised in the *Encyclopaedia*. And we find him later attributing perception to atoms, which correspond to Leibniz's monads. In certain combinations these atoms constitute animal organisms in which consciousness arises on the basis of the continuum formed by the atom.

The fluid character of Diderot's interpretation of Nature and man is connected with his insistence on the experimental method in science and philosophy. In his work *On the Interpretation of Nature* he declared, wrongly of course, that mathematical science would soon come to a standstill, and that in less than a century there would not be three great geometers left in Europe. His conviction was that mathematics was limited by its own self-made concepts, and that it was incapable of giving us direct acquaintance with concrete reality. This acquaintance could be obtained only by the use of the experimental method, by the new scientific approach which constituted a successful rival not only to metaphysics but also to mathematics. And once we study Nature itself we find that it is changeable and elastic, rich in fresh possibilities, characterized by diversity and heterogeneity. Who knows all the species which have preceded ours? Who knows the species which will follow ours? Everything changes; no two atoms or molecules are perfectly alike; only the infinite whole is permanent. The order of Nature is not something static, but it is being perpetually born anew. We cannot, therefore, give any permanent interpretation of Nature in terms of our conceptual schemes and classifications. And one of the prime needs of thought is that it should keep itself open to new points of view and to new aspects of empirical reality.

Some historians have emphasized the discrepancy between the materialistic elements in Diderot's thought and his ethical idealism. On the one hand, his materialism does away with freedom and seems to make repentance and remorse pointless and useless. On the other hand, he reproached himself with having written his early erotic romance, *Bijoux indiscrets*; and he upheld the ideals of self-sacrifice, benevolence and humanity. He had no sympathy with those materialists who united the profession of materialism and atheism with low moral ideals; and he objected to Helvétius's attempt to explain all moral impulses and ideals in terms of veiled egotism. Indeed, he asserted the existence of immutable laws of natural morality. And, as an art critic, he extolled the free, creative activity of the artist.

However, even though we may agree with Rosenkranz, in his work on Diderot, that there is an inconsistency between the philosopher's materialism and his ethics, Diderot himself did not see any inconsistency. In his opinion there was no essential relation between ethical ideals and a belief in a spiritual soul in man. The derivation of thought from more rudimentary psychical activities does not entail the denial of high moral ideals. Thus in his article on Locke in the *Encyclopaedia*, to which we alluded above, he asks what difference it makes whether matter does or does not think. 'How can it possibly affect the idea of justice or injustice?' No evil moral consequences follow from the theory that thought emerges or evolves from sensibility. For man remains precisely what he is, and he is judged according to the good or evil purposes to which he devotes his powers, not according to whether thought is an original creation or an emergent from sensibility. In modern terms Diderot, who anticipated the evolutionary theory of Lamarck, is saying that the hypothesis of evolution does not affect the validity of man's moral ideals.

To some extent Diderot formed his ethical ideas under the influence of Shaftesbury's writings. But these ideas were not precisely fixed, except in the sense that he always upheld ideals of benevolence and humanity. He began at least by maintaining a 'rationalist' idea of immutable moral laws. But he found the basis of these laws in man's nature, that is to say, in the organic unity of man's impulses, passions and appetites, rather than in *a priori* commands of the reason. And he was hostile to the ascetic ideal as being contrary to nature. In other words, even if Diderot continued to uphold the idea of a natural law, he came to lay emphasis on its empirical basis and on its pragmatic effectiveness, when contrasted with a theological ethic, in promoting the common welfare.

(ii) Jean le Rond d'Alembert (1717–83) was born out of wedlock and was abandoned by his parents. He owed his name Jean le Rond or Lerond to the fact that he was found near the church of S. Jean le Rond at Paris. The surname was added later by himself. He was cared for by the wife of a glazier named Rousseau; but his real father, a certain Chevalier Destouches, settled an annuity on him, and he was thus enabled to study.

In 1738 d'Alembert was admitted as an advocate, but he did not practise as such. He then turned to medicine; but in a very short time he decided to give himself entirely to mathematics. He presented several papers, including his *Mémoire sur le calcul intégral* (1739) to the Academy of Sciences, and in 1741 he was made a member of this academy. His work in mathematics and science was of considerable importance. In 1741 he published his *Mémoire sur le réfraction des corps solides* and in 1743 his *Traité de dynamique*. In this treatise on dynamics he developed what is still known as 'd'Alembert's principle', and in 1744 he applied it in his *Traité de l'équilibre et du mouvement des fluides*. Subsequently he discovered the calculus of partial differences and applied it in his *Réflexion sur la cause générale des vents* (1747), which was crowned by the Prussian Academy. Among other writings we may mention his *Essai d'une nouvelle théorie sur la résistance des fluides* (1752) and his *Recherches sur différents points importants du système du monde* (1754–6).

As we have seen, d'Alembert was associated with Diderot in editing the *Encyclopaedia*, and he was the author of the *Discours préliminaire*. He also wrote a number of articles, chiefly, though not exclusively, on mathematical topics. But in 1758 he withdrew from collaboration in the work, wearied with opposition and the hazards of publication. In 1752 he had published *Mélanges de littérature, d'histoire et de philosophie*, and in 1759 there appeared his *Essai sur les éléments de philosophie*. In 1763 he visited Berlin, but he refused Frederick the Great's offer of the presidency of the Academy, just as in the previous year he had refused the invitation of Catherine of Russia to become tutor to her son on very generous terms. D'Alembert was a friend of David Hume, who held him in high esteem for his moral character and abilities and left him a legacy of £200 in his will. Being primarily a mathematician and scientist, d'Alembert was less exposed than other Encyclopaedists to suspicion and attack, and in 1755 he had been made a member of the Institute of Bologna on the recommendation of Pope Benedict XIV.

In his preliminary discourse in the *Encyclopaedia* d'Alembert declared that Locke was the creator of scientific philosophy, occupying a position which corresponded to that of Newton in physics. And in the *Elements of Philosophy* he asserted that the eighteenth century was the century of philosophy in a special sense. Natural philosophy had been revolutionized, and nearly all other fields of knowledge had made progress and assumed new forms. 'From the principles of the secular sciences to the foundations of religious revelation, from metaphysics to matters of taste, from music to morals, from the scholastic disputes of theologians to matters of trade, from the laws of princes to those of peoples, from natural law to the arbitrary laws of nations . . . everything has been discussed and analysed, or at least mentioned. The fruit or consequence of this general effervescence of minds has been to cast new light on some things and new shadows on others, just as the effect of the ebb and flow of the tides is to leave some things on the shore and to wash others away.'[1]

This does not mean that for d'Alembert intellectual progress consists simply, or even primarily, in the mere accumulation of new facts. In a manner reminiscent of Descartes he maintains that all the sciences put together are the unfolding of the human intelligence. And he stresses the function of unification. He assumes that the system of phenomena is homogeneous and uniform; and the aim of scientific knowledge is to show the unity and coherence of this system in the light of the principles which it exemplifies.

But this point has to be rightly understood. D'Alembert is not concerned with metaphysical principles. Nor is he concerned with ascertaining the essences of things in a metaphysical sense. Metaphysical theories and speculations lead us into antinomies and result in scepticism; they are not a source of knowledge. We cannot know the why and wherefore of things. We cannot even know that there is an external world. True, we inevitably act on the assumption that there is such a world; but this is a matter of instinct rather than of theoretical knowledge. And it is in no way required for the purpose of scientific philosophy that we should solve problems of this sort. It makes no difference to us, for example, whether we can penetrate to the essences of bodies, 'provided that, matter being supposed such as we conceive it, we can deduce from properties which we regard as primitive other secondary properties which we perceive in matter, and that the general system of phenomena, always uniform and continuous, nowhere manifests to us a contradiction'.[2] To deduce phenomena from principles is not to deduce empirical data from metaphysical principles or from metaphysical essences; it is to deduce observed secondary properties from other observed properties which are regarded as more primitive. The business of scientific philosophy is to describe and correlate phenomena in a systematic way rather than to explain them in a metaphysical sense. Once we attempt to do the latter, we proceed beyond the bounds of what can properly be called knowledge.

We can say, therefore, that d'Alembert was a forerunner of positivism. Science has no need of occult qualities or substances or of metaphysical theories and explanations. And philosophy, like science, is concerned simply with phenomena, even if it considers a wider field of phenomena than is considered by the specialist in some particular limited branch of science. This does not mean, of course, that the natural philosopher is not concerned with explanation in any sense. On the basis of sense-experience he forms clear definitions, and he can deduce verifiable conclusions. But he cannot go beyond the range of phenomena or the empirically verifiable unless he wishes to enter a sphere where no sure knowledge is attainable. Metaphysics must either become a science of facts or remain the field of illusions. The study of the history of opinions shows us how men developed merely probable theories and how in some cases probability became, so to speak, truth, when it had been verified by patient investigation. So too the study of the history of the sciences suggests points of view for further investigation and theories which must be empirically tested.

In d'Alembert's moral theory we can see the same concern to separate ethics from theology and metaphysics which was commonly shared by the philosophers of the period. Morality is the consciousness of our duty towards our fellowmen. And the principles of morality all converge towards the same end, namely to showing us the intimate connection between our true interest and the performance of our social duty. The task of the moral philosopher is thus to make clear to man his place in society and his duty of employing his powers for the common welfare and happiness.

We cannot legitimately call d'Alembert a materialist. For he abstained from pronouncements about the ultimate nature of things and mistrusted the dogmatic materialists and mechanists. Apart from his importance as a mathematician, the salient feature of his thought is probably his insistence on positivist methodology. Like Diderot, he thought that progress could pretty well be taken for granted, in the sense that intellectual enlightenment would bring with it social and moral progress. But in his conception of intellectual and scientific development he was profoundly influenced by Newton and the experimental method. His thought moved within the field traced out by contemporary scientific advance rather than in the framework of controversy about the ultimately spiritual or material nature of reality.

2. There were, however, some outspoken materialists belonging to the period of the French Enlightenment; and in this section something will be said about La Mettrie, d'Holbach and Cabanis.

(i) Julien Offray de La Mettrie (1709–51) was a doctor who was stimulated by observation in himself of the effects of fever on the mind and thought to inquire into the relations between physiological factors and psychical operations. His *Histoire naturelle de l'âme* appeared in 1745, and in the following year he was banished from France. In 1748 he published at Leyden *L'homme machine*, and in the same year he was banished from Holland and sought refuge with Frederick the Great. *L'homme plante* appeared at Potsdam in 1748.

In his *Natural History of the Soul* (later called *Treatise on the Soul*) La Mettrie argues that man's psychical life of thought and volition arises out of sensations and is developed by education. Where there are no senses, there are no ideas; the fewer the senses the fewer the ideas; and where there is little education or instruction, there is a paucity of ideas. The soul or mind depends essentially on bodily organization, and its natural history must be studied by exact observation of physiological processes. The senses, says La Mettrie, are his philosophers. The theory of a spiritual soul, intrinsically independent of the body, is an unnecessary hypothesis.

In *Man a Machine* La Mettrie refers to Descartes' description of the living body as a machine. But in his opinion Descartes had no warrant for asserting dualism, that is, for speaking of man as composed of a thinking substance, immaterial and free, and of an extended substance, the body. He should have applied his interpretation of the physical organism to the whole man. At the same time La Mettrie differs considerably from Descartes in his idea of matter. For this is not mere extension: it also possesses the power of movement and the capacity of sensation. At least, organized matter possesses a principle of motion which differentiates it from unorganized matter; and sensation arises from motion. We may not be able to explain or thoroughly understand this emergence; but we cannot thoroughly understand matter itself and its basic properties. It is sufficient that observation assures us that motion, the principle of organized matter, does emerge. And, given the principle of motion, not only sensation but all other forms of psychical life can arise. In fine, all forms of life depend ultimately on different forms of physical organization. Of course, the analogy of a machine is not adequate for describing man. We can also use the analogy of a plant. (Hence *L'homme plante*.) But this does not mean that there are radically different levels in Nature. We find differences of degree rather than of kind.

In matters of religion La Mettrie professed a complete agnosticism. But he was popularly regarded as an atheist. And, indeed, he tried to improve upon Bayle's assertion that a State composed of atheists is possible by adding that it is not only possible but also desirable. In other words, religion is not only quite independent of morality but also inimical to it. As for La Mettrie's ethical ideas, their nature is sufficiently indicated by the title of his work, *The Art of Enjoyment or the School of Pleasure*.[3] He did not possess the moral idealism of Diderot. Incidentally, this work was but one of a number of treatises published in the eighteenth century which represented the views of the circle of so-called 'libertines', though the views expressed ranged from the emphasis on sense pleasure, which was characteristic of La Mettrie, to more refined and intellectualized programmes for enjoyment.

(ii) La Mettrie's writings exercised a considerable influence; but the chief statement of a materialist position was the *Système de la nature ou des lois du monde physique et du monde morale* (1770) by the Baron Paul von Holbach (1723–89). Born in Germany, he resided at Paris and is generally known as d'Holbach. His house at Paris was a meeting-place for *les philosophes*, where they were entertained with lavish hospitality by the Baron and his wife who, incidentally, had no sympathy with her husband's philosophy. Hume, while at Paris, took part in these gatherings, though he did not care for d'Holbach's dogmatic atheism. He expressed his attachment to the Baron, but among the members of the circle he preferred d'Alembert. Horace Walpole, however, who had no love for philosophers, remarks in his letters[4] that he had left off going to d'Holbach's dinners and that 'nonsense for nonsense, I like the Jesuits better than the philosophers'.

According to d'Holbach, Descartes was wrong in thinking that matter is inert of itself, so that motion has to be added from outside, as it were. Motion flows necessarily from the essence of matter, that is, from the nature of the atoms of which things are ultimately composed. Descartes was also wrong in thinking that matter is all of a piece, all of the same kind. Leibniz's principle of indiscernibles contains much more truth than the Cartesian notion of the homogeneity of matter. And there are different kinds of movement, each thing having its laws of motion which are inevitably obeyed.

Things as we know them empirically consist of different organizations of atoms, and their behaviours differ according to their several structures. Everywhere we find the phenomena of attraction and repulsion; but in the human sphere these take the form of love and hate. Further, each thing strives to preserve itself in being. And man too is impelled by self-love or self-interest. But this should not be taken as excluding a concern for the welfare of society. For man is a social being, and rational concern for one's own satisfaction and welfare goes hand in hand with concern for the general welfare. D'Holbach was a thorough-going materialist and determinist; but he did not intend to advocate a life of selfishness. As a man, he was known to have a humane and benevolent character. And among the anonymous works ascribed to him we find the *Système social ou principes naturels de la morale et de la politique* (London, 1773) and *La morale universelle* (Amsterdam, 1776).

The theory of a determined system of Nature, in which motion is not an extraneous element but an essential property of things, seemed to d'Holbach to rule out any need for postulating God or any supramundane being or beings. The order or system of the world is not the result of a divine plan, but of the nature of things and of their immanent laws. But d'Holbach was by no means content to profess agnosticism and to say that the religious hypothesis, as Hume called it, was unnecessary. In his opinion religion was the enemy of human happiness and progress. In a well-known passage of the second book of the *System of Nature* he declares that ignorance and fear created the gods, that fancy, enthusiasm and deceit have adorned or disfigured the pictures formed of them, that weakness worships them, that credulity preserves them, and that tyranny supports belief in them for its own purposes. Belief in God, so far from making men happy, increases their anxiety and fear.

If, therefore, religion, a powerful instrument of political tyranny, could be overthrown, it would be easier to ensure the development of a rational social system in place of the system which is responsible for so much suffering and misery. In his writings d'Holbach was more outspoken in denunciation of the *ancien régime* than was usual among his colleagues. But he rejected revolution as a solution to political problems, and in his *Social System* he declared that revolution is worse than the disease which it is supposed to cure.

It is sometimes said that in his *System of Nature* d'Holbach combined and then carried to extremes the different tendencies of the writers of the French Enlightenment. And this is doubtless true to some extent. But his ideas were too extreme for many of his fellow-philosophers. Voltaire, for example, denounced the work for its atheism. And in Germany Frederick the Great drew attention to what he regarded as a flagrant contradiction. According to d'Holbach, human beings are as much subject to determinism as are other things. Yet he does not hesitate to denounce priests and governments in passionate terms and to demand a new social order, though this way of speaking makes no sense unless men are free and can reasonably be praised or blamed for their actions.

Finally, there is an often-quoted estimate of d'Holbach's work from a very different quarter. In *Wahrheit und Dichtung* (Book XI) Goethe speaks of his studies at Strasbourg and remarks that out of curiosity he and his friends had a look at the *System of Nature*. 'We could not conceive how such a book could be dangerous. It appeared to us so grey, so Cimmerian, so corpselike that we had difficulty in enduring its presence and shuddered before it as before a spectre.' To Goethe, d'Holbach's work seemed to deprive Nature and life of all that is precious.

(iii) Particularly crude expressions of materialism can be found in the writings of Pierre Jean Georges Cabanis (1757–1808), a physician and author of *Rapports du physique et du moral de l'homme*. He summed up his view of man in the words *Les nerfs—voilà tout l'homme* and declared that the brain secretes thought as the liver secretes bile. In this case, one would have thought, there are simply different sets of secretions, and it is somewhat difficult to decide which possesses the greater truth-value. It would, however, be misleading to suggest that the whole French Enlightenment should be evaluated in the light of the crude assertions made by materialists such as Cabanis. Indeed, we miss the significance of the materialist current of thought itself if we pay attention simply to these crudities. For its importance lies in its programmatic aspect rather than in the dogmatism against which d'Alembert and others protested. That is to say, its long-term importance lies in its aspect as a programme for studying the connections between physiological and psychological phenomena rather than in its dogmatic reduction of the latter to the former.

Cabanis protested that his concentration on the physiological bases of psychical life should not be taken to imply metaphysical materialism. As regards ultimate causes, he professed agnosticism. But in his view morality must be cut adrift from metaphysical and theological presuppositions and given a firm basis in the scientific study of man. One of his contributions to their study was his insistence on the unity of man's life. It is inappropriate, for example, to speak with Condillac of conferring this or that sense on a statue. The senses are not only interdependent but also intimately connected with other organic functions.

3. Diderot gave it as his opinion that under certain circumstances nothing is more wasteful than preoccupation with method. This is especially true, he said, of natural history in general and of botany in particular. He did not mean, of course, that any science can be profitably studied in a purely haphazard manner. What he meant was that we are simply wasting time if we are preoccupied with discovering some universal method which will be applicable to all the sciences. It is absurd, for example, to suppose that the method applicable in mathematics is applicable also in botany. The form of method and of systematization which is appropriate in the study of botany must be derived from the special character of the subject-matter of this science.

In forming this point of view Diderot was influenced to some extent by the earlier volumes of Buffon's *Histoire naturelle générale et particulière* (1749–88).

(i) In his introductory reflections in the work just mentioned Georges-Louis Leclerc de Buffon (1707–88) maintains that it is a great mistake to form one ideal of scientific method and then to attempt to force all branches of scientific research into the framework of this method. For example, in mathematics we fix clearly the meanings of our symbols, and we can proceed deductively, unfolding the implications of our starting-point; but we cannot do this when we are concerned, not, as in mathematics, with our concepts or with the meanings of symbols, as determined by ourselves, but with existent Nature. Truth is different in mathematics from what it is in the natural sciences. In the latter we must start with observation of phenomena, and only on the basis of observation can we form general conclusions with the aid of analogies. In the end we can see how particular facts are connected together and how universal truths are exemplified in these particular facts. But we cannot employ the deductive method of mathematics. Buffon was the keeper of the royal garden, and it is, indeed, clear that what he says applies with force in the field of botany.

Buffon's rejection of any rigid conception of one ideal and universally applicable scientific method was accompanied by a rejection of the notion that organisms fall into sharply defined classes or species which are separated from one another by rigid boundaries or limits. Even Linnaeus, in his botanical studies, went wrong in this respect. For he arbitrarily selected certain characteristics of plants as the key to classification, whereas we cannot understand Nature in this way. In Nature there is continuity; there are gradual transitions and not rigidly fixed types. In other words, Buffon substituted for the idea of a hierarchy of sharply delimited classes the idea of a series or chain of classes in each of which the members are grasped according to observed kinship. He did not reject the whole notion of classes or species. But the species is a group of members which are more alike to one another, in virtue of observed characteristics, than they are to other things. It is a mistake to suppose that our classifications express the apprehension of fixed essences. We can say, if we like, that Buffon understood classification in terms of what Locke called the 'nominal essence'. But his great point is that we must follow Nature as observed and keep our class-concepts elastic instead of constructing a fixed conceptual scheme and forcing Nature to fit it. If we were concerned merely with our ideas or definitions and their implications, the latter procedure would be apposite. But in botany, for example, we are concerned with knowing reality, not with an ideal system akin to that of mathematics.

It is probably true to say that Buffon's views helped in some way to prepare the way for the theory of evolution. All the same one is not entitled to conclude from his idea of the series or chain of species that he himself maintained this theory. He thought, indeed, of the several types of organisms being brought into existence in a continuous series as external conditions rendered survival possible. But he did not say that one species undergoes a process of transformation into another. He thought rather of a kind of ideal archetype of the living thing, representing the unity of the divine plan, which can take an indefinite number of possible concrete forms. And even though these concrete types are not fixed and rigid, the creation of each is a special act.

(ii) The idea of a series is represented also in the writings of Jean-Baptiste Robinet (1735–1820). For him Nature is faced with the problem of realizing in the most perfect manner possible the three vital functions of nutrition, growth and reproduction, functions which are found in some sense in all matter. Nature's solution to this problem is found in man, who is, therefore, the culmination of the series as far as the material world is concerned. But we can envisage a gradual liberation of activity, which is an essential note of a substance, from matter and from dependence on material organs. And this conception leads us to the idea of pure intelligence.

(iii) There are, however, considerable difficulties in the theory of a purely linear series. And we find Charles Bonnet (1720–93) suggesting that Nature may produce different main lines in the series, which themselves produce subordinate lines. With the German naturalist and traveller, Peter Simon Pallas (1741–1811), we find the analogy of a tree with different branches. For the matter of that, we find with Buffon himself the analogy of a network.

4. The Jesuit, Roger Joseph Boscovich (1711–87), obviously cannot be accounted one of the philosophers of the Enlightenment, if one means by the Enlightenment a movement of thought opposed to all supernatural religion. But the term should not be used simply in this restricted

sense. True, we are dealing now with the French Enlightenment, and Boscovich, who was born at Ragusa, was not a
Frenchman. But for ten years (1773–83) he acted as director
of optics for the marine at Paris; and in any case this is the
most convenient place to make a few remarks about him.

In 1740 Boscovich was appointed professor of mathematics at the Roman College (now the Gregorian University), and while occupying this post he published essays on a
variety of mathematical and astronomical topics. In 1758 he
published at Vienna his *Philosophiae naturalis theoria, redacta ad unicam legem virium in natura existentium*. During
a stay in England he was elected a Fellow of the Royal Society, and in 1769 he was invited by the Royal Society to
undertake a journey to California to observe the transit of
Venus, though acceptance was prevented by the fact that
the Spanish Government had expelled the Jesuits from its
territories. In 1785, after he had returned to Italy from
Paris, he published *Opera pertinentia ad opticam et astronomiam* in five volumes. Among other works we may mention
his *Elementa universae matheseos* (1754).

In Boscovich's opinion there is no such thing as actual
contact between two bodies. The effect of Newton's theory
of gravitation has been to show that action is action at a distance. We cannot, therefore, any longer suppose that motion
or energy is communicated by immediate contact. Instead
we must postulate atoms which attract and repel one another, but which never actually touch each other. Each atom
has a position in space, and each possesses potential force,
in the sense that any two atoms attract or repel one another.
For all distances greater than a certain given distance this
force is an attraction which varies as the inverse square of the
distance. In the case of smaller distances the force is attraction in the case of one distance and repulsion in the case of
the other. But here the laws governing attraction and repulsion have not yet been discovered, though, according to
Boscovich, if we decrease the distance without limit, the
force of repulsion increases without limit. Hence two atoms
can never be in immediate contact. There are, of course,
systems of atoms; but no system can occupy the same space
as another. For when one system approaches another, there
is a point at which the repulsion between the atoms of the

two systems grows to such an extent that it cannot be overcome. Needless to say, Boscovich did not maintain that atoms
are the only reality. He was speaking simply of bodies, and
he went on to show how his theory of dynamic atomism could
be applied in problems of mechanics and physics.

5. The Encyclopaedists were animated by the idea of progress as shown in the growth of the sciences and in a corresponding liberation from superstition. Intellectual enlightenment would be accompanied by a growth of toleration
and by political and social reform. The idea of progress also
finds a place in the theories of the group of eighteenth-century French economists who are known as the 'physiocrats'.
This name was invented by Dupont de Nemours (1739–
1817), who belonged to the group. The physiocrats originally
called themselves economists, but their special name (com-
pounded from the Greek words *phusis*, nature, and *kratein*,
to rule) is an apt one because it draws attention to their
fundamental tenet. This was that there are natural economic
laws, and that economic progress depends on our allowing
these laws to have unrestricted play.

It follows from this position that the government should
interfere as little as possible in economic affairs. Society is
founded on a contract whereby the individual submits to the
limitation of his natural freedom in so far as its exercise is
incompatible with the rights of other people. And government should limit itself to securing the fulfilment of the
contract. If it tries to interfere in the field of economics, by
restricting competition, for example, or by maintaining privileges and monopolies, it is trying to interfere with the
operation of 'natural law'. And no good can come from such
interference: Nature knows best.

This does not mean that the physiocrats were enthusiastic
democrats, in the sense that they were zealous promoters of
the idea of popular rule. On the contrary, they tended to look
to enlightened autocracy as a means of implementing their
policy. The doctrines of non-interference and *laissez-faire*
lent themselves, indeed, to use in a revolutionary sense as
part of a general demand for freedom; and they came in
fact to be so used. But neither Quesnay nor Turgot, for instance, can be called an advocate of revolution or of the
substitution of popular for monarchic rule.

(i) François Quesnay (1694–1774) studied medicine and surgery and became physician to Louis XV. But he devoted himself while at court to the study of economics, and it was round him and Jean de Gournay (1712–59) that the group of physiocrats centred. Quesnay wrote some articles on economic matters for the *Encyclopaedia*. He also published, among other writings, *Maximes générales de gouvernement économique d'un royaume agricole* (1758) and, in the same year, a *Tableau économique avec son explication, ou extrait des économies royales de Sully*.

According to Quesnay, national wealth is dependent on agricultural productiveness. Those labours alone are truly productive which increase the quantity of raw materials. And national wealth depends on the excess of these products over the cost of producing them. Manufacture and commerce merely give new forms to the wealth produced (raw materials include, for instance, metals) and transfer wealth from one hand to another. They are therefore 'sterile', not 'productive', though to say this is not to say that they are not useful.

The interest of the landowner and of society are, therefore, one. The greater the agricultural production, the greater the national wealth. Or, as Quesnay put it, poor peasants, a poor kingdom; a poor kingdom, a poor king. The increase of the 'net product', therefore, should be the aim of the practical economist. Trade distributes wealth; but the trading and manufacturing classes make their gains at the expense of the nation, and the common good requires that this expense should be reduced as much as possible. The revenues of the State depend on the net product of agricultural labour; and they should be derived from a land tax.

This peculiar emphasis on agricultural production at the expense of industry and commerce was not shared by all the physiocrats, but it was characteristic of some prominent members of the group. Adam Smith, who made the acquaintance of Quesnay during his visit to Paris in 1764–6, had a high opinion of him; but though he was influenced to some extent by the physiocrats, he did not agree with the description of industry and commerce as 'sterile'.

(ii) Anne Robert Jacques Turgot, Baron de Laune (1727–81), first studied for the priesthood but abandoned these studies before ordination and subsequently occupied various parliamentary and administrative posts. A friend of Voltaire, he also became acquainted with Quesnay, Gournay, Dupont de Nemours and other economists of the physiocratic school. Besides concerning himself with practical economic reforms he wrote a number of essays and articles, some for the *Encyclopaedia*. In 1770 he wrote his *Lettres sur la liberté du commerce des grains,* and in 1776 he published as a separate book his *Réflexions sur la formation et la distribution des richesses,* which had first appeared in a journal in 1769–70. In 1774 he was appointed Minister of Marine and shortly afterwards Comptroller-General. In the latter position, which was effectively that of minister of finance, he insisted on economy and succeeded in raising the national credit. At first he enjoyed the support of the king, but his plans for the abolition of privilege, the subjection of all classes to taxation and freedom of trade in corn won for him many enemies, while his schemes for an educational system and for poor-relief proved too much for the king. In the end he was forced to resign in 1776. For the rest of his life he gave himself to his studies.

As an economist Turgot shared Quesnay's ideas about land as the only source of wealth and about complete freedom in industry and commerce. But he was much more than an economist. For example, in his article on existence in the *Encyclopaedia* he developed a positivist interpretation. The given is a multiplicity of phenomena, the mutual relations of which are constantly changing. Yet in certain groups there are relatively persistent relations of co-ordination. One of these groups is what we call the self or ego, a particular group of perceptions related to perceptions or feelings of pleasure and pain. To affirm the existence of the external world is to affirm that other groups of phenomena, either immediately given or postulated, stand to the self in spatial or causal relations. Existence thus means for us existence as a subject or for a subject in the system of spatial and causal relations. The question what existence is in itself or what existent things are apart from the system of spatio-temporal and causal relations, is not a question which we are competent to answer. In other words we cannot solve metaphysical problems. Science is concerned with the description of phenomena, not with 'ultimate questions'.

Turgot is of importance in the development of a positivist interpretation of history. In human as distinct from animal history there is progress, in the sense that the intellectual achievements of one generation are taken over by, widened and surpassed by, the next. In each cultural period we can, indeed, find a certain recurring pattern. But by and large the intellectual advance of the human race passes through three main phases, the religious, the philosophical or metaphysical, and the scientific. In this third phase the mathematical and natural sciences triumph over speculative metaphysics and lay the foundation for further scientific advance and for new forms of social and economic life. Thus Turgot anticipated the interpretation of history which was to be expounded in the next century by Auguste Comte. And though from the point of view of economics he must be classed with Quesnay and the other physiocrats, from the wider philosophical point of view he can be classed with the editors of the *Encyclopaedia*, d'Alembert and Diderot.

6. The French Enlightenment is often associated, doubtless understandably, with the crude materialism and the anti-religious polemics of men such as Helvétius, La Mettrie and d'Holbach. And this is, of course, a real aspect of eighteenth-century French philosophy. But the spirit of the movement is probably better represented by men such as d'Alembert, Diderot and Turgot who tended to abstain from making dogmatic pronouncements about ultimate reality and who looked to scientific progress and the growth of toleration to bring about new and more rational forms of social and political life. Eighteenth-century French philosophy doubtless helped to prepare the way for the Revolution; but the philosophers themselves aimed, not at bloody revolution, but rather at the spread of knowledge and through the diffusion of knowledge at social reform. I do not mean to imply that the philosophical outlook of *les philosophes* was adequate or that I agree with their anti-metaphysical point of view. At the same time it is a mistake to regard them simply in the light of the dogmatic materialism of certain writers. As has been already indicated, to do this is to overlook the programmatic aspect of their work, the programme of extending the sphere of empirically verified knowledge as far as it will go. Crudities apart, they look forward, for instance, to the

growth of empirical psychology and biology, to the development of sociological studies, and to the rise of political economy. In the next century the idealists felt the need for reconciling and synthesizing the religious, metaphysical and scientific outlooks. But this ideal presupposed, of course, the presence of the scientific and positivist outlook, and in helping to produce it the eighteenth-century philosophers were of considerable importance. As the idealists of the nineteenth century saw, the scientific outlook did not call for negation but rather for modification by incorporation in a wider synthesis. Whether they succeeded in providing this synthesis, is, of course, another question.

Chapter Three

ROUSSEAU (1)

Life and writings – The evils of civilization – The origin of inequality – The appearance of the theory of the general will – Rousseau's philosophy of feeling.

1. Jean-Jacques Rousseau was born at Geneva on June 28th, 1712, the son of a watchmaker. In 1725 he was apprenticed for five years to an engraver; but after a while he ran away. The priest of Confignon, a village near Geneva, introduced the boy to the Baronne de Warens, who was to figure prominently in his life. Under her influence Rousseau was converted to Catholicism, and in 1728 he was received into the Church at Turin in a hospice for catechumens, an institution of which he has given us a most unfavourable picture in his *Confessions*. After a period of wandering and unsettled existence he rejoined Mme de Warens in 1731. His life with her, first at Chambéry and afterwards at Les Charmettes, was later idealized by him as an idyllic episode. It was in this period that he endeavoured by reading to make up for the deficiencies of his earlier unsystematic education.

From 1738 to 1740 Rousseau acted as tutor to the children of a M. de Mably, and while occupying this post he made the acquaintance of Condillac. In 1742 he went to Paris, only to proceed to Venice in 1743 as secretary to the new French ambassador, the Comte de Montaigu. The two men did not get on well together, and in the following year Rousseau, dismissed for insolence, returned to Paris. In 1745 he met Voltaire for the first time, and in 1749 Diderot invited him to write the articles on music for the *Encyclopaedia*. He was also introduced to d'Holbach's *salon*. In the same year the Academy of Dijon offered a prize for the best essay on the question whether the progress of the arts and sciences had tended to the purification or to the corruption of morality. Rousseau's *Discourse on the Arts and Sciences* was the prize-winning essay, and it was published in 1750. Its author became at once a famous man. But as he had indulged in an attack on civilization and its corrupting effects on man, his views not unnaturally met with strong opposition from *les philosophes*, and a battle of words ensued. Rousseau was already well on his way to a decisive break with the d'Holbach circle. However, undaunted by opposition, he decided to compete for another prize offered by the Dijon Academy, this time on the question, what is the origin of inequality among men and whether it is authorized by the natural law. His *Discourse on the Origin and Foundation of Inequality among Men* did not obtain the prize, but it was published in 1758. In it we are presented with a picture of natural man or man in the state of nature, that is to say, of man when the trappings and accretions of civilization have been stripped away. Man is naturally good, but civilization has brought with it inequality and a host of consequent evils. In the same year, 1755, Rousseau's article on political economy was printed in the *Encyclopaedia*. In 1758 it appeared separately as a *Discourse on Political Economy*. The idea of the general will makes its first appearance in this essay.

Rousseau had been for some time disgusted with life at Paris, a disgust which was reflected in his first two *Discourses*. And his mind turned towards his native city. Hence in 1754 he turned his back on the French capital and set out for Geneva. He was there received back into the Protestant Church. This change did not, indeed, signify any religious upheaval. For, as Rousseau observed, if his philosophical friends at Paris had done nothing else for him, they had at least undermined any belief he may have had in Catholic dogma. His main reason for formally returning to Protestantism was, as he admits, his wish to regain Genevan citizenship. But the philosopher did not remain long at Geneva. Returning to Paris in October 1754 he sent a copy of his *Discourse on Inequality*, when it appeared in the following year, to Voltaire who wrote to thank him for 'your new book against the human race'.

From 1756 until 1762 Rousseau lived in retirement at Montmorency. This was a period of great literary activity. In 1758 he wrote his *Lettre à d'Alembert sur les spectacles* relating to the article on Geneva in the *Encyclopaedia* in which d'Alembert had criticized the Genevan prohibition of theatrical performances. The year 1761 saw the publication of *La Nouvelle Héloïse*, Rousseau's novel. And in 1762 there appeared not only his most famous work, the *Social Contract* (*Du contrat social*) but also *Émile*, his book on education. By this time Rousseau had already quarrelled with Diderot. His decisive break with *les philosophes* found expression in his *Lettres morales*, though these were not published until 1861.

As a result of the publication of the *Social Contract* and *Émile* in 1762 Rousseau had to take refuge in Switzerland. But the reaction to his works at Geneva was also hostile, and in 1763 he formally renounced his Genevan citizenship. In 1765 he set out for Berlin, but on the way he decided to go to England; and in January 1766 he crossed the Channel with David Hume who had offered him sanctuary in England. It cannot be said that this visit was altogether successful. By this time Rousseau, always sensitive and suspicious, was suffering from persecution mania, and he became convinced that Hume was in league with his enemies. Hume, not understanding Rousseau's abnormal state of mind, was very angry, especially as he was engaged in procuring a royal pension for his friend; and, disregarding any advice to the contrary, he published in London and Paris his account of the affair. In May 1766 Rousseau returned to France, where he was received as a guest by the Prince de Conti. In 1770, after various wanderings, he returned to Paris, neglecting the fact that he was liable to arrest. But as a matter of fact he was left undisturbed by the police, though he was subjected to a campaign of literary vilification, especially by Grimm and Diderot. In May 1778 he left for Erménonville, as guest of the Marquis de Girardin, and it was there that he died on July 2nd. His *Confessions* and the *Rêveries du Promeneur Solitaire* were published posthumously (1782–9). The *Considerations on the Government of Poland* appeared in 1782.

The character and life of Rousseau provide ample material for the psychologist. True, some of the troubles were due to physical ill-health. He suffered for years from a bladder complaint, and he most probably died of uraemia. But from the beginning social adjustment was difficult for him; and though he was capable of deep affection and attachment, he was too sensitive, suspicious and intolerant to maintain constant friendships. A man much given to self-analysis, he often failed to understand either himself or others. A philosopher, he yet possessed a highly emotional temperament, and he drew attention to the tension between emotion and thought, heart and mind, which oppressed him. Romantic, emotional, possessing a genuine religious feeling yet self-centred and mentally unbalanced, it is in no way surprising that Rousseau broke with *les philosophes*. D'Holbach warned Hume that he was contemplating warming a viper in his bosom. And Hume later referred to Rousseau as 'the most singular of all human beings', though he afterwards acutely remarked that the latter had only felt during the whole course of his life and that in him sensibility had risen to an unexampled pitch. But all this, of course, in no way affects Rousseau's importance in the history of philosophy.[1]

2. 'It is a noble and beautiful spectacle to see man raising himself, so to speak, from nothing by his own exertions.'[2] These words form the beginning of the first part of Rousseau's *Discourse on the Arts and Sciences*. And we would naturally expect to find them followed by a laudatory account of the blessings of civilization. If they had been written by d'Alembert, for example, our expectations would doubtless have been fulfilled. But not so in the case of Rousseau. We are soon told that 'the mind, as well as the body, has its needs: those of the body are the basis of society, those of the mind its ornaments'.[3] These words can, indeed, be taken in a quite innocuous sense, even if they seem to imply that the fulfilment of all non-physical needs is no more than an unessential ornament of society. But we straightway learn that the arts, literature and the sciences fling garlands of flowers over the chains which weigh men down and stifle in men's breasts the sense of liberty for which they seem to have been born. These 'ornaments' make men love their slavery. 'Necessity raised up thrones; the arts and sciences have made them strong.'[4]

The way is thus prepared for a rhetorical attack on so-called civilized society. Rousseau draws special attention to the artificiality of social life. In more rudimentary forms of society human nature may not have been fundamentally better than it is now; but men were sincere and open, letting themselves be seen as they were. Now 'we no longer dare to seem what we really are, but lie under a perpetual restraint'.[5] The herd of men all act exactly alike, unless some very powerful motive intervenes; and sincere friendship and real confidence are banished. The veil of conventional politeness covers all sorts of unworthy attitudes. Again, we may not take the name of God in vain by vulgar oaths; but real blasphemy does not disturb us. We do not indulge in extravagant boasting; instead we subtly decry the merits of others and artfully calumniate them. 'Our hatred of other nations diminishes, but patriotism dies with it. Ignorance is held in contempt; but a dangerous scepticism has succeeded it.'[6] Rousseau disliked and disapproved of the cosmopolitan spirit of the Enlightenment.

In his picture of civilized society Rousseau was obviously universalizing his experience at Paris, where he had hitherto appeared in fashionable society not on his own merits but in a humiliating position of dependence. However, some of what he says is doubtless true enough and provides material for the preacher. It is true, for instance, that in sophisticated society extravagant boasting is considered ludicrous but that the same end is sought for by the device of subtle depreciation of others. Rousseau, however, goes on to ascribe this state of affairs to the growth of the arts and sciences. 'Our minds have been corrupted in proportion as the arts and sciences have improved.'[7] And scientific advance is ascribed to 'vain curiosity'.[8] But it is one thing to draw attention to certain shadows in eighteenth-century society, and it is quite another thing to assign the advance of the arts and sciences as the cause of these defects.

To be sure, Rousseau endeavours to support his thesis by reference to history. Egypt, we are told, became the mother of philosophy (a very questionable proposition) and the fine arts, but soon she was conquered by Cambyses and subsequently by the Greeks, the Romans, the Arabs, and finally the Turks. In Greece, Rousseau tells us, the progress of the sciences soon produced dissolute manners and led to the imposition of the Macedonian yoke. 'Not all the eloquence of Demosthenes could breathe life into a body which luxury and the arts had once enervated.'[9] We can consider by contrast the virtues of the early Persians and of the Scythians, not to speak of the 'simplicity, innocence and virtue'[10] of the Germanic tribes who conquered the Romans. And we must not forget Sparta, 'eternal proof of the vanity of science'.[11]

In the second part of the *Discourse* we are roundly informed that 'astronomy was born of superstition, eloquence of ambition, hatred, falsehood and flattery; geometry of avarice; physics of an idle curiosity; and even moral philosophy of human pride. Thus the arts and sciences owe their birth to our vices.'[12] They arise out of evil, and they lead to evil consequences. They produce luxury and generate weakness. The military virtues of the Romans were extinguished in proportion as the latter cultivated the fine arts. And 'if the cultivation of the sciences is prejudicial to military qualities, it is still more so to moral qualities'.[13] An expensive education is provided which teaches everything but moral probity and integrity. Literary, artistic and scientific proficiency are honoured, but moral virtue goes unrewarded. Towards the end of his *Discourse* Rousseau does, indeed, recall to mind the fact that he is addressing the Academy of Dijon and that he is competing for a literary prize. And he finds it advisable to say something in favour of men such as Francis Bacon, Descartes and Newton, 'those teachers of mankind'.[14] But he contrasts these geniuses, who were intended by Nature herself to be her disciples, with 'the herd of text-book authors',[15] who have indiscreetly broken open the doors of the sanctuary of the sciences and admitted an unworthy populace to information and ideas which it would be all the better for lacking. There can be little doubt whom Rousseau has in mind.

Rousseau's critics had no difficulty in showing the deficiencies in his historical knowledge and the weakness of his arguments in favour of the thesis that moral degeneration was caused by the growth of the arts and sciences. If he were alive today, he would doubtless point out how military needs have stimulated the development of scientific research in certain departments. And he would doubtless maintain that such advance has arisen from human vice and leads to evil consequences. But there is obviously another side to the pictures. Even if advance in atomic physics, for instance, has been stimulated in some sense by war, the fruits of research can be used for other than destructive purposes.

Again, it is easy to criticize Rousseau's idealization of Sparta at the expense of Athens and his panegyric of the virtues of the Germanic tribes. However, Rousseau himself explicitly admitted the lack of logic and order in the work and its weakness in argument. In spite, however, of its obvious shortcomings the first *Discourse* possesses some importance as a counterblast to the Encyclopaedists' assumption that the advancement of the arts and sciences represents human progress in a general sense. True, it should not be taken as a complete and wholesale rejection of civilized society. It was the expression of feeling, of an attitude adopted in the light of an idea which came to Rousseau with the force of a sudden illumination. But later on, above all in the *Social Contract*, he undertakes to justify the transition from man's primitive state to that of organized society, and to inquire what form of social institution is most compatible with man's natural goodness and is least likely to corrupt and deprave him. Moreover, it appears that in 1750 or 1751 Rousseau began to plan a work on *Political Institutions* which he later abandoned after having extracted from his notes the substance of the *Social Contract*. And in this case he can hardly have held seriously, even at the time when he composed the first *Discourse*, that civilized society is so essentially evil that it must be totally rejected. At the same time it would be quite wrong to conclude that Rousseau was not sincere in what he said about the arts and sciences. The general idea that man has been corrupted by the growth of an artificial civilization and by rationalism remained with him, even if, to obtain an adequate picture of his philosophy, we have to balance it by his positive doctrine concerning the State and its function. In his later writings there is, indeed, a certain change of attitude, but it does not amount to a wholesale recantation of his earlier works.

3. If we assume that man has been corrupted by an artificial civilization, what is the natural state, the state of nature, from which he has been removed? That is to say, what positive meaning is to be attached to the term 'state of nature'? This question is discussed by Rousseau in his *Discourse on the Origin and Foundation of the Inequality among Men*.

We cannot, of course, observe the state of nature; for we are acquainted only with man in society. The really primitive

condition of man eludes empirical investigation. Our interpretation, therefore, must take the form of a hypothetical
account. 'Let us begin, then, by laying facts aside, as they
do not affect the question. The investigations into which we
may enter, in treating this subject, must not be considered as
historical truths, but only as mere conditional and hypothetical reasonings, calculated to explain the nature of things
rather than to ascertain their actual origin, just like the hypotheses which our physicists daily form about the formation of the world.'[16] In practice this means that we have
to take man as we know him and then abstract from all supernatural gifts and from those faculties which he can acquire
only in the course of a long process of social development.
Indeed, we have to abstract from society itself.

When we act in this way, we find man 'satisfying his hunger at the first oak and slaking his thirst at the first brook;
finding his bed at the foot of the tree which afforded him a
repast; and, with that, all his wants supplied'.[17] Such a man
would be physically robust, unafraid of the animals which
he surpasses in skill, if not in strength, subject to few causes
of sickness and so standing in little need of medicines, and
still less of doctors. His chief concern would be self-preservation. His senses of sight, hearing and smell would be refined,
but not the senses of touch and taste, which are perfected
by softness and sensuality.

How does savage man differ from the animal? 'It is not so
much the understanding that constitutes the specific difference between the man and the brute, as the human quality
of freedom . . . and it is particularly in his consciousness of
this liberty that the spirituality of his soul is displayed. For
physics may explain in some degree the mechanism of the
senses and the formation of ideas; but in the power of willing or rather of choosing, and in the feeling of this power,
nothing is to be found but acts which are purely spiritual and
wholly inexplicable by the laws of mechanism.'[18] Rousseau
thus rejects outright the adequacy of a purely materialistic
and mechanistic interpretation of man.

A further quality which distinguishes man from the brute
is the former's faculty of self-improvement, his perfectibility.
But man was first governed by immediate wants and by instinct and feeling. 'To will and not to will, to desire and to

fear, must be the first and almost the only operations of his soul until new circumstances occasion new development of his faculties.'[19] The desires of the savage never go beyond his physical wants. 'The only goods he recognizes in the universe are food, a female and sleep; the only evil he fears are pain and hunger.'[20]

Rousseau is imagining man 'wandering up and down the forests, without industry, without speech and without home, an equal stranger to war and to all ties, neither standing in need of his fellow-creatures nor having any desire to hurt them'.[21] Man is pictured, therefore, as devoid of social life and as not yet having reached the level of reflection. Can we say of such a man that he possesses moral qualities? In a strict sense, no; but it does not follow that man in a state of nature can be called vicious. We are not entitled to conclude that because man in his most primitive state had no idea of goodness, he was therefore bad. Again, where there are no 'mine' and 'thine', there are no clear concepts of justice and injustice; but it does not follow that in the absence of these concepts men must behave in a violent and ruthless manner. Hobbes's picture of the state of nature as a state of war of all against all was unjustified. He was right in saying that self-love was the fundamental impulse; but self-love, in the sense of the impulse to self-preservation, does not of itself involve badness and violence. In the beginning the individual took little note of his fellows; and when he did so, the natural or innate feeling of compassion came into operation. It precedes all reflection, and even the brutes sometimes show it. To this theme of natural compassion and to its relation to self-love I shall return in the concluding section of this chapter. Meanwhile it is sufficient to note that for Rousseau man in the primitive state of nature is good. Even if he cannot be called good in a strictly moral sense, morality is simply a development of his natural feelings and impulses. Thus in his letter to Christophe de Beaumont, archbishop of Paris, which was printed in 1763, he could say roundly that the fundamental ethical principle is that man is naturally good and that there is no original perversity or sin in human nature.

It will have been noted that Rousseau pictures primitive man as without speech. And in the first part of the *Discourse on Inequality* he makes some reflections about the origins of language and about its importance in man's intellectual development. Language originated in 'the simple cry of nature';[22] but in the course of time conventional signs were established by common consent, a particular name being given to a particular thing. But Rousseau does not profess to be able to explain how the transition took place from this stage of linguistic development to the use of general terms expressing general ideas. 'General ideas cannot be introduced into the mind without the assistance of words, nor can the understanding seize them except by means of propositions.'[23] But the words seem to postulate ideas or thoughts. We are left, therefore, with a problem. There is also the problem of the relation of language to society. 'I leave to anyone who will undertake it the discussion of the difficult problem, which was most necessary, the existence of society for the invention of language, or the invention of language for the establishment of society.'[24] However, whatever the answers to such problems may be, the development of man's intellectual life would be unthinkable apart from the development of language.

In the second part of the *Discourse on Inequality* Rousseau discusses the transition from the state of nature to organized society. He imagines how men gradually came to experience the advantage of common undertakings and how they thus came, on separate occasions at least, to develop a sense of social bonds. But the point on which Rousseau lays special emphasis is the establishment of private property. 'The first man who, having enclosed a piece of ground, bethought himself of saying *This is mine*, and found people simple enough to believe him, was the real founder of civil society.'[25] Property was introduced, equality disappeared, forests became smiling fields, slavery and misery arose with the crops. 'Metallurgy and agriculture were the two arts which produced this great revolution.'[26] Moral distinctions between justice and injustice also appeared. But this is not to say that men were better than they had been in the state of nature. 'Usurpations by the rich, robbery by the poor, and the unbridled passions of both, suppressed the cries of natural compassion and the still feeble voice of justice and filled men with avarice, ambition and vice. . . . The new-born state of society thus gave rise to a horrible state of war.'[27] In other words, private property was the result of man's departure from his state of primitive simplicity, and it brought untold evils in its train.

We have seen that Rousseau's primitive state of nature did not correspond to Hobbes's state of nature; it was not a condition of affairs of which it would be true to say, *Homo homini lupus*. But the form of society which has just been described was likened by Rousseau to a state of war, and in this respect it is similar to Hobbes's state of nature, though in some other important respects it is dissimilar. For example, moral distinctions arise for Rousseau in the state of civil society which, considered in abstraction, precedes the formation of political society,[28] whereas for Hobbes moral distinctions really follow the covenant whereby political society and government are established.

Given the insecurity and other evils which attend the establishment and development of the institution of private property, the establishment of political society, government and law was a foregone conclusion. 'All ran headlong to their chains in hope of securing their liberty; or they had just wit enough to perceive the advantage of political institutions, without sufficient experience to enable them to foresee the dangers.'[29] Government and law were thus established by common consent. But Rousseau is not the man to wax enthusiastic over this development. On the contrary, the institution of political society 'bound new fetters on the poor and gave new powers to the rich; irretrievably destroyed natural liberty, fixed eternally the law of property and inequality, converted clever usurpation into unalterable right, and, for the advantage of a few ambitious individuals, subjected all mankind to perpetual labour, slavery and wretchedness'.[30]

Rousseau declares, therefore, that he is content to adopt the common opinion and to regard the establishment of political society as 'a real contract between the people and the chiefs chosen by them; a contract by which both parties bind themselves to observe the laws therein expressed, which form the bonds of their union'.[31] But we can go on to ask, what was the course of development of political society? Did it begin with arbitrary power and despotism, or was despotism a later development? Rousseau's answer to this question is unequivocal. 'I regard it then as certain that government did not begin with arbitrary power, but that this is the depravation, the extreme term, of government and brings it back finally to just that law of the strongest which it was originally designed to remedy.'[32]

In the state of nature there was only natural or physical inequality, which consists in inequality of natural gifts and talents, whether physical or mental. And it is useless to ask, what is its source? For the very name shows that it is established by Nature. The subject of the *Discourse*, therefore, is what Rousseau calls 'moral or political inequality'.[33] This is due originally to the development of our faculties, and it is 'rendered permanent and legitimate by the establishment of property and laws'.[34] We can say, in addition, that whenever it is not proportionate to natural or physical inequality, it is at variance with natural right. It is wrong, for instance, that 'the privileged few should gorge themselves with superfluities while the starving multitude is in want of the bare necessities of life'.[35] And when we arrive at despotism, we have come, as it were, full circle. The subjects, being all reduced to slaves, return to their first equality. And as their master is unrestrained, all moral distinctions and principles of equity vanish. Men have then returned to a state of nature. Yet it differs from the original state of nature. For the latter was a state of innocence and simplicity, whereas the former is the result of corruption.

As we saw, Rousseau proposed to begin his *Discourse* by laying facts aside and by developing an hypothesis, that is, an hypothetical account of the origin of inequality. And according to his hypothesis moral or political inequality can be attributed not only to the improvement of the human faculties but also, and above all, to the establishment first of private property and then of political society, government and law. In the end we have a sharp antithesis between the natural goodness and simplicity of primitive man on the one hand and, on the other, the corruption of civilized man and the evils of organized society. At the same time perfectibility was assigned as one of the distinguishing marks of man as distinct from the brute. We can understand, therefore, the objection raised by Charles Bonnet (1720–93), writing under the pseudonym of Philopolis, that if perfectibility is a natural attribute of man, civilized society is natural. And this is obviously by no means the only objection which can be brought against the *Discourse on Inequality*.

But though Rousseau repeats in this *Discourse* the attack on the idea of progress which he had made in the first *Discourse*, he makes it clear at the end that he does not advocate the absurd idea of destroying society. 'What, then, is to be done? Must societies be totally abolished? Must *meum* and *tuum* be annihilated, and must we return to the forests to live among bears?'[36] Those who wish can return to the woods; but those who, like Rousseau, cannot subsist on acorns or live without laws or magistrates will, while maintaining a healthy contempt for the edifice of civilization, show concern for the reform of society. The way thus lies open for a more positive doctrine of political society. And in point of fact one of Rousseau's main ideas, that of the social or political contract, appears, as we have seen, in the *Discourse on Inequality*.

4. Another of Rousseau's leading ideas, that of the general will, makes its appearance in the *Discourse on Political Economy*. Having distinguished between the State and the family, Rousseau goes on to say that the former is 'a moral being possessed of a will'.[37] This 'general will', which always tends to the preservation and welfare of the whole and of every part, and which is the source of the laws, constitutes for all the members of the State, in their relations to one another and to it, the rule of what is just or unjust'.[38] It is idle, for instance, to say that Spartan children were morally guilty of theft when they stole to supplement their meagre repasts. For they were acting in accordance with the general will of the Spartan State. And this was for them the measure of just and unjust, right and wrong.

When one remembers that the *Discourse on Political Economy* was written about the same time as the *Discourse on Inequality*, and possibly even just before the latter, one may well be astonished at the difference in tone between the two works. But, as was mentioned in the second section of this chapter, it appears that Rousseau had formed positive ideas about the State before he competed for the prizes offered by the Dijon Academy by writing rhetorical essays on set subjects. In the *Discourse on Inequality* the ideas of the state of

nature and of the transition to organized society are discussed, and the theory of political society as resting on a contract makes its appearance; but neither of the first two *Discourses* was intended to be a systematic treatise on political
theory. Then in the *Discourse on Political Economy* we find
a sketch of the theory of the general will. This work gives,
indeed, the impression of being closer in spirit to the *Social
Contract* than to the first two *Discourses*; but the concept of
the general will is not proposed as though it had just been
thought of by Rousseau for the first time.

To return to the theory of the general will. If we take a particular society within the State, say a religious body, this
society possesses a will which is general in relation to its members; that is to say, it possesses a common will directed to the
attainment of the ends of the society. But this will is particular if it is considered in relation to the general will of the
State. Now, moral goodness involves identification of one's
particular will with the general will. It follows, therefore, that
a man may be a good member of some religious body, for
example, but a bad citizen. For though his will may be at
one with the general will of the former, this general will may
be at variance with the general will of the State which com-
prises the religious body within itself.

Rousseau assumes that the general will is directed towards
the common good or interest, that 'the most general will is
always the most just also, and that the voice of the people
is in fact the voice of God'.[39] The general will of the State,
being more general than the general will of any society within
the State, must prevail; for it is more just and directed to a
more universal good. We can conclude, therefore, that 'the
first and most important rule of legitimate or popular government, that is to say, of government whose object is the
good of the people, is . . . to follow in everything the general
will'.[40] Again, 'if you would have the general will accomplished, bring all the particular wills into conformity with it;
in other words, as virtue is nothing more than this conformity
of the particular wills with the general will, establish the
reign of virtue'.[41] But if virtue is nothing more than conformity with the general will, to establish the reign of virtue
can be nothing more than to conform all particular wills to
the general will. Hence public education, on the necessity of

which Rousseau lays stress, must be directed to facilitating and securing this conformity.

A distinction is drawn by Rousseau between sovereignty and government. The sovereign is the power which possesses the right of legislation; the government's function is executive and administrative, that is, to administer the law. 'The first duty of the legislator is to make the laws conformable to the general will.'[42] And 'the general will is always on the side which is most favourable to the public interest, that is to say, most equitable; so that it is needful only to act justly to be certain of following the general will'.[43]

What are we to understand by the general will? There is a natural temptation to interpret Rousseau as identifying the infallible general will with the voice of the people as expressed by vote in assembly. But he does not make this identification. In a large State such general assemblies of the whole people are impracticable; but even when a general assembly is practicable, 'it is by no means certain that its decision would be the expression of the general will'.[44] Of course, if one speaks at all about a quasi-mystical general will of the State, which stands in need of articulate expression, one will inevitably tend to identify it with the expressed decision of the legislature or with the expressed will of some supposed mouthpiece of the people. And this tendency is certainly present in Rousseau. It could hardly be otherwise, given his premises. But it is no more than a tendency; it is not a position which he formally adopts. He explicitly allows, for instance, that an actual decision of the sovereign legislature may fail to be a true expression of the general will. It may be the expression of private interests which for some reason or other have wrongly prevailed. To say, for example, that the general will is the criterion of what is just and what is unjust is not, therefore, to say that no criticism of the laws of the State on the score of injustice is possible. That is why Rousseau can say that the legislator's first duty is to make the laws conform to the general will, and that it is needful only to act justly to be certain of following the general will. Such statements obviously suppose that law is not necessarily or inevitably the true expression of the general will, and that not even common decisions of a general assembly are immune from moral criticism.

As far as the *Discourse on Political Economy* is concerned, Rousseau evidently assumes that there is something higher than the State. We have seen that, according to him, the more general will is also the most just. We can say, therefore, that just as the wills of individuals and of particular societies within the State are particular wills in relation to the general will of the State, so is the will of an individual State a particular will if it is looked at in relation to 'the great city of the world . . . whose general will is always the will of nature, and of which the different States and peoples are individual members'.[45] In other words, there seems to be at the back of Rousseau's mind the traditional concept of a natural moral law, engraven on men's hearts, obedience to which necessarily conduces to human happiness and welfare. And the general will of a political society is a particular canalization, so to speak, of the universal orientation of the human will to the good. The legislator's task is to conform the laws to this general will; and the citizen's task is to bring his particular will into harmony with the general will.

If this general will represents, in a given political society, the universal orientation of the human will to the good of man, it represents what every member of the society 'really' wills. This enables Rousseau to answer the objection that membership of society and obedience to law involve restraint and curtailment of liberty. Men are free by nature. And they unite in societies to assure not only their property and life but also their liberty. In point of fact, however, they become subject to restraint when they form organized societies; they become subjects instead of masters. And is it not paradoxical in the extreme to suggest that men become free or preserve freedom by becoming subjects? Rousseau answers by appealing to the idea of law. 'It is to law alone that men owe justice and liberty.'[46] But this answer can be effective only in so far as law expresses the general will and in so far as the latter represents the 'real' will of everyone and what everyone's reason 'really' dictates. In obeying the law a man is thus obeying his own reason and judgment and following his own real will. And to follow one's own judgment and will is to be free. Hence the obedient citizen is the truly free man; for he obeys a law which expresses his own real will.

This notion was to be of considerable importance in later philosophy.

In the *Discourse on Political Economy*, therefore, which, as has been already remarked, differs strikingly in tone from the first two *Discourses*, we find an emphatic statement of the most significant theory of the *Social Contract*, namely that of the general will. The theory gives rise to considerable difficulties and problems; but further discussion is best postponed to the next chapter. The concluding section of this chapter, however, may help to throw a little more light on Rousseau's general outlook.

In the final pages of the *Discourse on Political Economy* Rousseau deals with the subject of taxation. In his opinion the most equitable system of taxation, and consequently the one best suited to a society of free men, would be a capitation tax in proportion to the amount of property which a man possesses over and above the necessities of life. Those who possess only the latter should pay nothing at all. As for the other citizens, the tax should be levied, not in simple ratio to the property of the taxed, but in compound ratio to the difference of their conditions and the superfluity of their possessions. It is perfectly just that the more wealthy a man is, the more he should pay in taxation. For one thing, the rich derive great advantages from the social contract. Society protects their possessions and opens to them easy access to lucrative positions of eminence and power. They enjoy many advantages which the poor fail to enjoy. Hence, as the richer a man is, the more he gets out of the State, so to speak, he should be taxed in proportion to his wealth. There should also be heavy taxes on all luxuries. For then either the rich will substitute socially useful for socially useless expenses or the State will receive high taxes. In either case the State will gain.

If we care to translate Rousseau's ideas into modern terms, we can say that he advocated a system of graduated income-tax, according to which those with very low incomes would pay nothing at all while those possessing incomes above a certain level would pay a tax constantly increasing as we go up the scale. This is not, of course, exactly what he says. For he thinks in terms of property and of 'superfluities' rather than in terms of income. But it indicates the spirit of his

proposals. And it is significant that he speaks of these proposals as tending insensibly 'to bring all fortunes nearer to
that middle condition which constitutes the genuine strength
of the State'.[47]

5. It was Rousseau's constant thesis that the fundamental
impulse in man is self-love. Our wants give rise to our passions; and as primitive man's wants were purely physical, self-
preservation was 'his chief and almost sole concern'.[48] In
Émile we are told that 'our first duties are to ourselves; our
first feelings are centred on self; all our instincts are at first
directed to our own preservation and on our own welfare'.[49]
Again, 'the origin of our passions, the root and spring of all
the rest, the only one which is born with man, which never
leaves him as long as he lives, is self-love; this passion is
primitive, instinctive, it precedes all the rest, which are in
a sense only modifications of it'.[50]

But this fundamental passion of self-love is not to be confused with egoism. For egoism is a feeling which arises only
in society, and which leads a man always to prefer himself to
others. 'In the true state of nature egoism did not exist.'[51]
For primitive man did not make the comparisons which are
required for egoism to be possible. Self-love, considered in
itself, is 'always good, always in accordance with the order of
nature'.[52] In his letter to the archbishop of Paris Rousseau
says that self-love is 'a passion indifferent in itself to good
and evil; it becomes good or evil only by accident and according to the circumstances in which it develops'.[53] But
whether it is called good or indifferent, it is certainly not
evil, and it is not to be identified with what is called egoism.

Primitive man is also depicted as moved by natural pity or
compassion, which Rousseau describes as 'the pure emotion
of nature, prior to all kinds of reflection'.[54] This feeling
comes into operation, of course, only when a man has taken
note in some sense of his fellows; but he does not reason to
the desirability of compassion; he simply feels it. It is a natural impulse.

Rousseau may sometimes seem to imply that compassion
is a feeling or passion different from and originally independent of self-love. Thus he speaks of compassion as 'a natural feeling which, by moderating the violence of love of self
in each individual, contributes to the preservation of the

whole species'.[55] And he goes on to add that in the hypothetical state of nature compassion supplies the place of laws,
morals and virtues. But though we can distinguish between
self-love and compassion, the latter is really a derivative of
the former. We are told in Émile that 'the child's first sentiment is self-love (and that) his second, which is derived
from it, is love of those about him'.[56] True, Rousseau is here
speaking of something which goes beyond natural pity or compassion. But later he undertakes to tell us how pity, 'the first
relative sentiment which touches the human heart according
to the order of nature'[57] is born. We are informed that the
individual sympathizes with or feels compassion for, not those
who are happier than himself, but only those who are more
unfortunate than he is and who are suffering from ills from
which he does not believe himself to be immune. In other
words, man originally feels pity because he identifies himself
with the sufferer. And in this case it is not so much that the
original impulse of self-love is accompanied and modified by
an independent natural feeling of pity and compassion as
that the latter is comprised in the former and grows out of
it when man takes note of his fellows. In this sense it is the
'first relative sentiment'.

Now, all morality is founded on these natural feelings. In
his letter to the archbishop of Paris, Rousseau remarks that
love of self is not a simple passion. For man is a composite
being, sensitive and intelligent. Sense-appetite tends to the
good of the body, while the desire of the intelligent part of
man, the desire or love of order, tends to the good of the
soul. 'This last love, developed and rendered active, bears
the name conscience';[58] but the operations of conscience, the
love of order, postulate knowledge of order. It is, therefore,
only when man has begun to take note of his fellows and to
apprehend relations and make comparisons that he comes to
have such ideas as justice and order, and that conscience can
operate. Given the necessary reflection, moral concepts are
formed and virtues and vices arise. But all these are founded
on man's fundamental feelings. The concept of justice, for
example, is founded on self-love. 'Thus the first notion of
justice springs not from what we owe to others, but from
what is due to us.'[59] Again, from the natural emotion of
compassion 'flow all those social virtues of which he (Mande-

ville) denied man the possession. What is generosity, clemency or humanity but compassion applied to the weak, to the guilty, or to mankind in general?'[60] And conscience, as we have seen, is founded on love of self as present in man as an intelligent or rational being.

If our whole moral life depends on our fundamental impulses or passions, it is not surprising to find Rousseau attacking those who maintain that moral education consists in extirpating them. 'Our passions are the chief means of self-preservation; to try to destroy them is therefore as absurd as it is useless; this would be to overcome nature, to reshape God's handiwork.'[61] In point of fact moral development consists in the right direction and extension of the fundamental passion of self-love. 'Extend self-love to others and it is transformed into virtue, a virtue which has its root in the heart of every one of us.'[62] Self-love is capable of development into the love of all mankind and the promotion of the general happiness which are the concern of every truly virtuous man.

Morality is thus the unthwarted and unprevented development of man's natural passions and feelings. Vice is not natural to man; it constitutes a distortion of his nature. 'Our natural passions are few in number; they are the means to freedom, they tend to self-preservation. All those which enslave and destroy us have another source; nature does not bestow them on us; we seize on them in her despite.'[63] For instance, the rise of civilization has multiplied man's wants and needs, and this has given rise to selfishness and to the 'hateful and angry passions'. It is easy, therefore, to understand Rousseau's insistence that it is the simple, those who stand nearest to nature and whose feelings and passions have been least corrupted by an artificial civilization, who are most open to the voice of conscience. 'Virtue! Sublime science of simple minds, are such industry and preparation needed if we are to know you? Are not your principles graven on every heart? Need we do more, to learn your laws, than examine ourselves and listen to the voice of conscience, when the passions are silent? This is the true philosophy, with which we must learn to be content.'[64] And Rousseau makes the Savoyard priest assert that 'there is therefore at the bottom of our hearts an innate principle of justice and virtue by which, in spite of our maxims, we judge our own actions or those of others to be good or evil; and it is this principle which I call conscience'.[65] 'To exist is to feel; our feeling is undoubtedly earlier than our intelligence, and we had feelings before we had ideas. . . . To know good is not to love it; this knowledge is not innate in man. But as soon as his reason leads him to perceive it, his conscience impels him to love it. It is this feeling which is innate.'[66] Hence, although Rousseau does not deny, but rather asserts, that reason and reflection have a part to play in the development of morality, he lays the emphasis on feeling. 'What I feel to be right is right, what I feel to be wrong is wrong . . . it is only when we haggle with conscience that we have recourse to the subtleties of argument.'[67] These words are put into the mouth of the simple Savoyard priest, it is true; but they represent a real element in Rousseau's thought.

The word 'feeling', when used in the last quotation, signifies, of course, immediate apprehension or intuition rather than feeling in the sense in which the sentiment of pity is a feeling. And the word has more or less the same meaning when the Savoyard priest uses it in connection with recognition of God's existence. The world is an ordered system of interrelated entities, and this fact manifests the existence of divine intelligence. 'Let us listen to the inner voice of feeling; what healthy mind can reject its evidence?'[68] 'I believe, therefore, that the world is governed by a wise and powerful will; I see it or rather I feel it, and it is a great thing to know this.'[69] 'I see God everywhere in his works; I feel him within myself.'[70] Again, I know that I am a free, active being. 'In vain do you argue this point with me; I feel it, and it is this feeling which speaks to me more forcibly than the reason which disputes it.'[71]

We have seen that morality develops when man begins to recognize his relations with his fellows. Rousseau can say, therefore, that 'society must be studied in the individual and the individual in society; those who desire to treat politics and morals apart from one another will never understand either'.[72] If one is acquainted only with the *Social Contract*, one might perhaps be inclined to interpret this statement as meaning that moral distinctions are settled simply by the general will expressed in positive legislation. But we ought to bear in mind the first part of the statement, namely that society must be studied in the individual. What we have said hitherto shows that for Rousseau Nature herself has directed our will to the good for man. But we possess no innate idea of this good. Hence we can form erroneous ideas of it. There is no guarantee, therefore, that what individual citizens, even when they are gathered together in assembly, think to be for the common good actually is for the common good. At the same time there is, underlying all distorted passions and erroneous ideas, a universal and natural direction of the will to the good. Hence it is the business of the legislator to interpret this will and to bring the laws into conformity with it. And this is why Rousseau can say in the *Social Contract* that 'the general will is always right and tends to the public advantage; but it does not follow that the deliberations of the people are always equally correct. Our will is always for our own good, but we do not always see what that is; the people is never corrupted, but it is often deceived, and on such occasions only does it seem to will what is bad.'[73]

I do not suggest that this aspect of Rousseau's theory of the general will, a theory which owes much to the traditional conception of natural law, is the most significant aspect from the point of view of the historical development of political theory. And other aspects will be discussed in the next chapter. But if we bear in mind the relation between the concept of the infallible general will and Rousseau's moral theory as developed in other writings, it becomes easier to understand how he came to propose this concept in the first place.

Rousseau's exaltation of intuition and of inner feeling or sentiment (*sentiment intérieur*) gave expression to a revulsion against arid rationalism which was not uncommon in the second half of the eighteenth century. It also gave to this revolt a powerful impetus. The cult of intuition and sensibility owed much to Rousseau. As for the profession of faith of the Savoyard priest, with its founding of belief in God and in immortality on feeling rather than on sheer reasoning, this exercised a considerable influence on Robespierre and his followers. But in the long run Rousseau's sentimental deism perhaps worked more in favour of the restoration of Catholicism than against it.

Chapter Four

ROUSSEAU (2)

The social contract – Sovereignty, the general will and freedom – Government – Concluding remarks.

1. Rousseau states the first problem to be considered in the *Social Contract* in these terms: 'Man is born free; and everywhere he is in chains. One thinks himself the master of others, and still remains a greater slave than they. How did this change come about? I do not know. What can make it legitimate? This question I think I can answer.'[1] Having postulated an original state of nature in which men were free, Rousseau is obliged either to condemn the social order in which man's primitive freedom no longer exists and to say that men should shake off their bonds as soon as possible or to justify it in some way. The first course is ruled out, because 'the social order is a sacred right which is the basis of all other rights'.[2] Hence Rousseau is compelled to show that the social order is justified and legitimate.

In solving his problem Rousseau has recourse to the contractual theory which we have already met in different forms in the philosophies of Hobbes and Locke. He is unwilling to found the social order on force; for might does not confer right. 'Force is a physical power, and I fail to see what moral effect it can have. To yield to force is an act of necessity, not of will—at most it is an act of prudence. In what sense can it be called a duty?'[3] If citizens have a duty of obedience, it cannot be founded simply on the possession of power by the person or persons to whom obedience is rendered. At the same time there is no natural right to legislate for society. For society and the state of nature are distinct. The social order, therefore, to be legitimate and justified, must be founded on agreement or convention.

Rousseau proposes the hypothesis that men have reached the point at which the obstacles to their preservation in the state of nature are greater than their resources for maintaining themselves in this state. They must, therefore, unite together and form an association. But the problem is not simply to find a form of association which will protect the persons and goods of each member. It is also that of finding an association in which each member will still obey himself alone and remain as free as before. 'This is the fundamental problem of which the *Social Contract* provides the solution.'⁴

In essence the social compact or contract can be expressed as follows. 'Each of us puts his person and all his power in common under the supreme direction of the general will, and, in our corporate capacity, we receive each member as an indivisible part of the whole.'⁵ This act of association immediately creates a moral and collective body, a public person, the republic or body politic. It is called the State when considered as passive, the Sovereign when considered as active, and a Power when compared with other similar bodies. Its members are called collectively the people, while, taken individually, they are called citizens, as sharing in the sovereign power, and subjects, as being under the laws of the State.

This theory of the social contract obviously differs from that of Hobbes. According to the latter's theory individuals agree to hand over their rights to a sovereign who stands outside the covenant, not being a party to it. Government is thus set up by the same agreement that creates an organized society: in fact, the existence of the body politic really depends on its relation to the sovereign who might, indeed, be an assembly and not an individual, but who is distinguishable from the contracting parties. In Rousseau's theory, however, the original contract creates a sovereign which is identical with the contracting parties taken collectively, and nothing at all is said about government. For Rousseau, the government is simply an executive power which is dependent for its power on the sovereign assembly or body politic. Hobbes's problem was one of social cohesion. Given his view of man and of the state of nature, he was faced with the task of finding an effective counterbalance to the centrifugal forces in human nature. Or, more concretely, he was faced with the problem of finding an effective remedy for the greatest evil of society, namely civil war. He found the solution in centralized government, in a theory of sovereignty which emphasized above all things the position of the government. And as he accepted the hypothesis of the state of nature, he had to incorporate this emphasis on government into his account of the covenant whereby the transition from the state of nature to that of organized society is effected. Rousseau's problem, however, was different. Given his insistence on liberty, and given his desire to show that the change from the state of nature to that of organized society was not a substitution of slavery for freedom for the sake of mere security, he felt himself compelled to show that in society a higher form of liberty is acquired than the one enjoyed in the state of nature. One would not, therefore, expect to find him emphasizing the idea of government in his account of the social contract or the idea of the contracting parties handing over their rights to a sovereign who stands outside the contract. Instead, we find him emphasizing a mutual agreement between the contracting parties which creates a new moral entity in which each member realizes himself more fully than he could do in the state of nature.

Obviously, this signifies a marked change of attitude and tone between the first two *Discourses* and the *Social Contract*. True, in the *Discourse on Inequality* we can see, as was remarked in the last chapter, some elements of Rousseau's mature political theory making their appearance. But the first *Discourse* inevitably gives the impression that for Rousseau political society is an evil, whereas in the *Social Contract* we find man's true nature being fulfilled, as it were, in the social order. He becomes, 'instead of a stupid and unimaginative animal . . . an intelligent being and a man'.[6] There is not, indeed, a pure contradiction between the first *Discourse* and the *Social Contract*. In the former Rousseau is speaking of the evils of civilized society as it actually existed, particularly in France, whereas in the *Social Contract* he is speaking rather of political society as it ought to be. And even in the latter work, while extolling the benefits which man acquires by the social contract, he remarks that 'the abuses of this new condition often degrade him below that which he left'.[7] At the same time it can hardly be denied that there is a remarkable change of tone and emphasis. And the same is true of the relation of the *Social Contract* to the *Discourse on Inequality*. The impression given by the latter is that man, naturally good, acquires moral ideas and moral qualities in the strict sense during a gradual process of development in which civil society, in the sense of loose social bonds, precedes the formation of organized political society. But in the *Social Contract* Rousseau speaks as though through the institution of political society man passes at once from a non-moral to a moral state. 'The passage from the state of nature to the civil state produces a very remarkable change in man, by substituting justice for instinct in his conduct, and giving his actions the morality which they had formerly lacked.'[8] The State becomes the source of justice and the basis of rights. Here again there is perhaps no sheer contradiction. The social contract is after all nothing but a philosophical fiction, as Hume puts it; and we can, if we like, regard Rousseau as making a theoretical or logical, rather than an historical, distinction between man in society and man considered in abstraction from society. As a mere isolated individual, man, while not vicious or bad in himself, is not properly a moral being: it is only in society that his intellectual and moral life develops. And this is substantially what Rousseau had said in the *Discourse on Inequality*. At the same time there is a change of tone. True, this change of tone can be explained in large part by difference of purpose. In the *Discourse* Rousseau was concerned with the origins of inequality, and he ascribes to the institution of society the origin of what he calls 'moral or political inequality'. The emphasis is on inequality, as is indicated by the title of the *Discourse*. In the *Social Contract* Rousseau is concerned with the benefits which man acquires from the institution of society, such as the substitution of civil and moral for merely 'natural' liberty. But though the change in tone is explicable largely in terms of difference of purpose, it is there none the less. In the *Social Contract*, a new, and more important, aspect of Rousseau's political theory is displayed.

We can see, therefore, how misleading the opening words of the first chapter of the *Social Contract* can be, if they are taken as an adequate statement of Rousseau's position. 'Man is born free; and everywhere he is in chains.' These words formulate a problem, not a solution. The solution is to be found in the idea of the transformation of natural into civil and moral liberty. 'What a man loses by the social contract is his natural liberty and an unlimited right to everything which he tries to get and succeeds in getting; what he gains is civil liberty and the proprietorship of all he possesses.'[9] Natural liberty is limited only by the strength of the individual; civil liberty is limited by the general will, with which the real will of each member of society is one. Mere possession is the effect of force or of the right of first occupation; proprietorship is founded on a positive title, it is a right conferred by the State. 'Over and above all this, we might add to what man acquires in the civil state moral liberty, which alone makes him truly master of himself. For the mere impulse of appetite is slavery while obedience to a law which we prescribe to ourselves is liberty.'[10] In some forms of society, in a tyrannical and capricious dictatorship for example, men are indeed reduced to slavery, and they may be worse off than in the state of nature. But this is accidental, in the sense that it does not follow from the essence of the State. If we consider the State in its essence, we must say that its institution is an incalculable benefit to man.

By accepting the contractual theory Rousseau is faced, of course, with the same difficulty with which Locke was faced. Are we to say that the original contracting parties bound not only themselves but also their descendants? And, if so, what is our justification for saying this? Rousseau does not appear to consider this problem explicitly, though he makes it clear that the citizens of a State can at any time agree to dissolve the contract. 'There neither is nor can be any kind of fundamental law binding on the body of the people—not even the social contract itself.'[11] Again, 'there is in the State no fundamental law that cannot be revoked, not excluding the social compact itself; for if all the citizens assembled of one accord to break the compact, it is impossible to doubt that it would be quite legitimately broken'.[12] As for individuals taken singly, Rousseau refers to Grotius's opinion that each man can renounce his membership of his own State and recover his natural liberty by leaving the country. He appears to endorse this opinion by adding that 'it would be indeed absurd if all the citizens in assembly could not do what each can do by himself'.[13] (Rousseau appends a note to say that flight from the country to escape one's obligations in the hour of need would be a criminal and punishable act.) Presumably he considered that as the social contract brings into existence a new moral being, this being continues to exist, in spite of the fact that some members die and new members are born, unless the members collectively dissolve the contract in one of their periodic assemblies. The membership in the State does not effect the latter's continual existence as a moral being.

2. We have seen that according to Rousseau the public person which is formed by the union of individuals through the social contract is called, when considered as active, the sovereign. This means in effect that the sovereign is the whole body of the people as legislating, as the source of law. Now, law is the expression of will. Rousseau can say, therefore, that sovereignty is 'nothing less than the exercise of the general will'.[14] Each citizen has a dual capacity. As a member of the moral being which is the source of law he is a member of the sovereign. Considered as standing under the law and bound to obey it, he is a subject. The individual possesses, of course, a particular will, and this may be at variance with the general will. It is his civic duty to conform his particular will to the general will of the sovereign, of which he is himself a member.

Sovereignty, Rousseau insists, is inalienable. For it consists in the exercise of the general will, and this will cannot be alienated or transferred. One may transfer power, but not will. This is why Rousseau later insists that the people cannot elect representatives in the full sense of the word; it can only elect deputies. 'Sovereignty, for the same reason as makes it inalienable, cannot be represented; it lies essentially in the general will, and will does not admit of representation. It is either the same or other; there is no intermediate possibility. The deputies of the people, therefore, are not and cannot be its representatives: they are merely its stewards, and can carry through no definitive acts. Every law the people has not ratified in person is null and void. . . .'[15] (Rousseau draws the conclusion that the people of England are free only during the election of members of parliament, and that then they relapse into slavery.)

For the same reason sovereignty is indivisible. For the will, the exercise of which is called sovereignty, is the general will, and this cannot be divided. Divide it, and you have only particular wills, and thus no sovereignty. We cannot divide sovereignty into various powers, such as legislative and executive powers. The executive power or government is neither the sovereign nor a part of it: it is concerned with the administration of law and is a mere instrument of the sovereign. For Rousseau, therefore, the sovereign is the legislative, and this is the people. In a given State the nominal sovereign may be a person or persons other than the people; but the true sovereign is always the people. Needless to say, by 'people' Rousseau does not mean one class in the State, as distinct from another class or from other classes; he means the whole body of citizens. We may also note that he uses the word 'legislator' in a technical sense of his own, to mean a person who draws up laws, as Lycurgus is said to have drawn up laws for the Spartans. But a legislator in this sense does not, of course, possess sovereign power. His function is advisory or illuminative, in the sense that his task is to enlighten the sovereign people so that it may act with a clear idea of what the common interest really is here and now.

Sovereignty, therefore, is said to be the exercise of the general will: and the sovereign is the people, in whom this will resides. But what is meant by the general will?

The natural temptation, of course, is to understand the term 'general will' primarily in relation to the willing subject, the sovereign people, in its legislative function. We may then be easily led to think that the general will can be identified to all intents and purposes with the decision expressed in a majority vote of the assembly. And if we interpret Rousseau in this sense, we shall be likely to comment that his description of the general will as infallible and as always tending to the public advantage is both absurd and pernicious. Absurd, because there is no guarantee that a law enacted by a popular assembly really will be to the public advantage; pernicious, because it encourages tyranny and intolerance. But the interpretation on which these conclusions are based is incorrect; in any case it places the emphasis wrongly.

We must recall to mind first of all Rousseau's famous distinction between the general will (*volonté générale*) and the will of all (*volonté de tous*). 'There is often a great deal of difference between the will of all and the general will. The latter considers only the common interest, while the former takes private interest into account and is no more than a sum of particular wills.'[16] The general will is, indeed, general in the sense that it is the will of a universal subject, the sovereign people; but the emphasis is placed by Rousseau on universality of object, namely the common interest or good or advantage. And this general will cannot be identified without more ado with the sum of particular wills as manifested in a majority, or even in a unanimous, vote. For the result of voting may give expression to a mistaken idea of what the common good involves and demands; and a law which is enacted as the result of voting may conceivably be detrimental to the public advantage. 'Of itself the people always wills the good, but of itself it by no means always sees it. The general will is always in the right, but the judgment which guides it is not always enlightened . . . the public wills the good it does not see.'[17] It is this fact which 'makes a legislator necessary',[18] in the sense described above.

The 'will of all', therefore, is not infallible; it is only the 'general will' which is infallible and always right. And this means that it is always directed to the common good. It is clear, I think, that Rousseau has extended his concept of the natural goodness of man to the new moral being which arises through the social contract. The individual, impelled fundamentally by self-love (not, we may recall, to be identified with egoism in a morally depreciative sense), naturally seeks his own good, though it does not necessarily follow that he has a clear idea of its true nature.[19] The 'public person' which the social contract brings into existence also seeks inevitably its own good, the common good. But the people do not always understand where their true good lies. Hence they stand in need of enlightenment in order that the general will may be properly expressed.

Let us suppose for the sake of argument that it makes sense to speak of the State as a moral entity which is capable of willing. If we say that its will, the general will, is always right, and if we distinguish between this will and the will of all considered as the sum of particular wills, then the statement that the general will is infallible does not commit us to the statement that every law which is passed by the popular assembly is necessarily the law which is most conducive to the public advantage in the given circumstances. There is still room for possibly justified criticism. At the same time we run the risk of being reduced to the utterance of a tautology. For if we say that the general will is always right, and if we mean by this that the general will is always directed to the common good, the question arises whether we are saying anything more than that the will for the common good is the will for the common good; if, that is to say, we define the general will in terms of a universal object, namely the common good or interest. It might be maintained, therefore, that Rousseau can be saved from an uncritical worship of the legislative decisions of public assemblies only by reducing what he says to an innocuous tautology.

The comment might then be made that what is really required is a clear account of what it means to speak about the State as a moral entity with a will. If this will is not identical with the will of all, what exactly is it? Is it something over and above all particular wills? Or is it rather particular wills taken collectively and considered according to their natural orientation towards the good rather than as directed by the particular concepts of the good in the minds of their owners? In the first case we are faced with an ontological problem. That is to say, we are faced with the problem of the ontological status of the subsistent general will. In the second case some reconsideration by Rousseau of his initial individualism would seem to be demanded. For the will of A is directed towards A's good, and the will of B is directed towards B's good. If, therefore, we wish to say that the wills of A, B, C, and so on, considered in their natural orientation towards the good, form collectively the general will (which is directed towards the common good), it seems that we ought to maintain that men are by nature and from the beginning social beings and that their wills are directed naturally not only towards their private good, but also to the common good, or to their private goods as comprised within the common good or as contributing to it. I think that something of this was, indeed, in the back of Rousseau's mind. But by first presenting us with an individualistic picture of man and by then advancing the idea of a new moral public person with a will of its own, he has left in obscurity the precise nature of the general will and its precise relation to particular wills. There is, indeed, little indication that Rousseau gave to these problems the prolonged reflection which they require. We can discern in his political philosophy various lines of thought which it is difficult to harmonize. The most significant line of thought is doubtless the idea of the State as an organic entity with a will of its own, which is in some rather undefined sense the 'true' will of each member of the State. To this notion I shall return presently.

I do not mean to imply that for Rousseau there is no connection between the general will and the legislative activity of the sovereign people. To say, as he does, that there is often a great deal of difference between the will of all and the general will, is not to say that they never coincide. And one of Rousseau's problems as a political theorist was to suggest means of ensuring, so far as this can be done, that the infallible general will attains concrete expression in law. One of the means which he suggests has already been noted, namely the employment of a wise 'legislator'. Another means is the prevention, so far as this is practicable, of partial societies within the State. The point is this. If each citizen votes entirely independently, the differences between them, according to Rousseau, will cancel out, 'and the general will remains as the sum of the differences'.[20] If, however, factions and parties are formed, each with its (relatively speaking) general will, the differences become less numerous, and the result is less general and less expressive of the general will. Worse still, when one association or party is so strong or numerous that its will inevitably prevails over those of the other citizens, the result is not expressive in any way of the general will of the State, but only of a particular will (particular, that is, in relation to the general will of the State, even if it is general in relation to the members of the association or party). Rousseau's conclusion is that 'it is therefore essential, if the general will is to be able to express itself, that there should be no partial society within the State, and that each citizen should think only his own thoughts'.[21]

This is, of course, one reason why Rousseau shows dislike of the Christian Church. 'Wherever the clergy is a corporate body, it is master and legislator in its own country. . . . Of all Christian writers, the philosopher Hobbes alone has seen the evil and how to remedy it, and has dared to propose the reunion of the two heads of the eagle, and the restoration throughout of political unity. . . . But he should have seen that the masterful spirit of Christianity is incompatible with his system, and that the priestly interest would always be stronger than that of the State.'[22] True, when Rousseau speaks against the Christian Church and in favour of a purely civil religion, he is not directly engaged in discussing the general will and its expression. But his remarks are none the less obviously relevant. For if the Church sets itself up as a quasi-sovereign, its influence will inevitably interfere with the expression of the general will of the true sovereign, namely the people.

It should be noted how Rousseau assumes that if the citizens are duly enlightened, and if partial societies within the State are suppressed (or, where this is not possible, rendered so numerous that their diverging interests and influences cancel out), the majority vote will inevitably express the general will. 'If, when the people, being furnished with adequate information, held its deliberations, the citizens had no communication one with another, the grand total of the small differences would always give the general will, and the decision would always be good.'[23] Again, 'there is but one law which, from its nature, needs unanimous consent. This is the social compact. . . . Apart from this primitive contract, the vote of the majority always binds the rest. . . . The general will is found by counting votes.'[24] This does not exactly contradict what Rousseau says about the distinction between the general will and the will of all. For the distinction is meant to allow for the possibility of private interests, especially the interest of partial groups and associations determining the decision of the people in assembly. And when this abuse takes place, the result of voting does not represent the general will. But when such abuses are avoided, the result will certainly give expression to the general will.

Of course, in one sense this is obviously true; namely in the sense that the will of a majority is more general than the will of a minority. But this is a truism. And it is not all that Rousseau has in mind. For a law which is the expression of the general will is for him a law which tends to or secures or preserves the common good or interest. If, therefore, the influence of group interests is avoided, the expressed will of the assembly is infallibly conducive to the public good. Criticism of the assembly's expressed will would seem to be legitimate only on the ground of undue influence by private party and group interests. If we assume that each citizen is 'thinking his own thoughts' and is not exposed to illegitimate pressures, there does not seem to be any ground left, on Rousseau's premises, for criticizing the expressed will of the assembly, even if it is expressed only by a majority vote. It is true that he asserts that the majority should approach unanimity in proportion to the gravity of the matters to be decided; but this does not alter the fact that 'the general will is formed by counting votes (and that) all the qualities of the general will still reside in the majority'.[25]

Rousseau's discussion of the general will is closely connected with the problem of freedom. As we have seen, he wished to justify the transition from the hypothetical state of nature to that of organized political society. Believing that man is naturally free and that freedom is an inestimable value, he felt himself compelled to show that through the social contract, which gives rise to the State, man, instead of losing freedom, acquires a higher kind of it. For 'to renounce liberty is to renounce being a man'.[26] Rousseau maintained, therefore, that by the social contract natural liberty is exchanged for civil liberty. But it is obvious that in society men are compelled to obey the law. If they do not do so, they are punished. And, given this situation, is it possible to hold that by exchanging the state of nature, in which man was free to do whatever he had the physical capacity for doing, for the state of political society he became more, and not less, free than before, or at least that he acquired a truer and fuller freedom? Rousseau's treatment of this problem is celebrated.

In the first place the social contract must be understood as including the tacit undertaking to submit to the general will and that whoever refuses to do this shall be subjected to compulsion. 'The citizen gives his consent to all the laws, including those which are passed in spite of his opposition, and even those which punish him when he dares to break any of them.'[27]

In the second place, and this is the salient point, the general will is each man's real will. And the expression of the general will is the expression of each citizen's real will. Now, to follow one's own will is to act freely. Hence to be compelled to conform one's will to the general will is to be compelled to be free. It is to be brought into a state where one wills what one 'really' wills.

Here we have Rousseau's famous paradox. 'In order that the social compact may not be an empty formula, it tacitly includes the undertaking, which alone can give force to the rest, that whoever refuses to obey the general will shall be compelled to do so by the whole body. This means nothing less than that he will be forced to be free.'[28] Again, '. . . the general will is found by counting votes. When, therefore, the opinion which is contrary to my own prevails, this proves neither more nor less than that I was mistaken, and that what I thought to be the general will was not so. If my particular will had carried the day I should have achieved the opposite of what was my will; and I should not have been free.'[29]

It is difficult to see how the fact that an opinion different from my own prevails by a majority vote 'proves' that I was mistaken. Rousseau simply assumes that it does. However, passing over this point we can draw attention to the ambiguous use of the word *free*. Another man might be content to say that if freedom means freedom to do whatever one wishes to do and is physically capable of doing, it is, indeed, curtailed by membership of the State. But curtailment of one's freedom by law is essential to the well-being of society, and, in view of the fact that the advantages of society outweigh its disadvantages, such curtailment needs no other justification than its utility. The only relevant problem is that of restricting it to the minimum required by the common good. This purely empirical and utilitarian approach was not, however, to the taste of Rousseau. He wishes to show that apparent curtailment of liberty is not really a curtailment at all. Hence he is led into the paradoxical position of maintaining that one can be forced to be free. And the very fact that the position immediately strikes one as being paradoxical suggests that the word *free* is being given a sense which, whatever it may be, is different from the sense or senses which it normally bears. To apply this word to a man who is forced, for example, to obey a certain law does not conduce to clarity. It is to suggest, by applying a word outside its normal range of meaning, that force and compulsion are not really force and compulsion.

Linguistic criticism may appear tiresome and superficial to some minds. But it has in reality a considerable practical importance. For the transference of laudatory names or epithets to situations which lie outside their normal range of meaning is a stock device of political propagandists who wish to render these situations more acceptable. Thus the term *democracy*, perhaps with the prefix 'true' or 'real', is sometimes applied to a state of affairs in which the few tyrannize over the many with the aid of force and terror. And to call compulsion 'being forced to be free' is an instance of the same kind of thing. Later we find Robespierre saying that the will of the Jacobins was the general will and calling the revolutionary government the despotism of liberty. Linguistic criticism can throw some much-needed light on these troubled waters.

These remarks are not, of course, intended to suggest that Rousseau himself was in any way a friend of despotism or tyranny or terror. His paradox proceeded, not from a desire to make people believe that black is white, but from the difficulty of justifying a normal feature of social life, restriction of personal caprice by universal laws, in face of the picture which he had given of the state of nature. And though it is only proper to point out the dangers inherent in the use of such paradoxes, it is also true that to confine oneself to linguistic criticism of the type to which I have alluded would be to fail to note the historical importance of Rousseau's theory of the general will and the different ways in which it is capable of development. This is perhaps one reason why such criticism can appear tiresome and superficial. But further remarks on Rousseau's theory will be reserved for the final section of this chapter. Meanwhile I turn to the subject of government.

3. Every free action, says Rousseau, is produced by the concurrence of two causes. One is a moral cause, namely the will which determines the act, the other a physical cause, namely the physical power which executes the act. Both causes are required. A paralytic may will to run; but, lacking the physical power to do so, he stays where he is.

Applying this distinction to the body politic we must distinguish between the legislative power, namely the sovereign people, and the executive power or government. The former gives expression to the general will in universal laws and does not concern itself with particular actions or persons. The latter applies and enforces the law, and it is concerned, therefore, with particular actions and persons. 'I call *government*, or supreme administration, the legitimate exercise of the executive power, and prince or magistrate the man or the body entrusted with this administration.'[30]

The action by which a people puts itself under a prince is not a contract: 'it is simply and solely a commission'.[31] It follows that the sovereign can limit or modify or recover the executive power at its pleasure. Indeed, Rousseau envisages periodic assemblies of the sovereign people in which two questions should be voted on separately: 'does it please the sovereign to preserve the present form of government?' and 'does it please the people to leave its administration in the hands of those who are actually in charge of it?'[32] Obviously, Rousseau is here envisaging small States like Swiss cantons, where it is physically possible for the people to meet together periodically. However, the general principle, that the government is merely the instrument or minister of the sovereign people, holds good for all States. Of course, to say that the people can 'recover' the executive power does not mean that it can decide to exercise this power itself. Not even in a small Swiss canton could the people carry on day-by-day administration. And, on Rousseau's principles, the sovereign people is concerned in any case with legislation, not with administration, except in the sense that if it is dissatisfied with the existing government's administration, it is entitled to dismiss it and entrust the executive power to another government.

The executive power, according to Rousseau, possesses 'a particular personality, a sensibility common to its members, and a force and will of its own making for its preservation'.[33] But this does not alter the fact that 'the State exists by itself and the government only through the sovereign'.[34] This dependence does not, indeed, prevent the government from acting with vigour and promptitude; but its dominant will ought to be the general will as expressed in law. If it comes to have a separate particular will which is more active and powerful

than that of the sovereign, 'there would be, so to speak, two
sovereigns, the one rightful and the other actual, the social
union would evaporate instantly, and the body politic would
be dissolved'.[35] Rousseau was no friend of capricious and
tyrannical princes or governments.[36] They should be servants,
and not masters, of the people.

Although Rousseau discusses types of government, it is unnecessary to say much about this subject. For he very sensibly
refuses to assert that there is one ideal form of government, suitable for all peoples and circumstances. 'The question "What absolutely is the best government?" is unanswer-
able as well as indeterminate; or, rather, there are as many
good answers as there are possible combinations in the absolute and relative situations of all nations.'[37] Again, 'there
has been at all times much dispute concerning the best form
of government, without consideration of the fact that each is
in some cases the best, and in other cases the worst'.[38] We
can say, however, that democratic governments suit small
States, aristocratic governments those of middle size, and
monarchical governments large States. But all forms of constitution are capable of abuse and degeneration. 'Were there
a people of gods, their government would be democratic. So
perfect a government is not for men.'[39] Rousseau is speaking here of democracy in the literal sense, which of all forms
of constitution is the one most likely to give rise to factions
and civil war. That monarchy is subject to abuse is obvious.
The 'best and most natural arrangement' is that 'the wisest
should govern the many, when it is assured that they will
govern for its profit, and not for their own'.[40] But this is not,
of course, assured. Aristocracy, like any other form of government, can degenerate. In fact, the tendency to degeneration
is, in all forms of constitution, natural and inevitable. 'The
body politic, as well as the human body, begins to die as soon
as it is born, and it carries within itself the causes of its destruction.'[41] True, men have to endeavour to preserve the
body politic in as healthy a condition as long as possible, just
as they do with their own bodies. And this can best be done
by separating clearly the executive from the legislative power
and by various constitutional devices. But even the best
constituted State will have an end, even if it survives longer
than others, apart from unforeseen circumstances, just as a

healthy and robust human body will eventually die, though of itself, and unforeseen accidents apart, it tends to outlive sickly and weak bodies.

4. A certain amount of what Rousseau says in the *Social Contract* is clearly related to his predilection for the small republic, like his own city of Geneva. It is only in a very small State that it would be possible, for example, for the citizens to meet together periodically and to exercise their legislative functions. The Greek city-State and the small Swiss republic furnished him with his ideal of the State in regard to size. Moreover, those extremes of wealth and poverty which disfigured contemporary France and which scandalized Rousseau were absent in the more simple life of the Swiss people. Again, the system of representation of which Rousseau disapproved is encouraged by the vastness of States, even if 'it comes to us from feudal government, from that iniquitous and absurd system which degrades humanity and dishonours the name of man'.[42] To be sure, Rousseau understood well enough that a very small State suffers from certain disadvantages, such as difficulty in defending itself; but he accepted the idea of federations of small States.

But Rousseau's predilection for small States constitutes a comparatively unimportant, though picturesque, aspect of his political theory. He was not so fanciful as to suppose that France, for instance, could in practice be reduced to a multiplicity of small States or to a confederation of such States. In any case his idea of the sovereignty of the people and his ideal of government for the people were of greater importance and influence than any of his ideas about the proper size for States. The idea of popular sovereignty was of some influence with Robespierre and the Jacobins. And we can say that when the slogans, Liberty and Equality, spread through Europe, it was in part Rousseau's ideas which were spreading, though he was not himself an advocate of revolution. Rousseau was not a cosmopolitan: he disliked the cosmopolitanism of the Enlightenment and deprecated the lack of that patriotism and love of country which was characteristic of Sparta, the early Roman Republic and the Swiss people. We can say, therefore, at least that Rousseau's idea of national popular sovereignty had some affinity with the growth of national democracy as distinct from international socialism.

To estimate the practical influence of Rousseau's writings on political and social developments is, however, scarcely possible; we are forced to confine ourselves more or less to general indications. It is much easier, of course, to trace the influence of his theories on other philosophers. And the two thinkers who come immediately to mind are Kant and Hegel.

Rousseau's theory of the social contract is of little or no importance in this respect. He gave it prominence, indeed, as the title of his chief political work clearly shows; but it was merely an artificial device, taken over from other writers, to justify the transition from the hypothetical state of nature to that of political society. It was not a theory which had any future. Far more important was the doctrine of the general will. But this doctrine could be developed in at least two ways.

In the original draft of the *Social Contract* Rousseau speaks of the general will as being in each man a pure act of the understanding, which reasons on what a man may demand of his neighbour and on what his neighbour has a right to demand of him. The will is here depicted as rational. Let us add to this the doctrine expressed in the *Social Contract* that 'the mere impulse of appetite is slavery, while obedience to a law which we prescribe to ourselves is liberty'.[43] We then have an autonomous, rational will or practical reason whereby man in his higher nature, so to speak, legislates for himself and pronounces a moral law to which he, in his lower nature, is subject. And this law is universal, in the sense that reason prescribes what is right and, implicitly at least, what every man in the same circumstances ought to do. This notion of the autonomous will which legislates in the moral sphere is an obvious anticipation of the Kantian ethic. It may be objected that the Kantian will is purely rational, whereas Rousseau emphasizes the fact that reason would be ineffective as a guide to action unless the law were graven on men's hearts in ineffaceable characters. The rational will needs a motive force which lies in man's fundamental impulses. This is true. It is true, that is to say, that Rousseau emphasizes the part played by *le sentiment intérieur* in man's moral life.

But there is no intention of suggesting that Rousseau's theory of the general will and Kant's theory of the practical reason are one and the same thing. The point is simply that there are elements in the former's theory which are susceptible of development in a Kantian direction. And Kant was certainly influenced by Rousseau's writings.

The general will is not, however, universal simply in relation to its object. For Rousseau it is also universal in relation to its subject. That is to say, it is the will of the sovereign people, of the moral being or public person which is brought into existence by the social contract. And we have here the germs of the organic theory of the State which was developed by Hegel. The latter criticized and rejected the theory of the social contract; but he commended Rousseau for assigning will as the principle of the State.[44] Hegel did not, of course, take over Rousseau's theories of the State and of the general will; but he studied him and was influenced and stimulated by him in the development of his own political theory.

We have noted that Rousseau expressed a predilection for small States. In the sort of political society which he looked on as an ideal the general will would be manifested in what we may call a straightforward democratic manner, namely by the citizens voting in a popular assembly. But if we assume a large State, in which such assemblies are quite impracticable, the general will cannot find expression in direct legislation. It can find partial expression in periodic elections, but for legislative expression it needs interpretation by a man or by men other than the sovereign people. And it is no very far step to the conception of the infallible national will finding articulate expression through the lips of some leader. I do not mean that Rousseau would have approved such an interpretation of his theory. On the contrary, it would have aroused his abhorrence. And he could have pointed to sections of his writings which militate against it. At the same time the notion of a quasi-mystical will seeking articulate expression lends itself to exploitation of this kind.

There is, however, yet another way in which the theory of the general will could be developed. We can think of a nation as possessing some operative ideal which is partially expressed in its history and traditions and institutions, and which is plastic in the sense that it is not a fixed, articulate ideal but one which is gradually built up and which demands modification and reformulation in the light of the nation's development. And we can then perhaps speak of the task of legislators and of political theorists as being, in part at least, that of endeavouring to give concrete expression to this ideal and thus to show the nation what it 'really wants'. I do not suggest that this conception is immune from criticism. My point is that it is possible to put forward a theory of the general will without being forced to conceive the organ of interpretation as an infallible mouthpiece. The legislative and government may endeavour to see what is best for the nation in the light of its traditions, institutions and historical circumstances; but it does not follow that the interpretation of what is best either is or need be regarded as correct. It is possible to keep the idea of the nation wanting what is best for it and of the government and legislative as trying, or as under an obligation to try, to give expression to this will, without supposing that there is any infallible organ of interpretation and expression. In other words, it would be possible to adapt Rousseau's theory to the life of a democratic State as it is found in our western culture.

One main reason why diverse developments of Rousseau's theory are possible is, of course, the ambiguity which can be found in his statement of the theory. One important ambiguity is the following. When Rousseau says that the social order is the basis of all rights, his statement can be taken in an innocuous sense if we understand by 'right' legal right. The statement then becomes a truism. But when he says that legislation gives birth to morality,[45] this suggests that the State is the fount of moral distinctions. And if we couple this with his attack on partial societies and with his defence of a civil religion, as distinct from a revealed religion mediated by the Church, it is easy to understand how the view can be put forward that Rousseau's political theory points in the direction of totalitarianism. Yet he did not in fact think that morality depends simply on the State. After all, he insisted on the need of virtuous citizens if the State itself is to be good. He was thus faced with Plato's dilemma. There cannot be a good State without good citizens. But the citizens will not be good if the State, in its legislation and government, tends to deprave and corrupt them. This is one reason why Rousseau had recourse to the idea of an enlightened 'legislator' after the style of Solon or Lycurgus. But the mere fact that he was faced with this dilemma shows that he did not think that morality depends simply on the State; in the sense that whatever the State declares to be right is right. Moreover, he believed that a natural law is written in the hearts of men. And if he considered that, given certain conditions and precautions, this natural law would certainly find articulate expression in the declared will of the sovereign people, this optimism was due to his belief in man's natural goodness rather than to ethical positivism. It cannot, however, be denied that he made statements which smack of ethical positivism, in the sense that they seem to imply the derivation of morality from legislation and social opinion. In other words, his theory, taken as a whole, is ambiguous. Man always wills the good, but he can be mistaken as to its nature. Who is to interpret the moral law? The answer is ambiguous. Sometimes we are told that it is conscience, sometimes that it is the legislative. On the one hand, the voice of the legislative is not necessarily infallible; it may be influenced by selfish interests, and then it does not express the general will. Conscience presumably must be the deciding factor. On the other hand, a man must conform himself to the decision of the sovereign people: if necessary, he must be forced to be free. It can hardly be claimed that there is no ambiguity here. Hence, even though Rousseau himself laid stress on the law engraven in indelible characters on men's hearts and on the voice of conscience, we can understand the contention that there are incompatible elements in his theory, and that the new element is the tendency to eliminate the traditional conception of a natural moral law.

A final remark. We have considered Rousseau under the general heading of the French Enlightenment. And in view of the fact that he dissociated himself from the Encyclopaedists and the d'Holbach circle this may seem to be an inappropriate classification. Further, in the development of literature Rousseau exercised a powerful influence not only on French but also on German literature, particularly of the *Sturm und Drang* period. And this may appear to be an additional reason for separating him from the French Enlightenment. But Rousseau was not the originator of the literature of sensibility, even if he gave to it a powerful impetus; nor was he alone among eighteenth-century French philosophers and writers in stressing the importance of the passions and of feeling in human life. We have only to think of Vauvenargues, for example. The situation seems to be this. If we single out as the main features of the Enlightenment in France an arid rationalism, religious scepticism and a tendency to materialism, then we must say, of course, that Rousseau overcame the Enlightenment or passed beyond it. But we can equally well revise our conception of the period to include Rousseau: we can find in it something more than arid rationalism, materialism and religious scepticism. The fact of the matter is, however, that while he had his roots in the general movement of thought in eighteenth-century France, he is too outstanding a figure in the history of philosophy and literature for it to be profitable to give him a simple class-label and think that one has then satisfied all justice. He is and remains Jean-Jacques Rousseau, not a mere example of a type. Some of his theories, such as that of the social contract, are typical of the age and of little more than historical interest. In other aspects of his thought, political, educational and psychological, he looked forward to the future. And some of his problems, such as that of the relation between the individual and the State, are obviously as real now as when he wrote, even if we would give to his questions different formulations.

PART II

THE GERMAN ENLIGHTENMENT

Chapter Five

THE GERMAN ENLIGHTENMENT (1)

Christian Thomasius – Christian Wolff – Followers and opponents of Wolff.

1. The first phase of the Enlightenment (*Aufklärung*) in Germany is perhaps best represented by Christian Thomasius (1655–1728), son of the Jakob Thomasius who had been one of Leibniz's teachers. As a young man Christian Thomasius emphasized the superiority of the French to the Germans in the sphere of philosophy. The latter have an inclination to metaphysical abstractions which promote neither the common good nor individual happiness. Metaphysics does not yield real knowledge. Moreover, the 'learned' philosophy, taught in the universities, presupposes that the end of rational reflection is contemplation of abstract truth for its own sake. But this presupposition is a mistake. The value of philosophy lies in its utility, in its tendency to contribute to the social or common good and to the happiness or well-being of the individual. Philosophy, in other words, is an instrument of progress.

This hostility towards metaphysics and pure intellectualism was grounded to a certain extent in empiricism. The mind, according to Thomasius, must be purified of prejudices and preconceptions, especially of those characteristic of Aristotelianism and Scholasticism. But if he rejected Aristotelian and Scholastic metaphysics, he did not do so in order to substitute another metaphysics in their place. Thus Thomasius attacked, for example, the *Medicina mentis* of Tschirnhaus (1651–1708) who under the influence of Descartes and Spinoza advocated the application of the mathematical method in a philosophy of discovery and who extolled the attainment of truth as the noblest ideal of human life. For Thomasius it is clear that our natural knowledge depends on the senses. We possess no innate ideas, and we cannot discover truths about the world by a purely deductive method. Experience and observation are the only trustworthy sources of knowledge; and the bounds of this knowledge are determined by our senses. On the one hand, if there is anything so small that it makes no impression on the senses, we cannot know it. On the other hand, there are things so great that they exceed the capacity of our minds. We can know, for example, that the objects of the senses depend on a First Cause; but we cannot know, by philosophy at least, the nature of this cause. The dependence of our minds on sense-perception and the consequent limitation of our range of knowledge show the emptiness of metaphysical speculation. Nor should we allow ourselves to be led back into metaphysics by doubting the trustworthiness of the senses and by then attempting to give a philosophical proof of their trustworthiness. Doubt has, indeed, its proper place in our mental lives. For we ought to subject to doubt the opinions of the past which have proved of no utility to man. But sound common sense places a limit to doubt. We ought to avoid being entangled either in scepticism or in metaphysics. Rather should we devote ourselves to attaining knowledge of the world presented by the senses, not for the sake of knowledge, but for the sake of its utility.

But though Thomasius's idea of philosophy, as it appears in the *Einleitung zur Vernunftlehre* and in the *Ausübung der Vernunftlehre* (both 1691), is to a certain extent the expression of an empiricist outlook, those historians are probably right who connect it not only with social developments but also with the outlook of the Protestant Reformation. Of course, if we simply assert that the prominence given to the idea of the common good is an expression of the rise of the middle class, we lay ourselves open to the charge of exaggeration. For the idea of the common good was prominent in, for example, mediaeval philosophy. At the same time it is probably true that the utilitarian conception of philosophy, with its concentration on the idea of the enlightened reason using its capacities for the promotion of the common good, had some connection with the post-mediaeval structure of society, and that it is not unreasonable to speak of it as 'bourgeois' philosophy, provided that this word is not used as a term of abuse. As for the religious connection, there seems to be some

truth in the view that this bourgeois philosophy was a secularized prolongation of the outlook of the Protestant Reformation. The true service of God is to be found in the ordinary forms of social life, not in the secluded contemplation
of eternal verities or in turning away from the world in asceti-
cism and mortification. This idea, when divorced from its
strictly religious setting, easily leads to the conclusion that
social progress and individual success in this world are marks
of divine favour. And if philosophical reflection, as Luther
thought, has little or no competence in the theological sphere,
it seems to follow that it should be devoted to the promotion
of the social good and of individual temporal happiness.
Utility, not contemplation of the truth for its own sake, will
be the chief motive of such reflection. That is to say, philosophy will be concerned with questions of ethics, social organization and law rather than with metaphysics and theology. It
will centre round man; but its chief aim in considering man
will be to promote his temporal good rather than to integrate
a philosophical anthropology into a general metaphysics of
Being. Man will be considered psychologically rather than
metaphysically or from a theological point of view.

This does not mean, of course, that philosophy has to be
anti-religious. As we have seen, the philosophy of the French
Enlightenment was frequently hostile to Catholicism and,
with certain thinkers, to religion in general, which was looked
at as an enemy of social progress; but this point of view was
certainly not characteristic either of the German Enlightenment in general or of Thomasius in particular. The latter was
far from being an irreligious man. On the contrary, he was or
came to be associated with pietism, a movement which arose
in the Lutheran Church towards the end of the seventeenth
century and which aimed at infusing a new devotional life
into this religious body. But though one cannot legitimately
say that pietism reduced religion simply to feeling, it had no
sympathy with metaphysics or with Scholastic theology but
laid emphasis on personal faith and interiority. Pietism, therefore, like empiricism, though for different reasons, contributed
to the turning of philosophy away from metaphysics and natural theology.[1]

The conclusion of the *Vernunftlehre* or *Doctrine of Reason*
is that metaphysics is useless and that reason should be em-

ployed to promote the good of man. Thomasius's ethical theory is set out in his *Einleitung zur Sittenlehre* (1692) and *Ausübung der Sittenlehre* (1696). But the theory undergoes a curious metamorphosis. We are first told that the highest good of man is tranquillity of soul, the way to which is pointed out by the reason, the will being the faculty which leads man away from the good. This appears to be an individualistic ideal. But Thomasius goes on to argue that man is by nature a social being and that only as a member of society is he, properly speaking, a man. It follows that man cannot attain tranquillity of soul without the social bond, without love for his fellow-men; and the individual ought to sacrifice himself to the common good. Through mutual love there arises a common will which transcends the merely private and egoistic will. From this it seems to follow that the will cannot be characterized as bad. For 'rational love' is a manifestation of will; and from rational love the virtues arise. But Thomasius none the less wishes to hold that the human will is bad. The will is the slave of the fundamental impulses or drives such as the desires for wealth, honour and pleasure. Selflessness is unobtainable by our own efforts. Human choice and action can produce only sin: it is divine grace alone which is capable of rescuing man from his moral powerlessness. In other words, it is pietism which has the last word in Thomasius's ethical writings, and he explicitly reproaches himself for having thought that a man could develop a natural morality by his own power.

Thomasius is best known for his works in jurisprudence and international law. In 1688 he published *Institutionum jurisprudentiae divinae libri tres, in quibus fundamenta juris naturae secundum hypotheses ill. Pufendorfii perspicue demonstrantur*. In this work he wrote, as the title indicates, in dependence on the famous jurist, Samuel Pufendorf (1632–94). But he showed a greater degree of originality and independence in his later publication, *Fundamenta juris naturae et gentium ex sensu communi deducta* (1705). In it he begins with a consideration of man which is psychological, and not metaphysical, in character. He finds in man three fundamental drives: the desire to live as long and as happily as possible, the instinctive recoil from death and pain, and the desire for property and mastery. So long as reason does not control these impulses or drives, there exists the natural state of human society, which is a mixture of war and peace, tending always to degenerate into the former. This condition of affairs can be remedied only when rational reflection gains the upper hand and is directed towards securing for man the longest and happiest life possible. But what is a happy life? In the first place it is a just life; and the principle of justice is that we should not do to others what we do not wish them to do to us. On this principle is based natural law in the narrower sense, namely as directed to the preservation of external peaceful relations. In the second place a happy life is characterized by decency (*decorum*); and the principle of decency or of what is fitting is that we should do to others what we wish them to do to us. On this principle is based politics which is directed to the promotion of peace by benevolent action. In the third place a happy life demands virtue and self-respect (*honestum*); and the principle here is that we should do to ourselves what we wish others to do to themselves according to their capacities. On this principle is based ethics, which is directed to the attainment of inner peace.

We have here a rather different outlook from that suggested by Thomasius's remarks in his *Ausübung der Sittenlehre* about man's incapacity to develop a moral life by his own efforts. For in the *Fundamenta juris naturae et gentium ex sensu communi deducta* he clearly takes up the position that a natural law is derivable from the human reason, and that by the exercise of the latter man can overcome his egoistic impulses and promote the useful, namely the common good. Pufendorf had also derived the natural law from reason; but Thomasius separated natural law from metaphysics and theology more sharply than his predecessor had done. We find, therefore, a characteristic idea of the Enlightenment, that reason can heal the wounds of human life, and that exercise of reason should be directed to the social good. The individual should find his own good in overcoming his egoistic desires and lusts and in subordinating himself to the good of society. This is not to say that Thomasius ever discarded belief in religion or in the supernatural. But he tended to separate religion, belonging to the sphere of faith, feeling and devotion, from the sphere of philosophical reflection. Calvinist emphasis on community appears in a secularized form; but it coexists for Thomasius with Lutheran pietism.

2. The chief representative of the second phase of the German Enlightenment is Christian Wolff (1679–1754). With Wolff, however, we find a very different outlook from that of Thomasius. The latter's hostility towards metaphysics, combined with pietism, is entirely absent. Instead we find a renewal of academic philosophy and School metaphysics, and a thorough-going rationalism. This must not be taken to imply that Wolff was a rationalist in the sense of being anti-religious; he was nothing of the kind. But he developed a complete rational system of philosophy which included metaphysics and natural theology, and which exercised a powerful influence in the universities. True, he emphasized the practical end of philosophy and his aim was that of promoting the spread of understanding and virtue among men. But the characteristic note of his thought is its confidence in and insistence on the power of the human reason to attain certainty in the field of metaphysics, including metaphysical knowledge of God. This rationalism finds expression in the titles of his German writings which frequently begin with the words 'Rational Ideas of . . .' ('*Vernünftige Gedanken von . . .*'); for example, '*Rational Ideas of God, the World and the Soul of Man*' (1719). And his Latin works form together the 'Rational Philosophy' (*Philosophia rationalis*). The pietistic sundering of the sphere of faith from the sphere of reason and the elimination of metaphysics as uncertain and useless were quite foreign to Wolff's mind. In this sense he continued the great rationalist tradition of post-Renaissance continental philosophy. He wrote in considerable dependence on Leibniz, whose thought he expressed in a Scholastic and academic form. But though he lacked the originality of Leibniz and his other leading predecessors, he is a figure of importance in German philosophy. And when Kant discusses metaphysics and metaphysical proofs, it is often the Wolffian philosophy which he has in mind. For in his pre-critical period he had studied and assimilated the ideas of Wolff and his followers.

Wolff was born at Breslau, and at first he was destined for the study of theology, though he soon devoted himself to philosophy and lectured on the subject at Leipzig. Some notes on the *Medicina mentis* of Tschirnhaus brought him into contact with Leibniz, and it was on the latter's recommendation that Wolff was appointed professor of mathematics at Halle, where he lectured not only on mathematics but also on the various branches of philosophy. His views aroused, however, the opposition of his pietistic colleagues, who accused him of godlessness and prevailed upon Frederick William I to deprive him of his chair (1723). Indeed, Wolff was ordered, under pain of death, to leave Prussia within two days. He was received at Marburg, where he continued his activity as lecturer and writer, while his case aroused lively discussion throughout Germany. In 1740 he was recalled as professor to Halle by Frederick II, and subsequently he was awarded a title. Meanwhile the influence of his ideas was spreading through the German universities. He died at Halle in 1754.

In some respects Wolff was a thorough rationalist. Thus the ideal method was for him the deductive method. Its use outside formal logic and pure mathematics is rendered possible by the fact that the highest principle, that of non-contradiction, applies to all reality. From this principle we can derive the principle of sufficient reason which, like that of non-contradiction, is an ontological and not merely a logical principle. And the principle of sufficient reason is of great importance in philosophy. The world, for instance, must have its sufficient reason in a transcendent Being, namely in God.

Wolff was, of course, aware that the deductive method alone will not suffice for building up a system of philosophy, and still less for developing the empirical sciences. We cannot get along in the latter without experience and induction, and even in philosophy we require empirical elements. We must often be content, therefore, with probability. Some propositions are absolutely certain; for we cannot assert their opposites without contradiction. But there are many propositions which cannot be reduced to the principle of non-contradiction but which enjoy varying degrees of probability.

In other words, Wolff adopted Leibniz's distinction between truths of reason, the opposites of which cannot be asserted without contradiction and which are necessarily true, and truths of fact, which are not necessarily but contingently true. He applied the distinction in, for example, this way. The world is the system of interrelated finite things, and it is like a machine which works or moves necessarily in a certain way because it is what it is. But this necessity is hypothetical. If God had so willed, the world could have been other than what it is. It follows that there are many true statements about the world, the truth of which is not absolutely necessary. At the same time the world is ultimately composed of substances, each one of which exemplifies an essence that can, ideally at least, be conceived in a clear idea and defined. And if we possessed a knowledge of these essences, we could deduce a series of necessary truths. For when we conceive essences, we abstract from concrete existence and consider the order of possibility, irrespective of God's choice of this particular world. It is, indeed, arguable that Wolff's view that the world could be different from what it is does not fit in with his theory of essences. For it might be maintained that, given the essences which compose the world, the world-order could only have been what it is. However, the point which I wish to make is that Wolff's rationalism, his emphasis on clear and distinct definable ideas and on deduction, leads him to describe philosophy as the science of the possible, of all possible things, a possible thing being anything which does not involve a contradiction.

Mention has been made of Leibniz, and there is no question, of course, that the latter's philosophy exercised a marked influence on Wolff's thought. We shall see examples of this influence shortly. But in reinstating the idea of essences Wolff makes explicit reference to the Scholastics; and though, given the widespread contempt for Scholasticism at the time, he is careful to maintain that he is improving on their ideas, he makes no secret of the fact that, following Leibniz, he has no sympathy with the wholesale condemnation of their opinions and work. And in point of fact it is quite clear that he was influenced by the Scholastics. But Wolff's concentration on being as essence puts one in mind of Scotus rather than of Aquinas. It was the later Scholasticism rather than the Thomist system which influenced his thought. Thus in his *Ontology* he refers with approval to Suárez, whose writings had enjoyed considerable success in the German universities, even in the Protestant ones.

The influence of Scholasticism can be seen in Wolff's division of philosophy. The fundamental division, which goes back, of course, to Aristotle, is into theoretical and practical philosophy. Theoretical philosophy or metaphysics is subdivided into ontology, dealing with being as such, rational psychology, concerned with the soul, cosmology, which treats of the cosmic system, and rational or natural theology which has as its subject-matter the existence and attributes of God. (Practical philosophy is divided, with Aristotle, into ethics, economics and politics.) The explicit separation of ontology or general metaphysics from natural theology does not go back to the Middle Ages; and it has sometimes been attributed to Wolff himself. But the separation had already been made by the Cartesian Clauberg (1622–65), who spoke of 'ontosophy' rather than of 'ontology', and the latter term had been used by Jean-Baptiste Duhamel (1624–1706), a Scholastic, in his *Philosophia universalis*. Moreover, in his *Ontology* Wolff explicitly aimed at improving on the definitions given by the Scholastics and on their treatment of the science of being as being. And although his division of philosophy differs from that, say, of St. Thomas Aquinas, his hierarchical arrangement of its branches was clearly developed under Scholastic influence.[2] This may not appear to be a matter of much importance; but it is at least interesting to observe that the Scholastic tradition found a continued life in the thought of one of the leading figures of the German Enlightenment, even if, from a strictly Thomist point of view, it was a rather debased form of Scholasticism which found a home in the Wolffian philosophy. This is certainly what is thought by those who, with Professor Gilson, contrast the 'existentialism' of Aquinas and his faithful followers with the 'essentialism' of later Scholastics.[3]

The Leibnizian influence can be clearly seen in Wolff's treatment of substance. Though he avoided the term 'monad', he postulated the existence of imperceptible simple substances which are without extension or figure, and no two of which are perfectly alike. The things which we perceive in the material world are aggregates of these substances or metaphysical atoms; and extension belongs, as with Leibniz, to the phenomenal order. The human body is, of course, also an aggregate of substances. But in man there is a soul which is a simple substance and the existence of which can be proved by reference to the fact of consciousness, self-consciousness and consciousness of the external world. Indeed, as far as the soul's existence is concerned, it is immediately evident to everyone in self-consciousness.

Wolff laid considerable emphasis on consciousness. The soul, as a simple substance, possesses active power; but this power consists in the soul's ability to represent to itself the world. And the different activities of the soul, of which the two fundamental forms are knowing and desiring, are simply different manifestations of this power of representation. As for the relation between soul and body, it must be described in terms of a pre-established harmony. As with Leibniz, there is no direct interaction between soul and body. God had so arranged things that the soul represents to itself the world according to the modifications which take place in the sense-organs of its body.

The principal proof of God's existence for Wolff is a cosmological argument. The world, the system of interrelated finite things, requires a sufficient reason for its existence and nature, and this sufficient reason is the divine will, though the divine choice has also its sufficient reason, namely in the attractive power of the best as conceived by God. This means, of course, that Wolff has to follow the main lines of the Leibnizian theodicy. Like Leibniz, he distinguishes between physical, moral and metaphysical evil. The latter, being the imperfection necessarily attendant on finitude, is inseparable from the world. As for physical and moral evil, the world requires at least their possibility. The question is really not whether God could have created the world without evil, but whether there is a sufficient reason for creating a world from which evil, or at least its possibility, cannot be absent. Wolff's answer is that God created the world with a view to being acknowledged, honoured and praised by man.

In all this we are obviously very far from Thomasius's view that the human mind is incapacitated for the attainment of truth in metaphysics and natural theology. Besides his cosmological proof of God's existence Wolff accepted the ontological argument, being persuaded that the development of this argument by Leibniz and himself had rendered it immune from the usual lines of criticism. The accusation of atheism which was brought against Wolff was absurd. But it is understandable that his enemies among pietists thought that he was putting reason in the place of faith and undermining their conception of religion.

Just as Wolff rejected the theory of man's intellectual incapacity in the sphere of metaphysics, so also did he reject the theory of man's moral incapacity, namely that man left to himself is incapable of doing anything but sin. His moral theory was based on the idea of perfection. The good is defined as that which makes us and our condition more perfect, while the bad is defined as that which makes us and our condition more imperfect. But Wolff admits that it was long ago recognized 'by the ancients' that we will only that which we regard as good, as in some way perfecting us, and that we will nothing which we regard as evil. In other words, he admits the Scholastic saying that man always chooses *sub specie boni*. Obviously, therefore, he has to find some criterion for distinguishing between good in the wide sense of the term, namely as including whatever is the object of the will's choice, and good in the moral sense, namely what we ought to strive for or choose. True, he emphasizes the idea of the perfection of our nature. But it is clear that this concept must be given some definite content which will enable us to discriminate between moral and immoral actions. In trying to do this Wolff gives prominence to the idea of the harmonization of the manifold elements of human nature under the rule of reason and of man's interior and exterior conditions. Some writers have maintained that by including external good in the *summum bonum* or end of human moral endeavour Wolff was giving expression to a 'Protestant ethic'. But, many centuries before, Aristotle had included a sufficiency of external goods in the good of man. In any case it must be noted that Wolff is anxious to avoid the individualism which may appear to be connected with an ethic of self-perfection. He therefore emphasizes the fact that man can perfect himself only if he strives to help his fellow-men and to rise above his purely egoistic impulses. Promotion of God's honour and of the common good belong to the idea of self-perfection. The 'natural law' ordains, therefore, that we should do that which makes ourselves and our condition and the condition of others more perfect, and that we should not do that which makes ourselves or others more imperfect.

Wolff asserts freedom as a condition of the moral life. But

it is not at all easy for him to explain how freedom is possible, if it means that a man could have made another choice than the one that he has actually made. For, as we have seen, he regards nature as analogous to a machine in which all movements are determined and (hypothetically) necessary. However, in spite of this difficulty Wolff continued to affirm that man is free. In justification of this position he appeals to the theory of the pre-established harmony between soul and body. There is no direct interaction between them. Hence, bodily conditions and sensual impulses, for example, cannot determine the soul's choices. Its choices spring from its own spontaneity, and they are therefore free.

But Wolff is also involved in difficulties about the relation of intellect to will in the moral life. According to him, a constant will to do only what corresponds with the natural moral law is the beginning and foundation of virtue. But can this constant direction of the will be produced by the intellect or reason, by knowledge of moral good and evil? Must not this production be an act of the will itself? As the constant direction of the will towards the objective moral good is not something which is given from the start, and as there is difficulty in showing how it can be produced by the intellect alone, Wolff stresses the need for and the important part played by education in the moral life. At the same time it is intellectual education, the formation of clear and distinct ideas, which he emphasizes. Hence, even if Wolff does not provide a completely satisfactory answer to the question how man by his own efforts can lead a truly moral life, it is clear that rationalism has for him the last word. The principal end of education is to produce those clear ideas of the moral vocation of man which can serve as motive-forces for the will. What is at the back of his mind seems clear enough. The will naturally seeks the good. But man can have mistaken ideas of the good. Hence the importance of developing true, clear and adequate ideas. The will can be rightly directed only by the intellect. Wolff may not succeed in explaining precisely how the intellect can govern the will and produce the right desires; but that it can do so in his opinion is beyond doubt.

Wolff sometimes speaks as though the aim of the education of the mind is to produce useful ideas. And if we bear in mind his insistence, when talking about our duties to ourselves and to our neighbour, that man ought to work and by this means maintain himself and promote the common good, we may perhaps be inclined to draw the conclusion that his moral ideal is simply that of the decent, hard-working citizen. We may conclude, in other words, that he has a thoroughly bourgeois conception of man's moral vocation, a conception which can be described as a secularized form of the Protestant notion of man's vocation in this world. But though this conception forms one element in his thought, it is not the only element. For he gives to the term 'useful' a wide range of meaning. Being useful to society does not mean simply faithful service as a manual labourer or as an official of some sort. The artist and the philosopher, for instance, develop their potentialities, perfect themselves, and are 'useful' to society. Education for life should not be taken in a narrow, Philistine sense. Wolff tries to combine a wide idea of education and self-perfection with an insistence on the duty of serving the common good, which he looks on as a characteristic note of his moral philosophy.

In view of Kant's idea that man has an obligation to seek moral perfection and that this perfection cannot be attained in a finite time, it is worth remarking that for Wolff before him moral perfection is not something which can be definitely attained here and now. Man cannot reach his objective and then rest on his oars, so to speak. The obligation to seek moral perfection involves an obligation to go on continually striving towards it, an obligation to strive endlessly after the complete harmonization of impulses and affects under the rule of reason. And this obligation falls both on the individual and on the human race in common.

On man's duties are based his rights. By nature all men are equal, and they have the same duties as men. They have, therefore, the same rights. For we have a natural right to all that enables us to fulfil our natural duties. There are also, of course, acquired rights; but as far as natural rights are concerned, all men are equal.

Wolff bases the State on a contract. But it has a natural justification in the fact that it is only in a large society that man can obtain for himself in sufficient measure the goods of life and defend them against aggression. The State exists, therefore, to promote the common good. As for government, this rests ultimately on the consent of the citizens, who may reserve to themselves the supreme power or transfer it to some form of government. Governmental power extends over only those activities of the citizens which are related to the attainment of the common good. However, Wolff conceded to the government wide powers of supervision with a view to the physical and spiritual well-being of the citizens. For he interpreted the common good in terms of human perfection, and not in purely economic terms.

Nations, says Wolff in his *Jus Gentium*,[4] are to be regarded as 'individual free persons living in a state of nature'. And just as there is a natural moral law which obliges individual men and gives rise to rights, so is there a natural law of nations or necessary law of nations, which is immutable and which gives rise to equal rights. This law is the natural moral law as applied to nations.

Further, all nations must be understood to have formed together, by presumed consent, a supreme State. For nature itself compels nations to form an international society for their common good. We must conclude, therefore, that the nations as a whole possess the right of compelling individual nations to fulfil their obligations towards the greater society. And just as in a democratic State the will of the majority must be considered to represent the will of the whole people, so in the supreme State the will of the majority of nations must be taken to represent the will of all nations. But how is this to be expressed, when nations cannot meet together in the way that is possible for groups of individuals? According to Wolff, we must take that to be the will of all nations upon which they would agree if they followed right reason. And from this he concludes that what has been approved by the 'more civilized nations' is the law of nations.

The law derived from the concept of a society of nations is called by Wolff the 'voluntary law of nations'. And he places it under the general heading of 'the positive law of nations', together with stipulative law, resting on the express consent of nations, and customary law, resting on their tacit consent. But, quite apart from possible criticism of the idea of a supreme State with a fictitious ruler, it would seem more natural to place what Wolff calls the *jus gentium voluntarium* under the heading of the *jus gentium naturale* rather than under that of the *jus positivum*. For the latter classification would seem to demand the existence of an actual supreme or universal society rather than of a presumed society of nations. However, in asserting the existence of 'the voluntary law of nations' Wolff was influenced by Grotius, to whom he appeals, though he finds fault with the latter for not having distinguished properly between voluntary, stipulative and customary law. In any case the idea of a society of nations is of unquestionable value, whether we accept or reject Wolff's use of the idea.

If Wolff is compared with thinkers such as Descartes, Spinoza and Leibniz, he must doubtless be reckoned a minor figure in the history of philosophy. But if he is looked at in the context of the development of German thought, one's judgment will be different. Apart from Leibniz, Germany had produced little in the way of philosophy: the great period of German philosophy lay in the future. But meanwhile Wolff acted as a kind of philosophical educator of his nation. He is often accused, no doubt with justice, of aridity, dogmatism and formalism. But because of its comprehensiveness and its formal and orderly arrangement his system was able to provide a school-philosophy for the German universities. His influence spread throughout Germany and beyond, and his ideas may be said to have dominated in the German universities until the rise of the Kantian criticism. The system, which was no mean achievement in itself, thus stimulated the growth of philosophical reflection. He triumphed over his theological opponents, even if his philosophy was to be conquered by that of Kant and his successors. In other words, he occupies an important place in the history of German thought, and no accusations of lack of originality or of formalism can rob him of it.

3. The term 'Leibniz-Wolffian philosophy', which was rejected by Wolff himself, was coined by Georg Bernhard Bilfinger (1693–1750), who was for a time professor of philosophy at St. Petersburg and later (from 1731) professor of theology at Tübingen. *Dilucidationes philosophicae de Deo, anima humana, mundo et generalibus rerum affectionibus* (1725) helped to spread Wolff's system, though he did not follow the latter in everything. Among other disciples of Wolff we may name Ludwig Philipp Thümmig (1697–1728), who

lost his chair at Halle at the same time as Wolff, and Johann Christoph Gottsched (1700–66), author of *Erste Gründe der gesamten Weltweisheit* (1733), who attempted to utilize the Wolffian philosophy in literary criticism. Mention must also be made of Martin Knutzen (1713–51), if for no other reason than that from 1734 he was professor of logic and metaphysics at Königsberg and numbered Kant among his hearers. He was a mathematician and astronomer as well as a philosopher, and he helped to arouse Kant's interest in New-tonian science. In the field of philosophy he was influenced by Leibniz and Wolff, but he was at the same time an in-dependent thinker. Thus he abandoned the theory of the pre-established harmony in favour of a theory of efficient causal-ity. Needless to say, Knutzen was not responsible for Kant's critical philosophy, but his lectures were one of the factors which contributed to form the latter's philosophical views in his pre-critical period. In religion Knutzen was inclined to pietism; but under the influence of Wolff he greatly modified the rejection of natural or philosophical theology which was one of the characteristics of the pietistic movement. Indeed, he published a *Philosophical Proof of the Truth of the Chris-tian Religion* (1740). In other words, he tried to combine pietistic spirituality with Wolffian 'rationalism'.

A more important figure is Alexander Gottlieb Baumgarten (1714–62), professor at Frankfurt on the Oder, who pro-duced a number of text-books in which he expounded and developed the Wolffian philosophy. His *Metaphysics*, for ex-ample, was used by Kant in his lectures, though not, of course, without criticism of its contents. But Baumgarten's impor-tance does not lie primarily in his relationship to Kant, nor in his enrichment of the German philosophical vocabulary by his translations of Latin terms; it lies in the fact that he was the real founder of German aesthetic theory. In his *Meditationes philosophicae de nonnullis ad poema pertinenti-bus* (1735), which has been translated into English under the title *Reflections on Poetry*, he coined the word 'aesthetics' (*aesthetica*), and he developed his theories in the two vol-umes of his *Aesthetica* (1750–8).

Baumgarten's approach to aesthetics was determined to a great extent by Wolff's philosophy. The latter had deliber-ately omitted a treatment of art and of the beautiful; for the subject did not fit into the scheme of his philosophy. He was concerned with 'distinct' concepts, that is, with concepts which are communicable in words: he was not concerned with concepts which are 'clear' but not 'distinct', that is, with concepts which are clear but not communicable in words, such as the concept of a particular colour. And as he believed that the concepts concerned with the enjoyment of beauty are not distinct, he omitted a treatment of aesthetics. Further, when considering man's powers or faculties, he concentrated on the 'higher powers' (*vires superiores*), leaving aside to all intents and purposes the 'lower powers' (*vires inferiores*). And his belief that aesthetic enjoyment is a function of the lower powers, the faculties of sensation, was thus also a reason for omitting consideration of aesthetic theory. There was, therefore, a gap in the Wolffian philosophy, which Baumgarten set out to fill. And for a disciple of Wolff this involved a consideration of man's sensitive powers. The need for such a consideration had been rendered all the more acute by the increasing knowledge in Germany of British empiricism.

Baumgarten's idea of aesthetics was humanistic in character, in the sense that it was bound up with a view of man. At the beginning of the *Aesthetics* he remarks that 'the philosopher is a man among men; nor does he rightly think so great a part of human knowledge alien to himself'.[5] The philosopher must strive after a knowledge of sensibility, which plays such an important part in human life, and though he may not be able to create the beautiful as the artist does, he should seek for a systematic knowledge of the beautiful. Indeed, Baumgarten defines aesthetics as the science of the beautiful and of beautiful things. But beauty is perfection in the field of sensibility or sense knowledge. Hence aesthetics is the science of the perfection of sense knowledge. 'The goal of aesthetics is the perfection of sense knowledge as such. And this is beauty.'[6]

Aesthetics is also described by Baumgarten as the art of thinking beautifully (*ars pulchre cogitandi*). This unfortunate description or definition obviously lends itself to misunderstanding and misuse. But Baumgarten was not saying that the science of aesthetics consists in knowing how to think 'beautiful thoughts'; he was referring to the art of using the so-called lower faculties properly with a view to their 'perfection'. And if we put his various definitions or descriptions together, we can say that he looked to aesthetics to provide a psychology of sensation, a logic of the senses, and a system for aesthetic criticism.

The idea of a logic of the senses is of importance. As a follower of Wolff, Baumgarten naturally arranged the philosophical sciences in a hierarchical order, and equally naturally he placed aesthetics in a subordinate position. For it is concerned with the inferior powers and with inferior knowledge. Aesthetics, if it is a science at all, must be the activity of thought; but as it does not treat of the province of distinct ideas, it must take an inferior place in the ladder, so to speak, of knowledge. At the same time Baumgarten saw that it will not do to treat aesthetic intuition as a form of purely logical thinking which has somehow failed to live up to the standards of logical thought. Yet it is not 'illogical'. Aesthetic intuition has its own inner law, its own logic. This is why he speaks of aesthetics as the art of the analogue of reason. 'Aesthetics (the theory of the liberal arts, inferior knowledge, the art of thinking beautifully, the analogue of reason) is the science of sensitive knowledge.'[7] Baumgarten may not always indicate very clearly whether he is speaking of aesthetic intuition itself or of our reflective and conceptual representation of it; but two things at least can be said. First, sensibility is not to be excluded from the sphere of knowledge on the ground that 'sense knowledge' is not purely logical or mathematical knowledge. Secondly, it is a peculiar kind of knowledge. For dealing with it we require a special epistemology, inferior knowledge or theory of knowledge (*gnoseologia inferior*). For the law which governs aesthetic intuition cannot be expressed in distinct and purely logical concepts; it is an 'analogue of reason'. Pure logic means abstraction, and abstraction means impoverishment, in the sense that the concrete and individual is sacrificed in favour of the abstract and universal. But aesthetic intuition bridges the gulf between the individual and the universal, the concrete and the abstract; its 'truth' is found within concrete qualities. And beauty is something which cannot be expressed in abstract concepts.

By including a variety of themes under the general heading

of aesthetics Baumgarten did not facilitate the making of clear generalizations. But the salient point of his aesthetic theory is his recognition of the fact that concepts such as beauty have their own peculiar use. He thus established aesthetics as an independent branch of philosophical inquiry. When speaking, for example, of the language of poetry, he makes it clear that we cannot force all uses of language into the same mould and interpret them in the same way. In poetry the words remain, as it were, saturated with immediate sensory content: 'the perfect language of sense is poetry'.[8] The language of poetry must be differentiated from the language of, say, physical science: the words do not function in the same way. But it does not follow that poetic statements are nonsense. They express and evoke vivid intuitions which are not irrational but possess their own analogue of reason. In Baumgarten's phrase they have the 'life of knowledge' (*vita cognitionis*).

We certainly ought not to exaggerate the importance of Baumgarten. In the first place he was not 'the father of aesthetics'. To go no further back in history, Shaftesbury and Hutcheson, for example, had already written on the subject in England. In the second place extravagant praise has sometimes been given to his achievements, and as an antidote we have only to consider the judgment of Benedetto Croce that 'save in its title and its first definitions Baumgarten's *Aesthetic* is covered with the mould of antiquity and commonplace'.[9] At the same time his importance in the development of aesthetic theory in Germany is undeniable. It is doubtless true, as Croce remarks, that he is of importance in the history of aesthetics as 'a science in formation . . . of aesthetics *condenda* not *condita*';[10] but he did at least recognize not only that there is such a thing as the philosophy of aesthetics but also that the language of aesthetics has its own peculiarities. He doubtless interpreted the subject in the light of the Wolffian philosophy; and he is open to the accusation of having spoken in too intellectualist terms, 'in terms of knowledge' and 'truth', for instance. But the point to remark is that he felt the inadequacy of a purely rationalist account of aesthetic intuition and enjoyment and that he paved the way for a further development of aesthetic theory. Whatever Baumgarten's shortcomings may have been he saw that there is a side of human life and activity which is a fit object of philosophical consideration but which cannot be understood by anyone who is determined to bring it into the sphere of abstract logical thinking on pain of exclusion from philosophy altogether.

Among the disciples of Baumgarten was Georg Friedrich Meier (1718–77) who expounded his master's doctrines at Halle and published *Principles of all the Beautiful Sciences* (*Anfangsgründe aller schönen Wissenschaften*) in three volumes (1748–50) and *Considerations on the First Principles of all Fine Arts and Sciences* (*Betrachtungen über den ersten Grundsätzen aller schönen Künste und Wissenschaften*) in 1757. As far as aesthetic theory is concerned, Moses Mendelssohn (1729–86), who will be mentioned again in the next chapter, was also influenced by Baumgarten. But there is no point in giving a list of names. It is sufficient to say that there was a plentiful crop of writings on aesthetics in the second half of the eighteenth century. Indeed in his *Sketch of the History and Literature of Aesthetics* (1799), J. Koller asserted that patriotic youth would be pleased to note that Germany had produced more literature on the subject than any other country.

Turning to Wolff's opponents and critics, we may mention first Joachim Lange (1670–1744) of Halle, who was one of the principal agents in obtaining Wolff's expulsion from the university in the name of orthodoxy and piety. A much more philosophically-minded thinker was Andrew Rüdiger (1673–1731), who lectured at Halle and Leipzig and attacked the notion that the mathematical method can be applied in philosophy. Mathematics is concerned with the sphere of the possible, whereas philosophy is concerned with the actual. The philosopher, therefore, should build on the foundation of experience, as given in sense-perception and self-consciousness; and he should derive his fundamental definitions and axioms from this source. Rüdiger also attacked, for example, the theory of a pre-established harmony between soul and body. The soul is extended, and there is physical interaction between soul and body.

Another opponent of Wolff was Christian August Crusius (1715–75), professor of philosophy and theology at Leipzig, who attacked the optimism and determinism of the Leibniz-

Wolffian philosophy. As there are free beings in the world, namely men, we cannot interpret the world-system as a pre-established harmony. Further, Crusius criticized the use made by Leibniz and Wolff of the principle of sufficient reason, though this did not prevent him from substituting a fundamental principle of his own, namely the proposition that what cannot be thought is false and that what cannot be thought of as false is true.[11] From this illuminating proposition he derived three other principles; the principle of contradiction, that nothing can be and not be at the same time; the principle of inseparables, that those things which cannot be thought of separately cannot exist separately; and the principle of incompatibles, that those things which cannot be thought of as conjoined cannot exist in a state of conjunction. Obviously, Crusius was not really opposed to the spirit of Wolff's philosophy, even if he appeared to his contemporaries to be an opponent of Wolff because he rejected some of the latter's characteristic theses. Incidentally, Kant had a high opinion of Crusius, though he criticized his notion of metaphysics.

Chapter Six

THE GERMAN ENLIGHTENMENT (2)

Introductory remarks; Frederick the Great; the 'popular philosophers'—Deism: Reimarus; Mendelssohn—Lessing —Psychology—Educational theory.

1. (i) The philosophy of Wolff and of his followers was in one sense a high point of the German *Aufklärung*. It constituted a programme, as it were, for bringing all provinces of human mental activity before the bar of reason. This was, of course, the reason why the pietistic Lutheran theologians opposed Wolff; for they thought that his rationalism was the enemy of faith. The Wolffian system also represented the rise of the educated middle class. Reason should judge, for example, what is and what is not acceptable in belief about God; the personal convictions of the monarch or local sovereign should not be the deciding factor in settling the religion of a people. Again, 'taste' and aesthetic judgment are not the prerogative of the aristocracy or of genius: the philosophic reason can extend its sway to cover the aesthetic field. Philosophy, it is true, is carried on by comparatively few people; but reason is in itself universal. Belief, morals, forms of State and government, aesthetics, all are subject to reason's impersonal judgment.

These aspects of the Wolffian philosophy and its derivatives link it with the general movement of the Enlightenment. At the same time Wolff's system was, as we have seen, closely connected with the thought of Leibniz, and so with the movement of rationalist metaphysics in post-Renaissance philosophy on the European continent. It thus stands somewhat apart from the spirit of the Enlightenment as manifested in France and England. But in the phase of the *Aufklärung* which will be briefly considered in this chapter the influence of French and English thought becomes more marked.

(ii) If one wishes to find a symbol of this influence, one can hardly do better than consider Frederick the Great (1712–86). Brought up by a French governess and tutor, he developed an enthusiasm for French thought and literature, accompanied by a certain contempt for German literature, which showed itself in his preference for speaking and writing in the French language. True, he had at one time a strong sympathy with the philosophies of Leibniz and Wolff. And, as we saw in the last chapter, he reinstated the latter at Halle. Frederick had no sympathy with the Lutheran theologians who had secured Wolff's dismissal by Frederick William I. As far as religious beliefs were concerned, he was strongly in favour of toleration, not only of different dogmatic systems, but also of rationalism, agnosticism and even atheism. That a man of Wolff's eminence should be exiled from Prussia because he was not an adherent of pietism was something which the king could not countenance. In the course of time, however, his opinion of Wolff as a thinker changed, and he came under the predominating influence of French and English thought. In the chapters on the French Enlightenment we saw how Frederick invited philosophers such as Voltaire and Maupertuis to Potsdam, where he liked to converse with them on philosophical and literary matters. As for English thought, he had a high opinion of Locke and arranged for lectures to be given on his philosophy at Halle.

Though Frederick the Great believed in God, he had a strong inclination to scepticism; and Bayle was a writer whom he greatly appreciated. The king was very much of a freethinker. At the same time he developed a veneration for Marcus Aurelius, the Stoic emperor, and, like the Stoics, he laid great emphasis on the sense of duty and on virtue. Thus in his *Essay on Self-love considered as the Principle of Morals* (1770) he tried to show that self-love can be satisfied only through the attainment and practice of virtue which is the true good of man.

In view of Frederick's military exploits and of his successful determination to raise the political and military status of Prussia one may be tempted to regard the 'philosopher of Sans souci', as he called himself, with a cynical eye. But his praise of Marcus Aurelius was not merely idle talk. Nobody would wish to depict the Prussian monarch as a kind of un-

canonized saint; but he undoubtedly possessed a strong sense
of duty and of his responsibilities, and his statement in
Antimachiavell (1740) that the prince should regard himself
as the first servant of his people was meant seriously. A
despot he may have been; but he was an enlightened despot
who concerned himself, for example, with enforcing the im-
partial administration of justice and with promoting the
spread of education, from elementary education up to the
reorganization and development of the Prussian Academy.[1]
Through this concern with education Frederick was one of
the leading figures of the German Enlightenment.

(iii) The spread of philosophical ideas in Germany was
promoted by the so-called 'popular philosophers' who, without being creative thinkers, endeavoured to purvey philosophy to the educated public. Thus Christian Garve (1742–98)
translated into German a number of works by English moralists, such as Ferguson, Paley and Adam Smith. Friedrich
Justus Riedel (1742–85) helped to spread aesthetic ideas by
his *Theory of the Fine Arts and Sciences* (1767), which has
been called a mere compilation. Christian Friedrich Nicolai
(1733–1811) exercised a considerable influence through his
editorship, first of the *Bibliothek der schönen Wissenschaften*
(1757–8), then of the *Briefe, die neueste Litteratur betref-
fend* (1759–65), and finally of the *Allgemeine deutsche Bibliothek* (1765–1805), literary journals which their editor succeeded in making pay for themselves. One may also mention,
though he was scarcely a philosopher in the academic sense,
Christoph Martin Wieland (1733–1813), first a pietist and
then a literary figure and poet, who translated into German
twenty-two plays of Shakespeare and, in his autobiographical
novel, *Agathon* (1766), traced the history of the self-develop-
ment of a young man, chiefly through the successive influences of different philosophies.

2. One effect of the influence of English and French
thought on German thought was the rise of deism. In 1741
Tindal's *Christianity as old as the Creation* had appeared in
German, and right at the beginning of the century John
Toland had spent some time visiting the Courts of Hanover
and Berlin.

(i) Prominent among the German deists was Hermann
Samuel Reimarus (1694–1768), professor of Hebrew and

oriental languages at the Hamburg Gymnasium. His chief work was an *Apology for or Defence of the rational Worshippers of God* (*Apologie oder Schutzschrift für die vernünftigen Verehrer Gottes*). Reimarus did not publish the work, but in 1774–7 Lessing published some portions under the title of the *Wolffenbüttel Fragments*. Lessing did not give the name of the author, but pretended that he had found these fragments at Wolffenbüttel. Another portion was published at Berlin in 1786 under the pseudonym of C. A. E. Schmidt, and further excerpts appeared in 1850–2.

On the one hand Reimarus was opposed to purely materialistic mechanism. The world, as an intelligible system, is the self-revelation of God: the world-order is inexplicable without God. On the other hand he was a strong opponent of supernatural religion. The world is itself the divine revelation, and other so-called revelations are human inventions. Further, the idea of the world as a causally interconnected mechanical system is the great achievement of modern thought; and we can no longer accept the idea of miraculous and supernatural divine revelation. Miracles would be unworthy of God; for God achieves His purposes through a rationally intelligible system. In other words, Reimarus's natural theology follows the familiar deistic pattern.

(ii) The Jewish philosopher, Moses Mendelssohn (1729–86), who was a friend of Lessing and a correspondent of Kant, may be reckoned as one of the 'popular philosophers', in the sense that he helped to popularize the religious and philosophical ideas of the Enlightenment. But he is of some interest for his own sake.

In 1755 Lessing and Mendelssohn published an essay with the, at first sight at least, startling title, *Pope a Metaphysician!* (*Pope ein Metaphysiker!*). The Prussian Academy had announced an essay competition on the subject of Alexander Pope's alleged philosophical system, which Maupertuis considered to have been a digest of the Leibnizian philosophy. (The object was apparently to deliver an indirect blow at the reputation of Leibniz.) Lessing and Mendelssohn argued, however, that Pope was either a poet or a metaphysician, but not both; and that in point of fact he had no philosophical system. Philosophy and poetry are two quite different things. This differentiation between the conceptual and the aesthetic was expressed by Mendelssohn in more general terms in his *Letters on Sensations* (*Briefe über die Empfindungen*, 1755) and elsewhere. We must discriminate, he says in his fifth *Letter*, between the 'heavenly Venus', which consists in the perfect adequacy of concepts, and the 'earthly Venus' or beauty. Experience of the beautiful is not a matter of knowledge: we cannot grasp it by a process of analysis and definition. It is wrong to think that we should experience more perfect aesthetic enjoyment if we possessed more perfect cognitive powers. Nor is the beautiful an object of desire. In so far as something is desired, it ceases to be, if it ever has been, the object of aesthetic contemplation and enjoyment. Mendelssohn postulates, therefore, a distinct faculty which he calls the 'faculty of approval' (*Billigungsvermögen*). It is a special sign of beauty, he says in *Morgenstunden* (7), that it is comtemplated with 'calm pleasure', whether we possess it or not. In thus insisting on the disinterested character of aesthetic contemplation Mendelssohn was writing to some extent under the influence of English aesthetic theory.

In the sphere of religion Mendelssohn maintained that the existence of God is capable of strict proof. His proofs, as given in *Morning Hours* (*Morgenstunden*, 1785), followed more or less the lines of the Wolffian system; and he accepted and defended the ontological argument. God is possible. But pure possibility is incompatible with the idea of a most perfect Being. Therefore God exists.

In his *Phaedo or on the Immortality of the Soul* (*Phädon oder über die Unsterblichkeit der Seele*, 1767) Mendelssohn tried to modernize Plato and argued that the soul is neither a mere harmony of the body nor a corruptible thing which can, as it were, waste away or disappear. Further, the soul has a natural and constant drive towards self-perfection; and it would be incompatible with the divine wisdom and goodness to create the human soul with this natural drive or impulse and then to render its fulfilment impossible by allowing the soul to relapse into nothingness.

The philosopher, therefore, can prove the existence of God and the immortality of the soul, the foundations of natural religion. In doing so he is simply giving a theoretical justification of truths which the human mind, left to itself, spontaneously recognizes, at least in a confused way. But this does not mean that the State is justified in trying to enforce uniform acceptance of specific religious beliefs. Nor is any religious body which demands of its members uniformity of belief entitled to invoke the aid of the State in attaining this end. The State is concerned with actions, not with beliefs. And though it should, of course, encourage, so far as this is compatible with freedom of thought, the formation of ideas which tend to issue in desirable activity, it should not extend its power of coercion from the sphere of action into that of thought. Toleration is the ideal, though, as Locke observed, we cannot tolerate those who seek to substitute intolerance for toleration.

Mendelssohn became involved in a famous dispute with Jacobi about Spinoza and pantheism. But something will be said about this in the section on Lessing, because the debate arose in connection with the latter's alleged Spinozism.

3. When Gotthöld Ephraim Lessing (1729–81) entered the University of Leipzig he enrolled as a student of theology. But he soon abandoned theological studies for a literary career; and he is best known, of course, as a dramatist and as a literary and art critic. He must, however, be accorded a place in the history of philosophy. For though he was never a professional and systematic philosopher in the sense that Wolff was, he was deeply interested in philosophical questions, and his somewhat fragmentary ideas exercised considerable influence. More important, however, than any individual idea or thesis is the fact that his writings tended to form a unified literary expression of the spirit of the *Aufklärung*. This should not be taken to mean that his works simply reflected the ideas of others, as a kind of mirror. They did do this to some extent, of course. For example, *Nathan the Wise* (*Nathan der Weise*, 1779) expressed in dramatic form the ideal of religious toleration which was a prominent feature of the Enlightenment. But at the same time he developed the ideas which he took over from others. For instance, though he was somewhat influenced by the deism of Reimarus, he developed it partly under the inspiration of his understanding of Spinoza in a direction which put one in mind of later idealism rather than of what is usually understood by deism.

Lessing, as has already been mentioned, published some

portions of Reimarus's chief work under the title of *Wolffen-büttel Fragments.* And this action led to his being attacked by some writers, especially, of course, by those who suspected that Lessing himself was the author and who at the same time disagreed with the views expressed in the *Fragments.* But as a matter of fact Lessing's view of religion was not that of Reimarus. The latter was convinced that the fundamental truths of natural religion can be strictly proved, whereas Lessing believed that no system of religious belief can be proved by universally valid arguments. Faith rests on inner experience, not on theoretical proofs.

Again, Lessing did not agree with Reimarus's attitude towards the positive, dogmatic religions. We cannot accept the radical distinction made by the rationalistic deists between the truths of natural religion, which can be proved by reason, and the dogmas of so-called revealed religion, which have to be rejected by the enlightened. I do not mean to suggest, of course, that Lessing accepted the idea of revelation in the orthodox sense. He rejected, for instance, the idea of the Bible as an unquestionable revelation, and he was himself a pioneer of the higher criticism which was to become so fashionable in the nineteenth century. But it was his conviction that the value of religious ideas and beliefs is to be judged by their effect on conduct or by their ability to affect conduct in a desirable way. The Christian way of life was already in existence not only before the canon of the New Testament was fixed but also before any of the Gospels were written. And criticism of the documents cannot affect the value of this way of life. Obviously, therefore, if all religious beliefs rest ultimately on experience, and if their value is to be estimated primarily by their tendency to promote moral perfection, the deistic distinction between the rationally provable truths of natural religion and the man-made dogmas of Christianity tends to fall away and disappear. Lessing's interpretation of the Christian dogmas was not the orthodox interpretation; but at the same time it allowed him to give a more positive valuation to Christianity than the rationalistic deists felt able to give it.

Lessing did not mean, of course, that in no case are better reasons available for accepting one religious or philosophical position rather than another. But for him it was a question of

comparative degrees of truth and of an unending approximation to absolute truth rather than one of attaining at any
given moment an absolute truth possessing final and universal
validity. This point of view is symbolized by his famous remark that if God were to offer him with the right hand the
complete truth and with the left the unending search for
truth, he would choose the latter, even if it meant that he
would always be in error. The possession of pure and final
truth is for God alone.

This attitude has not unnaturally been criticized on various grounds. For example, the objection has often been made
that, given his denial of man's possession of absolute and
immutable truth, Lessing has no criterion for distinguishing
degrees of truth. He can, indeed, maintain that degrees of
truth are to be judged by their tendencies to promote different lines of conduct. But a problem obviously recurs in regard
to distinguishing between more and less desirable types of
conduct, between the moral and the immoral, and so on. But
it is not possible to enter into discussion of these questions
here. It is sufficient to point out in passing that such problems
arise. The relevant point in a sketch of Lessing's ideas is
rather the shift from the rationalist attitude of the deists to a
'dynamic', not to say fluid, idea of truth. The latter re-
appeared later on in contexts very different from that of
Lessing's thought.

Lessing's idea of truth stands in close relation to his idea
of history. In the *Education of the Human Race* (*Die Erziehung des Menschengeschlechts*, 1780) he asserts that 'what
education is to the individual human being, that revelation
is to the whole human race'.[2] Education is revelation made
to the individual while revelation is the continual education
of the human race. For Lessing, therefore, revelation means
the divine education of the human race in history. It is a
process which has been always going on, which is still taking
place and which will continue in the future.

Further, revelation as the education of the human race in
general is analogous to the education of the individual. The
child is educated by means of sensible rewards and punishments. And in the childhood of the human race God could
give 'no other religion, no other law, than one through the
observance of or non-observance of which His people hoped

or feared to be happy or unhappy here on earth'.[3] The child-hood of the human race corresponds, therefore, more or less to the state of affairs depicted in the Old Testament. This is followed by the boyhood or youth of the human race, corresponding to the New Testament. Nobler motives for moral conduct than terrestrial punishments and rewards are brought to the fore; the immortality of the soul and eternal reward and punishment in the hereafter are preached. At the same time the conception of God as the God of Israel develops into the conception of the universal Father; and the ideal of inner purity of heart as a preparation for heaven takes the place of mere outward obedience to a law with a view to attaining temporal prosperity. To be sure, Christians have added theological speculations of their own to the teaching of Christ; but we should recognize in them a positive value. For they have stimulated the exercise of the reason and through them man has accustomed himself to think about spiritual things. Lessing mentions and rationalizes some particular dogmas; but the important point is not so much that he rationalizes them as that he sees in them a positive value. On this point he looks forward to Hegel rather than backwards to the deists. Finally, there is the manhood of the human race. 'It will certainly come, the time of a new, eternal Gospel, which has been promised to us in the ele-mentary books of the New Covenant.'[4] The term 'elementary books' is not a term of abuse. For Lessing the books of the Old Testament are *Elementarbücher* in comparison with the New Testament, while the books of the latter are *Elemen-tarbücher* in comparison with the further stage of divine revelation. In this third stage of revelation man will do good for the sake of the good and not for the sake of reward, either terrestrial or celestial. Lessing lays the emphasis, therefore, on the moral education of the human race. This is an unend-ing process; and Lessing even suggests a theory of palingenesis or reincarnation. To say that he asserts the theory would be to say too much: he suggests it in a series of questions. 'Why could not each individual human being not have been pres-ent more than once in this world? Is this hypothesis ridicu-lous because it is the oldest? . . . Why should I not return as often as I have been to acquire new knowledge, new capaci-ties?'[5]

In 1783 Jacobi (whose ideas will be outlined in the next chapter) wrote to Mendelssohn that when he had visited Lessing not long before the latter's death, Lessing had openly admitted that he was a Spinozist. To Jacobi this was a shocking admission; for he held that pantheism was simply atheism under another name. As for Mendelssohn, he was not a pantheist; but he was offended and upset by Jacobi's correspondence, which he took as an attack not only on Lessing but also, even if indirectly, on himself, as he was planning an edition of Lessing's works. He therefore in his turn attacked Jacobi in *Morning Hours*, whereupon the latter published a reply, together with his correspondence with Mendelssohn (1785). Both Herder and Goethe were drawn into the controversy, and both disagreed with Jacobi's identification of Spinoza's doctrine with atheism.

What Lessing said to Jacobi seems to have been that the orthodox ideas of God were no longer of any use to him, that God is one and all, and that if he had to call himself a disciple of anybody, he could name nobody but Spinoza. And even if we allow for the possibility of Lessing having taken a pleasure in shocking Jacobi, there seems to be no doubt that he had been influenced by Spinoza and that he recognized an affinity between his later ideas of God and those of the great Jewish philosopher. Lessing believed, for example, that human actions are determined. The world is one system in which God is ultimately the universal cause. Further, he clearly suggests that all things are comprised within the divine Being. To see this we have only to look, for example, at the paragraphs entitled *On the Reality of Things outside God*, a short essay written for Mendelssohn. Referring to the theory that existent things are different from the divine ideas of these things, he asks: 'Why should not the ideas which God has of real things be these real things themselves?' It will be objected that in this case there are contingent things in the immutable essence of God. But 'has it never occurred to you, who are compelled to attribute to God ideas of contingent things, that ideas of contingent things are contingent ideas?' Lessing doubtless attached much more value to individuality than Spinoza did, and, as we have seen, he laid great stress on the movement of history towards a goal, that of moral perfection. His theories thus looked forward to some extent to later idealism with its emphasis on historical development rather than backward to Spinoza. But the question is not whether Lessing interpreted Spinoza correctly but whether there was some autobiographical truth in his remarks to Jacobi. And it seems to be clear that there was.

In one sense, of course, the so-called *Pantheismusstreit* (pantheism controversy) was not very profitable. The question whether pantheism is atheism under another name, is one which is best dealt with by defining terms. But the controversy had the effect of stimulating interest in Spinoza's philosophy, ideas about which were vague and inexact.

In the field of aesthetic theory Lessing set himself in his *Laokoon* (1766) to analyse the specific differentiating characteristics of poetry and of formative art, that is, painting and sculpture. The great critic Winckelmann (1717–68) had remarked that the artistic effect of the Laokoon in the Vatican is the same as that of Virgil's description of the Laocoon story in the *Aeneid*. Lessing used this remark as a point of departure. We have already seen how, in connection with Pope, he made a sharp distinction between philosophy and poetry. In the *Laokoon* he maintained that poetry is concerned with presenting human actions, and through them the life of the soul; and for this reason he condemned pictorially descriptive poetry. Sculpture, however, is concerned with the presentation of the body, particularly of ideal corporeal beauty. Further, Lessing tried to show how the materials employed by the different arts determine their characteristics.

If human action is the specific theme of poetry, this is particularly true of the drama, a subject to which Lessing gave his attention in the *Hamburgische Dramaturgie* (1767–9). In this work he insisted on the unity of the drama, a unity which consists essentially in unity of action. According to Lessing, the *Poetics* of Aristotle, the fruit of reflection on the great Greek tragedies, is 'as much an infallible work as the *Elements of Euclid*' (*Hamburgische Dramaturgie*, last chapter). At the same time he strongly attacked the French preoccupation with the 'three unities'. They misunderstood Aristotle when they insisted on unity of time and place as essential characteristics of drama. If they were right, Shakespeare would be no true dramatist. Lessing also made his own

Aristotle's statement about the end of tragedy being 'the purging of pity and fear', interpreting pity as compassion, in a literal sense, and fear as self-regarding. Further, Aristotle was right in finding the essence of art in imitation. Drama imitates human actions; and tragedy imitates or presents a unity of human action in such a way as to ennoble man through its arousing of and 'purifying' of the passions of pity and fear. It has, therefore, a moral purpose.

These somewhat random, and in any case bald, observations give, it is true, a highly inadequate picture of Lessing as a writer on aesthetic theory and as a critic of the fine arts. He was not, indeed, an original thinker, in the sense of one who proposes new ideas in philosophy or in aesthetic theory. In the latter sphere he was much influenced by French, English and Swiss writers and, in regard to drama, by Aristotle. But though most of his ideas can be paralleled elsewhere, he had the gift of making these ideas live, and in this sense at least he was original and creative. In the preface to *Laokoon* he remarks that 'we Germans have no lack of systematic books'. His own work, he says, may not be as systematic and concise as that of Baumgarten, but he can flatter himself that whereas the latter admitted having taken many of the examples cited in his *Aesthetics* from Gesner's writings, 'my own example will taste more of the sources'. In other words, he endeavoured, as one would expect of a man who was himself a dramatist and poet, to base his aesthetic reflections on consideration of actual works of art and literature. It is thus doubtless true that Lessing's mind turned away from formalism and that, however dependent he may have been on other writers for his individual ideas, he presented them in a way which stimulated further, if different, reflections. The same can be said of his observations in the spheres of metaphysics and of the philosophy of history.

4. The period of the *Aufklärung* saw the beginnings of the study of psychology in Germany. An important figure in this field was Johann Nikolaus Tetens (1736–1807), who was professor of philosophy at Kiel for a time. In 1789 he accepted an invitation to take up a post at Copenhagen.

The general tendency of Tetens's thought was to mediate between the empiricist philosophy of England and the rationalist philosophy of the Continent. He was by no means an

anti-metaphysician. Indeed, he published works on metaphysics and on the proofs of God's existence in which he
affirmed the possibility and validity of metaphysics and of
metaphysical proofs, while at the same time he endeavoured
to ascertain why there are so few universally accepted metaphysical positions. But he insisted that in psychology we
must start, not with metaphysical pre-suppositions, but with
an analysis of psychical phenomena, though this analysis can
form the basis for metaphysical reflections on the soul. Here
we have an instance of the mediating tendency to which allusion has just been made.

Introspection must constitute the basis for scientific psychology, according to Tetens. But the soul is conscious of
itself only in its activities, and of its activities only in so far
as they are productive of psychical phenomena. The soul is
not its own immediate object of intuition. In classifying the
powers or faculties of the soul, therefore, and in attempting
to determine the nature of the soul itself as ground of its
activities we are necessarily dependent on hypotheses.

Together with the understanding, namely the activity of
the soul as thinking and as productive of images, and willing,
the activity whereby the soul produces changes (bodily movements, for instance) which are not themselves psychical
representations, Tetens recognizes feeling as a distinguishable
activity. We can distinguish, therefore, three powers of the
soul, understanding, will and feeling, the latter being described as the receptivity or modifiability of the soul. He suggests, however, the hypothesis that these three powers are
ultimately reducible to one fundamental power, the power of
feeling and of self-activity, which is capable of progressive
perfection. It is in the perfectibility of the soul's activity that
man's difference from the animals is particularly conspicuous.

Tetens's *Philosophical Essays on Human Nature and Its
Development* (2 vols., 1777) showed a predominantly analytic approach to psychology. A rather different approach was
represented by the *Essay on the Soul* (1753) of Karl Kasimir
von Creuz (1724–70). Like Tetens after him, von Creuz endeavoured to mediate between the English and continental
(Leibnizian) philosophies of the soul. And, again like Tetens,
he insisted on the empirical foundation of psychology. But
he was concerned with reconciling Leibniz's view of the soul

as a simple substance or monad with Hume's phenomenalistic analysis of the self. Von Creuz conceded to Hume that we cannot discover a point-like metaphysical ego which has no extension. At the same time he refused to allow that the self can be dissolved into discrete, separate phenomena. It has, indeed, parts, and in this sense it is extended; but the parts are not separable. And this inseparability of the parts of the soul distinguishes it from material things and constitutes a reason for affirming the soul's immortality, even if the ultimate grounds for this affirmation are to be found in divine revelation.

Of the two men Tetens was certainly of more importance for the development of psychology. He insisted, as we have seen, on a precise analytical approach. But at the same time he linked up analytical psychology with a general philosophy of human nature and its development, as the title of his chief work indicates. In his view we ought to study, not simply, for example, the origins of human ideas in experience, but the whole growth of the human intellectual life up to its expression in the different 'sciences. Again, his insistence on feeling as a distinct 'power' pointed towards a study of the expression of the life of feeling and sensibility in the world of art and literature.

5. The influence of Rousseau's *Émile* on educational theory in Germany during the *Aufklärung* was considerable. It was felt, for example, by Johann Bernhard Basedow (1723–90), author of, among other educational writings, a large tome named *Elementarwerk* (1774) which was designed as a kind of encyclopaedia for teachers and as a text for parents and children. But while Basedow was stimulated by Rousseau's idea of a 'natural' education, his pedagogical theory was not complicated by presuppositions about the deleterious effects of civilization on the human being. He was thus able to propose as the end and purpose of education preparation of children for a patriotic and happy life in the service of the common good. In his ideas about methods of teaching he was influenced by Comenius (1592–1671), author of *The Great Didactic*.

The stimulating effect of Rousseau was felt also by the famous Swiss educationalist, Johann Heinrich Pestalozzi (1746–1827), who influenced the development of the German *Volksschulen* or elementary schools. But with Pestalozzi, as with Basedow, we find an emphasis on education for social life. He laid great stress on education in the family and in a rural community, and on education in general as the best instrument of social reform, provided, of course, that it fosters moral, and not merely intellectual, development.

Basedow was for a time a professor of moral philosophy; but Pestalozzi can scarcely be called a philosopher, and it would be out of place to discuss here his particular ideas in the field of pedagogy, however famous his name may be in the history of educational theory. It is sufficient to note that the Enlightenment in Germany, as elsewhere, produced its educational theorists. In England there was Locke, in France Rousseau, in Germany and Switzerland Basedow and Pestalozzi. And the idea of education for social life, represented by the two latter names, was in conformity with the general direction of thought in the *Aufklärung*.

Chapter Seven

THE BREAK WITH THE
ENLIGHTENMENT

Hamann – Herder – Jacobi – Concluding remarks.

1. At the time of Wolff's death a very different type of man, Johann Georg Hamann (1730–88), was in his twenty-fourth year. Wolff was a great systematizer: Hamann had no use for philosophical systems. Wolff represented abstraction and the power of the discursive reason: Hamann hated what he regarded as one-sided abstraction and rejected the tyranny of the discursive reason. Wolff strove after clear and distinct ideas: Hamann dealt in oracular utterances which helped to earn for him the title of the Wizard (or Magus) of the North. In other words, Hamann set his face against the rationalism of the Enlightenment which represented for him the power of the devil rather than divine reason.

A native of Königsberg, Hamann was an unstable character who turned from one branch of study to another and from one occupation to another, ranging from posts as tutor in a family to minor posts in the commercial world. When reduced at one time to extreme poverty and an inner torment of spirit, he gave himself to the study of the Bible and developed the extreme pietism which was a characteristic of his writings. He numbered Herder and Jacobi among his friends, and he was also on friendly terms with Kant, though he vigorously criticized the latter's philosophy when Kant, awoken from his dogmatic slumbers, started to publish his *Critiques*.

It may seem that the Wizard of the North is out of place in a history of philosophy. But he gave expression, even if unsystematic and exaggerated expression, to ideas which were characteristic of the reaction against the Enlightenment, and he certainly exercised a considerable influence, even though his influence on Herder in particular has been exaggerated by some historians.

One of the main characteristics of Hamann's anti-rational-ism was its religious setting. Let us take, for example, the controversy about language. Against the rationalistic view that man invented language, as though it was a kind of mechanical product, Herder maintained that language is coeval with mankind. Hamann was and always had been of the same opinion. But he was not content with saying that language is not an artificial invention of the human reason and then assigning some other empirical cause or causes. In his opinion language was in some mysterious way a communication of God, a divine revelation. Again, Hamann was convinced that poetry in particular is not the product of reason. On the contrary, poetry, as he says in 'Aesthetics in a Nutshell' (con-tained in *Crusades of a Philologist*, 1762), was the mother-tongue of mankind. The speech of primitive men was sensa-tion and passion, and they understood nothing but images. It was in music, song and poetry that they expressed them-selves. Moreover, great poetry is not the product of a su-perior reason: it is not to be attributed to a superior capacity of understanding and observing rules. Homer and Shakespeare created their works by genius, not by applying intellectually apprehended rules. But what is genius? The genius is a prophet whose inspiration is divine. Language and the arts are products of revelation.

Of course, such statements could be given a simple and common-sense interpretation. For example, as Goethe re-marked, if it is true that God made man, and if language is natural to man as differentiated from the animals, it is true that God made language. Similarly, any theist (or pantheist for the matter of that) would be ready to attribute genius to the creative work of God. But Hamann expressed himself in an oracular style with a mystical colouring, which suggests that he meant something more, even if it is difficult to say what precisely he did mean.[1] In any case he was not content, for example, with insisting on the natural character of human speech and dissociating it from the idea of invention by rea-son: he insisted too on its divine origin.

Again, Hamann was not content with attacking the tyranny of the discursive reason and its pretended omnicompetence and with allowing a place in human life to faith in God and in divine revelation. His pietism led him to depreciate the reason and to find pleasure in the restriction of its power. It is significant that for him there is poetic, but not scientific, genius. We cannot speak of the great scientists as geniuses. For they work by reason, and this is not the organ of inspiration. And, in the religious sphere, it is not simply the case that the Wolffian natural theology is inadequate: it is thrown overboard in the name of faith. Again, while Hamann's view of history as a commentary on the word or self-expression of God exercised a powerful influence on Herder's mind, the former was rather disconcerted by the latter's use of profane sources and by his attempt to apply a scientific method in his interpretation of history. In Hamann's eyes history, like the Scriptures, possesses an inner mystical or 'true' sense which is revealed by God rather than attained by the patient and untiring effort of the reason. In other words, Hamann tended to apply to the understanding of history the Protestant conception of the true sense of Scripture being revealed by the Holy Spirit to the silent and prayerful individual believer. The deeper exegesis, whether of the Bible or of history, is the work of God alone.

We cannot, however, dismiss Hamann as a mere pietist who, if he deserves any consideration at all by the philosopher, deserves it only in the sense that one may pay some attention to one's opponents. His view of history as a divine revelation, as a work of divine providence, which was shared by Herder, was to have considerable importance in the near future. For this view, transposed, it is true, into a system of speculative philosophy which would have seemed to Hamann an intolerable expression of rationalism, was to form an integral part of the Hegelian philosophy of history. Further Hamann's anti-rationalism was bound up with a dislike of abstraction, which was not the product of mere prejudice. And a brief allusion must be made to this theme.

Goethe remarked[2] that Herder's utterances can be reduced to the principle that everything which man undertakes to perform, be it by word or by deed or in any other way, originates from the total, united powers of the personality. From the beginning man was poet, musician, thinker and worshipper in one. The rationalists of the Enlightenment, however, had, in Hamann's opinion, hypostatized the reason, speaking about 'the reason' and its performances as though it were something on its own and as though the ideal of human life consisted in reason's conquest of all spheres. Thus they tended to give man a false conception of himself and his activities. They abstracted one function of man's activity and turned it into the whole.

This hostility towards what he regards as false or one-sided abstractions is evident in Hamann's criticism of Kant's first *Critique*. In his *Metacritique on the Purism of Pure Reason*[3] Hamann attacked the Kantian separations between reason, understanding and sense, and between form and matter in sensation and conceptualization. Kant deals in abstractions. There certainly is, for example, an activity called 'reasoning'; but there is no such thing as 'the reason' or 'the understanding'. There are simply different activities which are performed by one being, one organism, one person. Obviously, even if this line of criticism does not dispose of the *Critique of Pure Reason*, Hamann is making a good point. It is one which is not infrequently made in other contexts by philosophers whose general outlook is far removed from that of the Magus of the North.

2. Hamann was clearly opposed to the rationalism of the Enlightenment. When we turn to Herder, however, we find a man who started from the point of view of the *Aufklärung* (so far as one is justified in speaking of 'a' point of view) and who worked his way out of it. While, therefore, historians are perfectly entitled to speak of his break with the Enlightenment, it is also possible to speak of his development of certain lines of thought within the movement. What we choose to say about this matter depends to some extent, of course, on the way in which we define certain terms. If we mean by the Enlightenment the Wolffian rationalism and the individualism of a number of thinkers, it is obvious that Herder made a break with the *Aufklärung*. But if we give the term a wider range of meaning, including under it the first germs or seeds of positions to which Herder gave expression, the word 'break' may seem to be too sharp. It makes, however, for clarity if one follows the traditional practice and represents Herder as having reacted against and broken with the Enlightenment.

Johann Gottfried Herder (1744–1803) was born at Mohrungen in East Prussia, the son of a pietist schoolmaster. In

1762 he enrolled as a student of medicine at the University of Königsberg, though he presently changed to theology. He attended the lectures of Kant who was expounding the traditional Wolffian philosophy and giving courses on astronomy and geography; and Kant introduced him to the writings of Rousseau and Hume. At Königsberg Herder also formed a friendship with Hamann, though he can hardly have been at once deeply influenced by his anti-rationalist friend; for when he moved to Riga in 1764 he contributed essays and reviews to organs of the Enlightenment. In 1765 he was ordained a Protestant clergyman.

In 1766 there appeared anonymously at Leipzig the first two parts of Herder's *Fragments concerning Recent German Literature* (*Ueber die neuere deutsche Literatur: Fragmente*). The work bore the date 1767, the year which saw its completion. In the course of this work Herder discussed problems concerning language, a subject which occupied a good deal of his thoughts. Like Mendelssohn and Lessing, he insisted on a distinction between poetic and scientific (in his terminology philosophical) language. But the distinction was given a genetic or historical setting. Herder distinguishes four stages of linguistic development, which are classified according to an analogy with human growth, an analogy suggested by Rousseau. First comes the childhood stage when language consists of signs of passions and feelings. Secondly there is the period of youth, the poetic age of language, when poetry and song are one. Thirdly there is the stage of manhood which, though it still possesses poetry, is marked by the development of prose. Fourthly and finally there is the old age of language, the philosophical age, when life and richness are sacrificed to pedantic accuracy.

The context in which this theory of language was placed was a discussion about the German language. We cannot enter here into the details of this discussion. It must suffice to say that Herder, because of his insistence on the difference between poetic and philosophical language, rejected the notion that what German poetry required was to develop logical clarity. This idea had been put forward by, for example, J. G. Sulzer (1720–79), for whom poets were mediators between speculative philosophy and the people. Herder also rejected the idea that the German language should be im-

proved by imitation of foreign literature. German poetry can
be great if it grows out of the spontaneous poetry of the people and is the fruit of national genius. Later on Herder was
to do much to foster a revival of interest in folk-poetry. In
this attitude he was opposed to those thinkers of the *Aufklärung* who despised the German language and thought that
the only hope for German literature lay in 'imitation'.

All this may seem to have little to do with philosophy. But
it is interesting to observe how Herder (and not Herder alone,
of course) distinguished between different types of language.
Further, Herder saw that the question of use is of great importance. If we investigate the origins of different types of
language, we do so in order to examine their uses more carefully, he tells us. And the uses of language is a subject which
is obviously much discussed in present-day English philosophy. Again, Herder's insistence on German and on the spontaneous poetry of the people as the basis for developed poetic
literature can be regarded as an initial stage in the growth of
his later philosophy of culture and history, which lays stress
on the development of national cultures considered as to-
talities in which languages play an extremely important part.

In *Critical Forests* (*Kritische Wälder*, 1769) Herder took
as his point of departure Lessing's *Laokoon*, though he had
other critics in view besides Lessing, whom he recognized as
an outstanding dramatist. In his work Herder touched on a
variety of points, distinguishing sculpture and painting, for
example, and arguing that though Homer was, indeed, the
greatest of Greek poets, the creations of his poetic genius
were historically conditioned and that his practice cannot be
taken as a norm. This is obvious enough to us; but Herder's
point of view is significant as representing an aspect of his
sense of historical development and of his rejection of purely
abstract and rationalistic criticism and theorizing.

In the fourth *Grove* of *Critical Forests*, which was not published in his lifetime, Herder subjected to trenchant criticism
the ideas of Friedrich Justus Riedel (1742–86), author of a
Theory of the Fine Arts and Sciences (1767). Riedel had
asserted the existence of three fundamental faculties of the
mind, common sense, conscience and taste, corresponding to
three absolutes, the true, the good and the beautiful. Herder
argued, for instance, that it is nonsense to suppose that there

is a faculty called 'common sense' whereby man apprehends absolute truth immediately without a process of reasoning. Anti-Wolffian notions of this sort would make one return to the philosophy of Wolff if one thought it acceptable. Again, the theory of a faculty of taste, with its implication that whatever pleases is beautiful or at least what pleases the greater number of people is the more beautiful, is an absurdity. Baumgarten was much more on the right lines when he distinguished between logic and aesthetics but maintained at the same time that there can be and ought to be a science of aesthetics, a science of sensation, which would be an important part of the philosophy of man. For Herder, aesthetics would examine the logic of artistic symbolization. Like Baumgarten, he saw that aesthetics must be distinguished from abstract logic and from science; but his approach was more historical. What is required is an historical analysis of different cultures and of the development and nature of their respective aesthetic ideals. But, while rejecting Riedel's theory of the universal faculty of taste, corresponding to the absolutely beautiful, Herder wavers in his discussion of absolute beauty. It may seem that his idea of an historical approach, with its accompanying psychological and physiological investigations, should lead to a relativistic conception of beauty; and Herder does, indeed, make artistic beauty relative to different cultures and to different periods of those cultures. At the same time he seems to hold that through an historical approach it would be impossible to find a common denominator. For an historical approach does not mean merely registering different conceptions of artistic beauty: it involves also an examination of the factors, psychological, physiological and environmental, determining these conceptions. It is true that Riedel had himself defended a psychological approach to aesthetics, using the psychology of Johann Georg Darjes (1714–91), who had been influenced by the faculty psychology of Crusius. But Herder's point was that the psychological approach must be integrated into an historical approach. We cannot legitimately take a short cut by postulating a faculty which remains uniform in its operations in all cultures and which is correlative to an absolute, universal and unchanging ideal.

In 1769 Herder resigned his post as pastor at Riga and set

out on a voyage to Nantes, going afterwards to Paris and then to Strasbourg, where he consorted with the young Goethe (1770–1). The literary fruit of his journey to Nantes was his *Travel Diary*. This work, though not intended for publication, is of considerable importance as manifesting a change of mind in its author. Looking backwards, he expresses his dissatisfaction with the lifeless technicalities of aesthetic criticism, describes his *Critical Forests* as useless, crude and miserable, and wishes that he had given himself to the study of French, of the natural sciences and of history; that is, to the acquisition of positive knowledge of the world and of men. If he had acted in this way, he says, he would not have become an inkpot and a repository of print. Looking forward, he envisages a new type of school and education in which the child will be led by gradual stages from acquaintance with its natural environment through a concrete presentation of geography, ethnography, physics and history to a systematic and more abstract study of such sciences. The method would thus be inductive, proceeding from the concrete to the abstract, so that abstract ideas would be grounded in experience. Religious and moral education would, of course, form an integral part of the general plan. And the result aimed at would be the development of a full and balanced human personality. In other words, Herder's mind in the *Travel Diary* is dominated by the ideas of positive knowledge and of education.

At Strasbourg Herder succeeded in conveying to Goethe some of his own interest in and appreciation for folk-poetry and the national cultural heritage. He also wrote his *Treatise on the Origin of Language* (*Abhandlung über den Ursprung der Sprache*). Written at the end of 1770, it won a prize at the beginning of 1771 which had been offered by the Berlin Academy. Rejecting the extreme opposing views of the divine origin of language on the one hand and of its 'invention' on the other, Herder insists that the question of the origin of language, so far as it has any sense, is one which can be solved only on the basis of empirical evidence concerning the development and use, or uses, of language: it cannot be settled by dogmatic statements and *a priori* theorizing. In the course of his discussion he attacks the faculty psychology, maintains that primitive language and primitive poetry were one, and emphasizes the social function of poetry.

Herder did not like Strasbourg, and in 1771 he went to Bückeburg as court preacher to the Count of Schaumburg-Lippe. Stimulated by James Macpherson's Ossianic forgeries, he contributed to a volume entitled *Of German Nature and Art* (*Von deutscher Art und Kunst,* 1773), an essay on Ossian and folk-songs, as well as another on Shakespeare. At this time Herder was revolting against the typical ideas of the Enlightenment, that it was the highest culmination of historical development and that the middle class was practically the unique source of enlightened reasonableness. He also asserted that the great rationalist systems of Descartes, Spinoza, Leibniz and others were poetic fictions, adding that the poetry of Berkeley was greater and better sustained. It is not surprising, therefore, that Herder completed his break with the *Enlightenment,* a break symbolized by *Another Philosophy of History* (*Auch eine Philosophie der Geschichte,* 1774).

In this work Herder gives an account of the successive ages of humanity, from the Golden Age of humanity's childhood onwards. But this scheme is not meant to be taken too seriously, as is clear from the fact that Herder states roundly that when one has depicted a whole age or a whole people, one is left with a general word. General characterizations are inherently weak. Indeed, there is a good deal of irony in Herder's account of historical ages. For Rome is said to represent the manhood of the human race. And the implication is that the eighteenth century, so lauded by the men of the Enlightenment, represents senility. And Herder does not hesitate to draw attention to the hollowness of some of the claims made on behalf of the eighteenth century. For instance, sublime ideas and principles are formed and expressed by the enlightened; but inclination and impulse to live with nobility and kindness are weakened. Again, enlightened Europe boasts its freedom, but the invisible slavery of class to class is passed over in silence, and the vices of Europe are exported to other continents.

More important, however, from a philosophical point of view than Herder's attack on the complacency of the men of the Enlightenment is his attack on their historiography. They approach history with a presupposition, namely that history represents an upward movement from religious mysticism and superstition to free and non-religious morality. But if we study history in the light of such presuppositions, we shall never succeed in understanding it in its concrete reality. We ought to study each culture and phase of culture on its own merits, seeking to enter into its complex life and to understand it, so far as possible, from within, without judgments about better and worse, happier and less happy. Each nation, says Herder, carries within itself its own happiness, and the same is true of each period of its development. We cannot say in general that youth is happier than childhood or that old age is more miserable than youth. Nor can we legitimately make analogous generalizations about nations in the course of their development.

Of course, there is a certain historicism in this attitude. But Herder is clearly insisting on an important truth, that if we wish really to understand the historical development of man, we must not force the historical data into the Procrustean bed of a preconceived scheme. This seems obvious enough to us now; but, given the general tendency of the Enlightenment to use history to prove a thesis, and a questionable thesis at that, Herder's point was by no means a truism at the time when he made it.

In 1776 Herder moved from Bückeburg to Weimar, where he was appointed General Superintendent or head of the Lutheran clergy. In 1778 he published an essay *Of the Cognition and Sensation of the Human Soul* (*Vom Erkennen und Empfinden der menschlichen Seele*), in which he expressed his opinion that no psychology is possible which is not physiology at every step. This statement is markedly behaviouristic, though Herder postulated in physiology a vital force. He also wrote extensively on literary subjects, such as folk-songs and their cultural significance, on theological questions, on certain books of the Bible, and on the spirit of Hebrew poetry. But the outstanding work of this period was his *Ideas for the Philosophy of the History of Mankind* (*Ideen zur Philosophie der Geschichte der Menschheit*) which appeared in four parts from 1784 to 1791, the production of the work being interrupted by a journey to Italy (1788–9). A projected fifth part was never written. As I propose to discuss the *Ideas* in a later chapter, when dealing specifically with the rise of the philosophy of history, I shall say nothing about its contents here.

In the period from 1793 to 1797 there appeared Herder's *Letters for the Advancement of Humanity* (*Briefe zur Beförderung der Humanität*), dealing with a heterogeneous collection of topics. One or two of the views which he expressed in the *Letters* will be mentioned later on in connection with the *Ideas*. The general theory of the work is that 'humanity', the ideal character of our race, is innate in us as a potentiality or predisposition and that it must be developed by formative education. The purpose of science, art and all other human institutions is to 'humanize' man, to develop the perfection of humanity. Herder raises the objection that this development would lead to the production of a Superman or of a being who was outside the human species; but he meets it by saying that perfect man would not be a Superman but simply the realization of 'humanity'. We may note that Herder's educational ideals were not confined simply to theory and writing; for he set himself to plan and carry into effect, so far as he could, a reform of education in the duchy of Weimar.

In his later years Herder published a number of theological writings, notably *Christian Writings* (1794–8), which are, in general, surprisingly rationalistic and much more what one would expect of a man of the Enlightenment than of a friend of Hamann. He also wrote in opposition to the critical philosophy of Kant of which he strongly disapproved. In 1799 he published a *Metacritique of the Critique of Pure Reason*, representing Kant's work as jugglery with words, as a linguistic monstrosity and as involving a wrong-headed perpetuation of the faculty psychology. This should not be taken to mean that Herder's criticism consisted of unintelligent abuse. On the contrary, it consisted of a reasoned examination of Kant's theories. For example, he maintained, as against the Kantian theory that mathematical propositions are synthetic, that they are 'identical', that is to say, that they are what Wittgenstein called 'tautologies'. Again, Herder rejected Kant's view of space and time. The geometer does not analyse the *a priori* form of space; for there is no such form. And even if Herder does not explain clearly what the geometer does analyse, it seems to be implied that he analyses the implications of his own axioms and fundamental postulates. But Herder's account of mathematics is only one particular instance of his criticism of Kant. His main line of thought is that Kant's whole enterprise is wrongly conceived. Even if there were a separate faculty called 'reason', it would be out of order to speak of 'criticizing' it. Rather should we start with language; for reasoning is not only expressed in language, it is also inseparable from it, though it is not coextensive with all the uses of language. Thinking, according to Herder, is inward speaking, while speaking in the ordinary sense is speaking aloud or thinking aloud, whichever you like. There is no 'reason' as an entity, there is only a process, an activity of man as a total personality, and language is an indispensable instrument of this process, merging with it. In fine, the *Critique of Pure Reason* is based, according to Herder, on an erroneous psychology.

In 1800 Herder published *Kalligone*, a criticism of Kant's *Critique of Judgment*. In his opinion Kant had no real understanding of aesthetics. Herder did not write a criticism of the second *Critique*; but this was not because he agreed with it. He intended to attack it but abandoned the idea, partly because he was advised not to do so and partly, probably more, because he was engaged on other work. Thus he undertook to edit a new literary periodical, *Adrastea* (1800-4), to which he was the main contributor, in the form of essays and poetic dramas.[4] The fifth volume of the periodical contained instalments of Herder's German translation of the *Romances of the Cid* (made from a French translation with consultation of a late Spanish version).

Herder died at Weimar on December 18th, 1803. From the foregoing account of his life and activity it should be clear that he was a man of many interests; and though he was not a great systematic philosopher, he was a fertile writer who exercised a great influence on German life and thought. He has been called the teacher of the *Sturm und Drang* (Storm and Stress) movement in German literature; but he certainly influenced also the succeeding romantic movement through his insistence on the significance of folk songs, through his idea of the all-important role of language in culture and in the development of the aesthetic consciousness, through his idea of history as a divine revelation and through his defence of Spinoza in the pantheism controversy. A. W. Schlegel (1767-1845) and F. Schlegel (1772-1829) were both in-

debted to Herder. However, as historians of German literature have remarked, it was the younger Herder, the rebel
against the rationalism of the Enlightenment, who most influenced the romantic movement. In his later years Herder
could not compete in the literary sphere with the influence
of Goethe, which was inevitably felt even by those who disagreed with him.[5]

3. Mention has already been made of Jacobi in connection
with the pantheism controversy. Friedrich Heinrich Jacobi
(1743–1819), who became president of the Academy of Sciences at Munich, was a philosopher of faith. He emphasized
the fact that it was never his intention to construct an academic system of philosophy; on the contrary, his writings
were the expression of his inner life and experience and were,
so to speak, forced from him, as he put it, by a higher and
irresistible power.

Jacobi had made a study of Spinoza, and in his opinion the
latter's philosophy was the only logical system. For the human reason can pass, in its process of demonstrating truths,
only from the conditioned to the conditioned: it cannot rise
above the conditioned to a transcendent Deity. All metaphysical demonstrations of an ultimate ground of existence must
lead, therefore, to monism, to the conception of a world-
system, which, as Jacobi maintained in his correspondence
with Mendelssohn, is equivalent to atheism. But this is not
to say that Spinozism is to be accepted. On the contrary, it
must be rejected in the name of faith, which is an affair of
the heart (Gemüt) rather than of the speculative reason.

The result of this position is, of course, a complete separation between philosophy on the one hand and the sphere of
faith on the other. To attempt to prove God's existence is
equivalent to trying to reduce God to a conditioned being;
and in the long run speculative metaphysics must result in
atheism. It is better to recognize Hume's services in exposing
the pretensions of metaphysics, provided that we attribute
full validity to faith. Just as we do not prove the existence of
the external world but enjoy an immediate intuition in sense-
perception of the existence of sense-objects, so do we have
(or can have) an immediate intuition of supersensible reality,
which we call 'faith'. In his later writings Jacobi spoke of the
higher reason (Vernunft as distinguished from Verstand)

whereby we apprehend immediately supersensible reality. If somebody denies the existence of God, we cannot prove this existence to him; but in his denial he shuts himself off from one whole aspect of human experience. Or, rather, his denial is a result of his blindness to all but our perception of the corporeal world and our knowledge of the relations between finite things. Light comes to us from the sphere of supersensible reality, but once we try to grasp by the discursive reason this light and what it renders visible to the higher or intuitive reason, the light fades and disappears.

To a certain extent Jacobi was in agreement with Kant. Thus he believed that the field of knowledge, that is to say of scientific or theoretical knowledge, is limited to the realm of possible experience, where experience means sense-experience, and he was in agreement with Kant about reason's incapacity to prove the existence of supersensible realities. To this extent, therefore, he welcomed the critical philosophy as making room for faith. But he rejected the Kantian theory of the postulates of the practical reason. Belief in God, for example, is not a practical postulate but the result of faith, of an inner illumination of the higher reason. Again, Jacobi rejected what he regarded as Kant's phenomenalism. What we perceive are not phenomena linked together by subjective forms of intuition and categories of the understanding; they are the real things themselves. Further, he insisted on the immediacy of moral intuition or sense as against what he looked on as the empty formalism of the Kantian theory of the categorical imperative. It may be argued that Jacobi misunderstood Kant; but the point in mentioning his criticism of the critical philosophy is to draw attention to the facts, first that he accepted it in so far as it fell in with his idea of the incompetence of the discursive reason to transcend the sphere of the sensible, and secondly that he rejected it in so far as it seemed to rule out immediate apprehension of God and of moral values. It is also to be noted that in Jacobi's view Kant's doctrine of the thing-in-itself was an anomaly, not in the sense that there are no metaphenomenal realities but in the sense that in the Kantian philosophy the affirmation of things-in-themselves can be justified only by use of the causal principle, though this is a subjectively grounded principle, according to Kant, and applicable only to phenomena.

4. We have seen that all three thinkers whom we have considered in this chapter not only opposed the rationalism of the Enlightenment but also subjected to criticism the new critical philosophy of Kant. It was from Kant, however, that the great movement of German speculative idealism in the first half of the nineteenth century took its rise. To be sure, some of the objections they brought against Kant were shared by the idealists. For instance, Jacobi's objection that the Kantian affirmation of the thing-in-itself, when taken together with his doctrine of the categories, placed Kant in an impossible position was raised also by Fichte. But the line of development taken by speculative idealism was not at all the line which either Hamann or Herder or Jacobi would have approved. (Jacobi charged Schelling with trying to conceal the Spinozistic consequences of his thought.) In this sense they were swimming against a current which was to prove too strong for them. At the same time Herder's idea of history as a progressive education of humanity and as a manifestation of providence, together with his insistence on organic totality, both in the cultural and in the psychological spheres, as against analytic splintering, were to be incorporated into the idealist movement, especially in the Hegelian system. It is true that Hamann also sponsored the idea of history as a kind of commentary on the divine *logos*. But his utterances were too oracular to have the effect of Herder's ideas. Historically speaking, therefore, the latter must be accounted the most important of the three.

It may be said that we ought to regard these three men, not simply in relation to subsequent philosophical development, but on their own merits, recognizing that they performed the useful function of drawing attention to and insisting on aspects of man's spiritual life which the rationalistic Enlightenment tended to ignore. This may well be true. At the same time one could hardly expect the human mind to rest content with the sort of dichotomy between faith and philosophy which was made by Hamann and Jacobi. If religion, as Herder maintained, is an integral part of human culture and not something man must grow out of, as some of the men of the Enlightenment had believed, man, in trying to understand his own cultural development, must try to understand religion. And this, of course, is one of the things which Hegel tried to do. In doing so he elevated the speculative reason above the immediacy of faith, and he thus adopted a position which was contrary to that of Hamann and Jacobi and which stimulated Kierkegaard to a reassertion of faith. We thus have the reaction of Hamann and Jacobi against the rationalism of the Enlightenment and, later, the reaction of Kierkegaard against the Hegelian form of rationalism. This suggests that Hamann and Jacobi in the late eighteenth century[6] and Kierkegaard in the nineteenth represent an important fact, the role of faith in human life. But it also suggests that a more satisfactory, that is, rationally satisfactory, synthesis of faith and philosophy is required than any which was offered by these protesters against an arid rationalism or an all-engulfing speculative intellect.

PART III

THE RISE OF THE PHILOSOPHY OF HISTORY

Chapter Eight

BOSSUET AND VICO

Introductory remarks; the Greeks, St. Augustine – Bossuet – Vico – Montesquieu.

1. According to Aristotle in the *Poetics*,[1] poetry is 'something more philosophical and of graver import than history, because its statements are of the nature rather of universals, whereas those of history are particular'.[2] Science and philosophy are concerned with the universal, whereas history is the sphere of the particular and of the contingent. Poetry, of course, is not philosophy or science; but it is 'more philosophical' than history. It is true that Aristotle makes general statements about historical development, which might possibly be classified under the heading of philosophy of history. For, like Plato before him, he speaks in the *Politics* of the various kinds of revolution which tend to occur under different institutions, of their causes and of the means of preventing them and of the tendencies in certain types of constitution to turn into other types. But such remarks are obviously general reflections on history of the kind which could perfectly well be made by the historian himself. If we mean by philosophy of history a total view of historical development purporting to show that this development, as made known by historical research, follows a rational pattern and fulfils some plan or exemplifies certain universal and necessary laws, we can hardly say that the Greeks elaborated a philosophy of history. They had, of course, their historians, such as Thucydides, but this is a different matter. True, the notion of a cyclic return in the history of the world was common enough, and this theory can, indeed, be called a philosophy of history. But it can scarcely be claimed that the Greeks elaborated the theory. And if we concentrate our attention on the tradition which ultimately came to dominate Greek philosophy, namely the Platonic tradition, we find a marked tendency to belittle the impor-

tance of historical development, a tendency connected, of course, with the Platonic insistence on unchanging spiritual reality as the sphere of true being in contrast with the sphere of becoming. The most impressive expression of this tendency is probably that found in Plotinus,[3] when he depicts historical events as so many incidents in a play which must be set in sharp contrast with the interior life, the spiritual return of the soul to God. True, Plotinus does not subtract history from the rule of law and of 'providence'. And his view of human history must be accounted a philosophy of history, inasmuch as it is closely linked with his general philosophical outlook: it is part of his system, just as the Stoics' view of cosmic history as a series of cycles was part of their system. But the tendency of Plotinus is to belittle the events to which prominence is accorded by the historian. And in any case there is no idea of human history in general as a development towards a goal which is attained in and through history.

The idea of history not as a series of cycles but as a process of progressive development towards an ultimate goal is characteristic, not of Greek but of Jewish and Christian thought. But the intimate connection between this idea and the doctrines of the Messias in Judaism and of the Incarnation in Christianity, as well as with Jewish and Christian eschatological doctrines, leads to a theory of historical development which is theological in character, in the sense that it presupposes theological doctrines. The most notable example of a specifically Christian philosophy of history is, of course, the theory of St. Augustine as presented in his *De civitate Dei*, in which the history of the Jewish people and the foundation and growth of the Christian Church play important roles. I do not wish to repeat here what I have said in the second volume of this *History*[4] about St. Augustine's philosophy of history. It is sufficient to remark that he thought in terms of a total 'Christian wisdom' rather than in terms of a systematic distinction between theology and philosophy. The fact, therefore, that his view of history is largely a theological interpretation with reference to God's providential dealings with the Jews as manifested in the Old Testament and with reference to the Incarnation and its prolongation, so to speak, in the Church, Christ's mystical body, is in no way inconsistent with his general outlook. And it is, in-

deed, arguable, at least from a Christian point of view, both
that an interpretation of history as a process of development
towards a determinate goal cannot be anything else but a
theological interpretation and that a non-theological interpretation of history, so far as it is capable of validity, is reducible to the sort of statements about history which historians themselves are competent to make. In other words, it
is arguable, from a Christian point of view, that there can be
no such thing as a philosophy of history, if this term is
understood to mean an interpretation of the whole of history
as an intelligible movement towards a determinate goal and if
a systematic distinction between philosophy and theology is
presupposed. However, if it is claimed that there can be no
such thing as a philosophy of history in this sense, the claim
must obviously be understood with reference to a valid philosophy of history. For it is clear enough that philosophies
of history which do not presuppose theological doctrines have
been and are presented. The Marxist philosophy of history
is a case in point. And though we are not concerned with
Marxism in this volume, we are concerned with the transition
from a theological to a non-theological interpretation of history.

2. Jacques Bénigne Bossuet (1627–1704), the great orator
who was bishop first of Condom and afterwards of Meaux,
expounded a theological interpretation of history in his *Discourse on Universal History* (*Discours sur l'histoire universelle*, 1681). In his preface to the work, dedicated to the
Dauphin, he emphasizes two aspects of universal history, the
development of religion and that of empires. For 'religion
and political government are the two points on which human
affairs turn'.[5] Through a study of history princes can be
made aware of the abiding presence and importance of religion in its successive forms and of the causes of political
changes and of the transition from one empire to another.

Obviously, these two themes could be treated by a non-
religious historian, without any theological presuppositions.
But in his *Discourse on Universal History* Bossuet has apologetic considerations in mind. In the first part he outlines
twelve epochs: Adam, or creation; Noe, or the Deluge; the
vocation of Abraham; Moses, or the written Law; the taking
of Troy; Solomon, or the building of the Temple; Romulus,

or the foundation of Rome; Cyrus, or the re-establishment of the Jews; Scipio, or the conquest of Carthage; the birth of Jesus Christ; Constantine, or the peace of the Church; and Charlemagne, or the establishment of the new empire. In other words, Bossuet is concerned with the providential dealings of God with the chosen people, with the spread of the Roman empire as a preparation for Christianity, with the Incarnation and with the establishment of the Church and of Christian society. Oriental empires enter upon the scene only in function of their relations with the Jewish people. India and China are omitted. The theological doctrines of creation, of divine providence, and of the Incarnation form the framework of the author's historical scheme. And the twelve epochs fall under seven 'ages of the world', the birth of Christ ushering in the seventh and last.

In the second part, devoted to the development of religion, apologetic considerations are again dominant. We pass from the creation through the time of the Patriarchs to the revelation of the Law to Moses; and from the kings and prophets to the Christian revelation. Bossuet discusses, indeed, some religions, such as those of Rome and Egypt, other than Judaism and Christianity; but his remarks are incidental to his main theme, that Christianity is the perfect development of religion. 'This Church, always attacked and never conquered, is a perpetual miracle and a striking testimony to the changelessness of the counsels of God.'[6]

The idea of divine providence is prominent also in the third part of the Discourse, which deals with the fortunes of empires. Thus we are told that 'these empires have for the most part a necessary connection with the history of the people of God'.[7] God used the Assyrians and Babylonians to punish the Jews, the Persians to re-establish them in their land, Alexander and his first successors to protect them, and the Romans to maintain their liberty against the kings of Syria. And when the Jews rejected Christ, God used these same Romans to chastise them, though the Romans did not understand the significance of the destruction of Jerusalem. Bossuet does not, of course, confine himself to such general familiar statements. He discusses the particular causes of the falls of a number of empires and States from Egypt to Rome, and he endeavours to draw lessons for the Dauphin from these discussions. His final conclusion is that no man can rule the course of history according to his own plans and wishes. A prince may intend to produce one effect by his actions and in actual fact produce another. 'There is no human power which does not serve, despite itself, other designs than its own: God alone knows how to reduce all to His will. That is why everything is surprising if we regard only particular causes; and yet everything proceeds according to an ordered development.'[8] In other words, historical changes have their particular causes, and the way in which these causes operate is by no means always foreseen or willed by men. But at the same time divine providence is fulfilled in and through the operations of these particular causes.

Perhaps we can say, therefore, that for Bossuet there are, as it were, two historical levels. There is the level of particular causes which are considered by the historian. The latter can determine, for instance, the particular causes which contributed to the fall of the Babylonian empire or of imperial Rome. But there is also the level of theological interpretation, according to which divine providence is fulfilled in and through historical events. But we are restricted in our knowledge of how divine providence is thus fulfilled in the cause of history. And this is obviously one reason why Bossuet dwells on the relations of Egypt, Assyria, Babylon and Persia to the Jewish people; for here he can have recourse to the teaching of the Old Testament.

Bossuet thus renewed in the seventeenth century St. Augustine's attempt to develop a philosophy of history. But, as has been remarked and as Bossuet was doubtless well aware, our ability to develop this sort of philosophy of history, namely in terms of the idea of divine providence, is very restricted. The chief significance of his *Discourse* is probably that it helped to draw attention to human history as the subject-matter of philosophical reflection.

3. A much more important figure in the rise of the philosophy of history is Giambattista Vico (1688–1744), one of the greatest of Italian philosophers. During Vico's lifetime a considerable amount of historical research was carried on. The Reformation and Counter-Reformation had both stimulated this work; and a further impetus, as historians have noted, was given by the rise of the national States and by

dynastic interests. Thus Leibniz engaged in writing the history of the House of Brunswick, while in Italy Muratori, who was librarian to the Duke of Modena in the first half of the eighteenth century, was commissioned by his patron to prepare a history of the House of Este.[9] But historical research and accumulation of material for the writing of history is not the same thing as historiography; and historiography or the writing of history is not the same thing as a theory or philosophy of history. For the latter we have to turn to Vico.

In 1699 Vico became professor of rhetoric in the university of Naples, a post which he held until 1741.[10] And in this capacity he delivered a number of inaugural lectures. The earlier ones show the influence of Cartesianism; but in that of 1708 he adopts a different attitude. The moderns, he says, have introduced great improvements in certain sciences, namely the physical sciences; but they have underestimated and depreciated the branches of study whose subject-matter depends on the human will and cannot be treated by the same method as, for instance, mathematics. These sciences include poetry, history, language, politics and jurisprudence. Further, the moderns have tried to extend the application of the demonstrative mathematical method of sciences where it can yield only apparent demonstration.

This point of view was developed more fully in his *Ancient Wisdom of the Italians* (*De antiquissima italorum sapientia*, 1710). In this work Vico attacks the philosophy of Descartes. In the first place, the *Cogito, ergo sum* cannot serve as an adequate refutation of scepticism or as a basis for scientific knowledge. For the certainty that one is thinking belongs to the level of unreflecting consciousness and not to the level of science. In the second place, clarity and distinctness of idea will not serve as a universal criterion of truth. It may appear to serve as a criterion of truth in mathematics. But it is applicable in geometry, for example, because geometry is a constructive science, in which the mind constructs or makes its own entities. Mathematical entities are not realities in the sense in which the objects of natural sciences are realities; they are fictions made by man. They are indeed clear and distinct; but they are so because the mind has itself constructed them. Construction of the object is therefore more fundamental than clarity and distinctness; and it provides us with the criterion of truth. 'The rule and criterion of truth is to have made it.'[11] But construction of the object does not mean precisely the same in physics, for instance, as in pure geometry. In the latter the objects are unreal entities, mental fictions; in the former they are not. Construction of the object in physics means using the experimental method. The things which we can prove in physics are those to which we can perform something similar. And the ideas of natural things which are clearest are those which we can support by experiments which imitate nature.

The statement of the principle *verum factum*, namely that the criterion of truth is to have made it, does not, therefore, lead to the conclusion that the geometrical method is of universal applicability in all sciences. Nor should it be taken to mean that the mind creates physical objects in the same sense in which it creates mathematical entities. We should not interpret Vico as maintaining that things are mental fictions or mere ideas. The making or constructing of the object should be understood in a cognitive rather than in an existential sense. When the mind reconstructs the structure of the object out of its elements, it attains certainty of truth in the very act of reconstruction. In this sense knowing and making are identified, *verum* and *factum* becoming one. God, creating all things, necessarily knows all things clearly. And a strict analogue to this truth is found only in human mathematical knowledge, where the objects or entities are mental fictions. We do not create Nature in the existential order. At the same time we have a scientific knowledge of Nature only in so far as we remake, as it were, the structure of the object in the cognitive order. And we cannot know that we are doing this correctly without the help of the experimental method. A deduction from purely abstract concepts created by ourselves cannot guarantee a knowledge of existent Nature, however clear and distinct these concepts may be.

The application of these ideas to history was not made in the *Ancient Wisdom of the Italians*; but it is easy to anticipate the general line which Vico's thought was to take. Human history is made by man; it is therefore understandable by man. The principles of historical science are to be found in the modifications of the human mind, in man's nature.

Indeed, history lends itself to scientific investigation and reflection more easily than physical Nature. Nature was made by God alone, not man; hence God alone can have a full, adequate knowledge of Nature. But human society, human laws, language and literature, are all made by man. Hence man can truly understand them and the principles of their development. Here we have a reversal of the Cartesian position. The sciences which Descartes belittled in favour of physical science are given a position superior to the latter.

The principles of this new science were discussed by Vico in his great work, *Principles of a New Science concerning the Common Nature of the Nations* (*Principi di una scienza nuova d'intorno alla comune natura delle nazioni*, 1725; 2nd edition, 1730; 3rd edition, 1744). In his autobiography Vico remarks that up to a certain date he admired two men above all, namely Plato and Tacitus. 'For with an incomparable metaphysical mind Tacitus contemplates man as he is, Plato as he should be.'[12] And we can connect with his admiration for these two men his aim in the *New Science* of determining the universal and eternal law of history and the ways in which this eternal law works itself out in the histories of individual peoples. The 'esoteric wisdom' of Plato is to be combined with the 'common wisdom' of Tacitus. But Vico adds the names of two other men to whom he recognizes a special debt. The first of these is Francis Bacon, from whose *De augmentis scientiarum* and *Novum organum* he derived a powerful inspiration in the development of his new science. (The title *New Science* may have been suggested by Bacon's *Novum organum*.) The second name is Grotius. Bacon saw that the sum of knowledge as existing in his time stood in need of being supplemented and amended, but, as far as law was concerned, he did not succeed in working out the laws governing human history. 'Grotius, however, embraces in a system of universal law the whole of philosophy and philology, including both parts of the latter, the history on the one hand of facts and events, both fabulous and real, and on the other of the three languages, Hebrew, Greek and Latin; that is to say, the three learned languages of antiquity that have been handed down to us by the Christian religion.'[13] Vico desired to carry further the work of Grotius. And we can connect with his reading of the philosophers of natural law, such as Grotius and Pufendorf (we may add Hobbes), his formulation of the problem of history as, in a large part, a problem concerning the origins of civilization. This is a theme to which he gives special attention in the *New Science*.

Vico was unwilling to start with Hobbes's 'licentious and violent men', Grotius's 'solitary, weak and needy simpletons' or Pufendorf's 'vagrants cast into the world without divine care or help', as he expresses the matter at the beginning of the first book of the first edition of the *New Science*. That is to say, he was unwilling to make an absolute start with men in these conditions. For Genesis does not suggest that Adam was originally in the state of nature described, for example, by Hobbes. So Vico allows a lapse of time for the process of man's bestialization to take place, among the Gentile races, that is to say. And then the problem arises how civilization developed.

Vico supposes that the first beginnings of civilization came with settled dwellings. The thunder and lightning of the sky god drove men, together with their women, into the shelter of caves. And these primitive habitations made possible the rise of the first stage of civilization, 'the age of the gods' or 'state of the families', when the father of the family was king, priest, moral arbiter and judge. This family-stage of civilization had three principles, namely, religion, marriage and burial of the dead.

In this primitive stage of civilization there were, however, ever-present tensions and inequalities. Among the vagrants, for instance, those who had not yet formed themselves into settled families which worshipped deities and tilled the soil in common, some were strong, others weak. And one can picture the weak taking refuge with settled families as dependents or serfs, to save themselves from their stronger and more violent fellows. We can then imagine the fathers of families uniting together against the serfs. That is to say, patrician and plebeian orders were gradually formed, and so there arose 'heroic states', in which the magistrates belonged to the patrician order. This was the second stage in the development of civilization; it was 'the age of the heroes'.

But this stage was inherently unstable. The patricians or nobles naturally wished to conserve the structure of society as it was; for they wished to preserve their position and privileges intact. But, equally naturally, the plebeians wished to change the structure of society. And in the course of time they succeeded in winning for themselves a share in one privilege after another, from a legal recognition of their marriages up to citizenship and eligibility for office. The age of the heroes thus gradually gave place to 'the age of men', characterized by democratic republics. It was the age of men, because the dignity of man as man, as a rational being, was at length recognized.

However, this third stage in the development of civilization held within itself the seeds of its own decay. Religion, which had been present from the start and which had been an all-important agent in man's rise to a civilized condition, tended, with the flowering of rationality, to give place to philosophy and barren intellectualism. Equality gave birth to a decline in public spirit and to the growth of licence. The laws certainly became more humane, and toleration increased; but decadence accompanied this process of humanization, until in the end society disintegrated from within or succumbed to external attack. This led, as at the close of the Roman empire, to a reversion to barbarism.

After the completion of the cycle a new cycle begins. Thus in the West the coming of Christianity heralded a new age of the gods. The Middle Ages represented the age of the heroes in the new cycle. And the seventeenth century, the century of the philosophies, was a phase of a renewed age of men. We find cycles in the histories of individual peoples; and their particular cycles are the working-out of a universal law. But this theory of cycles, which Vico believed to be confirmed inductively, must not be misunderstood. Vico does not mean that historical events are determined or that precisely similar sets of particular events occur in each cycle. Nor does he mean, for instance, that Christianity is a temporary religious phenomenon which possesses a value relative to one particular cycle, so that it must give place to another religion in the future. What recurs is not the particular historical facts or events but rather the general framework in which the events occur. Or, better, it is the cycle of mentalities which recur. Thus the primitive mentality, expressed in the language of sense, imagination and passion is gradually succeeded by the emergence of reflective rationality. This in turn becomes, as it were, cut off from other layers of human nature and tends to develop into the dissolvent criticism of the sceptical reason. And the dissolution of society is not arrested until man recaptures the spontaneous primitive mentality which brings with it a renewed contact with God, a renewal of religion. Civilization 'in every case began with religion and was completed by sciences, disciplines and arts'.[14] There is a cycle of mentalities, of the forms of historical development, but not of the contents, the particular historical facts and events. Vico's idea does, indeed, recall Greek theories of the cyclic return; but he has no intention of affirming a fatalistic theory of the necessary repetition of similar particular events. Nor does his theory of cycles preclude all progress. For instance, Christianity may correspond in a new cycle to what Vico calls the 'frightful religions' of the first age of the gods; but it does not follow that Christianity is not superior to them.

It is a great mistake to think that Vico offered nothing else in his philosophy of history but a theory of cycles. There is much more to it than a tidy map of the development of each people or nation. For one thing we can find in his work a healthy counterblast to rationalism in the sense of an over-intellectualist interpretation of man and his history. The philosophers, says Vico, are incapable of forming for themselves a true idea of the origins of society; for they tend constantly to read back into the past their own ways of looking at things and to rationalize what was not the work of reason in the sense which they give to this word. Thus the philosophers of natural law depict for us men in the state of nature as making a contract or covenant which gives rise to society. But the real origins of society cannot have been of this kind. The factor which drove the vagrants or vagabonds into caves and suchlike primitive dwellings, there to establish more or less settled habitations, was fear; or, more generally, felt need.

This idea can be applied, not only to the philosophers of the seventeenth century, but also to those of the ancient world. The latter, subject to the same rationalizing tendency as their modern successors, attributed the laws of States to enlightened law-givers, such as Lycurgus at Sparta. But laws did not begin as the product of reflective reason, though in the course of time, as civilization developed, they have been subjected to revision by reason. The trouble is that philosophers, worshipping the reflective reason, find the essence of man in this reason. They think that it is reason alone which unites men and acts as a common bond, so that it must be the source of law, which is a unifying factor. The imagination, the senses and the passions separate men from one another. In reality, however, men in the first stages of development were ruled by imagination and feeling rather than by the reflective reason. True, reason was present; but it expressed itself in forms proper to imagination and feeling. Primitive religion was, psychologically, the spontaneous product of fear and of a sense of helplessness, not of reason in the philosophic sense; and primitive law was intimately associated with primitive religion. Both were the product, not of the philosophical reason, but of a logic of feeling and imagination. Law, in its origins, was custom as a natural growth, not the fruit of the planning intellect.

Vico laid great emphasis on poetry and mythology. Indeed, the third book of the *New Science* is entitled *On the Discovery of the True Homer*. If we wish to study the early stages of religion, morality, law, social organization and economics, we must refrain from mere abstract theorizing and study the data of philology, namely poetry and myth. And in interpreting, for instance, the Homeric poems we must avoid two erroneous ideas. First, we should not look on the myths as deliberate impostures, useful lies of the type commended by Plato in the *Republic*. Secondly, we should not rationalize them, as though their authors were giving allegorical expression to clearly conceived and rationally formulated ideas and theories. Rather are they the expression of the 'vulgar wisdom', the 'poetic wisdom', of a people; and they give us the key to the manner of thinking of peoples at the time when the myths were born. The Homeric poems, for instance, express in 'poetic characters' the religion, customs, social organization, economics and even scientific ideas of the Greeks in the heroic age. They are, as it were, the spontaneous literary expression or deposit of the mentality and life of a people at a given period of its development. Hence comes their great value for a reconstruction of history. Obviously, we are not called upon to accept everything as literal truth. Zeus, for instance, was not a real person, in the form in which he and his activities are described in the Homeric poems. At the same time he is not a mere literary device, symbolizing some abstract philosophical notion of deity. He is rather the imaginative expression of an early stage of contact with the divine. It is not that poetical descriptions of the divine covered, as it were, a philosophical theory of the divine, which was clearly formulated in reflective reason: the religious thinking of the period was poetical thinking. It had its own logic, but this was the logic of imagination and feeling rather than the abstract logic of the philosopher.

Another point to notice in Vico's philosophy of history is his insistence on the complex unity of each cultural period. Each 'age' or stage in a cycle has its own types of religion, law, social organization, and economics. Vico doubtless over-schematized; but he provided a programme, as it were, for a study of history which would not be confined to the narration of dynastic, political and military events but which would delve into the lives of peoples in successive phases of their histories and explore these lives in all their ramifications, exhibiting the connections between religion, morality, custom and law, social and political organization, economics, literature and art. At the same time he outlined programmes for the comparative study of the development both of human mentality in general and of particular sciences and arts.

History, therefore, reveals to us human nature. We cannot attain a knowledge of human nature by simply considering man as he is, say, in the second period of the 'age of men' or by taking the philosopher as a standard. We have to turn to the gradual revelation of man's nature in history, in his poems, in his art, in his development of society and law, and so on. History is made by man; it is therefore understandable by man. And in studying history man attains a reflective awareness of his own nature, of what it has been and is and can be. It is silly to extol the achievements of the age of reason, the age of the philosophers, and despise the past and the primitive, for the whole course of history is the revelation of man. In the primitive age of the gods we see man as sense; in the age of heroes we see man as imagination; in the age of men we see man as reason.

The fact that history, whether we consider human actions or the monuments of art and literature or institutions, is made by man does not mean, however, that it is cut off from divine providence and that it is not in some sense the work of God. But for Vico divine providence operates primarily through the human mind and will; that is, through natural means and not primarily through miraculous intervention. Men have often intended one end and achieved another. For example, 'fathers meant to exercise without restraint their paternal power over their serfs, and they subjected them to the civil power from which cities arose. The ruling class of nobles meant to abuse their lordly freedom over the plebeians, and they had to submit to the laws which established popular freedom.'[15] Whatever individuals may have intended, through their actions civilization arose and developed. And in the second phase of the age of man, when free-thinkers, for instance, try to destroy religion, they contribute to the dissolution of society, to the end of a cultural cycle, and so to a rebirth of religion which is the chief factor in facilitating man's conquest of his egoistic passions and which leads to the growth of a new culture. Men act freely, but their free actions are the means by which the eternal purposes of divine providence are realized.

It is not quite accurate to say that Vico's *New Science* was entirely disregarded by his contemporaries. For certain particular theses became the subject of discussion. But the general significance of his ideas was certainly not appreciated; and Vico did not begin to come into his own until the nineteenth century. In 1787 Goethe visited Naples, and the *New Science* was brought to his attention. The great poet lent the work to Jacobi, and in 1811 Jacobi referred to what he considered to be Vico's anticipation of Kant. This passage was used by Coleridge in his *Theory of Life* (1816, published 1848), and in subsequent years he spoke with some enthusiasm of Vico. In France, Michelet published an abridged translation of Vico's main work (1827), and in 1835 he reissued it, accompanied by a translation of the autobiography and of some other writings. In Italy, Rosmini and Gioberti interested themselves in Vico, and so did the idealists, such as Spaventa, who maintained that the entry of Hegelianism into Italy was, as it were, the homecoming of Vico to his native soil, on the ground that the latter was the precursor of German philosophy. But the modern spread of interest in Vico has been due above all to Benedetto Croce who represented him as the man who 'discovered the true nature of poetry and art and, so to speak, invented the science of aesthetic'.[16]

4. Montesquieu (1689–1755) does not refer in his published writings to Vico; but it seems probable that he made the acquaintance of the *New Science* when he was travelling in Italy in 1728, that is to say, before the publication of his famous works on the causes of the greatness and decadence of the Romans (1734) and on the spirit of laws (1748). The fact that he undertook a comparative study of society, law and government with a view to ascertaining the principles of historical development at once suggests that Vico exercised some influence on his mind, at least by way of stimulus, though it does not of itself prove that there was such an influence. However, Montesquieu's personal notes seem to show that Vico's theory of cycles and of the decay of civilization did exercise some influence on his mind, though its extent can hardly be ascertained.

As Montesquieu's ideas have been outlined already in the first chapter of this volume, no more will be said about them here. It is sufficient to point out that with both Vico and Montesquieu we find the idea of a comparative historical method, and that both men set out to use historical data as a basis for determining the laws governing the historical development of peoples. Of the two men Montesquieu, a thinker of the Enlightenment with a passion for liberty, had incomparably the greater success as far as his own time was concerned. Vico's star did not really begin to shine until the Enlightenment had run its course.

Chapter Nine

VOLTAIRE TO HERDER

Introductory remarks – Voltaire – Condorcet – Lessing – Herder.

1. It has sometimes been maintained that the outlook of the eighteenth-century Enlightenment was unhistorical. If this were taken to mean that no history was written, the statement would be patently false. We have only to think of Montesquieu's *Histoire de la grandeur des Romains et de leur décadence* (1734), of Gibbon's *Decline and Fall of the Roman Empire* (1776–81), of Voltaire's *Histoire de Charles XII* (1731) and of his *Histoire du siècle de Louis XIV* (1751), and of Hume's historical works. Nor can it be said that the historiography of the eighteenth century was concerned simply with battles, diplomatic and political struggles and the doings of 'great men'. On the contrary, we see the rise of the idea of history as a history of human civilization. Charles Pinot Duclos, author of a *Histoire de Louis XI* (1745) and of *Considérations sur les mœurs de ce siècle* (1750), declared that he was concerned with the manners and customs of men rather than with wars or politics. In this attitude he was at one with Voltaire. The eighteenth century certainly saw a broadening of the idea of history.

When it is said that the outlook of the eighteenth-century Enlightenment was unhistorical, the statement may refer in part to the tendency shown by some writers to treat history as a form of *belles-lettres* and to make over-hasty judgments without real knowledge or understanding of the sources. More important, it refers to the tendency to treat the age of reason and enlightenment and its ideals as a kind of absolute standard of judgment and to despise the past except in so far as it could be interpreted as leading up to the age of *les philosophes*. This attitude of mind, with its accompanying tendency to use history to prove a thesis, namely the superiority of the eighteenth century in general and of the philosophers in particular, obviously did not conduce to an objective understanding of the past. It would be, indeed, an exaggeration to suggest that all the thinkers of the Enlightenment expounded a naïve theory of progress. A certain pessimism shows itself even in Voltaire. But, by and large, the philosophers were convinced that progress and the triumph of emancipated reason are synonymous; and their idea of reason made it difficult for them to understand either a primitive mentality or, for instance, the Middle Ages. When the philosophers wished to picture to themselves primitive man, they set before themselves modern man and stripped him of the qualities and habits which could be attributed to civilization, being careful to leave him the exercise of reason which would enable him to enter into the social contract. True, Vico saw the artificiality of this analytical method, and he looked to an examination of poetry, song, art, records of customs and of religious observance to afford a secure basis for an understanding of the mentality of earlier times. But Vico was a genius who stood somewhat apart from the Enlightenment, and who was consciously opposed to the exaggerated rationalism and intellectualism of so many of his contemporaries. His estimate of his own time was certainly not that of the average *philosophe*. As for the Middle Ages, the men of the Enlightenment were quite incapable of a sympathetic understanding of the mediaeval culture and outlook; the Middle Ages represented for them a darkness out of which the light of the reason had gradually emerged. Thus though they broadened the idea of historical study and made a valuable contribution to the future of historiography, they were too much inclined to use history to prove a thesis, to glorify the Enlightenment, and their prejudices made it difficult for them to penetrate with sympathetic understanding into cultures and outlooks which they felt to be very different from their own and which they were inclined to despise. It is in this sense that we should understand the accusation that the mentality of the Enlightenment was 'unhistorical'.

2. Voltaire, whose general philosophical position has been discussed in the first chapter of this volume, asserted that his *Essai sur les mœurs* (1740–9, published 1756) was intended as a continuation of the work of Bossuet. 'The illustrious

Bossuet, who in his discourse on a part of the universal history grasped its true spirit, stopped at Charlemagne.'[1] Voltaire wishes to continue from where Bossuet left off, and the full title of his work is *An Essay on General History and on the Manners and Spirit of Nations from Charlemagne up to Our Days*. In point of fact, however, he goes back much further and begins with China, passing to India, Persia and Arabia, and then coming to the Church in West and East before Charlemagne.

But though Voltaire announces his intention of continuing the work of Bossuet, it is obvious that his idea of history is very different from that of the bishop of Meaux. For Bossuet the important events in history are the creation, the dealings of God with the Jewish people, the Incarnation and the growth of the Church; and he envisages human history, from the creation to the last day, as a unity, as a manifestation of divine providence which is served even by human free choices. With Voltaire the theological outlook of St. Augustine and Bossuet is conspicuous by its absence. History is the field of the interplay of human wills and passions. Progress is possible in so far as man rises above the animal condition and in so far as reason dominates, particularly when it takes the form of that enlightened despotism which alone can bring true social reform. But the idea of history as the implementation of a divine plan and as moving towards a supernatural goal disappears. And with it there disappears any strong conviction about the unity and continuity of history.

In part, of course, Voltaire is simply putting forward the idea of an empirical study of history, without dogmatic presuppositions. He wrote a *Philosophie de l'histoire* (1765), which was prefixed to the 1769 edition of the *Essai sur les mœurs*; but there is little philosophy in it in any ordinary sense of the term. When he talks about the need for writing history in a philosophical spirit, he is referring to the need for excluding legends and fairy-stories. This is made clear, for instance, in his *Remarques sur l'histoire* where he asks whether a man of good sense, born in the eighteenth century, can be permitted to speak seriously about the oracles of Delphi. But Voltaire is ultimately demanding, of course, that supernatural explanations should be left out altogether. To write history in a philosophic spirit is to write in the spirit of a *philosophe*, a man of the Enlightenment. And 'the illustrious Bossuet' was not a *philosophe*.

The conviction that it is not the historian's business to entertain his reader with fabulous anecdotes and tall stories is one of the reasons why Voltaire advises people to study the history of modern, rather than of ancient, times. In his *Nouvelles considérations sur l'histoire* he remarks that to treat of ancient history is to mix a few truths with a thousand lies. But it is obvious that an historian of ancient times is not obliged to write in the chatty and gossipy manner of Herodotus or to accept as true all fable and legend. Quite apart from the fact that a study of such legends, and even of the oracles of Delphi can be, as Vico saw but Voltaire did not, of great use to the serious historian, the remedy for uncertain and fabulous history is patient research. But Voltaire had, of course, another reason for preferring the history of modern times, namely a conviction of the superiority of the modern world, and especially of the philosophers. In the brief *Remarques sur l'histoire* he expresses the wish that the young should begin a serious study of history 'at the time when it becomes really interesting for us; that is, it seems to me, towards the end of the fifteenth century'. It was then that Europe changed its aspect. In other words, the Middle Ages have no real interest for us.

This point of view comes out in a number of places in Voltaire's writings. We are told that past times are as if they had never been; that the world of the ancient Jews was so different from ours that one can hardly draw from it any rule of conduct applicable today; that study of ancient times satisfies curiosity, whereas study of modern times is a necessity; and so on. This attitude obviously constitutes a weak point in Voltaire as historian and philosopher of history.

But Voltaire has, of course, his strong points. In his little essay, *Nouvelles considérations sur l'histoire*, he remarks that after having read three or four thousand descriptions of battles and the contents of some hundreds of treaties he has scarcely found himself any wiser than before. 'I no more know the French and the Saracens by the battle of Charles Martel than I know the Tartars and the Turks by the victory which Tamerlane won over Bajazet.' Instead of a narration of battles and of the doings of kings and courts one should find in histories accounts of the dominant virtues and vices of nations, explanations of their power or feebleness, the story of the establishment and growth of arts and industries. In fine, for the man who wishes to read history 'as a citizen and philosopher' 'changes in manners and in the laws will be his great object of study'.[2] Similarly, at the beginning of the sixty-ninth chapter of the *Esprit des mœurs* Voltaire states: 'I should like to show what human society was at the time (the thirteenth and fourteenth centuries), how people lived in the intimacy of family life, which arts were cultivated, rather than to repeat so many disasters and combats, those deadly subjects of (ordinary) history, those well-worn examples of human malice.' The philosopher may have underestimated the importance of political and military history, but he certainly drew attention to aspects of human life which are now universally regarded as important parts of the subject-matter of the historian but which had been overlooked by chroniclers who were hypnotized by the deeds of generals and monarchs and heroes.

In his general ideas about history Voltaire was clearly not as profound as Montesquieu, whom he attacked, let alone Vico: but in his conception of social historiography we can see the expression of the development of the bourgeois consciousness. For him history should no longer be dynastic history, an instrument for the glorification or vilification, as the case might be, of potentates, but rather an account of the emergence of the life, arts, literature and science of the eighteenth century, or, more broadly, of the social life of man through the ages.

Finally, to balance what has been said about Voltaire's contempt for the pre-Renaissance world, it should be added that in the *Esprit des mœurs*, including the additions which he made to it, he paints on a vast canvas. He speaks not only of Europe but also of the Far East and of America, not only of the Christian world but also of the Mohammedan world and of the oriental religions. True, his knowledge is often very defective; but this does not alter the scope of his design. In one sense his history was less universal than that of Bossuet. For the latter's theological framework held together in an intelligible unity the whole history of the race. But in another, and more obvious, sense Voltaire's *Esprit des mœurs* was more universal than the bishop's *Discours sur l'histoire universelle*, namely in the sense that the former wrote about nations and cultures on which the latter did not touch.

3. In the section on the physiocrats in the second chapter of this volume attention was drawn to the theory of progress proposed by Turgot, who anticipated the view of history which was expounded in the nineteenth century by Auguste Comte. Turgot was, indeed, much more of a believer in progress than Voltaire had been. For in spite of his convictions about the superiority of the age of the Enlightenment the latter had no belief in laws governing human history. But I have no wish to repeat what has been already said about Turgot, and I turn instead to another leading exponent of the idea of progress in the later part of the eighteenth century, namely Condorcet.

Marie Jean Antoine Nicolas Caritat, Marquis de Condorcet (1743–94), was a mathematician as well as a philosopher. At the early age of twenty-two he composed a treatise on the integral calculus, which won for him the esteem of d'Alembert. For the latter, as well as for Voltaire and Turgot, whose lives he subsequently wrote (Turgot's in 1786 and Voltaire's in 1787), he had a great admiration. He took part in the preparation of the *Encyclopaedia*, and he was elected to the Academy of Sciences (1769) and to the French Academy (1782). In 1785 he published an essay on probability, a second edition of which, revised and enlarged, appeared in 1804 with the title *Éléments du calcul des probabilités et son application aux jeux de hasard, à la loterie et aux jugements des hommes*.

Condorcet also interested himself in economic matters, writing, under Turgot's influence, in defence of free trade in corn. In politics he was an enthusiastic democrat and republican. He welcomed the revolution and was elected a deputy in the Convention. But he possessed too independent a mind to survive for long in those tempestuous years. He criticized the constitution which had been adopted by the Convention in favour of the one which he had sponsored; he denounced the arrest of the Girondists; and, objecting on principle to the death penalty, he opposed the conduct of the Mountain, the left-wing group headed by Robespierre, Marat and Danton. His critical attitude resulted in his being declared an enemy of the Republic and an outlaw. For a time he lay in hiding in the house of a widow, Madame Vernet; but, becoming convinced that the house was watched and that he was endangering the life of his benefactress, he fled. In the end he was captured and died in a cell at Bourg-la-Reine. Whether he succumbed to a stroke, was poisoned or poisoned himself does not seem to be clear.

While in hiding from his enemies Condorcet wrote his work on progress, *Esquisse d'un tableau historique des progrès de l'esprit humain* (1794), which is his chief title to fame as a philosopher. His main general ideas are those of the perfectibility of man, of the history of the human race as a gradual progress from darkness to light, from barbarism to civilization, and of indefinite progress in the future. Thus, although he wrote the work in the shadow of the guillotine, it is pervaded by a spirit of optimism. The violence and evil of the times he explained principally in terms of the bad institutions and laws which had been created by rulers and priests. For he was an enemy, not only of the monarchy, but also of the priesthood, indeed of all religion. He looked to constitutional reform and to education as the chief means of promoting progress. In 1792 he was one of those who presented to the Assembly a plan for organizing State secularist education, which became the basis for the plan subsequently adopted by the Convention. According to his plan mathematics, natural, technical, moral and political science would form the chief subject-matters for instruction in more advanced education, the study of languages, living or dead, occupying a comparatively minor place in the syllabus. In other words, the emphasis would be put on the science of Nature and on the science of Man.

Condorcet's interpretation of past history is developed in the light of this idea of scientific culture. He distinguishes nine stages or epochs. In the first epoch men, emerging from a state of barbarism in which they differed only physically from the animals, united together into groups of hunters and fishers, recognizing family relationships and using language. In the second or pastoral stage of development inequality and slavery make their appearance, together with some rudimentary arts; and in the third period, the agricultural period, there is further progress. These three preliminary epochs are admittedly conjectural; but with the invention of the alphabetic script we pass from conjecture to historic fact. The culture of Greece represents for Condorcet the fourth epoch, and that of Rome the fifth. He then divides the mediaeval period into two epochs. The sixth closes with the Crusades, the seventh with the great invention of printing. The eighth epoch is more or less synonymous with the Renaissance, opening with the invention of printing and closing with the new turn given to philosophy by Descartes. The ninth epoch closes with the revolution of 1789. It embraces Newton's discovery of the true system of Nature, Locke's opening-up of the science of Man, that is, of human nature, and the discovery of the system of human society by Turgot, Rousseau and Price.

A future and tenth epoch is then envisaged by Condorcet. In it, he says, there will be progress towards equality between nations, towards equality between classes, and in the physical, moral and intellectual improvement of individuals. Equality for him does not mean mathematical equality, but rather freedom, accompanied by equality of rights.

Progress in the past is thus regarded as issuing in future progress. The justification for this optimistic belief is obviously the assumption that there is a kind of law of progress or of human development which permits inferences from the past to the future. But the factor on which Condorcet lays most stress as securing future progress is not some hypothetical law operating inevitably but education, that is, rational enlightenment, political reform and moral formation. In his view we can set no limits in advance to human progress and perfectibility. When treating of the tenth epoch he insists that indefinite progress is possible, not only in moral science (in, for instance, the reconciliation of self-interest with the common good), but also in physical science, technical science and even (as against Diderot's view) in mathematics.

Obviously, the interpretations of history given by Turgot and Condorcet prepared the way for the positivist system of Auguste Comte. Theology is regarded as disappearing as the light of the scientific reason grows in strength; and the same can be said of metaphysical philosophy, except in so far as this can be reduced to a synthesis of scientific laws. We can hardly say that Condorcet worshipped *les philosophes* and regarded them as the peak of historical advance. He admired

Voltaire, it is true, and shared his violent anticlericalism. But he did not share his faith in enlightened despotism or his contempt for the people. He looked forward to a democratic and scientific civilization; and in spite of the defects of his *Essay*, both in its schematic framework and in many of its particular statements, he is in a sense much more modern than Voltaire. He does not so much canonize the eighteenth century as point to the future. Unfortunately he was blind to important aspects of reality and of man; but this blindness was shared, of course, by his nineteenth-century successors. And as for the dogma of progress, this has suffered a serious setback in the twentieth century.

4. The idea of progress was represented in Germany by Lessing. But, as we saw in the sixth chapter of this volume, his theory of progress in history had a theological setting. In *The Education of the Human Race* (1780) he declared that what education is to the individual human being, that revelation is to the whole human race. Progress is first and foremost the moral education of mankind by God. True, Lessing's conception of history differs very much from that of St. Augustine and Bossuet. For he did not, like them, regard Christianity as God's definitive revelation to man. Just as the Old Testament consisted of 'elementary books' in comparison with the New, so the New Testament consists of 'elementary books' with the further stage of divine revelation when men will be educated to the doing of good for its own sake and not for the sake of reward either in this life or the next. In this idea of passing beyond Christian morality, with its doctrine of sanctions, Lessing was in tune with the general current of moral theory characteristic of the Enlightenment. At the same time his conception of history as a progressive divine revelation permits at least some analogy between it and the philosophies of history of St. Augustine and Bossuet. It certainly bears the stamp of the eighteenth century; but it obviously differs very much from the theory of Condorcet, for whom historical progress is not the work of God but rather a liberation from religion.[3]

5. When we turn to Herder's philosophy of history, we find important differences from the characteristic theories of the Enlightenment. As we saw in the seventh chapter of this volume,[4] Herder attacked the self-complacency of the En-

lightenment, the tendency of eighteenth-century philosophers to think that history led up to their own times by a process of progressive development. But, as we also saw, he did not base this attack simply on a disagreement with their interpretation of the Enlightenment: he attacked their general approach to history. For in his view they approached history with presuppositions, and they used it to prove a preconceived thesis. Their thesis certainly differed from that of Bossuet, but it was none the less a preconceived theory, namely that history represents an upward movement from religious mysticism and the slavery of superstition towards a free and non-religious morality. To be sure, the philosophers of the Enlightenment might reply that their interpretation was based on induction rather than on presuppositions. But Herder could retort that their selection of facts on which to base a general interpretation was itself guided by presuppositions. And his great point was that their approach to history prevented them from studying and understanding each culture on its own merits, according to its own spirit and complex unity. In his *Another Philosophy of History* (1774) Herder himself divided up history into ages or periods; but he also drew attention to the danger of such a proceeding. When we delimit an 'age' and describe it in a few generalizations, we tend to be left with mere words: the reality, the rich life of a people escapes us. It is only patient and thorough study of the data which will enable us to understand the development of a people. And he himself laid emphasis, as we saw, on the poetry and early folk-songs of peoples as an important source for understanding the development of the human spirit. We can, indeed, hardly say that an emphasis on the understanding of the development of language and literature was in contradiction with the ideas of the Enlightenment. But Herder drew attention to the importance of the comparatively primitive in interpreting man and his history. We shall fail to appreciate the significance of earlier cultural phases if we persist in judging them simply with reference to a standard based on the rationalist ideals and presuppositions of eighteenth-century philosophers.

Herder's great work, *Ideas for the Philosophy of the History of Mankind* (*Ideen zur Philosophie der Geschichte der Menschheit*, 1784–91) was conceived on a gigantic scale. For, in the first two parts of the work, each of which contains five books, he treats of man's physical environment and organization, with anthropology and, to speak paradoxically, with the prehistorical period of man's development. It is only in the third part, comprising books XI–XV, that he comes to recorded history, carrying his account up to the fall of the Roman empire. This account is continued in the fourth part (books XVI–XX) up to about A.D. 1500. The fifth part was not written. However, ambitious as the scheme of his work certainly was, Herder did not make extravagant claims on its behalf. The very title, *Ideas for the Philosophy of the History of Mankind*, is significant in its modesty. And the author explicitly states that the work consists of 'stones for a building which only centuries can finish'.[5] He was not so foolish as to suppose that he could complete the edifice.

After treating of man's physical environment, that is, of the forces of the physical cosmos and of the position and history of the earth, Herder comes to the subject of organic life and of man himself. He does not expound evolution in the sense of maintaining that man has evolved from some species of animal; but he regards genera and species as forming a kind of pyramid, at the apex of which is man. Throughout all organic life we find, according to Herder, the manifestation of a vital force (obviously corresponding to Aristotle's *entelechy*), which, as we ascend the scale of genera and species, expresses itself in ever-increasing differentiation of function. Herder's conception of this hierarchy is frankly teleological in character. The lower species in their ascending order prepare the way for the appearance of man as being capable of conceptual thinking, a rational and free being. Man in his appearance fulfils the purpose of Nature, that is, of God. But Herder notes that whereas on the level of pure instinct the fundamental drives of the organism function in an unerring manner, the possibility of error increases with the growth of the will. 'The weaker instinct becomes, the more does it fall under the command of arbitrary will (or caprice) and therefore also of error.'[6]

For Herder history is the natural history of human powers, actions and propensities, as modified by time and place. Though not expounding, at least not in any explicit fashion, the theory of transformistic evolution, he emphasizes man's continuity, so to speak, with his physical environment and with lower forms of life. He also emphasizes man's organization. Man is 'organized for' reason and freedom. He has come into the world to learn reason and acquire freedom. He can speak, therefore, of humanity (*Humanität*) being latent in man, as something which has to be developed. At first sight it may appear to constitute a contradiction in terms if one speaks of humanity being latent in man. But Herder uses the term in two senses. It may mean the ideal which man is capable of attaining; or it may mean the potentiality for attaining this ideal. The ideal is thus latent in man, and Herder can speak of man as being organized for humanity. As a physical entity, of course, man is already there. But he has a potentiality for the perfection of man, for 'humanity'.

Man is also said to be organized for religion. Indeed, religion and humanity are intimately connected, so that the former is described as the highest humanity. As for the origin of religion, this is due, according to Herder, to man's spontaneous inference from visible phenomena to their invisible cause. To say that religion is due to fear (to fear, for instance, of hostile, dangerous or threatening meteorological phenomena) is to assign a totally inadequate cause. 'It is saying nothing to say that fear invented the gods of most peoples. For fear, considered as such, does not invent anything; it simply awakens the understanding.'[7] Even false religions bear witness to man's power of recognizing God. He may infer the existence of beings which do not exist as he conceives them; but he is justified in his inference from the visible to the invisible, from the phenomena to a hidden cause.

When treating of Herder in *Chapter Seven*, we mentioned his statement in *Of the Cognition and Sensation of the Human Soul* (1778) that no psychology is possible which is not physiology at every step. It is worth mentioning, therefore, that in the fifth book of the first part of his *Ideas* Herder explicitly affirms the spirituality and immortality of the human soul. He describes the mind as a unity. The phenomena of association of ideas cannot be used as a proof of the contrary. Associated ideas belong to a being which 'calls up memories from its own energy . . . and connects ideas according to an internal attraction or repulsion, not according to some external mechanics'.[8] There are purely psychological laws according to which the soul carries out its activities and combines its concepts. This certainly takes place in conjunction with organic changes; but this does not alter the nature of the soul or mind. 'If the tool is worthless, the artist can do nothing.'[9] In other words, Herder has clarified his position as against materialism.

The second part of Herder's *Ideas* can be regarded as a sustained polemic against the tendency of the thinkers of the Enlightenment to despise the primitive. Certainly, there has been development from the more to the less primitive, a development in which reaction to physical environment (as with Montesquieu) was an important factor. And Herder gives a conjectural account of the development of the family into the clan, of the clan into a tribe with an elected leader, and of the tribe into a society with an hereditary monarch. But it is nonsense to suggest that primitive peoples were without any culture; and it is still greater nonsense to suggest that they were unhappy and miserable because they did not share the supposed privileges of the eighteenth century.

Further, Herder attacks the idea that history should be interpreted as a movement of progress towards the modern State. He implies at least that the development of a modern State had little to do with reason, and that it was due rather to purely historical factors. The members of a tribe may very well have been happier than many inhabitants of a great modern State, in which 'hundreds must go hungry so that one can strut and wallow in luxury'.[10] And Herder's dislike for authoritarian government is plain enough. When he published the second part he had to omit the statements that the best ruler is the one who contributes the most to making rulers unnecessary, and that governments are like bad doctors who treat their patients in such a way that the latter are in constant need of them. But what he did say was clear enough. In his view, 'the man who needs a lord is an animal; as soon as he becomes a human being he no longer needs a lord'.[11] So much for the ideal of enlightened despotism.

In all this Herder was partly engaged in an indirect attack on Kant. The latter had published a hostile review of the first part of *Ideas;* and in the second part Herder took the opportunity of attacking, indirectly, Kant's *Idea for a General History from a Cosmopolitan Point of View (Idee zu einer allgemeinen Geschichte in weltbürgerlicher Absicht*, 1784). Kant was prepared to neglect all stages of social organization except in so far as they could be seen as contributing to the development of the rational State. And a rational State must have a 'lord'; for man is so defective that he cannot live in society without one. Kant may very well have been right on this point; but Herder preferred to believe in man's natural goodness and perfectibility. In any case he was intent on rejecting the notion that history can profitably be interpreted as a progress towards the modern State, in the light of which all other forms of social organization must be judged.

In the third part of his *Ideas* Herder comes to recorded history. His general principle for the historian is that the latter's mind should be free from hypotheses, and that he ought not to take any particular nation or people as his favourite, despising or belittling other peoples. The historian of mankind must judge impartially and dispassionately, 'like the Creator of our race'.[12] Generally speaking, Herder makes a point of endeavouring to live up to this principle, though an animus against Rome manifests itself, with an accompanying indulgence towards the civilization of the Phoenicians.

Herder does not confine himself to Europe, but considers also the cultures of, for example, China, India, Egypt and the Jews, though his knowledge of China and India was, not unnaturally, deficient. Coming to Greece,[13] he finds a complete cultural cycle, the rise and decline of one people, and uses it to draw general conclusions. Every culture has its centre of gravity, and the deeper this centre of gravity lies in a balance of the culture's living, active forces, the more solid and lasting is the culture. We can say, therefore, that the peak of a culture is found when its active forces are most in equilibrium. But this peak is, of course, a point; that is to say, the centre of gravity inevitably moves, and the equilibrium is disturbed. The active forces may be so deployed that equilibrium is temporarily restored; but it cannot last for ever. Decline comes without fail sooner or later. Herder speaks as though the life of a culture were determined by natural laws: it is analogous to the life of a biological organism. The fate of Rome was predetermined not by divine intervention but by natural factors. Environment forced the Romans to become a military people, and this development shaped their history, their rise to greatness and their eventual decline. The empire became unbalanced, and it could not sustain itself.

In the fourth part of his *Ideas* Herder continues his account of European history from the fall of the Roman empire. In it he lays stress on the part played by Christianity in the development of European culture. It is true that we find an awareness of the importance of economic factors. Herder's account of the Crusades is a case in point. And he is by no means blind to the importance of technical inventions and of new scientific knowledge. But he is very far removed from the mentality of the Enlightenment, which regarded the desirable development of civilization as a movement away from religion. Herder may have been a liberal Christian, but he was profoundly convinced of the indispensable role of religion in human culture.

Inasmuch as Herder emphasizes ethnic groups, nations and cultures, and inasmuch as he emphasizes the part played by the Germanic peoples in the rise of Christian culture, a few misguided people, Nazis for instance, have tried to depict him as a nationalist and even as an adherent of a race-theory. But this interpretation is quite beside the mark. He nowhere suggests that the Germans should rule other nations. Indeed, he condemns, for instance, the behaviour of the Teutonic knights towards Germany's eastern neighbours; and in his writings he frequently attacks militarism and imperialism. His ideal was that of a harmonious unfolding of national cultures. Just as individuals are, or should be, free and yet united in society, so different nations should form a family, each making its own contribution to the development of 'humanity'. As for the race-theory, Herder believed that ethnic groupings form the most natural bases for States. And in his view one of the factors which contributed to the instability of Rome was precisely the way in which conquest of other peoples destroyed its ethnic unity. But this idea, whether valid or not, has nothing to do with the race-theory, if this is taken to mean the notion that one race is inherently superior to other races and has a right to rule them. As for the Jews, Herder was far from being an anti-Semite. But it would be waste of time to dwell more on this topic. No sensible, objective historian supposes that Herder's theory of history as a development of national cultures involves nationalism in the pejorative sense, militarism and imperialism, or the theory of the inherent superiority of a given race. Of course, in some sense he was a nationalist, but not in the sense that he claimed on behalf of his own nation rights which he was unwilling to concede to other nations.

Herder's philosophy of history is somewhat complex. In the first place we have his insistence on the need for an objective and dispassionate examination, free from preconceived theories, of each culture on its own merits. This is obviously an excellent rule for an historian. In the second place we have his theory of the life of a culture, on an analogy with the life of the organism; and this theory may appear to lend itself to interpretation in a manner reminiscent of Vico's theory of cycles. In the third place, however, we have his idea of 'humanity', which fits in better with a theory of progress than with a theory of cycles. But a harmonization is doubtless possible. Each culture has its cycle; but the general movement is towards the realization of man's immanent potentiality for 'humanity'.

Whether the progressive approximation to the ideal of humanity is inevitable or not for Herder, does not seem to be altogether clear. In his *Ideas* he remarks that 'the philosophy of final purposes has brought no advantage to natural history'.[14] It is absurd to suggest, for example, that the bad actions of Rome were necessary and required in order that Roman culture might develop and attain its peak. At the same time, although we cannot legitimately justify all actions in history on the ground that they were required for the fulfilment of some specific providential plan, Herder certainly appears to say that the gradual development of 'humanity' is inevitable. Thus he informs his readers that anything which can happen within the limits of given national, temporal and spatial circumstances, does happen.[15] And this appears to imply that if progressive approximation to the ideal of humanity is possible, it will inevitably take place. Indeed, we are told that all destructive forces must ultimately yield to conserving forces and work for the development of the whole.[16]

A similar ambiguity appears in the series of *Letters for the Advancement of Humanity* (*Briefe zur Beförderung der Hu-*

manität, 1793–7). In these *Letters*, in which Herder shows a greater readiness than before to recognize the capacity of political changes to contribute to the advance of mankind,[17] his general point of view seems to be that there is, and will be, by and large, a progressive movement towards the realization of the ideal of humanity. At the same time he insists on the necessity for education to develop man's innate potentialities. Without this unceasing formative education man would sink back into bestiality.[18] And such statements do not seem to imply the inevitability of progress. According to Herder, we can distinguish three phases in the development of the European spirit. First, there was that mixture of Roman and Germanic culture which produced the organization, religious and political, of Europe. Secondly, there were the Renaissance and Reformation. And, thirdly, there is the present phase, the result of which we are unable to predict.[19] Here again there seems to be some doubt about the future, though this doubt could, of course, be reconciled with a general belief in the forward march of humanity towards the ultimate development of its highest potentialities.

The situation can perhaps be expressed in this way. As an historian, hostile to the tendency to judge all cultures in the light of the civilization of his time, Herder was strongly inclined to historicism and relativism, which hardly fitted in with a dogma of progress. But as a philosopher, believing not only in man's natural goodness and perfectibility but also in the working of divine providence in and through men's actions, he was naturally inclined to the conclusion that man's highest potentialities will be eventually actualized in spite of all setbacks on the way.

Part IV

KANT

Chapter Ten

KANT (1): LIFE AND WRITINGS

Kant's life and character – Earlier writings and the New-tonian physics – Philosophical writings of the pre-critical period – The dissertation of 1770 and its context – The conception of the critical philosophy.

1. If we prescind from the history of his intellectual develop-ment and from the results of this development, we do not need to spend much time in recounting the facts of Kant's life. For it was singularly uneventful and devoid of dramatic incident. True, any philosopher's life is devoted primarily to reflection, not to external activity on the stage of public life. He is not a commander in the field or an Arctic explorer. And unless he is forced to drink poison like Socrates or is burned at the stake like Giordano Bruno, his life naturally tends to be undramatic. But Kant was not even a travelled man of the world like Leibniz. For he spent all his life in East Prussia. Nor did he occupy the position of a philosophical dictator in the university of a capital city, as Hegel later did at Ber-lin. He was simply an excellent professor in the not very dis-tinguished university of a provincial town. Nor was his char-acter such as to provide a happy hunting-ground for psychological analysts, as with Kierkegaard and Nietzsche. In his later years he was noted for his methodical regularity of life and for his punctuality; but it would hardly occur to any-one to think of him as an abnormal personality. But perhaps one can say that the contrast between his quiet and compara-tively uneventful life and the greatness of his influence has itself a dramatic quality.

Immanuel Kant was born at Königsberg on April 22nd, 1724, the son of a saddler. Both as a child at home and at the Collegium Fridericianum, where he studied from 1732 until 1740, he was brought up in the spirit of the pietist movement. He continued throughout his life to appreciate the good qualities of sincere pietists; but it is evident that he reacted rather sharply against the religious observances to which he had to conform at the college. As for his formal schooling, he acquired a good knowledge of Latin.

In 1740 Kant entered upon his university studies in his home town and attended lectures in a wide variety of subjects. The main influence upon his mind, however, was that of Martin Knutzen, professor of logic and metaphysics. Knutzen was a disciple of Wolff; but he had a particular interest in natural science, lecturing in physics, astronomy and mathematics, as well as in philosophy. And Kant, who enjoyed the use of the professor's library, was stimulated by him to acquire a knowledge of Newtonian science. Indeed, Kant's first writings were mostly of a scientific nature, and he always retained a deep interest in the subject.

At the conclusion of his university studies Kant was driven by financial reasons to take posts as a family tutor in East Prussia; and this period of his life lasted some seven or eight years, finishing in 1755 when he took what we would call the doctorate and received permission to set up as a *Privatdozent* or lecturer. In 1756 he tried to obtain Knutzen's chair, rendered vacant by the latter's death. But Knutzen had been an 'extraordinary' professor, and the government, influenced by financial considerations, left the post unfilled. In 1764 Kant was offered the chair of poetry, but he declined it, no doubt wisely. In 1769 he refused a similar offer from Jena. Finally in March 1770 he was appointed 'ordinary' professor of logic and metaphysics at Königsberg. His period as a *Privatdozent* lasted, therefore, from 1755 until 1770, though for the last four years of this period a post as assistant librarian afforded him some additional financial support. (In 1772 he resigned this post as incompatible with his professorship.)

During these fifteen years, which belong to what is generally called Kant's pre-critical period, the philosopher gave an enormous number of lectures on a wide variety of topics. Thus at various times he lectured not only on logic, metaphysics and moral philosophy but also on physics, mathematics, geography, anthropology, pedagogy and mineralogy. From all accounts he was an excellent lecturer. It was the rule for professors and lecturers to expound text-books, and Kant had, of course, to conform to this rule. Thus he made use of Baumgarten's *Metaphysics*. But he did not hesitate to depart from his text or to criticize it, and his lectures were salted with humour, and even with stories. In his philosophical courses his main aim was to stimulate his hearers to think for themselves, to stand on their own feet, as he put it.

It must not be thought that Kant was a recluse. Later on he found himself compelled to economize with his time, but at the period of which we are writing he went a good deal into local society. Indeed, throughout his life he enjoyed social intercourse. Moreover, though he was far from being a travelled man, he took pleasure in meeting people who had experience of other countries, and he sometimes astonished them by his own knowledge, though this had been gained, of course, by reading. His interests were fairly wide. Thus the influence of Rousseau's writings stimulated a lively interest in educational reform, besides helping to develop his political views in a radical direction.

It is hardly to be expected, of course, that one should be able to designate the exact moment at which the pre-critical period of Kant's thought ended and the critical period began. That is to say, it would be unreasonable to expect that one should be able to state exactly when Kant rejected the Leibniz-Wolffian system of philosophy and began to work out his own system. However, for general purposes one can take his appointment as professor in 1770 as a convenient date. But the *Critique of Pure Reason* did not appear until 1781. During the intervening eleven years Kant was thinking out his philosophy. At the same time (or, rather, until 1796 inclusive) he was also engaged in lecturing. He continued to use Wolffian text-books in philosophy, and he also continued to give courses of lectures on non-philosophical subjects, those on anthropology and physical geography being particularly popular. It was his conviction that students needed factual knowledge of this kind, in order that they might understand the part played by experience in our knowledge. Philosophical theorizing in the void was by no means a Kantian ideal, even though a cursory glance at the first *Critique* might suggest that it was.

Once the first edition of the *Critique of Pure Reason* had appeared in 1781, Kant's other famous writings followed in quick succession. In 1783 he published *Prolegomena to any*

Future Metaphysics, in 1785 the *Fundamental Principles of the Metaphysics of Morals*, in 1786 the *Metaphysical First Principles of Natural Science*, in 1787 the second edition of the *Critique of Pure Reason*, in 1788 the *Critique of Practical Reason*, in 1790 the *Critique of Judgment*, in 1793 *Religion within the Bounds of Reason Alone*, in 1795 a little treatise *On Perpetual Peace*, and in 1797 the *Metaphysics of Morals*. It is understandable, therefore, that with this heavy programme Kant had to husband his time. And his order of the day, to which he faithfully adhered during his years as a professor, has become famous. Rising shortly before five in the morning, he spent the hour from five to six drinking tea, smoking a pipe, and thinking over his day's work. From six to seven he prepared his lecture, which began at seven or eight, according to the time of year, and lasted until nine or ten. He then devoted himself to writing until the midday meal, at which he always had company and which was prolonged for several hours, as Kant enjoyed conversation. Afterwards he took a daily walk of an hour or so, and the evening was given to reading and reflection. He retired to bed at ten o'clock.

Only once did Kant come into collision with political authority. This was in connection with his *Religion within the Bounds of Reason Alone*. In 1792 the first part of this work, entitled 'On the Radical Evil in Human Nature', had been passed by the censor on the ground that, like Kant's other writings, it was not intended for the general reader. But the second part, 'On the Conflict of the Good Principle with the Evil', failed to satisfy the censorship, on the ground that it attacked biblical theology. However, the whole work, consisting of four parts, was approved by the theological faculty of Königsberg and the philosophical faculty of Jena, and was published in 1793. Then trouble arose. In 1794 Frederick William II, successor to Frederick the Great on the throne of Prussia, expressed his displeasure at the book and accused Kant of misrepresenting and depreciating many fundamental principles of the Scriptures and of Christianity. The king threatened Kant with penalties if he should venture to repeat the offence. The philosopher declined to retract his opinions, but he promised to refrain from making any further public pronouncements, whether in lectures or in writing, on religion either natural or revealed. On the king's death, however, Kant considered that he was released from his promise, and in 1798 he published *The Conflict of the Faculties*, in which he discussed the relation between theology, in the sense of biblical belief, and philosophy or the critical reason.

Kant died on February 12th, 1804. He was already fifty-seven years old when he published his first famous work, the *Critique of Pure Reason*, and his literary production between 1781 and the time of his death constitutes an astonishing performance. In his last years he was working at a restatement of his philosophy, and the notes which were designed as material for a revised version of his system were published in a critical edition by Erich Adickes in 1920 under the title *Kants opus postumum*.

The salient trait in Kant's character was probably his moral earnestness and his devotion to the idea of duty, a devotion which found theoretical expression in his ethical writings. He was, as we have seen, a sociable man; he was also a kindly and benevolent one. Never rich, he was systematically careful in money matters; but he regularly assisted a number of poor persons. His thrift was certainly not accompanied by selfishness or hard-heartedness. Though scarcely a sentimental man, he was a sincere and loyal friend, and his conduct was marked by courtesy and respect for others. As regards religion, Kant was not given to the ordinary observances, and nobody could claim that he was inclined to mysticism. Nor was he precisely an orthodox Christian. But he certainly possessed a real belief in God. Though he maintained that morality is autonomous, in the sense that its principles are underived from theology, natural or revealed, he was also convinced that it implies or ultimately involves belief in God, in a sense which will be explained later. It would be an exaggeration to say that he had no idea of religious experience. And if one did say this, one would unfailingly arouse indignant references to Kant's reverence for the starry heavens above and the moral law within. At the same time he showed no real appreciation of the activities of adoration and prayer and of what Baron von Hügel called the mystical element in religion. But this does not mean, of course, that he had no reverence for God, even if his approach to religion was practically exclusively through the consciousness of moral obligation. The fact of the matter seems to be that just as Kant wrote on aesthetics and aesthetic experience without apparently possessing any personal and lively taste for, say, music, so he wrote on religion without possessing any deep understanding either of Christian piety or, for instance, of oriental mysticism. He was characterized by moral earnestness rather than by religious devotion, provided that this statement is not understood to mean that he was an irreligious man or that his assertion of belief in God was insincere. It was only on formal occasions which required his presence that he attended church services, and his remark to a friend that advance in moral goodness is accompanied by disuse of prayer reveals something of his character.

In politics Kant was inclined to republicanism, if this term is taken to include limited, constitutional monarchy. He sympathized with the Americans in the War of Independence, and later with the ideals at least of the French Revolution. Militarism and chauvinism were quite alien to his mind: the author of the treatise On Perpetual Peace was not the kind of thinker of whom the Nazis were able to make plausible use. His political ideas were, of course, intimately associated with his conception of the value of the free, moral personality.

2. As we have seen, Kant's interest in scientific matters was stimulated by Martin Knutzen at the university of Königsberg. It is also evident that during the period which he spent as a family tutor in East Prussia he read extensively in scientific literature. For the doctorate dissertation which he submitted to the university in 1755 was on Fire (De igne): and in the same year he published a General Natural History and Theory of the Heavens (Allgemeine Naturgeschichte und Theorie des Himmels). This work had grown out of two previous essays (1754), one on the earth's motion round its axis, the other on the physical question whether the earth is growing old. In it he proposed an original anticipation of the nebular hypothesis advanced later by Laplace.

Instead, therefore, of the customary twofold division of Kant's intellectual life into the pre-critical period, when he was under the influence of the Leibniz-Wolffian system, and the critical period, when he was thinking out and expressing his own philosophy, some historians prefer a threefold division. That is to say, they think that we should recognize the existence of an initial period in which Kant was primarily concerned with problems of a scientific nature. This period would have lasted until 1755 or 1756, and the pre-critical philosophical period would fall more or less in the sixties.

There is, of course, something to be said in favour of this threefold division. For it serves to draw attention to the predominantly scientific character of Kant's earlier writing. But for general purposes the traditional twofold division seems to me to be quite sufficient. After all, Kant did not abandon Newtonian physics for any other kind of physics. But he did abandon the Wolffian philosophical tradition in favour of an original philosophy. And this remains the important fact in his mental development. Further, the threefold division can be misleading. On the one hand Kant's earlier writings, though predominantly scientific, were not exclusively so. For instance, in 1755 his *De igne* was followed by another Latin dissertation entitled A *New Explanation of the First Principles of Metaphysical Knowledge* (*Principiorum primorum cognitionis metaphysicae nova dilucidatio*), which was composed in connection with receiving permission to lecture in the university as *Privatdozent*. On the other hand Kant published some scientific papers even during the critical period. Thus in 1785 he published an essay *On Volcanoes in the Moon* (*Ueber die Vulkane in Monde*).

It would, however, be a waste of time to pursue this question any further. The important point is that Kant, though never, so to speak, a practising physicist or astronomer, acquired a knowledge of Newtonian science, and that the validity of the scientific conception of the world remained for him a firm fact. The nature of scientific knowledge was, of course, open to discussion; and the range of applicability of scientific categories and concepts constituted a problem. But Kant never doubted the general validity of Newtonian physics within its own field; and his later problems arose on the basis of this conviction. How, for example, can we reconcile with the scientific conception of the world as a law-governed system, in which each event has its determinate and determining course, the world of moral experience which implies freedom? Again, what theoretical justification can we

find for the universality of scientific statements and for the
validity of scientific prediction in face of the empiricism of
David Hume, which appears to deprive the scientific conception of the world of any rational, theoretical justification?
I do not mean to imply that such problems were present
from the beginning in Kant's mind; nor do I wish to anticipate at this point a discussion of the questions which gave
rise at a later stage to his critical philosophy. But for an appreciation of his characteristic problematic it is essential to
understand from the start that he accepted and continued to
accept the validity of Newtonian science. Given this acceptance and given the empiricism of Hume, Kant found
himself compelled in the course of time to raise questions
about the nature of scientific knowledge. Again, given his
acceptance of the scientific conception of the world and
given at the same time his acceptance of the validity of moral
experience, Kant found himself compelled in the course of
time to discuss the reconciliation of the world of necessity
with the world of freedom. Finally, given the facts of scientific advance and of the common acceptance of the classical
physics, he found himself driven to ask whether the lack of
comparable advance in metaphysics and of a common acceptance of any one metaphysical system did not demand a
radical revision of our ideas of the nature and function of
metaphysics. Kant's treatment of these problems lay in the
future; but it presupposed that acceptance of Newtonian
science which is manifested in his earlier writings.

3. When we speak of the pre-critical period in Kant's
intellectual development, the reference is, of course, to the
period which precedes the conception and working-out of his
own original philosophy. In other words, the term must be
taken in a technical sense and not in the sense of 'uncritical'.
In this period he adhered more or less to the standpoint of
the Wolffian philosophy; but he never accepted this philosophy in a slavish and uncritical manner. Already in 1755 he
had criticized some doctrines of Leibniz and Wolff, such as
the use made by them of the principle of sufficient reason, in
his Latin work, A *New Explanation of the First Principles of
Metaphysical Knowledge*. At this time his knowledge of the
philosophy of Leibniz, as distinct from the scholasticized
version of it elaborated by Wolff and his followers, was re-

stricted and inadequate; but in the writings during the sixties we can see an increasingly critical attitude towards the Leibniz-Wolffian system, though it was not until the end of the decade that the critical point of view, in a technical sense of the term, made its appearance.

In 1762 Kant published *The False Subtlety of the Four Syllogistic Figures (Die falsche Spitzfindigkeit der vier syllogistischen Figuren)*, in which he maintained that the logical division of the syllogism into four figures is over-subtle and unnecessary. And at the end of the same year he published *The Only Possible Ground for a Demonstration of God's Existence (Der einzig mögliche Beweisgrund zu einer Demonstration des Daseins Gottes)*. As this work is of some interest a few brief remarks can be made about it here.

At the end of the essay Kant remarks that though 'it is thoroughly necessary to be convinced of God's existence, it is not quite so necessary that one should demonstrate it'.[1] For Providence has not willed that the only way of coming to a knowledge of God should be by way of metaphysical subtleties. Indeed, if this were the case, we should be in a sorry plight. For no really cogent demonstration, affording a certainty analogous to that of mathematics, has yet been provided. However, it is natural that the professional philosopher should inquire whether a strict demonstration of God's existence is possible. And Kant's intention is to make a contribution to this inquiry.

All proofs of the existence of God must rest either on the concept of the possible or on the empirical idea of the existent. Further, each class can be divided into two sub-classes. In the first place we may attempt to argue either from possibility as a ground to the existence of God as a consequence or from possibility as a consequence to God's existence as the ground of this possibility. In the second place, that is, if we start with existing things, two courses are open to us. Either we can try to prove the existence of a first and independent cause of these things, and then show that such a cause must possess certain attributes, which make it proper to speak of it as God. Or we can try to prove at the same time both the existence and the attributes of God. Any proof of the existence of God must, according to Kant,[2] take one of these four forms.

The first line of argument mentioned, namely that from possibility as a ground to the existence of God as consequence, corresponds to the so-called ontological argument, from the idea of God to the divine existence, which was proposed in different forms by St. Anselm and Descartes and which was restated and accepted by Leibniz. It is rejected by Kant in *The Only Possible Ground* because, as he maintains, it presupposes that existence is a predicate, which is a false presupposition. The third line of argument, which corresponds to what Kant later calls the cosmological argument and which, he remarks, is much used by philosophers of the Wolffian School, is ruled out on the ground that we cannot demonstrate that a first cause must be what we call God. For the fourth line of argument, which corresponds to a teleological proof or proof from design, Kant shows, as he will continue to show in future, considerable respect, provided that emphasis is placed on the immanent teleology of the organism. None the less it does not, and cannot, amount to a demonstration of God's existence. For it brings us at best to a divine mind or intelligence which produces system and order and teleology in the world, not to a creator. In other words, it leaves us with a dualism, with superterrestrial mind on the one hand and with the material to be shaped on the other. As far as this argument alone is concerned, we are left in doubt whether this material is independent of or dependent on God.

There remains, therefore, the second line of argument, that from possibility as consequence to the existence of God as its ground. And it is this line of argument which Kant proposes as the only possible basis for a demonstration of God's existence. There is, he tells us, no intrinsic logical contradiction in denying all existence whatsoever. But what we cannot legitimately do is to affirm possibility and at the same time to deny that there is an existent ground of possibility. And we must admit possibility. For we cannot deny it without thinking, and to think is to affirm implicitly the realm of possibility. And Kant proceeds to argue that this being must be one, simple, immutable, eternal, spiritual and whatever else is included in the meaning of the term 'God' as used in metaphysics.

As far as mediaeval philosophy is concerned, this line of

argument reminds one much more of Duns Scotus, who tried to argue from possibility to the existence and attributes of God, than of St. Thomas Aquinas. True, in his Third Way Aquinas bases his argument on the concept of 'possible' beings; but his concept of possibility is derived from the empirical fact that some things come into being and pass away and are therefore 'possible' (what Scholastics generally call 'contingent'). And Kant is arguing that the existence of God is implied by all thinking rather than that the existence of contingent things manifests the existence of God. Perhaps we can say that what Kant is demanding is that the Leibnizian argument from eternal truths should be turned into a strict demonstration. In any case it is interesting to observe that his line of thought, though different from that of the ontological argument, is of an *a priori* character in comparison with, say, the argument from design, and that it presupposes a Leibnizian view of metaphysics as a non-empirical science. But this does not mean that he did not see any intrinsic difference between mathematics and metaphysics. A difference is clearly affirmed in a work to which reference will now be made.

In *The Only Possible Ground*[3] Kant spoke of metaphysics as 'a bottomless abyss' and as 'a dark ocean without shore and without lighthouses'. We hear something more explicit about the nature of metaphysics in his *Enquiry into the Distinctness of the Principles of Natural Theology and Morals* (*Untersuchung über die Deutlichkeit der Grundsätze der natürlichen Theologie und der Moral*, 1764). In the preceding year the Berlin Academy had offered a prize for an essay on the question whether metaphysical truths in general and, in particular, the first principles of natural theology and morals are capable of the same degree of demonstrative certainty as the truths of geometry. If not, what are the peculiar nature and degree of the certainty which they enjoy? And is this degree sufficient to justify full conviction? Kant's essay did not win the prize, which went to a contribution by Mendelssohn; but it is naturally of considerable interest.

Kant insists that there are fundamental differences between mathematics and metaphysics.[4] Thus mathematics is a constructive science in the sense that it proceeds 'syntheti-

cally' constructing its definitions arbitrarily. The definition
of a geometrical figure is not the result of analysing a previously possessed concept or idea: the concept arises through
the definition. In philosophy (which Kant calls 'world-wis-
dom', *Weltweisheit*), however, definitions are obtained, when
they are obtained, by analysis. That is to say, we have first of
all an idea of something, though this idea is confused or
inadequate; and we then endeavour to clarify it by comparing
instances of its application and by performing a work of
abstraction. In this sense philosophy proceeds analytically,
and not synthetically. To illustrate the difference, Kant takes
the example of time. We already have some idea and knowledge of time before we undertake a philosophical investigation of it. And this investigation takes the form of comparing
and analysing diverse instances of the experience of time with
a view to forming an adequate, abstract concept. 'But if I
wished to try to arrive synthetically at a definition of time,
what a happy chance I should have to meet with, for this
concept to be precisely the one which completely expressed
the previously given idea.'[5] That is to say, if I constructed a
definition of time arbitrarily, as the geometer constructs his
definitions, it would be a matter of mere chance if it happened to give explicit, abstract expression to the concrete idea
of time which I, like anyone else, already possess.

It may be said that philosophers do as a matter of fact construct definitions 'synthetically'. For instance, Leibniz conceived for himself a simple substance possessing only obscure or confused representations and called it a slumbering
monad. This is perfectly true. But the point is that when
philosophers construct definitions arbitrarily, these definitions
are not properly speaking *philosophical* definitions. 'Such
determinations of the meaning of a word are never philosophical definitions; but if they are to be called clarifications
at all, they are only grammatical clarifications.'[6] I can explain, if I wish, in what sense I intend to use the term 'slumbering monad'; but then I am acting as a grammarian rather
than as a philosopher. Leibniz 'had not explained this monad,
but imagined it; for the idea of it was not something given
to him but something which he had himself created'.[7] Analo-
gously, the mathematician often enough deals with concepts
which are capable of philosophical analysis and which are

not mere arbitrary constructions. The concept of space is a
case in point. But such concepts are received by the mathematician; they are not, technically speaking, mathematical
concepts in the same sense as the concept of, say, a polygon.

We can say, then, that while in mathematics I have no
concept at all of my object until the definition provides one,
in metaphysics[8] I have a concept which is already given to
me, although it is confused, and I should try to make it
clear, explicit and definite.[9] As St. Augustine says, I know
very well what time is as long as nobody asks me for a definition. And in metaphysics I can very well know some truths
about an object of thought and draw valid conclusions from
these truths without being able to define the object. Kant
gives the example of desire. There is much that I can say with
truth about the nature of desire without being able to define
it. In short, while in mathematics one begins with definitions,
in metaphysics it is rather the other way about. And Kant
concludes that the principal rule to be observed if certainty
is to be obtained in metaphysics is to ascertain what it is that
one knows immediately and with certainty of the subject-
matter in question, and to determine the judgments to which
this knowledge gives rise.

Metaphysics is thus different from mathematics. At the
same time we must admit that philosophical theories have
been for the most part like meteors, the brightness of which
is no guarantee of their longevity. 'Metaphysics is without a
doubt the most difficult of all human studies; only no metaphysics has yet been written.'[10] What is required is a change
of method. 'The genuine method of metaphysics is fundamentally of the same kind as that which Newton introduced
into natural science and which was there so fruitful.'[11] The
metaphysician should start with some phenomena of 'inner
experience', describe them accurately and ascertain the immediate judgments to which they give rise and of which we are
certain. He can later inquire whether the diverse phenomena
can be brought together under a single concept or definition,
analogous to, say, the general law of gravitation. Kant, as we
have seen, used Wolffian text-books in philosophy, and in
metaphysics he made use of Baumgarten. Now, Baumgarten's
method was that of starting with very general definitions and
then proceeding to the more particular. And it is precisely

this method which Kant rejects. The metaphysician is not concerned primarily with the relation of ground to consequent in a purely logical and formal sense. He is concerned with 'real grounds'; and he must start with the given.

As regards the particular questions proposed by the Berlin Academy concerning natural theology and morals, Kant still maintains in the *Enquiry* that the principles of natural theology are, or can be, certain. And he refers briefly to his demonstration of the existence of God as the actual ground of possibility. But in morals the situation is somewhat different. For one thing we must recognize the part played by feeling in the moral life. Kant refers to 'Hutcheson and others', and he remarks that 'it is first of all in our days that people have begun to see that while the power of representing truth is *knowledge*, that of perceiving the good is *feeling*, and that these two must not be confused with one another'.[12] (The influence of British moralists and writers on aesthetics is apparent also in Kant's *Observations on the Feeling of the Beautiful and Sublime* [*Beobachtungen über das Gefühl des Schönen und Erhabenen*, 1764].) But, quite apart from the part played by feeling in the moral life, the first principles of morality have not yet been made sufficiently clear. We find some anticipation of Kant's later ethical theory in the distinction which he makes between 'problematical necessity' (to attain end X, you must take means Y) and 'legal necessity' (you are obliged to do this, not as a means to something else, but as an end). At the same time he tells us that after much thought he has come to the conclusion that the first formal principle of obligation is 'Do the most perfect thing which is possible for you'.[13] But we cannot deduce from this principle particular obligations, unless 'material' first principles are also given. All these themes need to be carefully examined and thought through before we can give to the first principles of morals the highest degree of philosophical certainty.

Kant's remarks in the *Enquiry* about clarifying our idea of time may perhaps suggest to the contemporary English reader that he is engaged in reducing philosophy to 'linguistic analysis', to an analysis of the use of terms. But he does not intend to deny the existential import of metaphysics. This is made clear, for instance, by what he has to say on natural theology.

His point in this work is that a metaphysics which really employs the mathematical method will be confined to exhibiting relations of formal implication. If the metaphysician is to increase our knowledge of reality, he must cease trying to ape the mathematician and turn rather to a method analogous to that which was employed so successfully by Newton in natural science. He should, indeed, begin by clarifying the confused concepts of experience and giving them adequate and abstract expression; but he may then be able to proceed to inference and to the building-up of a metaphysics. It does not follow, however, that Kant possesses any great faith in the capacity of metaphysics for extending our theoretical knowledge beyond the sphere of the sciences. And when we are already aware of the later development of his thought, certain remarks in the *Enquiry* naturally suggest to our minds a tentative anticipation of his later point of view. Such a remark is the statement that metaphysics is concerned with the first principles of our knowledge. We should not, however, be justified in trying to father upon Kant at this stage the critical point of view. What we can say is that his recommendation to metaphysicians to substitute the Newtonian for the mathematical method should not blind us to his growing scepticism about the pretensions of speculative metaphysics. Indeed, the recommendation is partly an expression of this scepticism, or at least doubt. For it is linked with the conviction that whereas natural science has made good its claim to increase our knowledge of the world, metaphysics has not yet done so. And a suggestion as to how it might do so does not mean that Kant commits himself to the claims of speculative metaphysics. Indeed, he very soon makes it clear that this is far from being the case.

In 1766 Kant published anonymously (though the author's identity was never a secret) a partly serious, partly humorous work entitled *Dreams of a Ghost-seer explained by Dreams of Metaphysics (Träume eines Geistersehers, erläutert durch Träume der Metaphysik)*. For some time he had been curious about the visionary experiences of Immanuel Swedenborg; and he studied the latter's *Arcana coelestia*, the result of his reflections being *Dreams of a Ghost-seer*. As regards visionary experiences, Kant does not definitely either accept or reject their possible origin in the influence exerted by a

world of spirits. On the one hand he gives us what he calls 'a
fragment of esoteric philosophy',[14] in which, given the (un-
proved) assumption of a world of spirits, he suggests a way
in which the influence of spirits on men's souls might be
projected in imaginative visions. On the other hand he follows this up with 'a fragment of vulgar philosophy',[15] in
which he suggests an explanation of experiences such as
those of Swedenborg which would make their subjects fit
candidates for medical attention and treatment. The reader
is left to adopt which explanation he chooses. But the main
point is not Kant's discussion of visionary experiences but
rather his question whether the theories of speculative metaphysics, so far as they pretend to transcend experience, are
in any stronger position than Swedenborg's visions. And he
makes it clear that they are, in his opinion, in a weaker position. It may be that Swedenborg's visions were caused by
contact with a world of spirits, even if this cannot be proved.
But metaphysical theories are supposed to be rationally demonstrated; and this is what metaphysical theories about spiritual beings cannot be. We cannot even have positive conceptions of spirits. True, we can try to describe them by the aid
of negations. But the possibility of this procedure rests, according to Kant, neither on experience nor on rational inference: it rests on our ignorance, on the limitations of our
knowledge. The conclusion is that the doctrine of spirits
must be excluded from metaphysics which, if it is to be scientific at all, must consist in determining 'the limits of knowledge which have been set by the nature of the human reason'.[16]

In adopting this attitude towards metaphysics Kant was
influenced by the criticism of Hume. This seems to be made
abundantly clear by what is said in *Dreams of a Ghost-seer*
about the causal relation. This must not be confused with
the relation of logical implication. No logical contradiction
is ever involved in affirming the cause and denying the effect.
Causes and effects can be known only through experience.
We cannot, therefore, employ the idea of causality to transcend experience (that is, sense-experience) and to attain
knowledge of supersensible reality. Kant does not deny that
there is supersensible reality: what he denies is that meta-

physics can open the door to it in the way that metaphysicians of the past have thought that it could.

It is no good saying, Kant remarks, that traditional metaphysics is necessary for morality, in the sense that moral principles are dependent on metaphysical truths, such as the immortality of the soul and divine reward and punishment in the next life. Moral principles are not conclusions drawn from speculative metaphysics. At the same time moral faith (*der moralische Glaube*) may well point beyond the empirical world. 'It seems to be more in accordance with human nature and the purity of morals to ground the expectation of the future world on the experience of a virtuous soul than, conversely, to base its moral attitude on the hope of another world.'[17]

In the *Dreams of a Ghost-seer*, therefore, we find anticipations of Kant's later views. Speculative metaphysics of the traditional type is not, and cannot be, a source of scientific, demonstrated knowledge. Morality is autonomous and not dependent on metaphysics or on theology. That is to say, moral principles are not conclusions drawn from metaphysical or theological premises. At the same time morality may point beyond itself, in the sense that moral experience produces a (reasonable) moral faith in certain truths which cannot be demonstrated by the metaphysicians. But beyond the suggestion that metaphysics should take the form of a science of the limits of human knowledge Kant has not yet arrived at his characteristic conception of philosophy. The negative side of his thought is still prominent, namely the sceptical criticism of speculative metaphysics.

That Kant has not yet arrived at the critical standpoint is clear, for example, from the essay on space which he published in 1768. In this essay he developed some ideas of Leonard Euler (1707–83), for whom he had a great admiration, and maintained that 'absolute space possesses a reality of its own independently of the existence of all matter. . . .'[18] At the same time he shows himself conscious of the difficulties attending the theory that space is an independent, objective reality. And he remarks that absolute space is not an object of external perception but a fundamental concept which makes external perception possible.[19] This point of view was to be developed in his inaugural dissertation.

4. Kant's statement in the introduction to the *Prolegomena to Any Future Metaphysics* that it was David Hume who first interrupted his dogmatic slumbers is so often quoted or referred to that one may be inclined to overlook or underestimate the influence of Leibniz. In 1765 the latter's *New Essays concerning the Human Understanding* were at last published, and in 1768 there appeared Duten's edition of Leibniz's writings, containing the Leibniz-Clarke correspondence. Before these publications Kant had seen the thought of his great predecessor largely through the medium of the Wolffian philosophy; and it is clear that the fresh light shed on Leibniz had a profound effect on his mind. The first results of his reflections found expression in his inaugural dissertation as professor *On the Form and Principles of the Sensible and Intelligible World* (*De mundi sensibilis atque intelligibilis forma et principiis*, 1770).

To start with a particular point. As regards the Leibniz-Clarke correspondence, Kant was convinced that the former was right in maintaining against Newton and Clarke that space and time cannot be absolute realities or properties of things-in-themselves. If we try to retain Clarke's position, we shall find ourselves hopelessly involved in antinomies. Kant accepted, therefore, the view of Leibniz that space and time are phenomenal, and that they are not properties of things-in-themselves. At the same time he was not prepared to accept Leibniz's notion that they are confused ideas or representations. For in this case geometry, for instance, would not be the exact and certain science which it is. Kant speaks, therefore, of space and time as 'pure intuitions'.

In order to understand this position, we must go further back. In his inaugural dissertation Kant divides human knowledge into sensitive knowledge and intellectual knowledge. This distinction must not be understood as being between confused and distinct knowledge. For sensitive knowledge can be perfectly distinct, as it is, indeed, in the case of geometry, the prototype of such knowledge. And intellectual knowledge can be confused, as it not infrequently is in the case of metaphysics. The distinction must be understood rather in terms of objects, the objects of sensitive knowledge being sensible things, *sensibilia*, capable of affecting the sensibility (*sensualitas*) of the subject, which is the latter's receptivity or capacity for being affected by the presence of an object so as to produce a representation of it.

Leaving aside intellectual knowledge for the moment and attending to sensitive knowledge, we must distinguish therein between the matter and the form. The matter is what is given, namely sensations, that which is produced by the presence of sensible objects. The form is that which co-ordinates the matter; it is contributed, as it were, by the knowing subject and is the condition of sensitive knowledge. There are two such conditions, namely space and time. In the inaugural dissertation Kant speaks of them as 'concepts'. But he is careful to observe that they are not universal concepts *under* which sensible things are grouped but singular concepts *in* which *sensibilia* become the object of knowledge. These 'singular concepts' are described as 'pure intuitions'. The divine intuition is the archetype and active principle of things; but this is not the case with our intuitions which are said to be passive. Their function is simply to co-ordinate the sensations which are received and thus to make sensitive knowledge possible. *'Time is not something objective and real;* it is neither an accident, nor a substance, nor a relation; it is the subjective condition, necessary because of the nature of the human mind, of co-ordinating all *sensibilia* by a certain law, and it is a *pure intuition.* For we co-ordinate substances and accidents alike, as well according to simultaneity as to succession, only through the concept of time. . . .'[20] Again, *'space is not anything objective* and real; it is neither a substance nor an accident nor a relation; but it is *subjective* and ideal and proceeding from the nature of the mind by a stable law, as the scheme (*schema*) of co-ordinating all external *sensa*'.[21] The pure intuition of time is thus the necessary condition for all sensitive knowledge whatsoever. I cannot, for instance, be aware of my internal desires except in time. The pure intuition of space is the necessary condition for all knowledge of external *sensa*.

In order, therefore, to avoid the difficulties and antinomies which are involved if we hold either that space and time are independent, absolute realities or that they are real and objective properties of things, Kant suggests that they are subjective pure (that is, of themselves empty of all empirical content) intuitions which, together with sensations, the matter of sensitive knowledge, form what he calls in the dissertation 'appearances' (*apparentiae*). But this should obviously not be taken to mean that the human being consciously and deliberately applies these pure intuitions to sensations. The union of form and matter precedes all reflection. That is to say, because the human subject is what it is it necessarily perceives sensible objects in space and time. The act of distinguishing between form and matter is the work of philosophical reflection. But as far as our first awareness is concerned the union is something given, even though in subsequent reflection we can distinguish between what is due to the presence of sensible objects and what is contributed by the subject.

One can interpret Kant's point of view in this way. Let us assume with Hume that in sense-knowledge the given consists ultimately of impressions or sensations. The world of experience obviously does not consist simply of impressions or sensations or sense-data. The question arises, therefore, how the ultimately given is synthesized to form the world of experience. In Kant's terminology in the inaugural dissertation what are the form and principles of the sensible world? First of all (that is, first of all from the point of view of logical priority) the given elements are perceived in the pure intuitions or 'concepts' of space and time. There is spatial and temporal co-ordination. We then have 'appearances'. The mind then, through what Kant calls the logical use of the intellect, organizes the data of sense intuition, while leaving their fundamentally sensuous character intact. We then have the phenomenal world of 'experience'. 'From appearance to experience there is no way except by reflection according to the logical use of the intellect.'[22] In its logical use or function the mind simply organizes the data of sense intuition; and we then have the empirical concepts of experience. The empirical sciences are thus rendered possible by the logical use of the intellect. They belong to the sphere of sensitive knowledge, not in the sense that the intellect or understanding is not employed in these sciences (which would be an absurd notion), but in the sense that it does not provide new concepts out of its own resources, so to speak, but simply organizes logically the materials drawn from a sensuous source. The logical use of the intellect is not, indeed, confined to the organization of material derived from a sensuous source; but, when it is used in this way, its use does not turn sensitive knowledge into intellectual knowledge, in the sense in which Kant uses these terms in the dissertation.

What, then, does Kant mean by intellectual knowledge and by the intelligible world? Intellectual or rational knowledge is knowledge of objects which do not affect the senses: that is to say, it is knowledge, not of *sensibilia*, but of *intelligibilia*. And the latter together form the intelligible world. Sensitive knowledge is knowledge of objects as they *appear*, that is, as subjected to what Kant calls 'the laws of sensibility', namely the *a priori* conditions of space and time, whereas intellectual knowledge is knowledge of things *as they are (sicuti sunt)*.[23] The empirical sciences come under the heading of sensitive knowledge, while metaphysics is the prime example of intellectual knowledge.

Now, this obviously suggests that in metaphysics the mind apprehends objects which transcend the senses; above all, God. But do we enjoy intuition of spiritual realities? Kant explicitly denies this. 'An *intuition* of intelligible objects is not given to man, but only a *symbolic knowledge*.'[24] That is to say, we conceive supersensible objects by means of universal concepts, not by direct intuition. What, then, is the justification for thinking that our conceptual representations of supersensible realities are valid?

The difficulty can be put in this way. Kant spoke, as we have seen, of the logical use of the understanding or intellect, the latter's function, that is, of comparing and organizing material derived from either a sensuous or a supersensuous source. In the case of material derived from a sensuous source the understanding has something to work on, namely the data derived from sense intuition, from the marriage, as it were, between sensations and the pure intuitions of space and time. But if we enjoy no intuition of supersensible reality, the understanding appears to have nothing to work on. For in its logical use it does not supply materials but logically organizes them.

The problem can be developed thus. Kant distinguished between the logical use of understanding or intellect and its 'real use'. According to its real use the intellect produces concepts from itself; that is, it forms concepts which are non-empirical in character. In the *New Essays* Leibniz had criticized Locke's empiricism. We do not, as the latter had maintained, derive all our concepts empirically. On this matter Kant sided with Leibniz, though he did not follow the latter in speaking of innate ideas. 'Since, then, in metaphysics we do not find empirical principles, the concepts encountered therein must be sought, not in the senses, but in the very nature of the pure intellect, not as *innate* (*connati*) concepts, but as abstracted from the intrinsic laws of the mind (attending to its actions on the occasion of experience), and so as *acquired*. Of this kind are possibility, existence, necessity, substance, cause, etc., together with their opposites or correlates. . . .'[25] Thus the concepts of substance and cause, for instance, are derived, not from sense-experience, but from the mind itself on the occasion of experience. The question arises, however, whether in the absence of intuitive material as far as the intelligible world is concerned, these concepts can be used to grasp supersensible realities in such a way that we can make positive and certainly true statements about them. In other words, can there be a dogmatic metaphysics which has any valid claim to embodying knowledge of *intelligibilia*?

We have seen that Kant divides not only knowledge into sensitive and intellectual knowledge but also the world into the sensible and intelligible worlds. And this naturally suggests that intellectual knowledge is knowledge of *intelligibilia*, just as sensitive knowledge is knowledge of *sensibilia*. And inasmuch as supersensible realities belong to the class of *intelligibilia*, we would naturally expect Kant to maintain that dogmatic metaphysics, considered as a system of known truths, is possible. And in point of fact this twofold scheme of knowledge and of objects of knowledge, proposed under the influence of Leibniz, makes it difficult for him to throw dogmatic metaphysics overboard. At the same time he says enough in the dissertation to weaken very considerably the position of dogmatic metaphysics and to cast doubt upon its claims, even if he does not reject it outright and in so many words. And it is worth while dwelling briefly on this point which is of importance in the development of Kant's thought.

In the first place Kant asserts, as we have seen, that the 'real use' of the intellect in the sphere of *intelligibilia* gives us only symbolic knowledge. And this might suggest to someone trained in the Thomist tradition that Kant is saying that we can have valid knowledge of supersensible realities, though this knowledge is analogical in character. But what he seems to mean is that in the absence of intuitive material the extension of the 'real use' of the intellect (as producing from itself its concepts and axioms on the occasion of experience) into its dogmatic use provides us only with symbolic indications of supersensible realities, so that the description, for example, of God as first cause would be an instance of symbolism. And from this position to Kant's later position the distance is not very great. That is to say, it is easy to take the further step of maintaining that the primary function of concepts such as cause and substance is to synthesize further the data of sense intuition, and though it is, of course, psychologically possible to apply such concepts to supersensible realities the application does not yield scientific knowledge of these realities.

In the second place Kant discusses the following important point. In the natural sciences and in mathematics, where sense intuition supplies the data or material and where the intellect is employed only according to its logical use (that is, logically comparing and organizing the data but not supplying concepts and axioms from its own inner nature), 'use provides the method'.[26] That is to say, it is only after these sciences have already acquired a certain degree of development that we reflect on and analyse the method employed, considering how the method can be improved in detail. The situation is analogous to that obtaining in the case of language. Man did not first elaborate grammatical rules and then begin to employ language. The development of grammar followed, not preceded, the use of language. 'But in pure philosophy, such as is metaphysics, in which *the use of the intellect* concerning the principles is *real*, that is, where primitive concepts of things and relations and the very axioms are originally provided by the pure intellect itself, and where, since there are no intuitions, we are not immune from error, *method precedes all science*; and whatever is undertaken before the precepts of this method have been duly worked out and firmly established, seems to be rashly conceived and fit to be rejected as a vain and ridiculous activity of the mind.'[27] In dealing with material things, which affect the senses, we can come to know much about them without having first worked out a scientific method. But when we are dealing with supersensible realities, such as God, or with things in themselves as distinct from the way in which they appear to us in sense intuition, it is essential to ascertain first *how* we can come to know them. For in the absence of intuition the problem of method becomes all-important.

The chief rule of method, Kant tells us, must be to see that the principles of sensitive knowledge are not extended from sensible to supersensible realities. As we have seen, he made a sharp distinction between the sensuous and intellectual levels in human knowledge. And he insists that we must be on our guard against applying to supersensible realities concepts which are applicable only in the sphere of sensitive knowledge and against turning into universal principles the principles of sensitive knowledge. He gives as an example the axiom that whatever exists, exists somewhere and at some time. We are not entitled to state this universally, thus drawing down God, for example, into the spatio-temporal sphere. And the intellect in what Kant calls its 'critical use' (*usus elencticus*) has the office of exposing the unjustifiable character of such universal statements. The intellect in its critical use can thus keep the sphere of supersensible reality free, as it were, from contamination by the application of concepts and principles peculiar to sensitive knowledge.

But the critical use of the intellect must be distinguished from its dogmatic use. The fact that we can say, for instance, that God is not in space or time does not necessarily mean that we can attain positive and certain knowledge about God by the pure intellect. And, as has been already remarked, Kant has only to go on to say that the cognitive function of the primitive concepts of the pure intellect is that of further synthesizing the data of sense intuition for dogmatic metaphysics to be ruled out, if we mean by dogmatic metaphysics a system of certain truths about supersensible realities such as God and the immortal soul of man. Strictly speaking, the concept of cause, for instance, would then be inapplicable to God. Psychologically speaking, we could, of course, so apply it; but its use would give us only a symbolic indication of God, not scientific knowledge.

Kant does not maintain, and indeed never maintained, that there are no supersensible realities. And it may be objected that, given the doubt cast upon dogmatic metaphysics, he has no warrant for asserting that there are any such realities. But in the dissertation he does not reject dogmatic metaphysics in so many words, in explicit and clear terms. When he later comes to do so he also develops his theory of the postulates of the moral law, a theme which must be left aside for the present.

In the dissertation Kant speaks of the dogmatic use of the intellect as an extension of the general principles of the pure intellect to conceive a perfect *noumenon* or purely intelligible reality as the measure of all other realities. In the theoretical sphere (that is, in the sphere of being, of what is) this measure or exemplar is God, the supreme being. In the practical sphere (in the sphere of what ought to be effected through free action) it is moral perfection. Moral philosophy, therefore, as far as its fundamental principles are concerned, is said to belong to pure philosophy. Kant is saying that these principles depend on the reason itself, and not on sense-perception. He agreed with Hume that we cannot found moral principles on sense-perception. At the same time he was not prepared to make them the expression of feeling and to abandon the attempt to give them a purely rational foundation. Epicurus, accordingly, is worthy of severe reproof; and so are those, 'such as Shaftesbury and his followers',[28] who follow him to a certain extent. But Kant does not develop the subject. The elaboration of his moral philosophy lies in the future.

5. At the beginning of September 1770 Kant wrote to J. H. Lambert that he proposed during the winter to pursue his inquiries into pure moral philosophy, 'in which there are no empirical principles'.[29] He also mentioned his intention of revising and extending certain sections of his inaugural dissertation. In particular he wished to develop the idea of a particular, though negative, science which must precede metaphysics. This science, described as 'general phenomenology',[30] makes clear the range of validity of the principles of

sensitive knowledge and thus prevents the unwarranted application of these principles in metaphysics. We have already seen that Kant spoke about this science in his dissertation, where, as afterwards in the letter, it is referred to as a 'propaedeutic' in relation to metaphysics.[31]

His reflections during the winter of 1770-1, however, led Kant to abandon the idea of extending the inaugural dissertation and to project instead a new work. Thus in June 1771 he wrote to Marcus Herz,[32] who had been one of his pupils, that he was engaged on a book which would bear the title *The Bounds of Sensibility and Reason* (*Die Grenzen der Sinnlichkeit und der Vernunft*). In this work he proposed to deal with the relations of the fundamental principles and laws, taken to be determined before experience of the sensible world, to the subjects involved in the theory of taste, in metaphysics and in morals. We have seen that in the inaugural dissertation of 1770 Kant expounded the theory that space and time are subjective 'laws' of the co-ordination of sensations, and that in the same dissertation he embraced the theory that the pure intellect derives from itself on the occasion of experience the fundamental concepts of metaphysics, and also the theory that the fundamental principles of morals are derived from the reason alone. He now proposes to undertake an investigation into the fundamental concepts and laws which originate in the nature of the subject and which are applied to the experiential data of aesthetics, metaphysics and morals. In other words, he proposes to cover in one volume the subjects which proved in the end to need three, namely the three *Critiques*. In this letter he speaks of the subjective principles 'not only of sensibility but also of the understanding' (*des Verstandes*).[33] He is thus well on his way to conceiving his great enterprise of isolating the *a priori* elements in human knowledge. The distinction between form and matter in knowledge must be investigated not merely in relation to sensibility, where the subjective elements are the pure intuitions of space and time, but also in relation to the understanding and to the part which it plays in synthesizing the given. And the range of inquiry is to cover not only theoretical knowledge but also moral and aesthetic experience.

In another letter to Herz, written in February 1772, Kant

refers again to his projected book on *The Bounds of Sensibility and Reason*. According to his original plan the book would have consisted of two parts, one theoretical, the other practical. The first part would have been subdivided into two sections, treating respectively of general phenomenology and of metaphysics considered according to its nature and method. The second part would also have consisted of two sections, dealing respectively with the general principles of the feeling of taste and with the ultimate grounds of morality. But while thinking out the first part Kant noticed, he tells Herz, that something essential was wanting, namely a thorough treatment of the relation of mental presentations (*Vorstellungen*) to the objects of knowledge. And something must be said here about Kant's remarks on this theme; for they show him at grips with his critical problem.

Our sensuous representations do not create a problem, provided that they are the result of the subject's being affected by the object. True, sensible objects appear to us in a certain way because we are what we are, that is, because of the *a priori* intuitions of space and time. But in sensitive knowledge the form is applied to a matter which is passively received; our sensibility is affected by things external to us. Hence there is no great problem about the objective reference of our sensuous representations. But the situation is different when we turn to intellectual presentations. Abstractly speaking, the objective conformity of concept with object would be guaranteed if the intellect produced its objects through its concepts; that is, if it created the objects by conceiving or thinking them. But it is only the divine intellect which is an archetypal intellect in this sense. We cannot suppose that the human intellect creates its objects by thinking them. Kant never accepted pure idealism in this sense. At the same time the pure concepts of the understanding are not, according to Kant, abstracted from sense-experience. The pure concepts of the understanding must 'have their origins in the nature of the soul, yet so that they neither are caused by the object nor bring the object into being'.[34] But in this case the question immediately arises how these concepts refer to objects and how objects conform to the concepts. Kant remarks that in his inaugural dissertation he had contented himself with a negative account of the matter. That is to say, he had contented himself with saying that 'intellectual presentations . . . are not modifications of the soul by the object',[35] passing over in silence the question how these intellectual presentations or pure concepts of the understanding refer to objects when they are not affected by the latter.

Given Kant's assumption, namely that the pure concepts of the understanding and the axioms of the pure reason[36] are not empirically derived, this question is obviously a pertinent one. And the only way of answering it in the end, if the assumption is to be maintained, will be to abandon the statement of the dissertation that sensuous presentations present us with objects as they appear while intellectual presentations give us objects as they are, and to say instead that the pure concepts of the understanding have as their cognitive function the further synthesizing of the data of sense intuition. That is to say, Kant will have to maintain that pure concepts of the understanding are, as it were, subjective forms by which we necessarily conceive (because the mind is what it is) the data of sense intuition. Objects will then conform to our concepts, and our concepts will refer to objects, because these concepts are *a priori* conditions of the possibility of objects of knowledge, performing a function analogous to that of the pure intuitions of space and time, though at a higher, namely an intellectual, level. In other words, Kant will be able to maintain his sharp distinction between sense and intellect; but he will have to abandon the notion that while sense presentations give us things as they appear, intellectual presentations give us things as they are in themselves. Instead there will be an ascending process of synthesis whereby empirical reality is constituted. The sensuous and intellectual forms of the human subject remaining constant, and things being knowable only in so far as subjected to these forms, there will always be conformity between objects and our concepts.

To return to the letter to Herz. Plato, says Kant, postulated an intuition of the divinity in a previous existence as the source of the pure concepts and fundamental principles of the understanding. Malebranche postulated a present and continuing intuition of divine ideas. Crusius assumed that God implanted in the soul certain rules of judgment and certain concepts such that they will agree with objects according to a pre-established harmony. But all such theories have recourse to a *Deus ex machina* and they raise more problems than they solve. Some other explanations of the conformity between concepts and objects must therefore be sought. And Kant informs Herz that his inquiry into 'transcendental philosophy' (namely his attempt to reduce the concepts of the pure reason to a certain number of categories) is now sufficiently advanced for him to offer a *Critique of the Pure Reason* (*eine Kritik der reinen Vernunft*),[37] which will deal with the nature both of theoretical and of practical (moral) knowledge. The first part should be published within three months; and it will treat of the sources, method and limits of metaphysics. In the second part, to be published later, he will deal with the basic principles of morality.

The work did not, however, progress as rapidly as Kant at first imagined that it would. As he struggled with his problems, he became more and more conscious of their complexity. After a time he saw that he would have to divide up the matter which he hoped to treat in one *Critique*. In the end he became worried about the delay and put together the *Critique of Pure Reason* (*Kritik der reinen Vernunft*) in four or five months. It appeared in 1781. In this famous work Kant treats of mathematical and scientific knowledge and endeavours to justify the objectivity of this knowledge in the face of the empiricism of David Hume. He does this by proposing his 'Copernican revolution', that is, the theory that objects conform to the mind rather than the other way round. Because the structure of human sensibility and of the human mind is constant, objects will aways appear to us in certain ways. We are thus enabled to make universal scientific judgments which hold good not only for actual but also for possible experience. The Newtonian science is thus theoretically justified despite the dissolvent tendencies of empiricism. From this position it follows, however, that the pure concepts of the understanding do not enable us to apprehend things in themselves, apart from the way in which they appear to us, or supersensible realities. And in the first *Critique* Kant tries to explain how speculative metaphysics of the traditional type arose and why it is foredoomed to failure. The problems which lie at the basis of the *Critique of Pure Reason* will be discussed in *Chapter Eleven*, PART II of this volume.

Kant found that the *Critique of Pure Reason* was misunderstood, and that there were complaints about its obscurity. He therefore published *Prolegomena to Any Future Metaphysics* (*Prolegomena zu einer jeden künftigen Metaphysik*, 1783), a shorter work which was designed, not to supplement the *Critique*, but to act as a kind of introduction or explanation. In 1787 he published a second edition of the *Critique*. In references the first edition is referred as to as A, the second as B.

Meanwhile Kant had turned his attention to the fundamental principles of morals. And in 1785 he published his *Fundamental Principles* (or *Groundwork*) *of the Metaphysics of Morals* (*Grundlegung zur Metaphysik der Sitten*). And this was followed in 1788 by the *Critique of Practical Reason* (*Kritik der praktischen Vernunft*), though in between he had published, not only the second edition of the *Critique of Pure Reason*, but also *Metaphysical First Principles of Natural Science* (*Metaphysische Anfangsgründe der Naturwissenschaft*, 1786). Kant's moral theory will be dealt with in a later chapter. It is sufficient to say here that, just as in the first *Critique* he endeavoured to isolate and give a systematic account of the *a priori* elements in scientific knowledge, so in his moral writings he tried to isolate and give a systematic account of the *a priori* or formal elements in morality. Thus he endeavoured to ground obligation and the universality of the moral law not on feeling but on the practical reason, that is, on reason as legislating for human conduct. This does not mean that he tried to deduce from reason alone all the concrete duties which Smith or Brown encounters in his life. Nor did he think that we could work out a set of concrete moral laws, binding on man as such, without any reference to empirically given material. But he believed that in the moral judgment there is, as it were, a 'form' which can be derived from the practical reason and which is applied to empirically given material. The situation in morals is thus analogous to some extent with that in science. Both in science and in man's moral life, that is, both in theoretical and in practical knowledge, there is the given, the 'matter', and there is the 'formal' and *a priori* element. And

it is with the latter that Kant is chiefly concerned in his
ethical writings. In this sense he is concerned with the 'metaphysics' of morals.

But Kant is also concerned in his ethical writings with
metaphysics in another sense. For he tries to establish as
postulates of the moral law the great truths of freedom, immortality and God. Thus the principal truths which, according to the first *Critique*, are incapable of scientific demonstration, are later re-introduced as postulates of moral or
practical faith. This theory is not a mere appendix to the
Kantian philosophy, still less a superfluous excrescence. For
it is an essential part of Kant's attempt to harmonize the
world of Newtonian science with the world of moral experience and of religious faith. The notion that pure concepts of
the understanding can give us theoretical knowledge of
things in themselves and of a supersensible world has been
ruled out in the first *Critique*. At the same time room has
been made for 'faith'. And in the ethical writings the truths
of human freedom, immortality and the existence of God
are brought in, not as scientifically demonstrable, but as
implications of the moral law, in the sense that recognition
of the fact of moral obligation is seen to demand or postulate
a practical faith in these truths. Thus Kant still maintains
that there is a supersensible sphere; but he finds the key to
it, not in dogmatic metaphysics, but in moral experience.

It will be recalled that in his projected work on *The Bounds
of Sensibility and Reason* Kant had intended to deal not
only with metaphysics and morals but also with the fundamental principles of the theory of taste (*die Geschmacks-
lehre*). The aesthetic judgment or judgment of taste was at
length treated in the third *Critique*, the *Critique of Judgment* (*Kritik der Urteilskraft*), which appeared in 1790.
This work consists of two main parts, the first dealing with
the aesthetic judgment, the second with the teleological judgment or judgment of purposiveness in Nature; and it is of
considerable importance. For in it Kant tries, as far as our
consciousness is concerned at least, to bridge the gulf between the mechanistic world of Nature as presented in physical science and the world of morality, freedom and faith.
That is to say, he tries to show how the mind passes from
the one to the other; and he attempts the rather difficult

task of showing how the transition is reasonable without at
the same time going back on what he has already said about
the vanity of dogmatic metaphysics and about the position
of moral or practical faith as our only means of access to the
supersensible world. The contents of the work will be discussed in PART II of this volume. But it is worth while noting
how deeply Kant was concerned with the reconciliation of the
scientific outlook with that of the moral and religious man.

In 1791 Kant published an article 'On the failure of all
Philosophical Attempts at a Theodicy' (*Ueber das Miszlin-
gen aller philosophischen Versuche in der Theologie*), in
which he maintained that in theodicy or philosophical theology we are concerned with matters of faith rather than with
scientifically demonstrable truth. And this was followed in
1793 by *Religion within the Bounds of Reason Alone* (*Die
Religion innerhalb der Grenzen der blossen Vernunft*).
Mention has been made in an earlier section of this chapter
of the trouble to which publication of this book gave rise.
Reference has also been made to the small treatise *On Perpetual Peace* (*Zum ewigen Frieden*, 1795) in which perpetual peace, grounded on a moral basis, is depicted as a practical ideal of historical and political development.[38] Finally,
in 1797, there appeared the two works which form the two
parts of the *Metaphysics of Morals* (*Metaphysik der Sitten*),
namely the *Metaphysical Elements of the Theory of Right*
(*Metaphysische Anfangsgründe der Rechtslehre*) and the
Metaphysical Elements of the Theory of Virtue (*Metaphysische Anfangsgründe der Tugendlehre*).

We have seen that the human mind does not, on Kant's
view, constitute or create the object in its totality. That is
to say, although things as perceived and known are relative
to us in the sense that we perceive and know them only
through the *a priori* forms embedded in the structure of the
human subject, there are things-in-themselves, even if we
cannot know them as they are in themselves. To put the matter crudely, we no more create things according to their
ontological existence than the man who wears red-tinted
spectacles creates the things which he sees. If we assume that
the spectacles can never be detached, the man will never see
things except as red, and their appearance will be due to a
factor in the perceiving subject. But it does not follow that

things do not exist independently of the perceiving subject. Hence Kant refused to allow that Fichte's suppression of the thing-in-itself represented a legitimate development of his own philosophy. At the same time it can hardly be denied that some of the notes which form part of the *Opus Postumum* indicate that towards the end of his life Kant was developing his thought in such a way that it is reasonable to see in it an anticipation of German speculative idealism. However, it is illegitimate to found one's interpretation of the direction of Kant's thought in his later years on one set of notes to the exclusion of other notes which express a somewhat different point of view. And if we take the *Opus Postumum* as a whole it seems that we must conclude that Kant never abandoned altogether the realistic elements in his thought. But something more will be said about the *Opus Postumum* at a later stage of the discussion of Kant's philosophy in PART II of this volume.

APPENDIX

A SHORT BIBLIOGRAPHY[1]

For general remarks and for General Works see the Bibliography at the end of Volume 4, *Descartes to Leibniz*.

For the benefit of the reader who desires some guidance in the selection of a few useful books in English about general movements of thought and the more prominent thinkers an asterisk has been added to some titles. But the absence of this sign must not be taken to indicate a negative judgment about the value of the book in question.

The following works relating to the period of the Enlightenment can be added.

Becker, C. L. *The Heavenly City of the Eighteenth-Century Philosophers*. New Haven, 1932.

Cassirer, E. *The Philosophy of the Enlightenment*, translated by F. Koelln and J. Pettegrove. Princeton and London, 1951.

Hazard, P. *La crise de la conscience européenne (1680–1715)*. 3 vols. Paris, 1935.

  The European Mind, 1680–1715, translated by J. L. May. London, 1953.

  La pensée européenne au XVIIIe siècle, de Montesquieu à Lessing. 3 vols. Paris, 1946.

  European Thought in the Eighteenth Century, from Montesquieu to Lessing, translated by J. L. May. London, 1954.

Hibben, J. G. *The Philosophy of the Enlightenment*. London and New York, 1910.

Wolff, H. M. *Die Weltanschauung der deutschen Aufklärung*. Berne, 1949.

Wundt, M. *Die deutsche Schulmetaphysik im Zeitalter der Aufklärung*. Tübingen, 1945.

[1] The abbreviation (E.L.) stands, as in previous volumes, for *Everyman's Library*.

Chapters One–Two: The French Enlightenment

I. BAYLE

Texts

Dictionnaire historique et critique. 2 vols., Rotterdam, 1695–7; 4 vols., 1730; and subsequent editions.

Œuvres diverses. 4 vols. The Hague, 1727–31.

Selections from Bayle's 'Dictionary', edited by E. A. Beller and M. Du P. Lee. Princeton and London, 1952.

Système de la philosophie. The Hague, 1737.

Studies

André, P. *Le jeunesse de Bayle.* Geneva, 1953.

Bolin, W. *P. Bayle, sein Leben und seine Schriften.* Stuttgart, 1905.

Cazes, A. *P. Bayle, sa vie, ses idées, son influence, son œuvre.* Paris, 1905.

Courtines, L. *P. Bayle's Relations with England and the English.* New York, 1938.

Deschamps, A. *La genèse du scepticisme érudit chez Bayle.* Brussels, 1878.

Devolve, J. *Essai sur Pierre Bayle, religion, critique et philosophie positive.* Paris, 1906.

Raymond, M. *Pierre Bayle.* Paris, 1948.

II. FONTENELLE

Texts

Œuvres. 1724 and subsequent editions. 3 vols., Paris, 1818; 5 vols., Paris, 1924–35.

De l'origine des fables, critical edition by J-R. Carré. Paris, 1932.

Studies

Carré, J-R. *La philosophie de Fontenelle ou le sourire de la raison.* Paris, 1932.

Edsall, H. Linn. *The Idea of History and Progress in Fontenelle and Voltaire* (in Studies by Members of the French Department of Yale University, New Haven, 1941, pp. 163–84).

Grégoire, F. *Fontenelle.* Paris, 1947.

Laborde-Milan, A. *Fontenelle.* Paris, 1905.

Maigron, L. *Fontenelle, l'homme, l'œuvre, l'influence*. Paris, 1906.

III. MONTESQUIEU

Texts

Œuvres, edited by E. Laboulaye. 7 vols. Paris, 1875–9.

Œuvres, edited by A. Masson. 3 vols. Paris, 1950–5.

De l'esprit des lois, edited with an introduction by G. Truc. 2 vols. Paris, 1945.

Studies

Barrière, P. *Un grand Provincial: Charles-Louis Secondat, baron de La Brède et de Montesquieu*. Bordeaux, 1946.

Carcassonne, E. *Montesquieu et le problème de la constitution française au XVIIIe siècle*. Paris, 1927.

Cotta, S. *Montesquieu e la scienza della società*. Turin, 1953.

Dedieu, J. *Montesquieu, l'homme et l'œuvre*. Paris, 1943.

Duconseil, N. *Machiavelli et Montesquieu*. Paris, 1943.

Durkheim, S. *Montesquieu et Rousseau, précurseurs de la sociologie*. Paris, 1953 (reprint of 1892 edition).

Fletcher, F. T. H. *Montesquieu and English Politics, 1750–1800*. London and New York, 1939.

Levin, L. M. *The Political Doctrine of Montesquieu's Esprit des lois: Its Classical Background* (dissert.). New York, 1936.

Raymond, M. *Montesquieu*, Fribourg, 1946.

Sorel, A. *Montesquieu*. Paris, 1887.

Struck, W. *Montesquieu als Politiker*. Berlin, 1933.

Trescher, H. *Montesquieus Einfluss auf die Geschichts- und Staatsphilosophie bis zum Anfang. des 19. Jahrhunderts*. Munich, 1918 (*Schmollers Jahrbuch*, vol. 42, pp. 267–304).

Montesquieus Einfluss auf die philosophischen Grundlagen der Staatslehre Hegels. Munich, 1918 (*Schmollers Jahrbuch*, vol. 42, pp. 471–501, 907–44).

Vidal, E. *Saggio sul Montesquieu*. Milan, 1950.

See also:

Cabeen, D. C. *Montesquieu: A Bibliography*. New York, 1947.

Deuxième centenaire de l'Esprit des lois de Montesquieu (lectures). Bordeaux, 1949.

Revue internationale de philosophie, 1955, nos. 3–4.

IV. MAUPERTUIS

Texts

Œuvres. 4 vols. Lyons, 1768 (2nd edition).

Studies

Brunet, P. *Maupertuis*. 2 vols. Paris, 1929.

V. VOLTAIRE

Texts

Œuvres, edited by Beuchot. 72 vols. Paris, 1828–34.

Œuvres, edited by Moland. 52 vols. Paris, 1878–85.

Traité de métaphysique, edited by H. T. Patterson. Manchester, 1937.

Dictionnaire philosophique, edited by J. Benda. Paris, 1954.

Philosophical Dictionary, selected and translated by H. I. Woolf. London, 1923.

Lettres philosophiques, edited by F. A. Taylor. Oxford, 1943.

Bengesco, G. Voltaire. *Bibliographie de ses œuvres*. 4 vols. Paris, 1882–92.

Studies

Aldington, R. *Voltaire*. London, 1926.

Alexander, J. W. *Voltaire and Metaphysics* (in *Philosophy* for 1944).

Bellesort, A. *Essai sur Voltaire*. Paris, 1950.

Bersot, E. *La philosophie de Voltaire*. Paris, 1848.

Brandes, G. *Voltaire*. 2 vols. Berlin, 1923.

Carré, J-R. *Consistence de Voltaire: le philosophe*. Paris, 1939.

Charpentier, J. *Voltaire*. Paris, 1955.

Craveri, R. *Voltaire, politico dell'illuminismo*. Turin, 1937.

Cresson, A. *Voltaire*. Paris, 1948.

Cuneo, N. *Sociologia di Voltaire*. Genoa, 1938.

Denoisterre, H. *Voltaire et la société au XVIIIe siècle*. 8 vols. Paris, 1867–76.

Fitch, R. E. *Voltaire's Philosophical Procedure*. Forest Grove, U.S.A., 1936.

Girnus, W. *Voltaire*. Berlin, 1947.

Labriola, A. *Voltaire y la filosofia de la liberación*. Buenos Aires, 1944.

Lanson, G. *Voltaire*. Paris, 1906.

Maurois, A. *Voltaire*. Paris, 1947.

Meyer, A. *Voltaire, Man of Justice*. New York, 1945.

Morley, J. *Voltaire*, London, 1923.

Naves, R. *Voltaire et l'Encyclopédie*. Paris, 1938.

    Voltaire, l'homme et l'œuvre. Paris, 1947 (2nd edition).

Noyes, A. *Voltaire*. London, 1938.

O'Flaherty, K. *Voltaire. Myth and Reality*. Cork and Oxford, 1945.

Pellissier, G. *Voltaire philosophe*. Paris, 1908.

Pomeau, R. *La religion de Voltaire*. Paris, 1956.

Rowe, C. *Voltaire and the State*. London, 1956.

Torrey, N. L. *The Spirit of Voltaire*. New York, 1938.

Wade, O. *Studies on Voltaire*. Princeton, 1947.

VI. VAUVENARGUES

Texts

Œuvres, edited by P. Varillon. 3 vols. Paris, 1929.

Œuvres choisies, with an introduction by H. Gaillard de Champris. Paris, 1942.

Réflexions et maximes. London, 1936.

Reflections and Maxims, translated by F. G. Stevens. Oxford, 1940.

Studies

Borel, A. *Essai sur Vauvenargues*. Neuchâtel, 1913.

Merlant, J. *De Montaigne à Vauvenargues*. Paris, 1914.

Paléologue, G. M. *Vauvenargues*. Paris, 1890.

Rocheblave, S. *Vauvenargues ou la symphonie inachevée*. Paris, 1934.

Souchon, P. *Vauvenargues, philosophe de la gloire*. Paris, 1947.

    Vauvenargues. Paris, 1954.

Vial, F. *Une philosophie et une morale du sentiment. Duc de Clapiers, Marquis de Vauvenargues*. Paris, 1938.

VII. CONDILLAC

Texts

Œuvres. 23 vols. Paris, 1798.

Œuvres philosophiques, edited by G. Le Roy. 3 vols. Paris, 1947–51.

Lettres inédites à Gabriel Cramer, edited by G. Le Roy. Paris, 1952.

Treatise on the Sensations, translated by G. Carr. London, 1930.

Studies

Baguenault de Puchesse G. *Condillac, sa vie, sa philosophie, son influence*. Paris, 1910.

Bianca, G. *La volontà nel pensiero di Condillac*. Catania, 1944.

Bizzarri, R. *Condillac*. Brescia, 1945.

Dal Pra, M. *Condillac*. Milan, 1947.

Dewaule, L. *Condillac et la psychologie anglaise contemporaine*. Paris, 1892.

Didier, J. *Condillac*. Paris, 1911.

Lenoir, R. *Condillac*. Paris, 1924.

Le Roy, G. *La psychologie de Condillac*. Paris, 1937.

Meyer, P. *Condillac*. Zürich, 1944.

Razzoli, L. *Pedagogia di Condillac*. Parma, 1935.

Torneucci, L. *Il problema dell'esperienza dal Locke al Condillac*. Messina, 1937.

VIII. HELVÉTIUS

Texts

Œuvres. 7 vols. Deux-Ports, 1784.

5 vols. Paris, 1792.

Choix de textes, edited with an introduction by J. B. Séverac, Paris, 1911.

A Treatise on Man, translated by W. Hooper. London, 1777.

Studies

Cumming, I. *Helvetius*. London, 1955.

Grossman, M. *The Philosophy of Helvetius*. New York, 1926.

Horowitz, I. L. *C. Helvetius, Philosopher of Democracy and Enlightenment*. New York, 1954.

Keim, A. *Helvétius, sa vie et son œuvre*. Paris, 1907.

Limentani, L. *Le teorie psichologiche di C. A. Helvétius*. Padua, 1902.

Mazzola, F. *La pedagogia d'Elvetio*. Palermo, 1920.

Mondolfo, R. *Saggi per la storia della morale utilitaria, II: Le teorie morali e politiche di C. A. Helvetius.* Padua, 1904.

Stanganelli, I. *La teoria pedagogica di Helvetius.* Naples, 1939.

IX. ENCYCLOPAEDIA

Texts

Encyclopédie ou Dictionnaire raisonné des sciences, des arts et des métiers. 28 vols. Paris, 1751–72.
Supplement in 5 vols.: Amsterdam, 1776–7.
Analytic tables in 2 vols., edited by F. Mouchon, Amsterdam, 1780–1.

The 'Encyclopédie' of Diderot and d'Alembert: selected articles edited with an introduction by J. Lough. Cambridge, 1954.

Studies

Charlier, G., and Mortier, R. *Une suite de l'Encyclopédie, le 'Journal Encyclopédique'* (1756–1793). Paris, 1952.

Ducros, L. *Les encyclopédistes.* Paris, 1900.

Duprat, P. *Les encyclopédistes, leurs travaux, leur doctrine et leur influence.* Paris, 1865.

Gordon, D. H., and Torrey, N. L. *The Censoring of Diderot's Encyclopaedia.* New York, 1949.

Grosclaude, P. *Un audacieux message, l'Encyclopédie.* Paris, 1951.

Hubert, R. *Les sciences sociales dans l'Encyclopédie.* Paris, 1923.

Mornet, D. *Les origines intellectuelles de la révolution française* (1715–87). Paris, 1933.

Mousnier, R., and Labrousse, E. *Le XVIIIe siècle. Révolution intellectuelle, technique et politique* (1715–1815). Paris, 1953.

Roustan, M. *Les philosophes et la société française au XVIIIe siècle.* Lyons, 1906.
The Pioneers of the French Revolution, translated by F. Whyte. Boston, 1926.

Schargo, N. N. *History in the Encyclopaedia.* New York, 1947.

Venturi, F. *Le origini dell'Enciclopedia.* Florence, 1946.

X. DIDEROT

Texts

Œuvres, edited by Assézat and Tournaux. 2 vols. Paris, 1875–9.

Œuvres, edited by A. Billy. Paris, 1952–.

Correspondance, edited by A. Babelon. Paris, 1931.

Diderot: Interpreter of Nature. Selected Writings, translated by J. Stewart and J. Kemp. New York, 1943.

Selected Philosophical Writings, edited by J. Lough. Cambridge, 1953.

Early Philosophical Works, translated by M. Jourdain. London and Chicago, 1916.

Studies

Barker, J. E. *Diderot's Treatment of the Christian Religion*. New York, 1931.

Billy, A. *Vie de Diderot*. Paris, 1943.

Cresson, A. *Diderot*. Paris, 1949.

Gerold, K. G. *Herder und Diderot. Ihr Einblick in die Kunst*. Frankfurt, 1941.

Gillot, H. *Denis Diderot. L'homme. Ses idées philosophiques, esthétiques et littéraires*. Paris, 1938.

Hermand, P. *Les idées morales de Diderot*. Paris, 1923.

Johannson, V. *Études sur Diderot*. Paris, 1928.

Le Gras, J. *Diderot et l'Encyclopédie*. Amiens, 1938.

Lefebvre, H. *Diderot*. Paris, 1949.

Löpelmann, M. *Der junge Diderot*. Berlin, 1934.

Loy, J. R. *Diderot's determined Fatalist. A critical Appreciation of 'Jacques le fataliste'*. New York, 1950.

Luc, J. *Diderot. L'artiste et le philosophe. Suivi de textes choisis de Diderot*. Paris, 1938.

Luppol, I. K. *Diderot. Ses idées philosophiques*. Paris, 1936.

Mauveaux, J. *Diderot, l'encyclopédiste et le penseur*. Montbéliard, 1914.

Mesnard, P. *Le cas Diderot, Etude de caractérologie littéraire*. Paris, 1952.

Morley, J. *Diderot and the Encyclopaedists*. 2 vols. London, 1878.

Mornet, D. *Diderot, l'homme et l'œuvre*. Paris, 1941.

Rosenkranz, K. *Diderots Leben und Werke*. 2 vols. Leipzig, 1886.

Thomas, J. *L'humanisme de Diderot.* 2 vols. Paris, 1938
(2nd edition).

Venturi, F. *Jeunesse de Diderot.* Paris, 1939.

XI. D'ALEMBERT

Texts

Œuvres philosophiques, edited by Bastien. 18 vols. Paris,
1805.

Œuvres et correspondance inédites, edited by C. Henry.
Paris, 1887.

Discours sur l'Encyclopédie, edited by F. Picavet. Paris,
1919.

Traité de dynamique. Paris, 1921.

Studies

Bertrand, J. *D'Alembert.* Paris, 1889.

Muller, M. *Essai sur la philosophie de Jean d'Alembert.*
Paris, 1926.

XII. LA METTRIE

Texts

Œuvres philosophiques. 2 vols. London, 1791; Berlin,
1796.

Man a Machine, annotated by G. C. Bussey. Chicago, 1912.

Studies

Bergmann, E. *Die Satiren des Herrn Machine.* Leipzig,
1913.

Boissier, R. *La Mettrie.* Paris, 1931.

Picavet, F. *La Mettrie et la critique allemande.* Paris, 1889.

Poritzky, Y. E. *J. O. de La Mettrie. Sein Leben und seine
Werke.* Berlin, 1900.

Rosenfeld-Cohen, L. D. *From Beast-machine to Man-ma-
chine. The Theme of Animal Soul in French Letters
from Descartes to La Mettrie*, with a preface by P. Hazard. New York and London, 1940.

Tuloup, G. F. *Un précurseur méconnu. Offray de La Mettrie, médicin-philosophe.* Paris, 1938.

XIII. D'HOLBACH

Texts

Système de la nature. Amsterdam, 1770.

Système sociale. London, 1773.

La politique naturelle. Amsterdam, 1773.
La morale universelle. Amsterdam, 1776.

Studies

Cushing, M. P. *Baron d'Holbach*. New York, 1914.
Hubert, R. *D'Holbach et ses amis*. Paris, 1928.
Naville, P. P. T. *D'Holbach et la philosophie scientifique au XVIIIe siècle*. Paris, 1943.
Plekhanov, G. V. *Essays in the History of Materialism*, translated by R. Fox. London, 1934.
Wickwaer, W. H. *Baron d'Holbach. A Prelude to the French Revolution*. London, 1935.

XIV. CABANIS

Texts

Œuvres, edited by Thurot. Paris, 1823–5.
Lettre à Fauriel sur les causes premières. Paris, 1828.

Studies

Picavet, F. *Les idéologues*. Paris, 1891.
Tencer, M. *La psycho-physiologie de Cabanis*. Toulouse, 1931.
Vermeil de Conchard, T. P. *Trois études sur Cabanis*. Paris, 1914.

XV. BUFFON

Texts

Histoire naturelle, générale et particulière. 44 vols. Paris, 1749–1804.
Nouveaux extraits, edited by F. Gohin. Paris, 1905.

Studies

Dandin, H. *Les méthodes de classification et l'idée de série en botanique et en zoologie de Linné à Lamarck* (1740–1790). Paris, 1926.
Dimier, L. *Buffon*. Paris, 1919.
Roule, L. *Buffon et la description de la nature*. Paris, 1924.

XVI. ROBINET

Texts

De la nature. 4 vols. Amsterdam, 1761–6.
Considérations sur la gradation naturelle des formes de

l'être, ou les essais de la nature qui apprend à faire l'homme. Paris, 1768.

Parallèle de la condition et des facultés de l'homme avec la condition et les facultés des autres animaux. Bouillon, 1769.

Studies

Albert, R. *Die Philosophie Robinets.* Leipzig, 1903.

Mayer, J. *Robinet, philosophe de la nature (Revue des sciences humaines,* Lille, 1954, pp. 295–309).

XVII. BONNET

Texts

Œuvres. 8 vols. Neuchâtel, 1779–83.

Mémoires autobiographiques, edited by R. Savioz. Paris, 1948.

Studies

Bonnet, G. *Ch. Bonnet.* Paris, 1929.

Claparède, E. *La psychologie animale de Ch. Bonnet.* Geneva, 1909.

Lemoine, A. *Ch. Bonnet de Genève, philosophe et naturaliste.* Paris, 1850.

Savioz, R. *La philosophie de Ch. Bonnet.* Paris, 1948.

Trembley, J. *Mémoires pour servir à l'histoire de la vie et des ouvrages de M. Bonnet.* Berne, 1794.

XVIII. BOSCOVICH

Texts

Theoria philosophiae naturalis redacta ad unicam legem virium in natura existentium. Vienna, 1758.
(The second edition, Venice, 1763, contains also *De anima et Deo* and *De spatio et tempore.*)

A *Theory of Natural Philosophy,* Latin (1763)—English edition, translated and edited by J. M. Child. Manchester, 1922.

Opera pertinentia ad opticam et astronomiam. 5 vols. Bassani, 1785.

Studies

Evellin, F. *Quid de rebus vel corporeis vel incorporeis senserit Boscovich.* Paris, 1880.

Gill, H. V., S.J. *Roger Boscovich, S.J. (1711–1787), Fore-runner of Modern Physical Theories.* Dublin, 1941.

Nedelkovitch, D. *La philosophie naturelle et relativiste de R. J. Boscovich.* Paris, 1922.

Oster, M. *Roger Joseph Boscovich als Naturphilosoph.* Bonn, 1909.

Whyte, L. L. *R. J. Boscovich, S.J., F.R.S. (1711–1787), and the Mathematics of Atomism.* (Notes and Records of the Royal Society of London, vol. 13, no. 1, June 1958, pp. 38–48.)

XIX. QUESNAY AND TURGOT

Texts

Œuvres économiques et philosophiques de F. Quesnay, edited by A. Oncken. Paris, 1888.

Œuvres de Turgot, edited by Dupont de Nemours. 9 vols. Paris, 1809–11. Supplement edited by Dupont, Daire and Duggard. 2 vols. Paris, 1884.

Œuvres de Turgot, edited by G. Schelle. 5 vols. Paris, 1913–32.

Studies

Bourthoumieux, C. *Essai sur le fondement philosophique des doctrines économiques. Rousseau contre Quesnay.* Paris, 1936.

Fiorot, D. *La filosofia politica dei fisiocrati.* Padua, 1952.

Gignoux, C. J. *Turgot.* Paris, 1946.

Schelle, G. *Turgot,* Paris, 1909.

Stephens, W. W. *Life and Writings of Turgot.* London, 1891.

Vigreux, P. *Turgot.* Paris, 1947.

Weuleresse, G. *Le mouvement physiocratique en France de 1756 à 1770.* Paris, 1910.
La physiocratie sous les ministères de Turgot et de Necker. Paris, 1950.

Chapters Three–Four: Rousseau

Texts

Œuvres complètes. 13 vols. Paris, 1910. (There are, of course, other editions of Rousseau's works; but there is as yet no complete critical edition.)

Correspondance générale de J. J. Rousseau, edited by T. Dufour and P. P. Plan. 20 vols. Paris, 1924–34.

Le Contrat social, édition comprenant, avec le texte définitif, les versions primitives de l'ouvrage collationnées sur les manuscrits autographes de Genève et de Neuchâtel. Edition Dreyfus-Brisac. Paris, 1916.

Du contrat social, with an introduction and notes by G. Beaulavon. Paris, 1938 (5th edition).

Discours sur l'origine et les fondements de l'inégalité parmi les hommes, edited with an introduction by F. C. Green. London, 1941.

J-J. Rousseau. Political Writings, selected and translated with an introduction by F. M. Watkins. Edinburgh, 1954.

The Political Writings of Jean Jacques Rousseau, edited by C. E. Vaughan. 2 vols. Cambridge, 1915.

The Social Contract and Discourses, edited with an introduction by G. D. H. Cole. London (*E.L.*).

Émile or Education, translated by B. Foxley. London (*E.L.*).

J-J. Rousseau. Selections, edited with an introduction by R. Rolland. London, 1939.

Citizen of Geneva: Selections from the Letters of J-J. Rousseau, edited by C. W. Hendel. New York and London, 1937.

For a thorough study of Rousseau the student should consult:

Annales de la Société J-J. Rousseau. Geneva, 1905 and onwards.

We can also mention:

Sénelier, J. *Bibliographie générale des œuvres de J-J. Rousseau*. Paris, 1949.

Studies

Attisani, A. *L'utilitarismo di G. G. Rousseau*. Rome, 1930.

Baldanzi, E. R. *Il pensiero religioso di G. G. Rousseau*. Florence, 1934.

Bouvier, B. *J-J. Rousseau*. Geneva, 1912.

Brunello, B. *G. G. Rousseau*. Modena, 1936.

Buck, R. *Rousseau und die deutsche Romantik*. Berlin, 1939.

Burgelin, P. *La philosophie de l'existence de J-J. Rousseau.* Paris, 1952.

Casotti, M. *Rousseau e l'educazione morale.* Brescia, 1952.

Cassirer, E. **Rousseau, Kant, Goethe,* translated by J. Gutman, P. O. Kristeller and J. H. Randall, Jr. Princeton, 1945.
The Question of J-J. Rousseau, translated and edited with introduction and additional notes by P. Gay. New York, 1954.

Chapman, J. W. *Rousseau, Totalitarian or Liberal?* New York, 1956.

Chaponnière, P. *Rousseau.* Zürich, 1942.

Cobban, A. *Rousseau and the Modern State.* London, 1934.

Cresson, A. *J-J. Rousseau. Sa vie, son œuvre, sa philosophie.* Paris, 1950 (3rd edition).

Derathé, R. *Le rationalisme de J-J. Rousseau.* Paris, 1948.
J-J. Rousseau et la science politique de son temps. Paris, 1950.

Di Napoli, G. *Il pensiero di G. G. Rousseau.* Brescia, 1953.

Ducros, L. *J-J. Rousseau.* 3 vols. Paris, 1908–18.

Erdmann, K. D. *Das Verhältnis von Staat und Religion nach der Sozialphilosophie Rousseaus. Der Begriff der 'religion civile'.* Berlin, 1935.

Faguet, E. *Rousseau penseur.* Paris, 1912.

Fester, R. *Rousseau und die deutsche Geschichtsphilosophie.* Stuttgart, 1890.

Flores d'Arcais, G. *Il problema pedagogico nell'Emilio di G. G. Rousseau.* Brescia, 1954 (2nd edition).

Frässdorf, W. *Die psychologischen Anschauungen J-J. Rousseaus und ihr Zusammenhang mit der französischen Psychologie des 18 Jahrhunderts.* Langensalza, 1929.

Gézin, R. *J-J. Rousseau.* Paris, 1930.

Green, F. C. **Jean-Jacques Rousseau. A Study of His Life and Writings.* Cambridge, 1955.

Groethuysen, B. *J-J. Rousseau.* Paris, 1950.

Guillemin, H. *Les philosophes contre Rousseau.* Paris, 1942.

Hellweg, M. *Der Begriff des Gewissens bei Rousseau.* Marburg-Lahn, 1936.

Hendel, C. W. **Jean-Jacques Rousseau, Moralist.* 2 vols. New York and London, 1934.

Höffding, H. *J-J. Rousseau and His Philosophy*, translated by W. Richards and L. E. Saidla. New Haven, 1930.

Hubert, R. *Rousseau et l'Encyclopédie. Essai sur la formation des idées politiques de Rousseau (1742–1756).* Paris, 1929.

Köhler, F. *Rousseau.* Bielefeld, 1922.

Lama, E. *Rousseau.* Milan, 1952.

Lemaître, J. *J-J. Rousseau.* Paris, 1907.

Léon, P.-L. *L'idée de volonté générale chez J-J. Rousseau et ses antécédents historiques.* Paris, 1936.

Lombardo, S. *Rousseau nel contratto sociale.* Messina, 1951.

Maritain, J. *Three Reformers: Luther, Descartes, Rousseau.* London, 1945 (reprint).

Masson, P. M. *La religion de Rousseau.* 3 vols. Paris, 1916.

Meinhold, P. *Rousseaus Geschichtsphilosophie.* Tübingen, 1936.

Mondolfo, R. *Rousseau e la coscienza moderna.* Florence, 1954.

Moreau, L. *J-J. Rousseau et le siècle philosophique.* Paris, 1870.

Morel, J. *Recherches sur les sources du discours de J-J. Rousseau sur l'origine et les fondements de l'inégalité.* Lausanne, 1910.

Morley, J. **Rousseau.* 2 vols. London, 1883 (2nd edition).

Pahlmann, F. *Mensch und Staat bei Rousseau.* Berlin, 1939.

Petruzzelis, N. *Il pensiero politico e pedagogico di G. G. Rousseau.* Milan, 1946.

Pons, J. *L'éducation en Angleterre entre 1750 et 1800. Aperçu sur l'influence de J-J. Rousseau en Angleterre.* Paris, 1919.

Proal, L. *La psychologie de J-J. Rousseau.* Paris, 1923.

Reiche, E. *Rousseau und das Naturrecht.* Berlin, 1935.

Roddier, H. *J-J. Rousseau en Angleterre au XVIIIe siècle.* Paris, 1950.

Saloni, A. *Rousseau.* Milan, 1949.

Schiefenbusch, A. *L'influence de J-J. Rousseau sur les beaux arts en France.* Geneva, 1930.

Schinz, A. *La pensée de J-J. Rousseau.* Paris, 1929.
La pensée religieuse de Rousseau et ses récents interprètes. Paris, 1927.

État présent des travaux sur J-J. Rousseau. Paris, 1941.

Sutton, C. *Farewell to Rousseau: a Critique of Liberal Democracy*, with an introduction by W. R. Inge. London, 1936.

Thomas, J. F. *Le pélagianisme de Rousseau.* Paris, 1956.

Valitutti, S. *La volontà generale nel pensiero di Rousseau.* Rome, 1939.

Vasalli, M. *La pedagogia di G. G. Rousseau.* Como, 1951.

Voisine, J. *J-J. Rousseau en Angleterre à l'époque romantique.* Paris, 1956.

Wright, E. H. *The Meaning of Rousseau.* London, 1929.

Ziegenfuss, W. *J-J. Rousseau.* Erlangen, 1952.

There are various collections of articles. For example:

F. Baldensperger, etc. *J-J. Rousseau, leçons faites à l'École des hautes études sociales.* Paris, 1912.

E. Boutroux, etc., in *Revue de métaphysique et de morale,* XX, 1912.

Chapters Five–Seven: The German Enlightenment

I. THOMASIUS

Texts

Institutionum iurisprudentiae divinae libri tres. Frankfurt and Leipzig, 1688.

Einleitung zu der Vernunftlehre. Halle, 1691.

Ausübung der Vernunftlehre. Halle, 1691.

Ausübung der Sittenlehre. Halle, 1696.

Versuch vom Wesen des Geistes. Halle, 1699.

Introductio in philosophiam rationalem. Leipzig, 1701.

Kleine deutsche Schriften. Halle, 1701.

Fundamenta iuris naturae et gentium ex sensu communi deducta in quibus secernuntur principia honesti, iusti ac decori. Halle, 1705.

Dissertationes academicae. 4 vols. Halle, 1733–80.

Studies

Battaglia, F. *Cristiano Thomasio, filosofo e giurista.* Rome, 1935.

Bieber, G. *Staat und Gesellschaft bei C. Thomasius.* Giessen, 1931.

Bienert, W. *Der Anbruch der christlichen deutschen Neu-*

zeit, dargestellt an Wissenschaft und Glauben des Christian Thomasius. Halle, 1934.
Die Philosophie des Christian Thomasius (dissert.). Halle, 1934.
Die Glaubenslehre des Christian Thomasius (dissert.). Halle, 1934.
Block, E. C. *Thomasius.* Berlin, 1953.
Lieberwirth, R. C. *Thomasius.* Weimar, 1955.
Neisser, K. *C. Thomasius und seine Beziehung zum Pietismus.* Heidelberg, 1928.
Schneider, F. *Thomasius und die deutsche Bildung.* Halle, 1928.

II. WOLFF

Texts

Philosophia rationalis, sive logica methodo scientifica pertractata et ad usum scientiarum atque vitae aptata. Frankfurt and Leipzig, 1728.
Philosophia prima sive Ontologia. Frankfurt, 1729.
Cosmologia generalis. Ibid., 1731.
Psychologia empirica. Ibid., 1732.
Psychologia rationalis. Ibid., 1734.
Theologia naturalis. 2 vols. *Ibid.,* 1736–7.
Philosophia practica universalis. 2 vols. *Ibid.,* 1738–9.
Gesammelte kleinere Schriften. 6 vols. Halle, 1736–40.
Ius naturae methodo scientifica pertractata. 8 vols. Frankfurt and Leipzig, 1740–48.
Ius gentium. Halle, 1750.
Oeconomica. Ibid., 1750.
Philosophia moralis sive Ethica. 5 vols. *Ibid.,* 1750–3.

Studies

Arnsperger, W. *Ch. Wolffs Verhältnis zu Leibniz.* Heidelberg, 1897.
Campo, M. *Ch. Wolff e il razionalismo precritico.* 2 vols. Milan, 1939.
Frank, R. *Die Wolffsche Strafrechtsphilosophie und ihr Verhältnis zur kriminalpolitischen Aufklärung im 18. Jahrhundert.* Göttingen, 1887.
Frauendienst, W. *Ch. Wolff als Staatsdenker.* Berlin, 1927.
Heilemann, P. A. *Die Gotteslehre des Ch. Wolff.* Leipzig, 1907.

Joesten, C. *Ch. Wolffs Grundlegung der praktischen Philosophie.* Leipzig, 1931.

Kohlmeyer, E. *Kosmos und Kosmonomie bei Ch. Wolff.* Göttingen, 1911.

Levy, H. *Die Religionsphilosophie Ch. Wolffs.* Würzburg, 1928.

Ludovici, C. G. *Ausführlicher Entwurf einer vollständigen Historie der Wolffschen Philosophie.* 3 vols. Leipzig, 1736–7.
Sammlung und Auszüge der sämmtlichen Streitschriften wegen der Wolffschen Philosophie. 2 vols. Leipzig, 1737–8.

Utitz, E. *Ch. Wolff.* Halle, 1929.

Wundt, M. *Christian Wolff und die deutsche Aufklärung* (in *Das Deutsche in der deutschen Philosophie,* edited by T. Haering, Stuttgart, 1941, pp. 227–46).

III. BAUMGARTEN

Texts

Meditationes philosophicae de nonnullis ad poema pertinentibus. Halle, 1735.

Reflections on Poetry, translated, with the original Latin text, an introduction and notes by K. Aschenbrenner and W. B. Hoelther. Berkeley and London, 1954.

Metaphysica. Halle, 1740.

Aesthetica acroamatica. 2 vols. Frankfurt, 1750–8.

Aesthetica. Iterum edita ad exemplar prioris editionis annorum MDCCL–LVIII spatio impressae.
Praepositae sunt: Meditationes philosophicae de nonnullis ad poema pertinentibus. Bari, 1936.

Ethica philosophica. Halle, 1765.

Philosophia generalis. Halle, 1769.

Studies

Bergmann, E. *Die Begründung der deutschen Aesthetik durch Baumgarten und G. F. Maier.* Leipzig, 1911.

Maier, G. F. *A. G. Baumgartens Leben.* Halle, 1763.

Peters, H. G. *Die Aesthetik A. G. Baumgartens und ihre Beziehungen zum Ethischen.* Berlin, 1934.

Poppe, B. *A. G. Baumgarten, seine Bedeutung und Stellung in der Leibniz-Wolffschen Philosophie.* Berne-Leipzig, 1907.

IV. FREDERICK THE GREAT

Texts

Antimachiavell. The Hague, 1740.

Essai sur l'amour propre envisagé comme principe de la morale. Berlin, 1770.

Œuvres de Frédéric le Grand. 30 vols. Berlin, 1847–57. Vols. 8 and 9 *Œuvres philosophiques.*

Briefwechsel mit Maupertuis, edited by R. Koser. Berlin, 1898.

Briefwechsel mit Voltaire, edited by R. Koser and H. Droysen. Berlin, 1908.

Studies

Berney, A. *Friedrich der Grosse. Entwicklungsgeschichte eines Staatsmannes.* Tübingen, 1934.

Berney, G. *Friedrich der Grosse.* Munich, 1935.

Dilthey, W. *Friedrich der Grosse und die deutsche Aufklärung.* Leipzig, 1927.

Gent, W. *Die geistige Kultur um Friedrich den Grossen.* Berlin, 1936.

Gooch, G. P. *Frederick the Great.* New York, 1947.

Koser, R. *Friedrich der Grosse.* 4 vols. Stockholm, 1912 (4th edition).

Langer, J. *Friedrich der Grosse und die geistige Welt Frankreichs.* Hamburg, 1932.

Muff, W. *Die Philosophie Friedrichs des Grossen* (in *Wissen und Wehr,* Berlin, 1943, pp. 117–33).
Friedrichs des Grossen philosophische Entwicklung (in *Forschungen und Fortschritte,* Berlin, 1943, pp. 156–7).

Pelletan, E. *Un roi philosophe, le grand Frédéric.* Paris, 1878.

Rigollot, G. *Frédéric II, philosophe.* Paris, 1876.

Spranger, E. *Der Philosoph von Sanssouci.* Berlin, 1942.

Zeller, E. *Friedrich der Grosse als Philosoph.* Berlin, 1886.

V. REIMARUS

Texts

Abhandlungen von den vornehmsten Wahrheiten der natürlichen Religion. Hamburg, 1754.

Vernunftlehre. Hamburg and Kiel, 1756.

Allgemeine Betrachtungen über die Triebe der Tiere, hauptsächlich über ihren Kunsttrieb. Hamburg, 1760.

Apologie oder Schutzschrift für die vernünftigen Verehrer Gottes. See p. 145, this volume.

Studies

Buettner, W. H. S. *Reimarus als Metaphysiker.* Würzburg, 1909.

Koestlin, H. *Das religiöse Erleben bei Reimarus.* Tübingen, 1919.

Loeser, M. *Die Kritik des H. S. Reimarus am alten Testament.* Berlin, 1941.

Lundsteen, A. C. *H. S. Reimarus und die Anfänge der Leben-Jesu Forschung.* Copenhagen, 1939.

VI. MENDELSSOHN

Texts

Werke, edited by G. B. Mendelssohn. 7 vols. Leipzig, 1843–4.

Gesammelte Schriften, edited by J. Elbogen, J. Guttmann and M. Mittwoch. Berlin, 1929–.

Studies

Bachi, E. D. *Sulla vita e sulle opere di M. Mendelssohn.* Turin, 1872.

Bamberger, F. *Der geistige Gestalt M. Mendelssohns.* Frankfurt, 1929.

Cohen, B. *Ueber die Erkenntnislehre M. Mendelssohns.* Giessen, 1921.

Goldstein, L. *M. Mendelssohn und die deutsche Aesthetik.* Königsberg, 1904.

Hoelters, H. *Der spinozistische Gottesbegriff bei M. Mendelssohn und F. H. Jacobi und der Gottesbegriff Spinozas.* Bonn, 1938.

VII. LESSING

Texts

Sämtliche Schriften. 30 vols. Berlin, 1771–94.

Sämtliche Werke, critical edition of Lachmann-Muncker (Leipzig, 1886 f.); 4th edition by J. Petersen. 25 vols. Berlin, 1925–35.

Die Erziehung des Menschengeschlechts. Nach dem Urtext von 1780 neu herausgegeben mit Anmerkungen und einem Nachwort von K. R. Riedler. Zürich, 1945.

Lessing's Theological Writings, translated and selected by H. Chadwick. London, 1956.

Studies

Arx A. von. *Lessing und die geschichtliche Welt*. Frankfurt, 1944.

Bach, A. *Der Aufbruch des deutschen Geistes. Lessing, Klopstock, Herder*. Markkleeberg, 1939.

Fischer, K. *Lessing als Reformator der deutschen Literatur*. 2 vols. Stockholm, 1881.

Fittbogen, G. *Die Religion Lessings*. Halle, 1915.

Flores d'Arcais, G. *L'estetica nel Laocoonte di Lessing*. Padua, 1935.

Garland, H. B. *Lessing, the Founder of Modern German Literature*. London, 1937.

Gonzenbach, H. *Lessings Gottesbegriff in seinem Verhältnis zu Leibniz und Spinoza*. Leipzig, 1940.

Kommerell, M. *Lessing und Aristoteles. Untersuchung über die Theorie der Tragödie*. Frankfurt, 1940.

Leander, F. *Lessing als aesthetischer Denker*. Göteborg, 1942.

Leisegang, H. *Lessings Weltanschauung*. Leipzig, 1931.

Milano, P. *Lessing*. Rome, 1930.

Oehlke, W. *Lessing und seine Zeit*. 2 vols. Munich, 1929 (2nd edition).

Robertson, G. *Lessing's Dramatic Theory*. Cambridge, 1939.

Schmitz, F. J. *Lessings Stellung in der Entfaltung des Individualismus*. Berkeley, U.S.A. and Cambridge, 1941.

Schrempf, C. *Lessing als Philosoph*. Stockholm, 1921 (2nd edition).

Wernle, P. *Lessing und das Christentum*. Leipzig, 1912.

VIII. TETENS

Texts

Gedanken über einige Ursachen, warum in der Metaphysik nur wenige ausgemachte Wahrheiten sind. Bützow, 1760.

Abhandlung von den vorzüglichsten Beweisen des Daseins Gottes. Ibid., 1761.

Commentatio de principio minimi. Ibid., 1769.

Abhandlung über den Ursprung der Sprache und der Schift. Ibid., 1772.

Ueber die allgemeine spekulative Philosophie. Ibid., 1775.

Philosophische Versuche über die menschliche Natur und ihre Entwicklung. 2 vols. Leipzig, 1776. (Reprinted, Berlin, 1913).

Studies

Schinz, M. *Die Moralphilosophie von Tetens.* Leipzig, 1906.

Schweig, H. *Die Psychologie des Erkennens bei Bonnet und Tetens* (dissert.). Bonn, 1921.

Seidel, A. *Tetens Einfluss auf die kritische Philosophie Kants* (dissert.). Leipzig, 1932.

Uebele, W. *J. N. Tetens nach seiner Gesamtentwicklung betrachtet mit besonderer Berücksichtigung des Verhältnisses zu Kant* (Kantstudien, Berlin, 1911, suppl. vol. 24, viii, 1–238).

Zergiebel, K. *Tetens und sein system der Philosophie* (Zeitschrift für Philosophie und Pädagogik, Langensalza, vol. 19, 1911–12, pp. 273–79, 321–6).

IX. BASEDOW

Texts

Philalethie. Lübeck, 1764.

Theoretisches System der gesunden Vernunft. Leipzig, 1765.

Vorstellung an Menschenfreunde und vermögende Männer über Schulen, Studien und ihren Einfluss in die öffentliche Wohlfahrt. Bremen, 1768.

Elementarwerk. 4 vols. Dessau, 1774.

Studies

Diestelmann, R. *Basedow.* Leipzig, 1897.

Pantano-Migneco, G. *G. B. Basedow e il filantropismo.* Catania, 1917.

Piazzi, A. *L'educazione filantropica nella dottrina e nell'opera di G. B. Basedow.* Milan, 1920.

Pinloche, A. *La réforme de l'éducation en Allemagne au XVIIIe siècle. Basedow et le philanthropisme.* Paris, 1889.

X. PESTALOZZI

Texts

Sämtliche Werke, edited by A. Buchenau, E. Spranger and H. Stettbacker. 19 vols. Berlin, 1927–56.

Sämtliche Werke, edited by P. Baumgartner. 8 vols. Zürich, 1943.

Sämtliche Briefe. 4 vols. Zürich, 1946–51.

Educational Writings. Translated and edited by J. A. Green, with the assistance of F. A. Collie. London, 1912.

Studies

Anderson, L. F. Pestalozzi. New York, 1931.

Bachmann, W. Die anthropologischen Grundlagen zu Pestalozzis Soziallehre. Berne, 1947.

Banfi, A. Pestalozzi. Florence, 1928.

Barth, H. Pestalozzis Philosophie der Politik. Zürich and Stockholm, 1954.

Green, J. A. Life and Work of Pestalozzi. London, 1913.

Hoffman, H. Die Religion im Leben und Denken Pestalozzis. Berne, 1944.

Jónasson, M. Recht und Sittlichkeit in Pestalozzis Kulturtheorie. Berlin, 1936.

Mayer, M. Die positive Moral bei Pestalozzi von 1766–1797 (dissert.). Charlottenburg, 1934.

Otto, H. Pestalozzi. Berlin, 1948.

Pinloche, A. Pestalozzi et l'éducation populaire moderne. Paris, 1902.

Reinhart, J. J. H. Pestalozzi. Basel, 1945.

Schönebaum, H. J. H. Pestalozzi. Berlin, 1954.

Sganzini, C. Pestalozzi. Palermo, 1928.

Spranger, E. Pestalozzis Denkformen. Zürich, 1945.

Wehnes, F. J. Pestalozzis Elementarmethode. Bonn, 1955.

Wittig, H. Studien zur Anthropologie Pestalozzis. Weinheim, 1952.

XI. HAMANN

Texts

Sämtliche Schriften. Edited by F. Roth. 8 vols. Berlin, 1821–43.

Sämtliche Schriften. Critical edition by J. Nadler. 6 vols. Vienna, 1949–57.

Briefwechsel. Edited by W. Ziesemer and A. Henkel. 2 vols. Wiesbaden, 1955–6.

Studies

Blum, J. *La vie et l'œuvre de J. G. Hamann, le Mage du Nord.* Paris, 1912.

Heinekamp, H. *Das Weltbild J. G. Hamanns.* Düsseldorf, 1934.

Metzger, W. *J. G. Hamann.* Frankfurt, 1944.

Metzke, E. *J. G. Hamanns Stellung in der Philosophie des 18. Jahrhunderts.* Halle, 1934.

Nadler, J. *Die Hamann-Ausgabe.* Halle-Saale, 1930.

J. G. Hamann. Der Zeuge des Corpus Mysticum. Salzburg, 1949.

O'Flaherty, J. C. *Unity and Language. A Study in the Philosophy of J. G. Hamann.* Chapel Hill, U.S.A., 1952.

Schoonhoven, J. *Natur en genade by Hamann.* Leyden, 1945.

Steege, H. *J. G. Hamann.* Basel, 1954.

Unger, R. *Hamann und die Aufklärung.* 2 vols. Jena, 1911.

XII. HERDER

Texts

Sämtliche Werke. Edited by B. Sulphan and others. 33 vols. Berlin, 1877–1913.

Treatise upon the Origin of Language. Translator anon. London, 1827.

Outlines of a Philosophy of the History of Man. Translated by T. Churchill. London, 1803 (2nd edition).

The Spirit of Hebrew Poetry. Translated by J. Marsh. 2 vols. Burlington, Vt., 1832.

God. Some Conversations. Translated by F. H. Burkhardt. New York, 1949 (2nd edition).

Studies

Andress, J. M. *J. G. Herder as an Educator.* New York, 1916.

Aron, E. *Die deutsche Erweckung des Griechentums durch Winckelmann und Herder* (dissert.). Heidelberg, 1929.

Bach, R. *Der Aufbruch des deutschen Geistes: Lessing, Klopstock, Herder.* Markkleeberg, 1940.

Baumgarten, O. *Herders Lebenzweck und die religiöse Frage der Gegenwart.* Tübingen, 1905.

Bäte, L. J. G. Herder. Der Weg, das Werk, die Zeit. Stuttgart, 1948.

Berger, F. Menschenbild und Menschenbildung. Die philosophisch-pädagogische Anthropologie J. G. Herders. Stuttgart, 1933.

Bernatzki, A. Herders Lehre von der aesthetischen Erziehung (dissert.). Breslau, 1925.

Blumenthal, E. Herders Auseinandersetzung mit der Philosophie Leibnizens (dissert.). Hamburg, 1934.

Boor, W. de. Herders Erkenntnislehre in ihrer Bedeutung für seinen religiösen Idealismus. Gutersloh, 1929.

Brändle, J. Das Problem der Innerlichkeit: Hamann, Herder, Goethe. Berne, 1950.

Clark, R. T., Jr. *Herder: His Life and Thought. Berkeley and London, 1955. (Contains full bibliographies.)

Dewey, M. H. Herder's Relation to the Aesthetic Theory of His Time (dissert.). Chicago, 1918.

Dobbek, W. J. G. Herders Humanitätsidee als Ausdruck seines Weltbildes und seiner Persönlichkeit. Braunschweig, 1949.

Erdmann, H. Herder als Religionsphilosoph. Hersfeld, 1868.

Fischer, W. Herders Erkenntnislehre und Metaphysik (dissert.). Leipzig, 1878.

Gerold, K. G. Herder und Diderot, ihr Einblick in die Kunst. Frankfurt, 1941.

Gillies, A. Herder. Oxford, 1945.

Grabowsky, I. Herders Metakritik und Kants Kritik der reinen Vernunft (dissert.). Dortmund, 1934.

Hatch, I. C. Der Einfluss Shaftesburys auf Herder (dissert.). Berlin, 1901.

Haym, R. Herder nach seinem Leben und seinen Werken dargestellt. 2 vols. Berlin, 1954. (Reprint of 1877–85 edition.)

Henry, H. Herder und Lessing: Umrisse ihrer Beziehung. Würzburg, 1941.

Joens, D. W. Begriff und Problem der historischen Zeit bei J. G. Herder. Göteborg, 1956.

Joret, C. Herder et la renaissance littéraire en Allemagne au XVIIIᵉ siècle. Paris, 1875.

Knorr, F. Das Problem der menschlichen Philosophie bei Herder (dissert.). Coburg, 1930.

Kronenberg, M. *Herders Philosophie nach ihrem Entwicklungsgang und ihrer historischen Stellung.* Heidelberg, 1889.

Kuhfuss, H. *Gott und Welt in Herders 'Ideen zur Philosophie der Geschichte der Menschheit'* (dissert.). Emsdetten, 1938.

Kühnemann, E. *Herder.* Munich, 1927 (2nd edition).

Landenberger, A. *J. G. Herder, sein Leben, Wirken und Charakterbild.* Stuttgart, 1903.

Litt, T. *Kant und Herder als Deuter der geistigen Welt.* Heidelberg, 1949 (2nd edition).
Die Befreiung des geschichtlichen Bewusstseins durch Herder. Leipzig, 1942.

McEachran, F. *The Life and Philosophy of J. G. Herder.* Oxford, 1929.

Nevinson, H. *A Sketch of Herder and His Times.* London, 1884.

Ninck, J. *Die Begründung der Religion bei Herder.* Leipzig, 1912.

Rasch, W. *Herder, sein Leben und Werk im Umriss.* Halle, 1938.

Rouché, M. *Herder précurseur de Darwin? Histoire d'un mythe.* Paris, 1940.
La philosophie de l'histoire de Herder (dissert.). Paris, 1940.

Salmony, H. A. *Die Philosophie des jungen Herder.* Zürich, 1949.

Siegel, K. *Herder als Philosoph.* Stuttgart, 1907.

Voigt, A. *Umrisse einer Staatslehre bei J. G. Herder.* Stuttgart and Berlin, 1939.

Weber, H. *Herders Sprachphilosophie. Eine Interpretation in Hinblick auf die moderne Sprachphilosophie* (dissert.). Berlin, 1939.

Werner, A. *Herder als Theologe: ein Beitrag zur Geschichte der protestantischen Theologie.* Berlin, 1871.

Wiese, B. von. *Volk und Dichtung von Herder bis zur Romantik.* Erlangen, 1938.
Herder, Grundzüge seines Weltbildes. Leipzig, 1939.

XIII. JACOBI

Texts

Werke. Edited by F. Roth. 6 vols. Leipzig, 1812–25.

Aus F. H. Jacobis Nachlass. Edited by R. Zöpporitz. 2 vols. Leipzig, 1869.

Auserlesener Briefwechsel. Edited by F. Roth. 2 vols. Leipzig, 1825–7.

Briefwechsel zwischen Goethe und F. H. Jacobi. Edited by M. Jacobi. Leipzig, 1846.

Briefe an Bouterwerk aus den Jahren 1800–1819. Edited by W. Meyer. Göttingen, 1868.

Studies

Bollnow, O. F. *Die Lebensphilosophie F. H. Jacobis.* Stockholm, 1933.

Fischer, G. J. M. *Sailer und F. H. Jacobi.* Fribourg, 1955.

Frank, A. *Jacobis Lehre vom Glauben.* Halle, 1910.

Heraens, O. F. *Jacobi und der Sturm und Drang.* Heidelberg, 1928.

Hoelters, H. *Der spinozistische Gottesbegriff bei Mendelssohn und Jacobi und der Gottesbegriff Spinozas* (dissert.). Bonn, 1938.

Lévy-Bruhl, L. *La philosophie de Jacobi.* Paris, 1894.

Schmid, F. A. *F. H. Jacobi.* Heidelberg, 1908.

Thilo, C. A. *Jacobis Religionsphilosophie.* Langensalza, 1905.

Zirngiebl, E. *F. H. Jacobis Leben, Dichten und Denken.* Vienna, 1867.

Chapters Eight–Nine: The Rise of the Philosophy of History

I. BOSSUET

Texts

Œuvres complètes. Edited by P. Guillaume. 10 vols. Bar-le-Duc, 1877.

Studies

Auneau, A. *Bossuet.* Avignon, 1949.

De Courten, C. *Bossuet e il suo 'Discours sur l'histoire universelle'.* Milan, 1927.

Nourisson, A. *Essai sur la philosophie de Bossuet.* Paris, 1852.

II. VICO

Texts

Opere. Edited by F. Nicolini. 8 vols. (11 'tomes'). Bari, 1914–41.

La Scienza Nuova seconda, giusta la edizione del 1744, con le varianti del 1730 e di due redazioni intermedie inedite. Edited by F. Nicolini. 2 vols. Bari, 1942 (3rd edition).

There are many other Italian editions of the *Scienza nuova*.

Commento storico alla Scienza seconda. By F. Nicolini. 2 vols. Rome, 1949.

The New Science of Giambattista Vico. Translated from the third edition (1744) by T. G. Bergin and M. H. Fisch. London, 1949.

Il diritto universale. Edited by F. Nicolini. Bari, 1936.

De nostri temporis studiorum ratione. With introduction, translation (Italian) and notes by V. De Ruvo. Padua, 1941.

Giambattista Vico. Autobiography. Translated by M. H. Fisch and T. G. Bergin. New York and London, 1944.

For Bibliography see *Bibliografia vichiana*. Edited by F. Nicolini. 2 vols. Naples, 1947.

Studies

Adams, H. P. The Life and Writings of Giambattista Vico. London, 1935.

Amerio, F. Introduzione allo studio di G. B. Vico. Turin, 1947.

Auerbach, E. G. B. Vico. Barcelona, 1936.

Banchetti, S. Il significato morale dell'estetica vichiana. Milan, 1957.

Bellofiore, L. La dottrina del diritto naturale in G. B. Vico. Milan, 1954.

Berry, T. The Historical Theory of G. B. Vico. Washington, 1949.

Cantone, C. Il concetto filosofico di diritto in G. B. Vico. Mazana, 1952.

Caponigri, A. R. Time and Idea, the Theory of History in Giambattista Vico. London, 1953.

Cappello, C. La dottrina della religione in G. B. Vico. Chieri, 1944.

Chaix-Ruy, J. *Vie de J. B. Vico.* Paris, 1945.
   La formation de la pensée philosophique de J. B. Vico.
   Paris, 1945.
Chiochetti, E. *La filosofia di Giambattista Vico.* Milan,
   1935.
Cochery, M. *Les grandes lignes de la philosophie his-
   torique et juridique de Vico.* Paris, 1923.
Corsano, A. *Umanesimo e religione in G. B. Vico.* Bari,
   1935.
   G. B. Vico. Bari, 1956.
Croce, B. *La filosofia di G. B. Vico.* Bari, 1911.
Donati, B. *Nuovi studi sulla filosofia civile di G. B. Vico.*
   Con documenti. Florence, 1936.
Federici, G. C. *Il principio animatore della filosofia vichi-
   ana.* Rome, 1947.
Flint, R. *Vico.* Edinburgh, 1884.
Fubini, M. *Stile e umanità in G. B. Vico.* Bari, 1946.
Gentile, G. *Studi vichiani.* Messina, 1915.
   Giambattista Vico. Florence, 1936.
Giusso, L. *G. B. Vico fra l'umanesimo e l'occasionalismo.*
   Rome, 1940.
   Le filosofia di G. B. Vico e l'età barocca. Rome, 1943.
Luginbühl, J. *Die Axiomatik bei Vico.* Berne, 1946.
   Die Geschichtsphilosophie G. Vicos. Bonn, 1946.
Nicolini, F. *La giovinezza di G. B. Vico.* Bari, 1932.
   Saggi vichiani. Naples, 1955.
Paci, E. *Ingens Sylva, Saggio su G. B. Vico.* Milan, 1949.
Peters, R. *Der Aufbau der Weltgeschichte bei G. Vico.*
   Stuttgart, 1929.
Sabarini, R. *Il tempo in G. B. Vico.* Milan, 1954.
Severgnini, D. *Nozze, tribunali ed are. Studi vichiani.*
   Turin, 1956.
Uscatescu, G. *Vico y el mundo histórico.* Madrid, 1956.
Villa, G. *La filosofia del mito secondo G. B. Vico.* Milan,
   1949.
Werner, K. *G. B. Vico als Philosoph und gelehrter
   Forscher.* Vienna, 1881.
There are some collections of articles; for example:
Vico y Herder. Ensayos conmemorativos del secondo cen-
   tenario de la muerte de Vico y del nacimiento de Herder.
   Buenos Aires, 1948.

III. MONTESQUIEU

See pp. 212–13.

IV. VOLTAIRE

See pp. 213–14.

V. CONDORCET

Texts

Œuvres. Edited by Mme Condorcet, Cabanis and Garat. 21 vols. Paris, 1801–4.

Œuvres. Edited by A. Condorcet, O'Connor and M. F. Arago. 12 vols. Paris, 1847–9.

Sketch for a Historical Picture of the Progress of the Human Mind. Translated by J. Barraclough, with an introduction by Stuart Hampshire. London, 1955.

Studies

Alengry, F. *Condorcet, guide de la révolution française.* Paris, 1904.

Brunello, B. *La pedagogia della rivoluzione francese.* Milan, 1951.

Caben, L. *Condorcet et la révolution française.* Paris, 1904.

Frazer, J. G. *Condorcet on the Progress of the Human Mind.* Oxford, 1933.

Jacovello, G. *Introduzione ad uno studio su Condorcet.* Bronte, 1914.

Martin, K. *Rise of French Liberal Thought in the 18th Century.* New York, 1954 (2nd edition).

VI. LESSING

See pp. 227–28.

VII. HERDER

See pp. 230–32.

Chapter Ten: Kant (1)

See Bibliography in PART II.

NOTES

CHAPTER ONE

1 *De l'esprit des lois*, Preface.
2 *Ibid.*, II, 1.
3 *Ibid.*, II, 4.
4 *Ibid.*, III, 1.
5 *Ibid.*, III, 11.
6 *Ibid.*, I, 3.
7 Laws in their most general sense are 'the necessary relations resulting from the nature of things' (*De l'esprit des lois*, I, 1).
8 *Ibid.*, I, 1.
9 *Ibid.*
10 *Ibid.*
11 *Ibid.*
12 *Ibid.*
13 *Ibid.*, XI, 3.
14 *Ibid.*
15 *Ibid.*, XI, 5.
16 *Ibid.*, XI, 6.
17 *Essai de cosmologie*, 2 partie; *Œuvres*, I, edit. 1756, pp. 29–30.
18 *Ibid.*, p. 30.
19 *Ibid.*, p. 31.
20 *Ibid.*, p. 42.
21 *Ibid.*, pp. 42–3.
22 *Ibid.*, p. 44.
23 *Système de la Nature*, LXII; *Œuvres*, II, pp. 164–5.
24 *Maupertuis*, Paris, 1929.
25 Voltaire never met Hume, though he greatly admired him. On his part Hume was somewhat reserved in his attitude towards the French philosopher, though he was persuaded to write him an appreciative letter from Paris when Voltaire was at Ferney.
26 *Philosophie de Newton*, I, 1.
27 *Ibid.*
28 *Ibid.*
29 *Ibid.*, I, 1.
30 I, 7.
31 7.
32 I, 4.
33 *Philosophie de Newton*, I, 4.
34 *Ibid.*
35 *Ibid.*
36 13.
37 9.
38 *Ibid.*
39 *Treatise on Metaphysics*, 8.
40 *Introduction to the Knowledge of the Human Mind*, II, 42.
41 *Ibid.*, I, 1.
42 *Ibid.*, I, 15.
43 *Ibid.*, II, 22.
44 *Ibid.*
45 *Ibid.*, II, 22.
46 *Ibid.*
47 *Ibid.*, III, 43.
48 *Ibid.*
49 *Ibid.*
50 *Ibid.*, III, 44.
51 *Réflexions et maximes*, 222.
52 *Introduction to the Knowledge of the Human Mind*, III, 44.

53 *Réflexions et maximes*, 124.
54 *Ibid.*, 127.
55 *Ibid.*, 151.
56 *Ibid.*, 154–5.
57 III, V.
58 *Treatise on Sensations*, I, i, 2.
59 *Ibid.*, I, i, 15.
60 *Ibid.*, I, iii, 1.
61 *Ibid.*, I, iii, 5.
62 *Ibid.*, I, iii, 9.
63 *Ibid.*, I, vi, 3.
64 *Ibid.*, I, vii, 1.
65 *Ibid.*, I, xii, 1–2.
66 *Ibid.*, II, v, 4.
67 *Ibid.*, II, v, 5.
68 *Ibid.*, I, iv, 7.
69 *Ibid.*, IV, ix, 1.
70 II, 21, 31 f.
71 *Ibid.*, 33.
72 II, 11.
73 *Ibid.*, IV, ix, 3.
74 *Treatise on Sensations*, IV, v, *note*.
75 *Ibid.*
76 *On Man*, 2, 7; translation by W. Hooper, 1777, I, 127.
77 *Ibid.*, Hooper, I, p. 121.
78 *Ibid.*, Hooper, I, p. 122.
79 *Ibid.*, 2, 18; Hooper, I, p. 199.
80 *Ibid.*, 2, 19; Hooper, I, p. 200.
81 *Ibid.*, 2, 17; Hooper, I, p. 194.
82 *Ibid.*, 10, 1; Hooper, II, pp. 392 and 395.
83 *Ibid.*, 10, 10; Hooper, II, p. 436.
84 *Ibid.*, Hooper, II, p. 433.
85 Hooper, I, p. vi.
86 *Ibid.*, 6, 9; Hooper, II, p. 105.
87 *Ibid.*, 1, 13; Hooper, I, pp. 58–9.
88 *Ibid.*, Hooper, I, p. 60.

CHAPTER TWO

1 *Eléments de Philosophie* in the 1759 edition of *Mélanges de littérature, d'histoire et de philosophie*, IV, pp. 3–6.
2 *Ibid.*, IV, p. 59.
3 *L'art de jouir ou l'école de la volupté*, 1751.
4 VI, 370.

CHAPTER THREE

1 In this and the next chapters the following abbreviations will be used: D.A. for the *Discourse on the Arts and Sciences*; D.I. for the *Discourse on the Origin of Inequality*; D.P. for the *Discourse on Political Economy*; É. for *Émile*; and S.C. for the *Social Contract*. For the convenience of the reader page-references will be given to the *Everyman's Library* editions of the *Social Contract* and *Discourses* and of *Émile*, as these editions are easily available.
2 D.A., p. 130.
3 *Ibid.*
4 *Ibid.*, p. 131.
5 *Ibid.*, p. 132.
6 *Ibid.*, p. 133.
7 *Ibid.*
8 *Ibid.*, p. 134.
9 *Ibid.*
10 *Ibid.*, p. 135.
11 *Ibid.*, p. 136.
12 *Ibid.*, p. 140.
13 *Ibid.*, p. 147.
14 *Ibid.*, p. 152.
15 *Ibid.*
16 D.I., Introduction, pp. 175–6.
17 *Ibid.*, p. 177.
18 *Ibid.*, p. 184.

19 *D.I.*, p. 185.
20 *Ibid.*, p. 186.
21 *Ibid.*, p. 203.
22 *Ibid.*, p. 191.
23 *Ibid.*, p. 192.
24 *Ibid.*, p. 194.
25 *Ibid.*, p. 207.
26 *Ibid.*, p. 215.
27 *Ibid.*, p. 219.
28 Hegel in the next century made a distinction between civil society and the State.
29 *D.I.*, p. 221.
30 *Ibid.*
31 *Ibid.*, p. 228.
32 *Ibid.*
33 *Ibid.*, p. 174.
34 *Ibid.*, p. 238.
35 *Ibid.*
36 *Ibid.*, p. 245.
37 *D.P.*, p. 253.
38 *Ibid.*
39 *Ibid.*, p. 254.
40 *Ibid.*, p. 255.
41 *Ibid.*, p. 260.
42 *Ibid.*, p. 258.
43 *Ibid.*, p. 259.
44 *Ibid.*
45 *Ibid.*, p. 253.
46 *Ibid.*, p. 256.
47 *Ibid.*, p. 286.
48 *D.I.*, p. 183.
49 *É.*, II, p. 61.
50 *Ibid.*, IV, p. 173.
51 *D.I.*, p. 197, note 2.
52 *É.*, IV, p. 174.
53 *Œuvres*, 1865, III, p. 647.
54 *D.I.*, p. 198.
55 *Ibid.*, p. 199.
56 *É.*, IV, p. 174.
57 *Ibid.*, p. 184.
58 *Œuvres*, 1865, III, p. 64.
59 *É.*, II, p. 61.
60 *D.I.*, p. 199.
61 *É.*, IV, p. 173.
62 *Ibid.*, p. 215.

63 *Ibid.*, p. 173.
64 *D.A.*, pp. 153–4.
65 *É.*, IV, p. 252.
66 *Ibid.*, p. 253.
67 *Ibid.*, p. 249.
68 *Ibid.*, p. 237.
69 *Ibid.*, p. 239.
70 *Ibid.*
71 *Ibid.*, p. 242.
72 *Ibid.*, p. 197.
73 *S.C.*, II, 3, p. 25.

CHAPTER FOUR

1 *S.C.*, I, 3, p. 5.
2 *Ibid.*
3 *Ibid.*, p. 8.
4 *Ibid.*, I, 6, p. 14.
5 *Ibid.*, p. 15.
6 *Ibid.*, I, 8, p. 19.
7 *Ibid.*
8 *Ibid.*, p. 18.
9 *Ibid.*, p. 19.
10 *Ibid.*
11 *Ibid.*, I, 7, p. 17.
12 *Ibid.*, III, 18, p. 89.
13 *Ibid.*
14 *Ibid.*, II, 1, p. 22.
15 *Ibid.*, III, 15, p. 83.
16 *Ibid.*, II, 3, p. 25.
17 *Ibid.*, II, 6, p. 34.
18 *Ibid.*
19 We may compare the Scholastic doctrine that, whatever a man wills, he wills *sub specie boni*.
20 *S.C.*, II, 3, p. 25.
21 *Ibid.*, p. 26.
22 *Ibid.*, IV, 8, p. 116.
23 *Ibid.*, II, 3, pp. 25–6.
24 *Ibid.*, IV, 2, p. 94.
25 *Ibid.*
26 *Ibid.*, I, 4, p. 10.
27 *Ibid.*, IV, 2, p. 93.
28 *Ibid.*, I, 7, p. 18.
29 *Ibid.*, IV, 2, p. 94.

30 *S.C.*, III, 1, p. 50.

31 *Ibid.*

32 *Ibid.*, III, 18, p. 89.

33 *Ibid.*, III, 1, p. 53.

34 *Ibid.*

35 *Ibid.*

36 The word tyrannical is here used in its ordinary sense. In Rousseau's technical language, however, a tyrant is one who usurps the royal authority, while a despot is one who usurps the sovereign power. 'Thus the tyrant cannot be a despot, but the despot is always a tyrant' (*S.C.*, III, 10, p. 77).

37 *S.C.*, III, 9, p. 73.

38 *Ibid.*, III, 3, p. 57.

39 *Ibid.*, III, 4, p. 59.

40 *Ibid.*, III, 5, pp. 60–1.

41 *Ibid.*, III, 11, p. 77.

42 *Ibid.*, III, 15, p. 83.

43 *Ibid.*, I, 8, p. 19.

44 Cf. *Philosophy of Right*, translated by T. M. Knox, Oxford, 1942, pp. 156–7.

45 *S.C.*, IV, 7, p. 111.

CHAPTER FIVE

1 This statement is true as regards the direct influence of pietism on Thomasius and his followers; for it tended to remove religion and theology from the sphere of philosophical reflection. But the statement stands in need of qualification. For example, some knowledge of pietism is necessary, as will be seen in the next volume, for an understanding of the development of Hegel's thought.

2 One must add that Wolff's division of philosophy had a considerable influence on subsequent Scholastic manuals and text-books.

3 On this matter cf. Gilson's *Being and Some Philosophers* (second edition, corrected and enlarged, Toronto, 1952).

4 *Prolegomena*, 2.

5 Section 6.

6 *Aesthetics*, section 14.

7 *Ibid.*, section 1; cf. also *Prolegomena*, section 1.

8 *Meditations*, section 9.

9 *Aesthetic*, translated by D. Ainslie, p. 218.

10 *Ibid.*, p. 219.

11 The principle is applied by Crusius in this way, for example. The non-existence of the world is thinkable. Therefore it must have been created. Therefore there is a God.

CHAPTER SIX

1 It was his concern with education which made Frederick refuse to allow the publication in his territories of Pope Clement XIV's Bull suppressing the Society of Jesus. He did not wish the schools maintained by the Jesuits to be dissolved.

2 Section 1.

3 *Education of the Human Race*, section 17.

4 *Ibid.*, section 86.

5 *Ibid.*, sections 94–8.

CHAPTER SEVEN

1 What Hamann says is that at the beginning every phenomenon of Nature was for man a sign, a symbol, a guarantee of a divine communication, a living word. Language was a natural

response to the perception of Nature as a divine word.

2 *Dichtung und Wahrheit*, III, 12.

3 This work, which was utilized by Herder in his own *Metacritique*, was not published during Hamann's lifetime. It was begun in 1781, the year in which the *Critique of Pure Reason* was published.

4 The fifth volume, dated 1803, appeared in 1804 after Herder's death. The sixth volume (1804) was also published posthumously.

5 In his later years Herder became estranged from Goethe, who found the former afflicted by an 'ill-tempered spirit of contradiction'. As for Schiller, the other great representative of German classicism, he was never particularly enamoured of Herder and, as an admirer of Kant, he was offended by Herder's attack on the critical philosophy, which attack, indeed, was unfashionable and helped to isolate its author.

6 Jacobi's activity continued into the early part of the nineteenth century.

CHAPTER EIGHT

1 1451b, 5–8.
2 On the meaning of this statement, as far as poetry is concerned, see Vol. 1, Part II, pp. 102, 103.
3 *Enneads*, III, 2.
4 See Vol. 2, Part I, pp. 100–5.
5 *Dessein général.*
6 *Discourse*, Part II, 13.

7 *Ibid.*, Part III, 1.
8 *Ibid.*, Part III, 7.
9 Muratori's great work was the *Rerum italicarum scriptores.*
10 In 1723 Vico competed for, but failed to obtain, the chair of civil law.
11 *Opere*, I, 136; Bari, 1929.
12 *The Autobiography of Giambattista Vico*, translated by M. H. Fisch and T. G. Bergin, Cornell U.P., 1944, p. 138.
13 *Autobiography*, p. 155.
14 *Opere*, III, 5.
15 *Opere*, IV, 2, 164.
16 B. Croce, *Aesthetic*, translated by D. Ainslie, London, 2nd edition, 1929, p. 220.

CHAPTER NINE

1 *Avant-propos.*
2 *Nouvelles considérations sur l'histoire.*
3 For further information about Lessing, the reader is referred back to Chapter VI, pp. 147–53.
4 Pp. 160–69, to which the reader is referred for a further account of Herder.
5 Preface, XIII, p. 6. References to the *Ideas* are, by volume and page, to the edition of Herder's works by A. Suphan, Berlin, 1877–1913.
6 XIII, p. 102.
7 *Ibid.*, p. 162.
8 *Ibid.*, p. 183.
9 *Ibid.*, p. 182.
10 *Ibid.*, p. 340.
11 *Ibid.*, p. 383.
12 XIV, p. 85.
13 Goethe consulted Herder as an authority on Greek culture.
14 XIV, p. 202.

15 XIV, p. 144.

16 Ibid., p. 213.

17 He is more appreciative, for example, of Frederick the Great's measures of reform. And he at first intended to write optimistically of the French Revolution, though the appearance of the Terror led him to omit these sections.

18 XVII, p. 138.

19 In connection with this phase Herder speaks of the world-spirit (Weltgeist), a term which recurs with Hegel.

CHAPTER TEN

1 3, 5; W., II, p. 163. References to volume and page, preceded by the letter W., are always to the edition of Kant's Works by the Prussian Academy of Sciences. Gesammelte Schriften, 22 vols. Berlin, 1902–42.

2 3, 1; W., II, pp. 154-5.

3 Preface; W., II, p. 66.

4 In an essay on the concept of negative quantity (1763) Kant had already explicitly rejected the notion that the mathematical method should be used in philosophy, though he also insisted that mathematical truths can be philosophically relevant and fertile (W., II, pp. 167-8).

5 Enquiry, 1, 1; W., II, p. 277.

6 Ibid.

7 Ibid.

8 Metaphysics is described by Kant as 'nothing else but philosophy about the ultimate principles of our knowledge' (Enquiry, 2; W., II, p. 283).

9 Ibid.

10 Enquiry, 1, 4; W., II, p. 283.

11 Enquiry, 2; W., II, p. 286.

12 Enquiry, 4, 2; W., II, pp. 299-300.

13 Ibid., p. 299.

14 Dreams, 1, 2; W., II, p. 329.

15 Dreams, 1, 3; W., II, p. 342.

16 Dreams, 2, 3; W., II, p. 369.

17 Ibid., p. 373.

18 W., II, p. 378.

19 W., II, p. 383.

20 On the Form and Principles, 3, 14, 5; W., II, p. 400.

21 On the Form and Principles, 3, 15, D; W., II, p. 403.

22 On the Form and Principles, 2, 5; W., II, p. 394.

23 On the Form and Principles, 2, 4; W., II, p. 392.

24 On the Form and Principles, 2, 10; W., II, p. 396.

25 On the Form and Principles, 2, 8; W., II, p. 395.

26 On the Form and Principles, 5, 23; W., II, p. 410.

27 Ibid., p. 411.

28 On the Form and Principles, 2, 9; W., II, p. 396.

29 W., x, p. 97.

30 Ibid., p. 98.

31 W., II, p. 395, and x, p. 98.

32 See W., x, p. 123.

33 See W., x, p. 122.

34 W., x, p. 130.

35 Ibid.

36 Kant's terminology is still fluid. He speaks of 'the pure concepts of the understanding' (die reinen Verstandesbegriffe), of 'intellectual presentations' (intellectuale [sic] Vorstellungen),

and of 'the axioms of the pure reason' (*die axiomata der reinen Vernunft*).

37 W., x, p. 132.

38 On history Kant had published in 1784 his *Idea for a General History from a Cosmopolitan Point of View* (*Idee zu einer allgemeinen Geschichte in weltbürgerlicher Absicht*).

OTHER IMAGE BOOKS

THE IMITATION OF CHRIST – Thomas à Kempis. Edited with an Introduction by Harold C. Gardiner, S.J. (D17) – $1.25

ST. FRANCIS OF ASSISI – G. K. Chesterton (D50) – $1.25

VIPER'S TANGLE – François Mauriac. A novel of evil and redemption (D51) – 95¢

THE CITY OF GOD – St. Augustine. Edited by Vernon J. Bourke. Introduction by Étienne Gilson. Specially abridged (D59) – $2.45

RELIGION AND THE RISE OF WESTERN CULTURE – Christopher Dawson (D64) – $1.25

JESUS AND HIS TIMES – Henri Daniel-Rops (D67b) – $1.25

THE LITTLE FLOWERS OF ST. FRANCIS – Translated by Raphael Brown (D69) – $1.75

THE IDEA OF A UNIVERSITY – John Henry Cardinal Newman. Introduction by G. N. Shuster (D75) – $1.65

DARK NIGHT OF THE SOUL – St. John of the Cross. Edited and translated by E. Allison Peers (D78) – $1.25

THE PILLAR OF FIRE – Karl Stern. A psychiatrist's spiritual journey from Judaism to Catholicism (D83) – 95¢

A POPULAR HISTORY OF THE REFORMATION – Philip Hughes (D92) – $1.25

THE CONFESSIONS OF ST. AUGUSTINE – Translated with an Introduction by John K. Ryan (D101) – $1.75

THE THIRD REVOLUTION: A Study of Psychiatry and Religion – Dr. Karl Stern (D113) – 95¢

A HISTORY OF PHILOSOPHY: VOLUME 1 – GREECE AND ROME (2 Parts) – Frederick Copleston, S.J. (D134a, D134b) – $1.75 ea.

A HISTORY OF PHILOSOPHY: VOLUME 2 – MEDIAEVAL PHILOSOPHY (2 Parts) – Frederick Copleston, S.J. Part I – Augustine to Bonaventure. Part II – Albert the Great to Duns Scotus (D135a, D135b) – $1.45 ea.

A HISTORY OF PHILOSOPHY: VOLUME 3 – LATE MEDIAEVAL AND RENAISSANCE PHILOSOPHY (2 Parts) – Frederick Copleston, S.J. Part I – Ockham to the Speculative Mystics. Part II – The Revival of Platonism to Suárez (D136a, D136b) – $1.45 ea.

A HISTORY OF PHILOSOPHY: VOLUME 4 – MODERN PHILOSOPHY: Descartes to Leibniz – Frederick Copleston, S.J. (D137) – $1.75

THE MODERN DANCE

JOSÉ LIMÓN

ANNA SOKOLOW

ERICK HAWKINS

DONALD McKAYLE

ALWIN NIKOLAIS

PAULINE KONER

PAUL TAYLOR

THE
MODERN
DANCE

Seven Statements of Belief

EDITED AND WITH AN INTRODUCTION BY *Selma Jeanne Cohen*

Wesleyan University Press, Middletown, Connecticut

The article by Anna Sokolow was first printed, under a different title, in *Dance Magazine,* July 1965; that by Paul Taylor in the same journal, February 1966. That by José Limón appeared, in somewhat different form, in the *Juilliard Review Annual* for 1965. The courtesy of the editors in assigning copyrights in these articles is gratefully acknowledged.

Library of Congress Catalog Card Number: 66–14663

Manufactured in the United States of America

First paperback edition 1969

Contents

Illustrations

THE MODERN DANCE

Introduction:

THE CATERPILLAR'S QUESTION

WHEN I asked these choreographers to write about the modern dance, I anticipated the possibility of their feeling somewhat as Alice did when the Caterpillar took the hookah out of its mouth and addressed her in a languid, sleepy voice, saying: "Who are *you*?" To which Alice replied: "I — I hardly know, Sir, just at present — at least I know who I *was* when I got up this morning, but I think I must have changed several times since then."

In the lifetimes of these artists, the modern dance has changed. All of them have been instrumental in bringing about the changes, and all of them have changed themselves — some radically — from what they were when their careers began. The modern dance was once a fairly homogeneous entity. Not that all its exponents were alike — in fact, they gloried in their diversity — but they quite obviously shared many principles of belief. Today, the situation is far less clear. The ranks are not only diversified, but divided within themselves. So the modern dance has been several things in the course of time, and seems to be several more things right now. After a bit of thought, I began to wonder if all these various manifestations should — or even could — be brought together under a single name. However, the term is used, and perhaps I should at least attempt to find a thread of unity among its many, and apparently conflicting, uses.

In the course of compiling this book, I deliberately refrained from asking any of the choreographers to define the modern dance. Why make them uncomfortably self-conscious? As I had hoped, however, the definitions cropped up, quite naturally, in the course of their discussions. Also, as I had expected, they were all different.

3

What each did, of course, was define what the modern dance meant to him. At this point, the temptation was to say: "Well, good. The modern dance, then, is whatever it is, and all that it is, to its various exponents. A many-splendored thing. And let's let it go at that." That would have been easy. But basically unsatisfactory.

Then there was the choice of any number of previous definitions — all clear, pat, ready to be quoted. Yet no one of them seemed to cover the present situation. Barefoot dance? No, sometimes they wear shoes. Expressive dance? No, some of these choreographers are vehemently anti-expression.

So then, another possibility: a definition so flexible as to include them all — easily, comfortably. "Freedom from traditional rules" came most quickly to mind. But freedom from what tradition? Is any non-balletic choreography modern dance? And the ignorant are free. Does that make them modern? Apparently, none of these solutions would be of much practical value.

The only chance of finding an answer seemed to be the one implied by Alice, who admitted that she knew what she had been. By recalling what the modern dance had been when it started and by tracing it through its various evolutions, we may get a perspective on what it is today. If not a complete definition, at least a perspective . . .

In 1933, John Martin (who was then, and would be for many years to come, the dance critic of *The New York Times*) stated that the modern dance was a point of view. It was movement devised not for spectacular display, as was the ballet; not for self-expression, as was the interpretive dance current at that time; but it was movement made "to externalize personal, authentic experience." The ballet aesthetic, he contended, was concerned with visual beauty rather than emotion; when the ballet did deal with emotion, it did so in a manner so remote, so abstracted from realistic feeling that its creators in no way expected, or even desired, the audience to respond to its emotional content. The interpretive dance, while it dealt with experience, was unconcerned with its communication; the expression was an end in itself (therapeutic, we would call it today), which made it essentially untheatrical. The modern dance, on the other hand, externalized — projected, communicated — an emotion that was not only personal but "authentic." The choreographer felt the emotion deeply, but — further — was convinced that, by revealing his experience, he was also revealing a basic truth.

For America, the story had started at the turn of the century, when Isadora Duncan and Ruth St. Denis each began groping toward a style of dance that would allow a freedom of expression they could not find in the contemporary ballet. Both objected to the rigid formality and artificiality of the classic technique, to the superficiality of the themes it was using, to the triviality of its current aims. Duncan found the answer in natural movement, the unrestrained response to nature and to art as she felt the ancient Greeks had conceived it. Her dances were sometimes lyrical, sometimes heroic; always imbued with her vision of the Good and the Beautiful. St. Denis turned to the Orient, where the religious view of dance gave support to her concern with the spiritual values of the art. Later, with her husband Ted Shawn, she explored less exotic areas, but always with the aim of ennobling the concept of dance.

In the late twenties, however, the nature of the outlook was utterly changed when two renegades from Denishawn — Martha Graham and Doris Humphrey — rejected the sweetness-and-light approach of their predecessors. They created dance works with a toughness of fibre that had been bred — far from ancient Greece and the old Orient — by an age of skyscrapers, labor problems, and neuroses. Where the choreographers of the first years of the century had turned to past civilizations, aiming to revitalize the dance by infusing it with the enlightened aura of earlier cultures, those of the twenties stood rooted in the present. But it was a present colored by the ideas of *The Golden Bough,* by the writings of Freud and T. S. Eliot, by the paintings of Picasso and the music of Bartók. They too looked to the past, but to a more distant past — to the era of pre-history, to the time when man, uninhibited by arbitrary codes of mores, had expressed the full range of his primitive instincts. If the attack of Graham and Humphrey was more violent, it was because they had

5

more un-doing to accomplish. Both generations were concerned with externalizing personal, authentic experience. They differed radically, however, in their ideas of what kind of experience was important.

The second generation of the modern dance had to reject the idioms not only of classical ballet but also of Duncan and Denishawn. In none of their predecessors could they find a vehicle for the expression of contemporary ideas, and they asserted that dance could be a vehicle for the expression of such ideas. Doris Humphrey remarked then that the dancer should not be "concerned entirely with the graceful line and the fine, animal ease" that technical study provided; "he should also be concerned with his existence as a human being played upon by life, bursting with opinions and compulsions to express them." In principle, the ballet abstracted, idealized, the prowess and beauty of the body; not "played upon by life," but playing on life. That was fine — for the ballet. The heroism and nobility of Duncan and Denishawn were also very fine — for them. Now all this was seen as inadequate for an art that wanted to be significantly creative in the contemporary world.

Martha Graham wrote: "I do not want to be a tree, a flower, or a wave. In a dancer's body, we as audience must see ourselves; not the imitated behavior of everyday actions, not the phenomena of nature, not exotic creatures from another planet, but something of the miracle that is a human being, motivated, disciplined, concentrated."

The classical ballet could never have been accused of imitating everyday actions. As the ballet saw it, the miraculous aspect of the human being was its potential for dominion over the forces of nature — over its own weight, in the exultant leap; over gravity, in the joyously sustained balance; over its natural stiffness and awkwardness, in the high extension of the leg, effortlessly attained. To Denishawn, the exotic creature was the appealing character — the Egyptian or Hindu goddess, who shed about her the pure light of Truth. For Duncan, it was a simple process of taking what was best and most beautiful of the natural man.

The second generation found it impossible to settle for only the good. They acknowledged that there was love in man. Yes. But there were also hate and fear and jealousy. They spoke of all these with intensity and passion. The sweetness and light, they saw, were beautiful. But so were the depths of terror and hostility. Because they were true. And because they made man's achievement of love more difficult, more significant, more — miraculous.

The miracle was there; it had always been there; it was real. People had only forgotten. The manners and gentility of the Victorian age still cast their obscuring shadow over the emotions that were not mentioned in polite society. Now the modern dance choreographers felt the time had come to break through the veneer to reveal the terrible and wonderful beauty that lay beneath it. In Martha Graham's words, "to make apparent once again the inner hidden realities behind the accepted symbols."

They had to be extreme. They made their point by shock, though they did not set out to shock. They simply had to discard all the trappings of the familiar traditions to make their audience see with fresh eyes. By eliminating the decorative, the superficial, the glib polish, they aimed to dig down to the essence of significant movement; movement that had long been disguised by distortion and ornament; movement that — when laid bare — would be recognized as the symbol of long-hidden realities.

Martha Graham and Doris Humphrey started by looking for basic sources of movement, sources related to the primary instincts of the human animal. The ballet had used as its source the decorous positions of the dances of the courts of seventeenth-century European royalty. For Denishawn, it had been the stylization of the dances of Eastern temples. Duncan alone had apparently found a completely natural source; she traced all movement to the solar plexus. She herself had used this point instinctively, unerringly. From it she had derived movements of joy and grief, but there were other emotions she had not touched — guilt, anguish, remorse. These, apparently, were foreign to her nature, and she had no need to express them. The modern dance, however, needed them, and it needed a language of movement to embody them. So the 1920's started over — from the beginning.

For Martha Graham, it began with the act of breath — the start of life itself. Allowing the body to follow the natural ebb and flow of breathing, she watched what happened to the shape of the torso as it contracted in exhalation, expanded in inhalation. The next step was to intensify the dynamics of the act, taking the contraction as a sudden, spasmodic impulse, which could send the body into a fall, into a turn, into — as it evolved — any number of motions. It was a primitive use of energy — utterly new as an initiator of dance movement. Dramatically, it provided a basically natural but excitingly theatrical means of portraying the human being in terror, in agony, in ecstasy.

The approach of Doris Humphrey was equally basic, though totally different. Rather than turning to movement within the body, she viewed the body in relation to space. She saw movement as generated by effort to resist the pull of gravity — gravity as symbolic of all the forces that threaten man's balance, his security. She too discovered a principle of duality; for her it was the contrast of fall and recovery. Where Graham depicted the conflict of man within himself, Humphrey was concerned with the conflict of man with his environment. In both approaches, drama was inherent. But it was a kind of drama the public was unaccustomed to seeing. It was brutally honest; it was not pretty; it was not "nice."

Everything about the Graham and Humphrey productions was uncompromising. The time is now remembered as the "long woolens" period. No pretty costumes, just plain dresses of unadorned black jersey; no pink slippers, just bare feet; no elaborate scenery, just a functionally lighted cyclorama (of course the modern dancers could not have afforded fancy trimmings even if they had wanted them; their homes were the basements and attic walk-ups of Greenwich Village). The movements that derived from the primitive sources were as unornamented and unornamental as the costumes of the dancers. No graceful arms to enhance the visual picture; no brilliant technical feats. Instead of lyrical flow, there were sharply percussive thrusts. Instead of soaring with ease into the air, the dancers stamped on the bare floor with their bare feet. When they did jump, they jumped like creatures of the earth, fighting their way out of the mud. The hidden realities were apparent, all right. A lot of people didn't like them at all.

This made the life of the modern dance choreographers anything but easy. Boos and jeers are unpleasant to hear, and they have the further disadvantage of keeping potential ticket-buyers away from the box office. In time, however, largely through sheer persistence — though the persuasive powers of Mr. Martin in the pages of *The Times* helped a great deal — the public resistance gradually weakened. Not that the modern dance became popular; it has never been that. But it ceased to shock so much. Freud was no longer being ridiculed either. Gradually certain facts of art, as of life, were being at least recognized as inescapable realities.

At this point, the subsidence of hostility held great significance for the modern dance choreographers. It meant they no longer had to hammer at stubborn minds with reiterations of basic concepts. It meant they could explore, develop, apply those concepts to still further depths of experience. Great works had been created from the beginning. Now, after the initial period of struggle, the masterpieces began to flow.

There were ventures into primitive ritual, Americana, Greek myth, and social commentary. There were excursions into pure dance, with no overt dramatic content, that nevertheless achieved strikingly dramatic effects through rhythmic and spatial designs. There were adventures with structure — with stream-of-consciousness continuity, with dance punctuated by lines of spoken poetry, with the intricate weavings of allegory. Musical accompaniments ranged from silence, to Bach, to commissioned scores by experimental composers. Costume and décor were reinstated in fresh ways, with the use of simple but suggestive properties; nothing was there for purely decorative effect.

In time, the movement vocabulary itself was enormously expanded, becoming less relentless in its pounding earthiness, allowing softness — even tenderness — to emerge. For these too were part of man's essential nature. They had been submerged before only

9

because the break with the past had had to be unmitigated in order to achieve the desired impact. Now, with the impact accomplished, the choreographers could safely broaden their palettes. Martha Graham and Doris Humphrey went from one revelation to another.

Yet the fever pitch of revolutionary fervor was passing. And with it was going that special sense of urgency, of combative aggressiveness, of excitement, that is engendered by revolutions. It was good to be rid of the jeering; the cheers were no less strong. Yet, without heated opposition, the triumphs were not quite so dazzling. As the masterpieces continued to appear, it was less necessary to fight in their defense. Though the revolution had been hard, it had been more stimulating.

To come to the modern dance in the course of this period of assimilation (as did all the writers in this book) has been, in some ways, more difficult than to enter the lists at the beginning. Faced with an idiom that was still new and working with choreographers who were still developing themselves, the novice was easily tempted to fall in line behind his elders. With the achievements of the leaders well in mind, the young choreographer had on the one hand a splendid precedent for innovation; on the other, a strong deterrent. It had been done; it did not need to be done again.

Besides, there were plenty of other problems to occupy the new generation. There were problems of refining the techniques, of making the dancers stronger and more versatile, of expanding theatricality and thematic range. There was plenty to do without trying to set out on a completely new road. It was really too soon anyway. The revolution was not that far away.

Looking back now, we can see that, actually, tremendous developments have taken place in the forty years since Graham and Humphrey broke the ties to Denishawn. The changes, however, occurred gradually; so they have seemed less drastic, less epoch-making in their repercussions. And there has been nothing so radical as the discovery of another new source of natural movement or of a completely different area of drama. Though the implications of the original concepts have been enormously extended, they have been extended within the framework of the thoughts of the founders. Remaining today are the ideas that initiated the American modern dance, but they are now applied in the context of a world that — while still dominated by the thinking of Freud — has now felt the impact of beatniks, astronauts, and the population explosion. To ignore these would be to reject the principles of the founders; they were vitally reality-oriented. Though some of the themes have altered and the technique has grown, the basic concept has not changed. The modern dance is still involved with the communication of personal, authentic experience.

However, this cannot be applied to all the choreographers now associated in the minds of the public with the modern dance; it cannot be applied even to all the choreographers represented in this volume. For the modern dance has not grown exclusively in the directions laid by its founders. Along the line of development, off-shoots have appeared, and their products are so different as to force us to question whether or not they really belong to the original shoot at all. Taller or shorter, Alice in Wonderland was still Alice — in the minds of her readers, at least, if not in her own. Yet this is simply not the case with the modern dance today. It has nothing to do with just the passage of time. Whether compared to the work of either the early or the late Graham or Humphrey, the new forms of choreography seem to have little, perhaps no, relation to what appears to be the main line of continuity in the modern dance.

What is so different? Well — just about everything. Gone are the movements derived from contraction and release, from fall and recovery, or from anything much resembling them. Gone, too, are the concern with terror and anguish and ecstasy. The new choreographers take their ideas from other sources — from chance juxtaposition, from serial music and action painting, from the current concepts of "happenings" and the theatre of the absurd. As for expressive purpose, they have none, save to say that the proper subject of dancing is dance. Why, they say, should we ask dancing to mean something beyond itself, which is so beautiful and exciting by itself? For the early modern dance, emotional motivation had been

11

essential; it was at once the cause and the aim of movement invention. With the new choreographers, emotional motivation has been deliberately eliminated from the scheme of composition, while other factors — chance, mathematics, musical or pictorial structure — have taken its place.

Even to an uninitiated public, the early modern dance was patently recognizable as an utterly personal and individual expression of deeply felt experience. The new choreographers counter everything about this. They are concerned with the movement rather than with the personality performing it, and they don't want the dance to express anything — especially feeling. The only experience in dance, they assert, should be the experience of the qualities of movement — fleet, spacious, soft, energetic, or whatever. But not emotion. That only takes the attention of the audience away from the essential thing, which is the kinetic image. Feeling is out; drama is out.

This had led the new choreographers to be accused of depersonalizing the dance, a verdict they answer in various ways: that it is impossible to depersonalize an art that uses the human body as its instrument; that they are seeking a transcendent form of identity; that it is depersonalized, but so what? Twenty years ago even the severest opponent of the modern dance would not have made such an accusation. If anything, he would have found the choreography embarrassingly personal.

Why did this new movement spring into being? The choreographers themselves assert that the modern dance was becoming so dramatic that it was turning into a kind of pantomime. The dance had lost sight of its true nature. Movement was no longer seen for its own beautiful sake; it was merely being used as a means to tell a story, and by such employment it was degraded. Their mission, therefore, is to bring the dance back to its true province by making it an end in itself. In this endeavor, they acknowledge the influence of trends toward abstraction, mechanization, and randomness in the other arts — this is the direction of our time, and after all they are modern. However, such concepts seem utterly remote from the original point of the modern dance. Can these new choreographers still be identified with the idiom of Duncan and Denishawn, of Graham and Humphrey?

Martha Graham had spoken of the function of dance in making apparent again the hidden realities behind the accepted symbols. To do this, an art must create new symbols, and in the beginning they are strange, uncomfortably unfamiliar — unacceptable. With time, however, the eye and the mind adjust to them; they become accepted. This is desirable, of course, since the point is to get the viewer to acknowledge the reality, the truth, behind the symbols. Yet, in the course of the process, the symbols lose their power. It is the shock that makes them work. They have to startle us into awareness, for it is only then that we are compelled to probe their meaning and discover what they have to tell us. The accepted symbol does not challenge us; we take it for granted.

When a symbol becomes accepted, an art may take either one of two courses in order to retain its vitality. The artist may keep the original symbol but develop and use it in fresh ways. Or he may discard it altogether, replacing it with a new one. Change the symbol he must, but he can do so either in degree or in kind. Which path he takes will depend on his view of reality: whether he agrees essentially with his predecessors but feels that areas of their vision remain to be explored; or whether he is convinced that the vision needs not simply extension but displacement. The modern dance choreographers of today are divided among themselves because some have chosen to explore, others to displace. Though the latter way is, to be sure, the more striking, the effect of the former is never so complacent as that of the reiteration of a comfortably familiar image. The modern dance choreographer is always concerned with the unacceptable symbol, the one that startles us into awareness. The pressure may be subtle or it may be obvious, but it is always there.

If the pressure is absent, the artist relinquishes his allegiance to the modern dance. If it shocks us into something less than awareness of realities — if the pressure is exerted only arbitrarily, to display ego or to attract the crowds — it does not belong to the modern dance. If, on the other hand, it permeates the creations of a so-called ballet choreographer (and the works of Antony Tudor, Jerome Robbins, and some of George Balanchine come immediately to mind), then those creations are modern. Theoretically, the ballet is opposed to the modern dance because it deliberately uses accepted symbols to depict an established ideology. When it ceases to do so, the categorical name becomes meaningless.

This has nothing to do with value judgments. A ballet is not bad because it employs accepted symbols; it merely serves a different function, and it may or may not serve that function well. A modern dance work may fail too. Many have. This does not invalidate the concept of function that identifies it. For it can be identified.

The modern dance is a point of view, an attitude toward the function of art in the contemporary world. As that world changes, the modern dance will change, for the symbols will again — as they become acceptable — lose their power to evoke the hidden realities. They will again have to be recharged, revitalized; even demolished and re-created anew in order to serve their function. Unless this happens, the modern dance is not modern — it is dead.

The modern dance is an art of iconoclasts.

EACH choreographer represented in this book was asked to divide his contribution into two parts. First, he was to set forth, generally, his ideas on the modern dance. Second, he was to describe what he would do if he were given a commission to create a dance under the most (unrealistically) favorable conditions — any number of dancers, any kind of music, costumes, etc. Also (most unrealistic) he was to assume that he had unlimited funds at his disposal. There was only one restriction: his dance had to deal with the theme of the Prodigal Son.

Here, then, are seven essays on the modern dance. And seven descriptions of dances on the theme of the Prodigal Son.

José Limón

AN AMERICAN ACCENT

I

THE ballet as an art is an old and established tradition, not the least of the many splendors of European civilization. One cannot fully savor the essence of European culture without recognizing the importance of the ballet, for nations make themselves known through their dances. We gain a more profound insight into the soul of Spain, of India, of Cambodia, Bali, China, Korea, and Japan from their dances than from any of their other arts.

Italy, the mother of the ballet; France, its nursemaid; and Imperial Russia, which saw it to its glittering maturity, reveal themselves to the world in every movement, gesture, and configuration of their prodigious creature. The great Medici were not only statesmen, rulers, and patrons of the arts; they were connoisseurs and lovers of the *ballo*. One of their daughters, the illustrious Catherine, transplanted it to the court of France, where — amidst the turmoil of a savage century — it grew and flourished, elegant and serene. Subsequently the *Roi Soleil* gave it the prestige of his august participation. The Italian immigrant was now as royal as the dynasty of the House of Bourbon, as French as Versailles, and henceforth its code of movement, its vocabulary, was to be expressed in the French tongue.

The Imperial Romanovs, in transforming Russia from an Asiatic despotism into a state with the outward trappings of a Western nation, took care that the ballet, that most Western of the arts, should certify and confirm the new status. So superbly did the ballet flourish in the climate of the Muscovite empire — favored by Imperial patronage and the astonishing aptitude of the Russian temperament

17

José Limón (photo: Jack Mitchell)

and physique — that before long it surpassed the product of the regions of its origins. The formidable Imperial Russian Ballet came to be to the nation what armies, scientific achievements, and ancient ruins were to other nations. The Russian Ballet became the envy and wonder of the Western world. It became not only an art but a *lingua franca* of urbanity and civilization.

Yet it is a curious property of human accomplishment that — when seemingly at its zenith — it contains the seeds of the dissolution that could destroy it. It was at this high noon of the popularity of the ballet that an American girl rose in the cultural firmament and incredibly seemed to eclipse its radiance. Isadora Duncan, a rebel, an iconoclast was — like all revolutionaries — bold and uncompromising in her attack. She declared that the ballet was decadent, effete, ugly, artificial; that its training and technique, its turned-out positions, its rigidities, its obsessive use of the pointes, were odious, distorted, and against all nature. It made the human entity into a mechanical puppet, moving jerkily from one affected pose to another to the accompaniment of execrable music. With peerless audacity, she flung out her accusations and defiance, not only in the capitals of the West but in that holy of holies of the ballet itself — St. Petersburg.

It is dangerous for an art, however "classical," to become so rigid, so fossilized, as to lose the freshness, resiliency, and vigor of its original impulse. The art of the ballet during this era, in Western Europe and especially in Russia, seems to have fallen into such a state as to justify the ardent accusations of Isadora Duncan. Where the Parisians, with their cynical predilection for *joie de vivre,* made of their ballet a toy — a *petit rien,* a bagatelle — the Russians, with a heavy, despotic hand, transformed it into an instrument of the Imperial order — as were the church, the apparatus of government, and the armed forces. And they made it, like these, impervious to new ideas and to change.

Duncan — a scandal, a danger, and a delight — split the artistic world in half. There were those who saw her as a crude amateur, a shameless exhibitionist with no technique; there were those who

José Limón: rehearsing Sally Stackhouse, Louis Falco

sensed in her a challenge, a revelation, and a portent for the future of the dance. It was fortunate for this future that artists of the caliber of Michel Fokine accepted the disturbing challenge to stagnation. So came into being, away from Czarist authority, in the freer ambient of the West, the glories of the Ballets Russes.

It has been said that the modern dance is a temporary phase — that it has not sent down roots like the ballet and cannot, like it, endure. Yet the modern dance began with Duncan shortly after 1900. Now, in 1966, one would have to be myopic not to see that it is far from finished. An art that has produced such figures as Ruth St. Denis, Ted Shawn, Martha Graham, Doris Humphrey, Charles Weidman, Helen Tamiris, Hanya Holm, Pauline Koner, Anna Sokolow, Alwin Nikolais, Sophie Maslow, Pearl Lang, and Merce Cunningham, and can look to the vigor of a new generation, has a more than fair prospect of enduring. Especially when its principles exist and flourish, not only in its own milieu but in the works of the leading ballet companies. Let us make no mistake about it: if by "modern dance" one means a state of mind, a cognizance of the necessity of the art of the dance to come to terms with our time, then that art cannot be relegated to the position of a merely transitory influence. The modern dance is here to stay, whether it is performed barefoot or *sur les pointes*.

Modern dance is not a "popular art." It is not suitable, as is the traditional ballet, to advertise automobiles, vacuum cleaners, rugs, or hair dyes in newspapers or magazines or on television. A pretty ballerina in a pert tutu and pink toe shoes is a much more fetching sales pitch than a vision of a barefoot dancer in a species of ecstasy or suffering. On the other hand, talented — or sometimes merely clever — choreographers have taken the modern dance and adapted it to serve very successfully in musical shows, television, and films, in much the same manner that adaptations of Debussy, Bartók, and Schönberg have found their way into popular songs and the sound tracks of films from Hollywood. The use of serious art in any of its forms for less than its exalted purpose may be open to question. The fact remains that the multitudes who flock to musicals and movies would have had no contact with the contemporary arts (however diluted their presentation in commercial form) if they had not encountered them in this way.

I discovered, however, early in my career, after I had appeared in Broadway shows as both a dancer and a choreographer, that the commercial form and the serious form of the modern dance were incompatible. One had to devote one's self exclusively to one or the other. They could not mix. The serious dance demands an incorruptibility that makes no concessions to so-called popular taste. This has resulted in a dance that not only is not popular, it is not fashionable — it is not chic.

Yet it is a reality and a necessity of our time. Not every artist is disposed toward the Academy, great as it is in tradition and accomplishment. An American idiom is needed to say what cannot be said within the vocabulary of the European dance. This idiom, created by generations of American artists, is in essence non-academic; in principle, experimental; in practice, eclectic and inclusive.

Doris Humphrey declared that, as a young dancer, she was trained to perform — besides the traditional ballet — Spanish, Hindu, Siamese, Balinese, Japanese, Chinese, and other exotic dances. The time came, however, when she became aware that she had no identity as an American, and that all her dancing was — in effect — an impersonation, a masquerade. It was always something borrowed from Europe or the Orient. She could very well have accepted this, as so many young artists did and still do. But she suffered a deep discontent, knowing that for her this was not the way. What to do? What was there to look to as an American dance? Square dances? The American Indian? Negro jazz? Tap dancing? None of these offered a solution. Even the great Duncan, in rejecting the ballet, had reverted to the Hellenistic era. Doris Humphrey saw that the dance idiom she sought would have to be invented. Its creation would be a hard and long voyage of discovery into the inner self; its origins, its awareness and experience and capacity as an American self living

21

in the twentieth century. This dance would spring from the temper of her time.

I was fortunate in coming as a novice to her studio at the precise moment when, in company with Charles Weidman, she had embarked on this voyage of discovery. My experience with the dance had been, in a sense, similar to hers, though — by comparison — miniscule. As a child in Mexico, I had been fascinated — as any child would be — by Spanish jotas, Mexican jarabes, and Indian bailes. Later, across the border, I had seen tap dancers and ballet dancers. All this seemed interesting enough to watch, but to me it was something for girls to do. It never occurred to me as something a man would be caught dead doing. Then pure accident brought me to a performance by Harald Kreutzberg. What I saw simply and irrevocably changed my life. I saw the dance as a vision of ineffable power. A man could, with dignity and a towering majesty, dance. Not mince, prance, cavort, do "fancy dancing" or "show-off" steps. No: dance as Michelangelo's visions dance and as the music of Bach dances.

Kreutzberg had given me the illumination to see the road. But he was a German; his visions were Gothic. They became him; but I was by origin a Mexican, reared in the United States. I must find the dance to say what I had to say about what I was. In Doris Humphrey I found a master who knew that every dancer, being an individual, was an instrument unique and distinct from any other, and that in consequence this dancer must ultimately find his own dance, as she had found hers. I was instructed, stimulated, trained, criticized, encouraged to look for and find my own dance. I was not to ape my teachers. Early, I was encouraged to compose dances. I was admonished: "You will compose one hundred bad dances before you compose one good one."

I view myself as a disciple and follower of Isadora Duncan and of the American impetus as exemplified by Doris Humphrey and Martha Graham, and by their vision of the dance as an art capable of the sublimity of tragedy and the Dionysian ecstasies. I try to compose works that are involved with man's basic tragedy and the grandeur of his spirit. I want to dig beneath empty formalisms, displays of

23

The Emperor Jones: Lucas Hoving, José Limón

technical virtuosity, and the slick surface; to probe the human entity for the powerful, often crude beauty of the gesture that speaks of man's humanity. I reach for demons, saints, martyrs, apostates, fools, and other impassioned visions. I go for inspiration and instruction to the artists who reveal the passion of man to me, who exemplify supreme artistic discipline and impeccable form: to Bach, Michelangelo, Shakespeare, Goya, Schönberg, Picasso, Orozco.

With the years, I have become blind to the blandishments and seductions of the romantics. I am impatient with the sounds of the Schumanns, the Mendelssohns, the Gounods, and the Massenets. The literature of the romantics, their architecture, and their fashions arouse in me a feeling of aversion. The undisciplined and sometimes fatuous exhibition of the romantic soul in exquisite torment — whether in music, painting, or dance — leaves me cold. This saccharine and maudlin view of the human condition is to me specious and decayed. I am happy that the Cézannes, the Debussys, the Duncans, the Ibsens, the Dreisers, and the O'Neills have given us back a more adult view of our humanity.

I deplore the artist who makes of his art a withdrawal from the travail of his time; who sterilizes and dehumanizes it into empty formalism; who renounces the vision of man as perfectable, a "golden impossibility," and makes him into the shabby scarecrow of the beatniks; who forgets that the artist's function is perpetually to be the voice and conscience of his time. It was Doris Humphrey who first taught me that man is the fittest subject for choreography. And Martha Graham continues triumphantly to prove that his passions, grandeurs, and vices are the ingredients of great dance, great theatre, and great art.

It is important to preserve the traditional. It is part of our heritage, and as such it is to be cherished. But the modern idioms should be left to the individual to be kept resilient, venturesome, experimental, unhampered. The individual contribution is what gave us cultural maturity and independence from Europe in all our arts. Were it not for this, dancers in America would have remained docile

Missa Brevis: choreography, José Limón

provincials, creating nothing original. By learning to speak in an American idiom, they have enriched the world.

II

The tie between father and son is one of the most baffling of human relationships. Every man looks for his son, hoping through him to achieve his immortality. Every son rejects the father, and every father suffers for this, yet remains ultimately loving and compassionate. The wound that the son inflicts comes as a kind of blessing, a benediction. I feel poignantly the wisdom and beauty of this parable.

In composing dances, I tend to turn to my own experience. Therefore, as I did in *The Traitor,* I would set this version of the Prodigal Son in the present time. I would try to find in it something cogent and pertinent to our time. *The Traitor* was the result of my horror at the execution of two Americans, husband and wife, in peacetime, for treason and espionage against their country; and the spectacle of Russians who, in turn, abandoned their country and defected to the West.

I have been a son, and I have known the adolescent's antagonism toward his father, that instinctive hostility and resentment of his authority. I rebelled, resolving to be the exact opposite of my father. Years later — too late — I realized that I had been wrong and had misjudged him completely. Then I discovered that he had always understood and had been forgiving.

My dance, therefore, would have only two characters, a protagonist and an antagonist, eternally opposed and irreconcilable. They would represent the conflict between authority and the rebel, orthodoxy and the heretic, order and chaos. The dancers would perform on an austere, bare stage, hung with black velour, superbly lit throughout the action. There would be, for the son, no adventures, festivities, or orgies during his flight from his father's house. In this case, such scenes would be obvious and superfluous. I would show the son's defection from the virtues of his father's love as a subjective analysis of my own rebellious excesses, typical of all youth, and I would show them in an evocative solo of some substance. I would then examine the father's reaction in a dance symbolic of the desolation of those rejected and abandoned. Compassion is a bitter thing, for it leaves the compassionate without the solace that hatred and contempt bring. They must endure with their understanding and their pity.

I would not show the return of the chastened Prodigal in a sentimental dénouement with a fatted calf. There would be no touching filial repentance, no tender paternal acceptance. For the son can never return to the paternal bosom; he can only come back and continue to face the adversary anew. So I would have only a confrontation with new eyes and a new awareness. It would be austerely restrained and unemotional. Ultimate repentance and ultimate forgiveness are serene beyond sentiment. They are resolved in utter and private loneliness, for each man — forgiving father and errant son — must fail to reach or know the other. Each can regard the other only across a dark gulf, a chasm. In this scene, the abyss would deepen and intensify as the two dancers, remote as two planets, would circle — ostensibly for an eternity — each in his own lonely orbit. This I have found is my experience, and this is how I would — and probably will — compose a dance on the theme of the Prodigal Son.

I would persist in my emulation of the artists whom I revere. I would work to the limit of my capacity to utilize the elements of this theme with the utmost passion, with complete formality, with all simplicity.

Anna Sokolow: at rehearsal (photo: Herbert Migdoll)

Anna Sokolow

THE REBEL AND THE BOURGEOIS

I

I hate academies. I hate fixed ideas of what a thing should be, of
how it should be done. I don't like imposing rules, because the person,
the artist, must do what he feels is right, what he — as an individual
— feels he must do. If we establish an academy, there can be no future for the modern dance. An art should be constantly changing; it
cannot have fixed rules.

The trouble with the modern dance now is that it is trying to
be respectable. The founders of the modern dance were rebels; their
followers are bourgeois. The younger generation is too anxious to
please, too eager to be accepted. For art, this is death. To young
dancers, I want to say: "Do what you feel you are, not what you think
you ought to be. Go ahead and be a bastard. Then you can be an
artist."

The modern dance should be non-conformist. We should not
try to create a tradition. The ballet has done that, and that's fine —
for the ballet. But not for us. Our strength lies in our lack of tradition.
Some say that the big change came in the late 1920's, and now is
the time for the modern dance to assimilate and solidify. That's all
wrong, because it is like building on still another tradition. Without
change there can be no growth, and not enough change is going on
today.

My quarrel with this generation is that they copy their teachers,
and it's their own fault. They don't want freedom; they want to be
told what to do. Why don't they realize they don't have to believe
everything teacher says? They ought to disagree; they ought to argue.

Of course it's not all the fault of the student. Too often, teachers are merely polite when they should be provocative. They ought to shock. Look at Louis Horst. At eighty, he was still fresh and bold. The good teacher does not teach rules; he stimulates. He shows the students what he knows and inspires them — to go and do something else.

Learning rules cannot produce an artist. What is an artist? What is the nature of the creative process? These are things we can't know; they can't be explained. The creative teacher opens doors for his students to see what life is, what they are. They have to take it from there.

It is easier and quicker to teach by rule, but in the end it's no good. To learn to choreograph, you just have to mess through it for a while. Most people feel they have to "fix" a dance, they have to make it "neat." No — it's better to have disordered life, but to have life. The modern dance is an individual quest for an individual expression of life.

The new generation have not really faced themselves; they don't know what it is they want to say. Most of their choreography is vague. It doesn't come organically from the person. It can't, because the choreographer doesn't know who he is or how he feels. So he tries to cover up his confusion by giving his dances fancy titles, by being intellectual. Dance is not intellectual. It deals with deep emotion.

Choreography always reflects the character of the creator. We see in the person's work what he asks from life and from art. Some want only to be entertained, so they offer us only entertainment. Others see life as a tremendous, mysterious force, and this is reflected in their work. Of course there are times when we want to be entertained. Life is not all deep emotion. Art should recognize all our needs.

I don't believe in ivory towers. The artist should belong to his society, yet without feeling that he has to conform to it. He must feel that there is a place for him in society, a place for what he is. He must see life fully, and then say what he feels about it. Then, although

30

The Question: choreography, Anna Sokolow: American Dance Theatre (photo: Herbert Migdoll)

he belongs to his society, he can change it, presenting it with fresh feelings, fresh ideas.

The important thing is that the art being created now be related to now, to our time. The artist must be influenced by his time, conditioned by the life around him. If he is not, his viewpoint is limited by the past, and turns back instead of going forward. If he draws on the ever-changing life around him, his work will always be fresh and new. Art should be a reflection and a comment on contemporary life.

Yet some people are afraid to use life, feeling that art should be something apart, something isolated from reality. I once had a student in Israel who had been in a German concentration camp. You would never have known it from the windblown *schöene tänze* that she composed for me. They amounted to — nothing. I asked her: "Why don't you use your experience?" Then she created a marvelously powerful study based on the reality she had known.

Anyone, however, can have a good idea for a dance. In itself, that's not enough. There must be form as well as concept; both matter — what you feel and how you express it. First, the choreographer sees his idea in terms of movement, as the painter see his in terms of color, line, and mass. This happens spontaneously. Movements are not intellectually contrived but are evoked by emotional images. The only intellectual process is the one that puts these spontaneously conceived movements together into a form that works as a whole.

A sense of form, a feeling for construction, can be learned. But there are no rules. How, then? Well, you look at forms, at structures around you. Look at the shape of a box or a bottle; look at the lines of a table. It is easier to see form in life today than it was in the era of the Baroque, when forms were all covered with ornamentation. I don't like elaborated design. I like naked structure. In the theatre, I am anti-décor and anti-costume.

Progress in art comes through the quest for new forms. The artists I most admire are the ones who have dared to break with traditional forms — artists such as Joyce and Picasso and Balanchine. Pure form is not cold, because it is an abstraction from reality; its

33

Odes: choreography, Anna Sokolow: American Dance Theatre (photo: Herbert Migdoll)

source is life itself. Form for form's sake is dull, contrived, intellectual. True form comes from reducing reality to its essential shape, as Cézanne did with the apple. In the hands of an artist, form is emotional, exciting. You feel that there is a reason for everything being there, just as it is. There is nothing superfluous, because the artist has stripped his work down to the bare essentials. And an audience responds emotionally to this purity, this inevitability of form, which is beauty.

It takes courage to be so simple. I dig Balanchine because he is daring in his simplicity. Look at the last movement of *Ivesiana* — the dancers just walk on their knees. This is bold; it's modern. It's ballet, but it's modern.

I think there will always be a basic, technical distinction between modern dance and ballet, because the modern conception of training is different. But in dance works there should be no idioms. It's not technique that makes a dance modern; you can have a modern dance on pointes. It's not subject matter, either. Tudor's *Pillar of Fire* has a romantic story like *Giselle,* but it doesn't reflect the conventional concept of romance. It's a difference in point of view. The modern attitude does not eliminate fantasy or romantic and poetic ideas. But we don't handle them the way the nineteenth century did. We are not representational; we are imaginative.

I have never told stories in dance, though I have always been strongly dramatic. I never plan a dance. I do it, look at it, and then say: "Yes, I see what I am trying to do."

For me, *Lyric Suite* was a turning point. It was then that I began to find a language of movement for myself. I see no reason to fight a personal language; it's an organic statement of the person. But one must not rest on it. The important thing is to stretch the personal vocabulary so that it does not remain static. This does not mean changing its essential nature. One can remain one's self without repeating a statement.

When I first heard the *Lyric Suite,* I was fascinated with Berg's music, because I could see nothing lyric about it. Then it began to evoke dance images for me. After it was done, I saw the first move-

Opus '65: choreography, Anna Sokolow: Robert Joffrey Ballet (photo: Herbert Migdoll)

ment as an expression of man; the second, as the quality of woman.

Rooms was choreographed without music. I wanted to do something about people in a big city. The theme of loneliness and non-communication evolved as I worked. I like to look into windows, to catch glimpses of unfinished lives. Then I ask: "What is there, and why?" Then I thought of using chairs as if they were rooms, each dancer on his own chair, in his own room, isolated from all the others though physically so close to them.

Jazz was the right music for *Rooms*. I have always been interested in jazz; I find it one of the greatest and most profound expressions of our times. It makes me think. In *Rooms,* jazz was used for the dramatic and psychological depiction of individuals. In *Opus 58* I used jazz for an over-all aura of the sounds and rhythms of today. I wanted the feeling of a new era, one where life is violent and precarious, and the individual seems unimportant.

Then came *Dreams,* which was my indictment of Nazi Germany. When I started, I had only the idea of dreams, but they became nightmares, and then I saw they were related to the concentration camps. Once this had happened, I intensified the theme by focusing on it.

In *Opus 63* I just started out to do something in unison movement. But the work talked back to me. After a wild Bossa Nova, with everyone going at each other, I ended it with the dancers just walking. It had a quality of strength, like religion; a belief that the spiritual thing will survive. But my works never have real endings; they just stop and fade out, because I don't believe there is any final solution to the problems of today. All I can do is provoke the audience into an awareness of them.

II

I have always been interested in the Bible and curious to see how I might arrive at a movement style that has a Biblical feeling. The Imbal company has achieved this in its way; I must find my own way. There is the influence of the landscape, of dryness and heat. There is the quality of a desert people. There is the feeling of the culture of the Middle East, a mixture of the Greek and the Oriental.

There is the Bible itself, which deals with big and eternal emotions. We are always tempted; we always sin, because we are human. There is nothing sentimental about the Bible. It is not bound by all those horrible, Victorian concepts of good manners and little, blown-up feelings, with everyone going around being "nice" and thinking that only minority groups have passions. The Bible has tremendous force and vitality. It is really modern.

So in my telling of *The Prodigal Son,* I would try to capture the qualities of the Bible. I think I would do it in modern dress. I would use music of today — probably the jazz of Teo Macero — but asking him to work in the qualities of such ancient instruments as the drum, harp, and flute. I might use words as well as movement — possibly poetry.

Erick Hawkins

PURE POETRY

I

THE first time I saw pictures of Isadora Duncan, I simply fell in love with her with all the ardent tenderness that a young man of seventeen brings to such a love. Later on I saw pictures of Shanta Rao and fell in love again, and later still, when I saw her on stage — with her irresistible, sensuous female radiance — I fell even more in love with all the passion that a grown man can bring to something he knows is a treasure. Whatever discoveries I have since made in perception or attention or the pure fact of movement I owe to these loves. Whenever I have the good fortune to find another tender gesture for some new dance, I owe it to them. They taught me that the important essence of all dancing is *movement quality*, and its excellence or lack of excellence. I quickly discovered that the wondrous, immediate knowledge of existence that you get in the pure fact of movement can come only if you find that inner quality. I soon realized that pure movement is decorative, instead of significant, if the inner quality is lacking.

Ballet did not satisfy me because it was too much like a diagram and, for me, too much of the indescribable pure poetry of movement had to be left out. It moved like a diagram because it had developed at a period in Western culture that emphasized theoretical knowledge and — if not puritanical — at least extremely unsensuous attitudes toward the body.

When Jacques Barzun speaks of "the treason of the artist," he speaks of the wonderful breakthrough of modern art at the turn of the century to an undiagrammatic way of thinking. Then, with the

39

current pressure of technology and one kind of scientific thought, the backtracking, or "treason," of the contemporary artist turned against this vision toward a kind of pseudo-scientific art, or really a science-fiction.

Today we are losing the poetry of art, and this poetry can never be conceptual or diagrammatic. It must preserve that initial innocence of the sensuous. We now have a taste for the overblown, the complex, the unsensuous, and the anonymous. When the composer Lucia Dlugoszewski shakes one of her delicate paper rattles, I know she has the chance of being more poetic than a whole symphony orchestra.

We have to recognize that we live in a transcending culture. Non-Western peoples, who have a traditional culture, merely keep rediscovering their unchanging, unhistorical intuition of excellence and the good life. But once science comes into the picture, we have history and a constantly changing attitude toward what is the good life, and this we call a transcending culture. It constantly demands a constantly changing justification for the arts. Since ballet and modern dance are both part of a transcending culture, they are both temporary, both on trial, until they prove and re-prove their excellence and their potential for the good life.

Modern dance came into existence because it had to. It came into existence in recognition of some obvious facts: namely, that the codification of movement, technique, and aesthetics called "ballet" was only a part of the way Westerners, including and especially Americans, could dance; that as the ideas of the good life altered with time, so the ideas of how dance could be danced altered; that as the philosophical ideas of the other arts were changing, so those of dance would change.

The turning point that led to the manifestation called "modern dance" came when Isadora Duncan had a new idea of the human being — specifically the human being in this specific place America, stemming in a direct line from Melville, Thoreau, Emerson, and Whitman, and going back for confirmation to the idea of the human being as stated in the classical period of Greece — the only place in all of Western history where the human body was considered beautiful, a worthy and loved and equal partner with the "soul-mind"; where the human body, male or female, was not distorted by costume, conduct, and pinched puritanical and partial concepts of the human body-soul. Only when the body was re-recognized and freed could a new art of dance arise in the West.

Then Ruth St. Denis and later Ted Shawn, in their search for antecedents, for some connection with a sensuous past that could accept dancing, went afield for confirmation of their intuition to the non-Western peoples, to the Orient. The intuitions of these three were glorious and are still to be built upon. All three were bright enough to see how much more was possible in dance movement than traditional ballet offered. They saw that, for all the virtues of its technique, it was partial in scope.

Isadora Duncan was the first dancer in the West to intuit a kinesiological truth: that human movement starts in the spine and pelvis, not in the extremities — the legs and arms. That is: human movement, when it obeys the nature of its functioning, when it is not distorted by erroneous concepts of the mind, starts in the body's center of gravity and then — in correct sequence — flows into the extremities.

Photographs and drawings of Isadora Duncan indicate — and her writings try to say this too — that she conceived the essence of movement to lie in transition, not in position. When she says "Study Nature," she means "flow organically," in arcs, like the spring of a cat, the wiggle of a water moccasin, the gallop of a horse, the wave on a beach, the toss of a ball, the bellying of a sail — not like a man's mind-contrived, inorganic machine, which essentially cannot move but only take positions.

It is significant that the official symbol of the School of American Ballet is Leonardo da Vinci's drawing of a man's body as it is arranged diagrammatically, geometrically, ready for scientific measurement and for scientific (rather than felt) relationships. The change to a fresher and more comprehensive principle is what makes modern dance.

41

"Love Shouts Itself Transparent," from *Here and Now with Watchers:* Erick Hawkins, Nancy Meehan

Ballet denies the sensuous body in technique, costume, and subject matter. The image of the woman on toe is the limited, erotic image, which was permitted men with all the baggage of erotic fears that characterized Western culture from the Middle Ages until the revolution of Freud. In its subject matter, the early modern dance merely expressed these fears; the fearless and radiant sensuality of Shanta Rao is still a thing for us to have the courage to learn.

On the cover of *Newsweek* in the spring of 1964, George Balanchine was photographed with a number of women dancers. The caption below was: "Ballet Is Woman." This was correctly stated. Ballet is geared for the woman dancer on toe. In 1903 Isadora Duncan saw that this was a false artistic and kinesthetic premise, and that we had better join the rest of the world, which does its dancing with the sensitivity of the beautiful, naked, undistorted, and felt human foot.

The emphasis on the technique of the toe shoe in ballet leaves the male dancer as a supernumerary (a little like the guy who carries a spear in *Aida*). But the wiser all races become, the more they find a beautiful, complementary equality between man and woman. Whether you read Erich Fromm or Edward Albee, it is clear that if we do not solve the conflict between men and women, our culture will destroy itself. One of the challenges of our moment in history is to find the true and beautiful meeting between men and women, and when dance uses the human body as its material, it of all the arts is required to meet the challenge most vividly. It cannot today afford a technique that jeopardizes this vision.

The modern dance has had two goals. One was to develop a larger and more comprehensive total technique with which to train the body so that it could fulfill the vision of a new beauty of human movement in the Western world. The other was to use this completely trained instrument to convey a more far-ranging subject matter in the art.

Before she returned to India after her last performance here in 1964, Shanta Rao remarked to me that while she had not seen much modern dance in America, she wondered from what she had seen why it was so full of "frustration." Frustration is certainly a mighty frail area of human experience on which to build a blossoming art. The challenge of a new modern dance is to take the responsibility of maturity.

Many fine, mature works of art were made in modern dance between 1931 and 1964, but there has always been an unhealthy aspect as well. This has stemmed from the work of certain dance artists who, like those in other fields, considered it appropriate to portray anxiety and neurosis, and to report our state of confusion. My opinion, however, is that the Western dance artist is ready to learn from the Oriental that his function is to present ideas of enlightenment, and in this way to reconfirm the intuitions that each member of the audience has latent within him about how he can mature and fulfill all the possibilities of a complete and meaningful life. I suspect that the neurotic quality, the wallowing in confusion of much of serious art in our time, is what has alienated the broad mass of people who gravitate toward "entertainment" rather than immature, self-expressive, unhealthy art.

Shanta Rao's objection to modern dance subject matter can be seen from the beginning of formal Western thought on aesthetics. The pros and cons of Plato's discussion of art in *The Republic* have cropped up ever since his time. But his reasoning is incontrovertible and is parallel to traditional Oriental aesthetics. Plato says if you desire the ideal of maturity in all human beings, you will show in your arts only models of maturity and will not wallow in "reporting" strife, inadequate ways of how men and women get along together. You will not titillate people with patterns of immature behavior and paltry, vulgar images of the self, and then say: "Life is like this; what a mess!" You will not end only in unresolved discouragement, negativism, and Shanta Rao's "frustration." Modern artists try to justify this negative titillation by saying that they are not Pollyannas. Actually they are another kind of Pollyanna, hanging onto little, private neuroses, because without them they would feel naked and insignificant. The resulting art forms are melodrama. Let us stop fooling ourselves that these ever reach the truth of tragedy.

44

It is currently a popular idea to unify the modern dance achievements the way ballet is unified and to produce an impersonal company that could perform all modern dances. To unify the modern dance in a universal, non-egotistical technique is a commendable idea. It is right that as soon as possible the truth of how the body would be trained as a dancing instrument, without limitations and personal eccentricities, should be arrived at and used. This would stop the technical self-indulgence of many modern dancers and would set aside the unfortunate myths of idiosyncratic dancers, who have claimed for their personal limitations the label of a universal technique. There would then be finally no need for modern dancers to study ballet, because what was useful in the balletic training of a complete instrument would be assimilated into this larger point of view.

However, to jeopardize the glorious, unparalleled vitality in the diversity of modern dance choreography by arbitrarily fixing an impersonal dance company geared to perform all works would be to deny the glorious reason for its coming into existence in the first place. Everyone in Manhattan who is aesthetically alive groans to see another standard skyscraper go up—standard because it is cheaper. We must not forget that the true American dream is that exact, intense individualism and lack of conformity and passionate diversity. We are challenged in our moment of history not to lose this treasure that is our unique cultural heritage. We are lucky to be modern dancers. We have ahead of us one of the most exciting paths given to human beings in their eternally challenging excitement of being alive. All we have to do is take it.

II

To convey the story of the Prodigal Son in dance would be one of the greatest challenges a contemporary choreographer could meet. But such a dance would have to be as short, simple, and sweet as the original telling in Luke.

It is a great question in my mind whether we have in our theatre dance found the vocabulary to tell such a story with the required

directness and simplicity. The movement language used for such a dance would have to be consonant with the way the story was originally told to succeed as a worthy work of art. The first requirement for the use of such a story in dance would be the sincerity of the choreographer in his desire to tell the story, and tell only the story and nothing but the story.

There are two errors that I believe would be immediate temptations: one, allowing a movement to be used that did not absolutely, directly contribute to the immediacy of the telling; second, using the lines "devoured thy living with harlots" and "wasted his substance with riotous living" as an excuse completely out of proportion to the main telling of the parable for a scene of titillation and display of sex for sex-starved Americans.

Unless the spiritual meaning of the parable was uppermost in the mind of the choreographer at every stage and moment of the work, he should not attempt it. He had better wait until he is inwardly ready.

Dr. F. S. C. Northrop of Yale, author of *The Meeting of East and West,* formulates the most important aesthetic distinction in the history of Western thought when he uses the term "art in its first function" for the art that is concerned only with the materials of art in and for their own sake, because of their ineffable capacity to pinpoint the wondrous, living moment. This is not to be confused with "art for art's sake." The meaning of "art in its first function" can be distinguished by defining "art in its second function" as the art that uses the materials — the colors, shapes, sounds, and movements — not just for their own sake but to convey by means of them something in human experience other than the mysterious, sensuous aliveness of these colors, shapes, sounds, and movements.

When the choreographer presents movement in and for its own sake, he is not communicating. He is then not using the movement as a language. He is not "saying" something. The movement just "is." This difficult innocence of the pure fact of movement just "being" in and for itself, before it communicates, yields that strange, holy center that is the only thing we know about being alive. Such movement has its own significant purpose of filling the audience with wonder and delight, and that is very special and very perfect and more valuable than anything in the world. But it is not communication. It is before and beyond communication. It simply is!

When the choreographer sets out to do more — to use the movements not for their own sake but for the sake of revealing some theme, some idea, some narrative — then he must make the movement into a language. He must communicate with this language. One can sum it up this way:

When uncommunicating, be wondrous.

When communicating, communicate.

To invent movement to keep pointing directly at the story of the Prodigal Son at the present stage of dance, without falling into mime, would be extremely difficult, if what one sees on the stage is to be powerful and equivalent in intensity to the Biblical telling. There is a double requirement in this case. Each movement invented for the story must be as beautiful and fresh as a movement done for its own sake, but it has a second necessity. It must serve the purpose and immediacy of the story and only that.

The charm and power of the parable, and of course the truth, would be the first concern. Certainly it charms us, for it is a beautiful *peripeteia* (reversal); though in the opposite sense to downfall, as in Greek tragedy. Here it is not catastrophe, but a return and upcoming, or rebirth, the courage of the hero to grow up. The story is poignant and, like all true tragedies, the ending shows new sight, growth, and especially joy. When we see the hero come to self-knowledge, we are full of joy, because we see there is the chance that we ourselves can come to self-knowledge and so to our maturity. When the theatre does this, each man and woman walks out renewed.

This is the most exciting and profound aim of art in its second function — to embody and convey to the audience the artist's deepest insights — and not just his own, but those of the wisest thinkers of his or any time. For the artist, most completely when he is using art in its second function, is a priest and not just a reporter.

Rather than be concerned with any personalized treatment of the parable, my goal would be to present it stark and naked.

The cast would have: the Father, the Younger Son who leaves home, the Older Son who stays, the Citizen of the Far Country, three Women of the Father's House. I would use the Citizen very briefly as an antagonist to register the Younger Son's disintegration and degradation. I would avoid using the harlots. I would convey the Younger Son's journey, his dissipation, and his degradation through a solo passage. The conclusion of it would be his confronting the Citizen of a Far Country to highlight his final humiliation.

The most beautiful addition of thought beyond the words of the parable could be the conclusion. It would be that the Son who stayed home joined too in the making merry with a glad heart and all jealousy vanished.

For the Father appears to have made a mistake. He appears never to have told the Older Son how much he loved him. And the Older Son always needs to be told that. Most of the time we are the Older Son. And the Father, way back in Near Eastern, ancient society, behaved much like an English father. In the story, the Older Son quite humanly begs for evidence of being loved too. So his acceptance of the Father's speech that this was so, even though it had not appeared so, would be the triumph. The registering of this acceptance by the Older Son's participating in the rejoicing would be to show the greatest maturity and completeness. The greatest triumph!

I would use no setting in the sense of painted backdrop or any other device that would make the place of the stage too fixed. I might delimit sections of the stage to show the Father's house at the beginning and end, and other sections for the journey, and maybe there would be a fairly delimited part in which all the action in the Far Country would be contained.

The beauty of the objects that the dancers use would visually enhance the action and clarify the narrative. So I see used the robe, the ring, the shoes, but not the fatted calf. Stage objects are worse than useless, however, if they are used only to convey meaning. I am satisfied only by the approach of artists like Isamu Noguchi and

Ralph Dorazio, who have known the principle that everything used on the stage must be beautiful in its own materials, in its own right. To me, the only meaningful theatre aesthetic would be one in which every object used on stage and the making of every costume must be as beautiful in its construction and material on the side never seen by the audience as on the side that is seen.

I would compose the dance first, complete to the last rhythmic subdivision of a pulse, as I have done in all choreography since 1951. Then I would commission the musical score. Especially for works with a plot line, this allows the choreographer to hew to the line of meaning, pulse by pulse. It avoids padding, because music written after the dance is finished can be composed to fit the dramatic or movement requirements exactly. Even a score written to a scenario cannot achieve this exactness. Likewise, it allows the choreographer to extend his action to complete his meaning. It keeps the musician from digressing into musical ends that may distract from the intent of the dance, or at least make that intent diffuse. Such a method is feasible only if a brilliant composer and theatre person like Lucia Dlugoszewski is willing to compose the score to the completed dance and yet make an equal work of art, not a subservient one. I would suggest that Miss Dlugoszewski score the work for five or six instruments. In general, too much "weight" of sound buries the appropriate kinesthetic experience in the dancer. The finest theatre and dance music all over the known world uses only a few instruments at a time to accompany dance — except in the greedy West.

I think it is almost impossible to speak of aspects of the movement, such as its style, before it is found, before it comes out of my body as I choreograph, as a spider spins its web out of its body. My goal, however, in terms of quality, would be to make it economical. I would like it to be as economical as Brancusi's Fish or Seal or Flying Turtle. The meaning is conveyed, and this is defined, clear, and beautiful. But the means to convey this meaning in themselves require meeting the greater challenge — that the means, the materials of the art, are defined and clear and beautiful and imaginative and inventive.

Because of the crumbling of a generally experienced ground of metaphysics, or myth, or doctrine, the artist in modern times has fallen into the trap of thinking that he is wise enough to originate ideas. What has developed is a notion that the artist's job is to express what Coomaraswamy calls the artist's "private emotional storms." In this day of commercialism and competition, the artist has allowed himself to capitalize on eccentricity and dreaming up personal styles, gimmicks, and expression. Coomaraswamy contrasts this with the traditional role of the artist in societies where art has been used as a total expression of everyone's common life, either before the Renaissance or in any non-Western society. There art has been used to lead the spectator to "liberation" — to self-knowledge, or truth. We in a transcending society have the added burden of restating and rediscovering these original intuitions, as science in its own way continually puts them on trial. Thus the idea of using the Prodigal Son as a dance serves the highest purpose of art. It could eternally remind an audience of a truth without weariness, as Indian dancers have for hundreds of years danced about Krishna and his beloved. For the parable of the Prodigal Son is based on the eternal truth that "the door is always open."

Donald McKayle

THE ACT OF THEATRE

I

DANCE is my medium and theatre is my home. It is here that I find
excitement and fulfillment. Anything so close and so immediate
must bear the personal stamp of the creator if it is to reach out to
the viewer in its ultimate role, which is communication. This is the
key factor: the communication between artist and audience. This is
what creates that indefinable electricity, which is essential to theatre.
Theatre is not architecture or tradition or effects — it is an act. It is
done in concert and demands collaboration all along the way from
the conception to the final moment of unveiling.

Good work may be found in all forms of dancing, for in reality
there are only two kinds — that which is well done and that which
is not. And while the finest dance can be found in the so-called concert field and the most banal in the commercial field, the words "concert" and "commercial" are not synonymous with "good" and "bad."
Some of the dances done in the commercial theatre far surpass many
of the things seen on the concert stage; some of the latter should never
have been presented at all. I believe that people come to the theatre
to be moved or entertained. They do not come to be lectured, per-
plexed by perversity, or bored by tedious obscurities, no matter how
sincerely felt. The final act of theatre is that sharing with the audience
— the collaboration that I call participation. If this can be accomplished only with a small coterie of well-versed followers, the chances
are that the artist has failed.

My thoughts are dedicated to those artists who are in the creative act of theatre, rather than to those who are engaged in preserv-

53

Donald McKayle (photo: Jack Mitchell)

ing and perfecting tradition. The creators include artists in many forms — modern, ballet, and the so-called ethnic idioms. The dance theatre of today has many fine practitioners of divergent schools or points of view — but each with that personal stamp which makes for greatness. Martha Graham, Alwin Nikolais, Jerome Robbins are a few. All these people are modern (if one must find a cubbyhole to put artists into), not because they share technical devices, but because their outlook is contemporary.

The need to categorize I consider a point of contention. To me, one's alliance is determined by the manner of one's work. Is it the act of creation, or preservation? Is its aim realization or anticipation? If one must make niches, let them be based on artistic value. Classification according to arbitrary, ethnic groups is ridiculous and misleading. Some critics have discussed the work of most dance artists along the lines of their basic artistic allegiances, and then — quite separately — they have discussed the Negro dance. Yet certainly such dancers as Carmen de Lavallade and Janet Collins have much in common with Melissa Hayden and Pauline Koner. Opposition to casting dancers according to ability, talent, and dance quality rather than coloring has been defended with the argument of theatrical verisimilitude — that is, if the artist concerned is a Negro. No question is raised of José Limón's essaying the role of the Moor Othello, or of Helen Tamiris's dancing Negro spirituals, or of Hadassah's excursions into the Hindu dance. Prevailing prejudices have led any number of fine Negro ballet dancers such as Billie Wilson, Sylvester Campbell, Ronnie Aul, and Ronald Frazier to seek positions in Europe. There they have been quickly employed in ballet companies, where there are no extra-dance barriers to obscure the vision of their real abilities — such as the most recent nonsense concerning the Negro physique or that fallacious old bromide about Negro rhythm.

One's cultural heritage serves to flavor one's work, and the groups that are segregated socially, politically, and economically from the body of society tend to keep their cultural identity strongly intact, most often giving the national culture its mark of uniqueness

— witness the music, dance, and crafts of the Yemenite Jew in Israel; the song and dance of the gypsy in Spain; the tremendous contribution of the Negro to American music. One cannot help but be moved by these forces, no matter what one's birthright, and they become national and international treasures, for art knows no boundaries. They become the property of mankind, and the ability to perform within them is limited only by personal, artistic temperament and inner comprehension. This is especially true of music and dance, which have no language barriers. One cannot deny the rightness of Maria Alba dancing the *soleares* because she was not born a Spanish gypsy, or of Gerry Mulligan playing jazz because he was not born an American Negro, or of Raven Wilkinson dancing classical ballet because she is an American Negro.

If an artist is to bring anything of value to his work, he must seek his inspiration outside of the narrow confines of the technique of his craft. This is as true in dance as in the other art forms. But there is an exception. There are those artists who are dedicated to delving solely into explorations of body textures, tensions, and juxtapositions. Yes, they are valuable, and some of them will be known to posterity much like the ballet greats who first rose *sur les pointes* and added the double revolution of the pirouette. Pure movement in dance has its own validity when its practitioners are able to make their audiences respond with the very fibre of their own musculatures. There is little as exciting as a fine, virile, masculine dancer, demonstrating the completeness of physical prowess; or as thrilling as a female dancer, perfectly attuned rhythmically, muscularly, and temperamentally. Some of the finest choreography celebrates these qualities. Specific characterization is not necessary for dance to be communicative on a human level.

In my own work, I always demand a certain vibrancy, an inner vitality that communicates through the viscera, not the mind. While the mind is never dormant, it does not hold sway in all areas, and definitely should not in dance. The senses must be reached before the mind. The reflection afterward, which is then basically a process of the mind, should — if the experience has been meaningful — once

Games: choreography, Donald McKayle (photo: Jack Mitchell)

more awaken this sensory network. This is what I aim for in my dances, whether they have definite plots or are more abstract in concept.

It was a childhood memory that triggered my first dance. . . . It was dusk, and the block was dimly lit by a street lamp around which we hovered choosing a game. The street, playground of tenement children, was soon ringing with calls and cries, the happy shouts of the young. The street lamp threw a shadow large and looming — the constant spectre of fear — "Chickee the Cop!" The cry was broken; the game became a sordid dance of terror.

Games opens with songs and dances of play. Imagination that seeps out in verse converts empty beer cans into the most wonderful toys in the world. But there was also the dance of hunger. How many times we sang:

> Old Aunt Dinah sick in the bed
> Called for the doctor, the doctor said,
> All you need's some short'ning bread.

And then to terror — the terror of old, of the plantation overseer . . .

> There is your master; there is your mister
> There is the one gonna bring you to blister.

To today . . .

> Chickee the Cop!
> I saw a cop a walkin' down the street
> Swingin' his billie and a struttin' his beat.
> He's gonna catch you, beat you hard,
> Bash all of your bones, so help me God.

From remembrance came a dance.

Nocturne is a lyric dance that grew out of a first love with the music of Moondog. Its basic material is pure movement, yet it is not movement in a void of mood or idea. The dance celebrates the qualities of man and woman. Man is depicted in his role of discoverer, protector; woman as inspirer. The male patterns are large, thrusting, laced with impulse, volatility, and expectation. The female movements are flowing, curved, inviting. The resulting duets are a blending of both qualities.

57

District Storyville: choreography, Donald McKayle: Carmen de Lavallade and ensemble (photo: Herbert Migdoll)

Then I became intrigued with the music of the Southern Negro chain gang. What first captured me were the pulsing, restless rhythms. They seemed wrapped in the chains that bound the suffering men together, and they seemed to explode in desperation and anger. The lyrics were sardonic and then, in turn, biting, sensual, and filled with protest. The incessant labor of the men is the background for the drama. Their dreams, as envisioned in their desire for freedom, come always in the guise of a woman — once as the essence of idealized femininity; then as the remembered figures of sweetheart, mother, and wife. In retrospect, I find in *Rainbow Round My Shoulder* the same theme that appeared in *Nocturne* — woman, the inspirer.

District Storyville and *Reflections in the Park* are both set in the jazz idiom. One is a period piece set in the notorious red-light district of New Orleans; the other is a contemporary statement of love, dreams, cruelties, and fantasies in the heart of a big city. The former draws its ideas from the beginnings of jazz, a kaleidoscope of ribaldry, decadence, and creation. In the latter, the scene is New York in its one bucolic spot — the park. Here the inhabitants of the city come to find that contrast necessary to their urban lives — but they cannot escape the encroachment of pavements, mortar, and brick. Both works have in common the urgency of the underlying jazz rhythms.

II

The scene is a ballroom in a West Indian community within an American city. The music comes from a small combination of piano, guitar, conga drum, various islands gourds, and saxophone. The combo is situated in a niche upstage, partly veiled by a series of draped gauzes, which also permit various upstage entrances. Two projected downstage balconies mark a horseshoe mezzanine arrangement. A globe dominates the overhead. Two small tables and chairs are situated upstage right and left, and glimpses of others can be seen within the wings. The flow of bias chiffon dresses, bertha collars, and the highlights of marcelled coiffures place the era in the 1930's, as do the piano player's riffs and the lilt of the movement. The mood of joviality is set in an opening dance. We are made aware of a close community feeling, and are introduced to the leading club members: an extravagant dowager, her rather quietly dignified mate, and their young daughter — the main debutante of the evening. At the end of this dance, the major characters enter: a family consisting of a young man, his father, and his mother. In the next dance, the young girl and boy are presented to each other to the strains of a West Indian waltz. The circling globe colors the moving figures, and within the changing and interweaving couples, we are made aware of filial responsibilities and parental approval and the budding of first awareness.

The following episode is a dynamic dance done as an entertainment by a dancer. Her partner is her paramour, and his role is to perform primarily as a musician, playing sticks on a long conga drum, which he straddles. The band backs up the dance, all the instruments being used in the manner of a percussion ensemble. The young boy, who is downstage left, is in a direct line of vision to the drummer, who is downstage right. Between them is the dancer. The attraction of the boy to the dancer is apparent to her. At the crescendo of the dance, she runs from the corner where the young boy is standing, leaps up on the drum — which has been driving her on relentlessly — and stops the drummer's hands.

As the entertainers take their bows and leave, the boy starts in the direction of the dancer, but is swept away by the dowager into position for the grand march. The young girl is crowned and accepts the boy's hand, as the party slips into the stately measures of the Castillian. Couples begin to take their leave. As the lights are dimmed, the boy returns to claim the forgotten sceptre of the young girl. It has been found by the dancer, who goes through a small, wistful pantomime. He crowns her from behind with the debutante's diadem, which he has been carrying. She returns his gallantry with a toast. Under the strum of the solo guitar, we hear the invitation of the maracatu. The dance grows wilder. We see the boy on the threshold of manhood, happy within the confines of his parents' world as typified by his acceptance of the graciousness of the young girl. Suddenly he tastes the strange fruits of another world and becomes intoxicated with this new excitement. The dancer, experienced in her ways, is touched by the ingenuousness of her new companion. The drummer enters. He attacks the boy brutally, and takes his possessions. The dancer defends the lad. The entertainers battle, and their conflict grows into an animalistic love dance. The drummer carries her off.

The theme of the waltz presentation is stated again as the young girl and her parents return to find the boy in what is apparently a drunken stupor; the crown at his side, the sceptre in his hand. The boy awakens to find them turning on him and leaving. His father enters. The boy looks desperately around for the dancer, but finds only the unfinished wine, which he consumes. He approaches his father, slowly falling into his arms, drunk with wine and with the physical and spiritual brutality of love that has been born and slaughtered. As they exit, the dancer enters on the upper balcony. The drummer's sticks can be heard in violent rhythmic contrast to the waltz as the curtain falls.

Alwin Nikolais

I

IT is impossible for me to be a purist; my loves are too many for that. I am excited by things very old and also very new, and by so many things in between as well.

Thus, I cannot be content as only a choreographer. As such, my dominant concern should be motion; yet I cannot forego my attraction to the shapes and forms of things. Therefore, I do not hesitate to stress a sculptural form to the exclusion of motional excitement. Nor can I divorce myself from strong passions for sound and color, so I invade the fields of the composer and the painter as well. In truth, then, I am not a devoted husband to dance, for I choose to marry the lot of my inamorati rather than swearing fixed fidelity to one.

I look upon this polygamy of motion, shape, color, and sound as the basic art of the theatre. To me, the art of drama is one thing; the art of theatre is another. In the latter, a magical panorama of things, sounds, colors, shapes, lights, illusions, and events happen before your eyes and your ears. I find my needs cannot be wholly satisfied by one art. I like to mix my magics.

We are now in a new period of modern dance, and it is a period of new freedom. All the arts, we find, are now becoming vitally concerned with the direct and poignant translation of those abstract elements that characterize and underline an art subject. Not that earlier periods have ignored the inner substance. They have, however, usually spelled it out in terms of a literal scene. Freedom from the domination of the concrete is a logical manifestation of our times.

One of the most striking characteristics of the new art is the

63

Alwin Nikolais (photo: Eric Sutherland: Walker Art Center)

freedom from the literal and peripheral self of man. The artist need no longer channel his subject through a finite scene, nor need he distort, enlarge, reduce, or eliminate part of it to release its inner content. What is more, he is free of the subject-vehicle demanded by fixation and reference to the literal scene.

The early modern dance explored the psyche. Its concepts involved man's concern with the joys and pains of self-discovery. The idea was poetically translated into a kinetic language enacted by the dance character through whom a moment of psychological drama transpired. In the new art, the dance character is no longer dominant. The new dance figure is significant more in its instrumental sensitivity and capacity to speak directly in terms of motion, shape, time, and space. It is the poetry of these elements, speaking directly out of themselves and their interrelationships rather than through a dominant character. The character may be present, but if it is, it is in equilibrium with the aggregate of all the elements in operation.

I see things best in abstract terms. To me, abstraction does not eliminate emotion. Certainly the comparison between a Bach fugue and MacDowell's "In an Indian Hunting Lodge" well illustrates this point. I look upon statements that describe my work as cold, calculating, and out-of-this-world dehumanization with considerable skepticism. I feel that some of these reflect a limited view of humanity. The greatest gifts given to man are his ability to think in terms of abstraction and his ability of transcendence. From these he derives his imaginative power. These are part of his major distinction from the lower animals. Although we need our moments of hearts and flowers, we need also to see the other side of the universal fence.

Today we hear much talk about the "non-verbal" aspects of communication. In the main, this refers to man's facility to sense meaning beyond the literal and materialistic surface. Now we can find meaning in this way, both with the hearts-and-flowers subject and with the dadaistic relation to a cigar-store Indian and a strip-teaser. Each can be an aesthetic triumph or a dud. The form of the communication is less important than the aesthetic semantics of the event itself. (In a recent review of a dance-theatre recital, I was appalled to find that the critic had singled out the piece that was the weakest aesthetically as the only worthy one of the evening. This judgment seemed to be made on the basis that this piece was more recognizable as dance. What a miserable criterion for art dance!) In any case, I feel that the so-called dehumanization can be equally, vitally communicative, and that time and the artist must decide the form.

I have particular points of view about the difference between the male and female mind in respect to abstraction, but I had better not get involved with that here. What I'd like to point out is that the male is far more inclined toward the abstract, and the field of dance is overpoweringly female and matriarchal. I hope fervently for the time when the socio-dynamic climate will re-establish the male in a more just position in the modern dance world.

The choreographer of the new period of the modern dance is concerned with basic and legitimate elements, and is imbued with the urgency of pursuing the fleeting banshee of the moment of art according to the dictates of his individual vision.

II

I was once asked to create the choreography for a proposed Broadway musical production of an adaptation of Aldous Huxley's *Brave New World*. After several conferences with the producer, writer, and sundry other people associated with the project, I asked myself if — left on my own — I would ever want to choreograph a "feelie." I concluded that I would not.

Now, faced with the hypothetical project of creating a dance-theatre piece based on *The Prodigal Son,* the same question arises. This particular subject excites me even less than the Huxley. The bribe of hypothetical, unlimited funds seems not to affect my view; although I can think of one kind of production that would require Canaveral-like financial launching (but this I'll go into later). For me, *Brave New World* would offer far greater aesthetic challenge then *The Prodigal Son,* and would do justice to a plump budget. Even so, I prefer to avoid it.

65

There are times when an artist must turn his creative machineries to an idea offered by someone else. I have done this many times. Usually, one does this either because of economic need or because the opportunity offers advantages to personal development. But for me — unless it were a very special commission, one well suited to me — I would consider such a situation only a distraction from what I really want to do. Assuming, however, that this circumstance was challenging, and the dancers had the prospect of a good salary, I might even enjoy working with someone else's idea.

I understand that this hypothetical project is only a device to reveal the process of a particular creator's mind. I'll go along with it, but my heart is not really involved.

The Prodigal Son is a literal and relatively simple parable. Because my mind works in the direction of the non-literal or abstract, the mountain will have to come to Mohammed. Of course, this has happened many times before in dance. In ballet, particularly, a simple, literal story line has often been the tomato on which a rose is grafted. Here the story offers a skeletal framework upon which the non-literal dances are hung. In any case, I prefer to eliminate the story line and almost all literal reference, to just concentrate on the dances and theatre elements, which I am inclined to integrate into a theatre (happening). (By this I do not mean theatre as drama, but theatre as a form of musicality, of motion, light, color, sound, etc.)

So you can see this whole project is out of the range of my present congenialities. Nevertheless, I'll go on.

The Prodigal Son is a simple parable, but it can be seen from many points of view. The restless son leaves home to spend his inheritance willy-nilly and sow his wild oats, while his brothers invest their cash and lives in homebody stock. The son returns home broke, and is given a loving, extravagant welcome by the parents — much to the outrage of the brothers.

The interpretations the parable offers are numerous. It could be comedy or tragedy. It could be looked upon politically, as a lesson in finance, philosophically, psychologically, or as any combination of these.

66

The reason the son leaves home is not wholly apparent in the Bible. So to establish his behavior pattern in dance, we would have to give him some background to explain his act. He could be a fool or a hero; lovable or obnoxious; a brilliant, witty, satirical character; or a dolt. We could endow him with the vitality and bravado of a restless, inquisitive spirit. We could generously endow him with a passion for exploration and the courage to rub shoulders expansively with the universe, paired with a willingness to take his consequences and measurement therefrom. The Bible implies that he is somewhat rash and unwise in his fling. Yet we could take some artistic liberty here by motivating his behavior. The more one analyzes, the more it is evident that the theme offers much to a writer — perhaps more than to a choreographer. As a matter of fact, we have elements here of the Oedipus story, *The Silver Cord, Waiting for Godot, You Can't Go Home Again*, and many others.

With a little deep thinking, we could go almost anywhere. The son could represent the healthy soul who defies tradition, conformity, adherence to the status quo, and all else that supposedly stagnates the evolution of human capacity. On the other hand, he could be villain of the piece; insensitive to the consequences of his acts, unrealistic about his responsibilities as a member of the family, and welcomed back only because of some peculiar psycho-biological factor indigenous to human parenthood.

The abstractionist cannot be excused from this analytical investigation. As a matter of fact, for him it is even more essential, for — as the superficial, literal physicalities are removed — the molecular substance beneath must then do the speaking.

Even as I write this, I must confess that the intellectualizing process above is not my way of doing. I prefer to drop a simple, single idea into my brain and let it rummage around for several months, with no particular efforts toward consciousness on my part. Then, two or three weeks before I begin to choreograph, I attempt to cast up the results of the Rorschach process. Then I like to choreograph swiftly and within a short span of time. I feel that in this outpouring I keep the channels of my subject open. Even here, I do not over-

67

Imago: choreography, Alwin Nikolais (photo: Robert Sosenko)

question it. I like very much what one fine critic wrote of my theatre piece *Imago*. It reflects somewhat on the process I have just described:

"*Imago* is mindful of the film *Ballet Méchanique* of 30 years ago . . . also suggests the playwrights Capek, *R.U.R.,* or even *The Life of Insects*. Passed through the alembic of the choreographer's own personality and studded with the astonishing stratagems and devices of his mind and eye, they come out new all over again in *Imago*. The chief impact is not the cozy comfort of meeting old friends, but its subtly disturbing feeling. It is an atavastic uneasiness dating to the paleo-times when unknown things haunted men. There is an undeniable bit of gooseflesh in *Imago*."

This writing reflects a vision and reception far beyond the usual dehumanized-man-from-Mars stuff I am often confronted with, and I am most grateful for it.

But to get down to brass tacks. In *The Prodigal Son* we are offered four basic narrative concerns: 1, the son leaves; 2, the brothers toil; 3, the son cavorts in the world; 4, the son returns. Let us stay with Scene One.

As you may suspect, I'm not about to choreograph the brothers performing brilliant but surly grands jetés and twirls; while the mother bourrées in sadness, supported in a lamenting pas de deux by the father; while the son moons about, itching to vault over the gate.

Neither would I go in for a sort of "togetherness" idea, with a rollicking, folksy dance of the brothers, with the son not quite in the togetherness spirit and perhaps a bit show-offy on his own. In such a scene, the mother and father would perhaps offer some folksy stamps with a few humorous limps thrown in to indicate that they're not quite what they used to be. Then there would be the moment of the son's departure. Here a little Method acting, slapped onto a slow, simple three-four choreography, could add realistic heart-rending depth to the scene. (As you may perhaps note, I am impatient with the implication that dancers should be actors and tell stories. Of course they can be, and we know of many such beautiful ballets and

sensation, imparting a generality of meaning that may hit deeply. All this could be accompanied by suitable electronic sounds, in the nature of clashing steel, reverberations, feedbacks, switch clicks, with an obbligato of finger-nail scratching on a blackboard. Train sounds, automobile exhausts, and rustling time tables would add a note of symbolic realism; while baby cryings, filtered and played backward, fast and slow — although not real — would actually get under the skin. Lighting could add its dimension by burning into the yellow, while other lights play kaleidoscopically on the remaining colors. An occasional light directed at the audience could give it an intimate "I mean you" sort of suggestion, while at the same time creating a retinal confusion that would add to the visual maelstrom.

There is the possibility of a dada, or absurd, approach to this scene. One of the major figures in this event could be a naked female with one foot in a steaming pot-au-feu and the other fitted with a bicycle wheel. On her head is a weathervane, and she holds a 1916 Baedeker in her hand. The mother keeps pouring whitewash over her son's head, and tries to towel it off while prancing violently. The father hammers large spikes into a tinker-toy construction, while the brothers play basketball with a garbage pail. Accompanying sounds could be sawing wood, a Florence Foster Jenkins rendition of "Home, Sweet Home," plus deep-sea recordings of the sounds of shrimps. Put all this together with the title *The Prodigal Son,* and it is bound to be meaningful to someone, and even several — if not all.

But there is the possibility of an extravagant version that might have some slight appeal to me. Perhaps you'd have difficulty understanding my descriptions if you haven't actually seen Bryce Canyon in Utah. This is an extravagantly beautiful canyon with literally thousands upon thousands of stalagmite shapes (caused by erosion), piercing upward from the canyon floor. The idea here would be to do *The Prodigal Son* in the form of a "lumière." This is a kind of spectacle popular in Europe, taking place usually at some historical edifice, castle, or palace. Colored light illuminates the building, changing color and location according to a broadcast script, sound effects,

Alwin Nikolais
NO MAN FROM MARS

73

Allegory: choreography, Alwin Nikolais (photo: David Berlin)

music, etc. Can you imagine the effectiveness of such an event at Bryce Canyon?

Here the stalagmites in their multitudinous shapes can be made to represent everything from cabbages to metropolises, or even to suggest abstractly any frame of mind. A cast of a few hundred, maneuvered in this wilderness of natural beauty, together with a vast number of lighting instruments (all controlled electronically), with sound score and occasional narration — this could make possible the production of almost anything from *Ben Hur* to *Fanny Hill*. It might even work out financially, with the State of Utah contributing generously because of its tourist-attraction potential. Anyway . . . there it is.

Although I have presented all the above possibilities in a somewhat snide way, I would like to say that I sincerely believe someone could manage any one of them with legitimate and elegant aesthetic results.

Whichever way it might be done, and aesthetically successful or no; some would like it . . . some would hate it . . . some would say it is dance . . . some would say not. Some would lament the lack of progress it offers to dance . . . some would lament that it does not have the old-fashioned values.

An art is not responsible for its own reception and quality. The responsibility rests with the state of culture out of which it arises. It is not a separate entity grafted upon a people. It arises from the qualities that characterize the society from which it stems. If the society is a crazy, mixed-up mess, then it is likely that the art will illuminate that fact. If it is tight and moralistic, the art will reflect that. As a matter of fact, this is part of the function of art. It defines the culture of a people. By itself, art cannot change its heritage.

So, as you perhaps guess, I have no intention of saying how I would do *The Prodigal Son*. Aside from my personal attitude toward it, I would have company difficulties. Murray Louis would play the son, and he would do well in any of the versions. Phyllis Lamhut or Gladys Bailin would get stuck with the role of the mother and would certainly hate it. (Phyllis would rather do the lady with the Bae-

74

deker.) Unless we could integrate the family, my Negro dancers, Bill Frank and Raymond Johnson, would be without roles.

In closing, I should probably reveal that I myself am a Prodigal Son. Except I haven't as yet spent my fortune, and — at the moment — I have no intention of returning home.

Pauline Koner

I

MODERN dance — I would rather think of it as intrinsic dance — basic, essential, organic, internal — as opposed to extrinsic, the kind of dance that is composed from the outside, not motivated by the inner necessity of the creator's being. I find so much in dance today that seems to come only from concern for peripheral movement and external design, rather than from the organic, emotional need. I don't feel there is the need to say something. There is the desire to say it, a rationalization, which is quite different. The inner urgency is lacking.

Most of what is done now goes about as deep as the epidermis; it is all designed from the skin out. Design is important, but what is more important is what goes from the skin in, right to the core — the center of our being. The early modern dance dug way in. One was often unaware of its external design because one was so concerned with its inner meaning. It filtered through the pores as well as through the visual line. There was something in it like the *cante jondo* (deep song) of Spanish flamenco, which is a seeking within, going into yourself to find the depth and stay with the source.

Dancers are asked, more and more, to be just bodies for the choreographer. And the choreographer uses these bodies for the design in space rather than for the artistic need to communicate. If the artistic need were there, he would demand depth of performance from each individual. With increasing neglect in this realm, sad things are happening to our new crop of young dancers. I have the feeling that in this younger generation there are more "doers" and fewer "dancers." The element of the doing has become the main goal,

77

Pauline Koner: in rehearsal (photo: Peter Basch)

the criterion, while the real essence of the dancing — the artistry — is lost sight of. There are few young dancers today who leave one with the feeling: "This is the person I cannot forget; I don't care what he did, I don't remember what he did. But I cannot forget the person; I cannot forget the presence."

Today's modern dancer thinks too technically. He becomes too involved with: "How do you do it? Where does the foot go? Where is the arm?" And I say: "Don't analyze. I want a particular quality; just do the shape of the movement and you will fall into the right lines, because I have not done it from the impulse of outer design. When you analyze too much, you are apt to lose the original movement. It does not come from outer analysis, but from an inner motivation, and therefore the dynamics and the urgency should force the muscles to go so far and no farther."

Nowadays one does not feel the sense of inner urgency in the performer. The face rarely reflects what is going on in intensity. Emotional changes, when they are really there, can't be hidden. There is something that comes out of an eye even when it is slanted down — or the angle of the head — the muscle tensions change in the face. I don't see this happening. The face is plain — it is plain because it is probably counting like mad. The design is visible, and the design is perfect to the count. It is all one color, because counts do not change in dynamics. If you listen to yourself, to the throbbing blood pulse of your body, to its breathing, to the inner singing, you find an entirely different color in your movement than if you are listening to a number.

Margot Fonteyn dances with her inner ear because she is listening to how she feels, because she experiences the moment of doing as a moment of living. Therefore she phrases. When she dances with a man, you feel she relates to the man. She "is" with the other person. Usually dancing a duet is "being" with another person; dancing with a man has to have a man-woman relationship even if you are a dryad. This awareness creates characterization, timing, and luminous quality.

It seems to me that, also in life today, people relate from the skin

out instead of from the inside. The emphasis is on external relationship, on being with people, hearing the noise, hearing the sounds of voices, but not understanding anything about the people the voices belong to. This cannot produce art. Compassion is the root of all art; the artist must know compassion to create real art. The great painters — El Greco, Goya, Michelangelo, Rembrandt — they are great not because of their craftsmanship (which is indeed monumental), but because of their tremendous knowledge of human beings and their feeling for humanity.

The artist has to search, to explore all the levels of human emotion and experience, to seek and know compassion earnestly, deeply. To distill this into the best possible conscious form that he is capable of and by so doing to share this experience with an audience, to illuminate and transcend a particular moment in time — this is the function of the artist. His aim is to reach men's hearts, to reveal to them that they are more than they think they are, to strip away the layers of veneer so they can look at themselves and say: "This is how I feel, this is how I think." It is the artist's duty to crack the shell and reach the kernel, giving from the inner being to the inner being. What hurts the modern dance today is the kind of superficiality that has replaced the substance — the coldness that has replaced the compassion.

I always need a reason to work. For me, it is not just turning out another dance, like a machine. Some people work this way. These I think of as "nothing" people; the ones who make a conscious effort to have no emotion, no idea, no anything. Then there are "thing" people. These get involved with gadgets and mechanisms, and the thing is more important to them than the person. Fortunately, there are also "people" people. They look and dig and ask questions and search for answers.

For me, the work of the "nothing" people has little validity. If they find the world meaningless and confusing and say just that, there is not much reason to make the statement. We don't go to the theatre to be presented with just reality as such. An artist should not only mirror his time, but reflect upon it.

79

The "thing" people have made some wonderful experiments, which have enlarged the potential, opened our imagination to what one can achieve in design, in space, and in sound. But if this is an end in itself, there is a point where it defeats itself. If these devices are used as a means to an end, however, and are used purposefully to make a statement or to transfer an experience beyond the experience of the design itself, then they become valid and vital.

It is easier to be a "nothing" person or a "thing" person than a "people" person. It is harder to dig, to try to fathom an experience of your own, to understand the truth of it, and to create something out of it. This is a longer process, a more difficult process — and it can be agonizing. Many people today do not want this; they want the easy way. They are afraid, so now we find ourselves in a kind of blinker period, where people think that, if they shut out an awareness of problems, the problems will cease to exist. They will not. When one does make the effort to say something — something that reaches people, that touches them, moves them — the experience is shared.

Doris Humphrey did this. She never resolved her pieces on a negative note. This was part of her greatness. No matter how desperate the material was, the resolution was positive. She always said she believed in the wonder of the human spirit. Since, for me, this is basic, I felt a complete rapport with her manner of thinking and doing. There are people to whom the negative attitude, the hopelessness, seems to be the purpose in making something. To me, in times of hopelessness, the only way to go on living is for the artist to point out some way of hope. The person who only mirrors his period is not doing what an artist should do: act as a catalyst in society. If he sees only what is, he is merely saying in other words what everyone already knows. He is not seeing beyond; he is not transcending the immediate. The artist should ask: "How does one challenge this? How does one make life meaningful?"

The artist must comment. I do not mean that he has to narrate a parable or leave a motto. But the reflex reaction to an experience is not enough; the work must have a viewpoint. There has to be a

Pauline Koner (photo: Peter Basch)

conscious rethinking that forces him to see objectively, to re-evaluate, and then comment is inevitable. In rethinking, reliving an experience, he puts himself in another dimension of that experience. In the creation of art, he must analyze his own experience, seeing it objectively even as he is feeling it subjectively. He tries to be at once the viewer and the viewed. When he understands his own feeling, he can create something consciously about that understanding. He must re-establish how he felt within the experience in order to perform it with complete conviction and utter truth. Then he has a double knowledge. This is vital to art, the integration of the subjective and the objective. With such understanding, one can communicate.

Dance is a marvelous medium for such communication. For we dancers ourselves, via ourselves, our own bodies, with nothing in between — no added element such as words or colors or musical instruments — we are able to transfer an experience to another. We can identify with the other, with the audience, with the receiver — and the receiver with us — in a closer way because that person has the identical instrument we have: the body. The body sends a message from a giving muscle to a receiving muscle; the spirit sends a current of emotion to a receiving emotion.

Though the primary level of communication in dance is emotional, there may be an intellectual level as well. We feel an emotional response in just being happy, but how happy and why happy involve the mind. Each person experiences his own "how" and his own "why." The artist can stimulate this in two ways. He can embody his personal attitudes in a specific narrative form. Or he can distill the essence of an emotion, letting the viewer use it as a springboard for an experience of his own. One should try to find the ultimate in the immediate.

When I choreographed *Cassandra,* I was dealing with a specific, dramatic character, but I saw her also as a symbol of woman lamenting for her nation or for the world or for the blindness of human beings. And in *The Farewell,* which was my tribute to Doris Humphrey, I thought of her immortality as what she had achieved in her lifetime and left as her legacy to young dancers. There are various un-

derstandings of immortality, and each viewer may interpret in his own way. In *Solitary Song,* however, I wanted to grasp the essence of aloneness, to provoke the viewer to feel his own kind of solitude in his own way.

The identification of performer and audience is much closer in the modern dance than it is in the classical ballet, for the modern dance uses the body in a more organic way. The ballet dancer first stood on her toes to look like an ethereal being. To use that technique for depicting human beings of today is, for me, a mistake. It always has an element of unreality, since we cannot really identify kinesthetically. In the intrinsic dance, true identification is possible. Its movements, though stylized, are not so completely removed from the movements of living, and the audience can relate to a human experience.

When formal ballet began, it was related to the thinking, the life, the manners of the court. But that living does not exist today. Ballet is still interesting, and I am not against it; I could not be, having come from that source. I feel it has a definite purpose, as decorative painting has a purpose. While we look at some kinds of dancing for the sheer display of pyrotechnics, we watch others in order to have a deep, emotional experience. Neither should eliminate the other. The complete human being needs both. We like to see a decorative ballet, and if getting up on the toes helps the decoration, makes the girl look more ethereal, and gives the body and the leg a more beautiful line, and it seems incredible to perform — that's fine. On the other hand, I don't see the need to use that technique for saying something pertinent to today. There are always exceptions to the rule, for such ballets as Antony Tudor's *Pillar of Fire* and *Lilac Garden,* Jerome Robbins' *The Cage,* and George Balanchine's *Ivesiana* evoke a deep response. But such works are rare.

The intrinsic dance should look for new movements, new styles. The realm of movement has to be broad in texture. Think of the range of colors in painting, the shades of each color, the dynamic values. In movement, I think, this has not been explored. What I see is usually done on one level of dynamics right through an entire per-

formance. One rarely sees even a change of emotion any more. The dynamic quality within the one emotion usually remains on the same level. Yet it is possible to have, for example, a gay emotion with tremendous changes of dynamic color within the realm of happiness. One can have sadness with the variations that a motivated sadness demands. For there are kinds of sadness — reminiscent, agonized, tragic. And pain. There is pain that comes from an emotional source, and there is physical pain. There are many levels of dynamics within one kind of feeling quality. This is rarely explored to the full. A dancer seems to start at one point and remain there. The subtleties, the shadings, the seeking for various kinds of intensity — the artistry, really — do not exist.

Still another element potential of dance is missing today. I rarely feel the sense of space, the vibrancy of the entire space, and the body's relation to that space — so that no matter where the body is, the whole space is alive. I see design in the arms and legs of the body. Yet the urgency to just cover space, or to make that space an integral part of the design, does not exist very much these days. This is what I call metric rather than organic movement. Air — you should touch air; handle it, breathe it, embrace it, cut through it, leap into it. It is not the "body" jumping up or running fast that is important. It is "you" leaping into the air or cutting across the stage.

Too often there are personal styles. Each dancer finds a style for himself and stays with it, repeating the language. I prefer a challenge: how can I say this in a different way for a new piece? And my methods of looking for different ways stem from Doris Humphrey, who sought movements from gesture. The result of the search, after it is worked into the dance, may be so far removed from the original source that it is hardly recognizable. But the sheer experimentation of it has yielded a different kind of movement language. When movement is derived from gesture, the design, the dynamics, and the shape of the movement take on an entirely different look.

In depicting the story of Helen Keller in *The Shining Dark,* I sought gesture themes in real sources. They are not recognizable in

Pauline Koner
INTRINSIC DANCE

85

Pauline Koner: in performance (photo: Peter Basch)

the dance, and are not supposed to be, but everything came from factual images. There was the "teaching theme"; the touching of space, the sense of an object in the hands, like the sense of the roundness of a bowl. And there was the movement of "feeling into the unknown." These gestures were so stylized and patterned that they became dance. But this choreographic approach made them different from any other kind of movements I might have created.

On the other hand, the sources of movement for *The Farewell* stem from poetic images, both those of the actual poetry used in the songs of Mahler's last movement of *Das Lied von der Erde* and from poetic and emotional images of my personal interpolation. I found inspiration for arm patterns in the ever changing shapes of tree branches, with tremor of leaves adding rhythmic color. The flowing of a brook delineated a floor design, the bubbling and gurgling was food for phrasing. The root that winds its way from a seedling to finally burst into bloom . . . images of nature spurred the imagination to seek new forms for the body. Then there is a phrase in the poem: "The leaves are falling"; and my personal reflection: "The leaves are falling, my tears are falling." The nature image and the gestures of weeping and pain offered sources for a phrase linked by the idea of "falling, dropping" — hands, isolated at the wrists, fall first high in air, then at the eyes, and finally at the viscera. This approach creates movement that is specific to the idea and an organic part of the whole. The possibilities are limited only by the measure of one's need to search and one's own imagination.

What I am seeking now is a language that is not personal to me, but that speaks the quintessence of a mood or feeling in terms that are universally recognizable. I see the possibility of this in other art forms. There are the works of the lithographer Kaethe Kollwitz, which have a tremendous sense of pathos and compassion for the human being. It is conveyed in the feeling of the body line. You cry when you look at these; the drawings themselves cry. Strangely enough, I found that the line of the back and the head that she had in all her drawings is exactly what I use in *Solitary Song,* though I was not conscious of this when I was working on it. I am making collec-

tions of such things now. They give me courage, for otherwise one can always feel that one is just manufacturing these things, which is wrong. I feel there are certain root manifestations that are indigenous to particular emotions, and all intrinsic artists draw upon them. It is through these elemental symbols that an experience is shared by artist and audience.

II

Music: LUKAS FOSS

Set: PETER LARKIN

Narration: ARCHIBALD MacLEISH

The settings and costumes should have a timeless quality. The entire mood should maintain a symbolic reference. The scenes are not connected in narrative form, but are flashes of isolated episodes.

Scene I. The Home.

A mother, father, and two sons perform a dance that has ritual overtones. The faces of the family are covered with a gauze, which opaques the features but is transparent from within. All but the youngest son carry masks on sticks with which they cover their faces as though at a masked ball. (The masks are identical.) The youngest son is presented with a mask which he is constantly inverting so that its face is down and his own face is revealed. When a gauze is about to be placed on his face as a sort of initiation rite, the young son, refusing to conform, ceremoniously hangs up his mask and exits. Blackout.

Scene II. Somewhere — anywhere.

The background is a huge computing machine — three-dimensional — upstage center on a level or suspended. Extended from the machine are poles from which hang strings like those used for marionettes. The machine is brilliantly lit. Ten dancers in deep colors are attached to the marionette strings. One harness is empty.

The narration is written as a monologue for the machine over a background of sparse sounds punctuated with silences. The machine thinks aloud, announces its findings about manners, mores, and emotions. The people respond accordingly in duets, trios, or ensembles. One of the announcements is about ideal mates, which motivates a duet that is mechanical, ironic, and macabre. The various dances run a gamut of emotional colors and ideas, always resolving with a leitmotif done in unison.

The Prodigal enters and tries to relate to various people. He does a duet with a boy, who suddenly is not taking inspiration from the machine but is following the Prodigal's movement. The Prodigal cuts the strings of this boy, who then goes berserk and finally falls limp. The Prodigal puts him back in the empty harness, and he functions again quite happily. The Prodigal exits. Blackout.

Scene III. Somewhere in a City.
A group of dancers, with faces blocked out by gauze, wear masks on the backs of their heads, all of which look individual. The Prodigal has a series of encounters. At the end of each, he is surrounded, swallowed up, or overwhelmed by a mass of uniform gauze faces. Each group wants to absorb him or crush him. Each group would have a particular characteristic — one of play, one of drinking, etc. The people in the background would maintain a monotonous ground base, which would stop and start in counterpoint to the actions of the focal group. Some of these sequences would be in silence, or to electronic sound or to voice, etc. From time to time, a girl, pinspotted, wanders through aimlessly, always at a distance, and disappears. The group slowly drifts offstage, leaving the girl alone. Only the Prodigal is onstage with her. They draw together and do a warm, touching duet. In finding her, he seems to find himself. But at the end of the dance, in a final embrace, he brushes her long hair forward to reveal a simpering mask on the back of her head. Simultaneously, heads with similar masks thrust in at him from the wings and from various levels of the stage. They begin to converge on him. He flees. Blackout.

Scene IV. Same as Scene I. *The Home.*

The Prodigal enters. The formal dance, the ritual, begins again. But this time the faces of the family are not covered with gauze. The real faces are there, the stick masks covering and then revealing the reality. The Prodigal takes up his own mask, and all do a dance of formal celebration, where the masks are used as an implement of design, while the people relate to each other as individuals. The Prodigal has returned.

Pauline Koner
INTRINSIC DANCE

Paul Taylor

DOWN WITH CHOREOGRAPHY

I

A lot of dance writers, it seems, neglect to write about what most people notice first when they go to see dancing. The writers go on about dance theories, dance history, the costumes, the music, the choreography, and even the audience. In short, everything but the thing that all dancing depends on first and last. It is time more should be said about the dancer.

Because I am closest to the members of my own company and find it easy to get enthusiastic about them, I would like to say a few things about Bettie de Jong, Elizabeth Walton, Dan Wagoner, Sharon Kinney, Danny Williams, Molly Moore, Karen Brooke, and Carolyn Adams. I do not intend to give a detailed exposé on these fine people, though that could be an interesting possibility. I just want to mention one or two things that you cannot help noticing when you work with them.

More often than not, the kind of dance we work on together turns out to be dependent on these different dancers as individuals. Sometimes their limitations are as interesting as their strong points. The finest choreography in the world does not mean a thing if the dancers are not suited to it and they look terrible. That figures.

A dancer is involved in learning to execute a dance movement precisely in shape and time. A dancer is occupied with placement, stage spacing, the quality of a leap, the softness of a foot — whether a movement goes out to the audience or spirals inward upon itself. These are some of the things a dancer is concerned with, but actually what we see is more than a foot or a curved back. We see an

91

individual, and we see what that individual is. All this exact training and dance stylization cannot abstract a body into a nonentity. A person is going to be revealed. Vanity, generosity, insecurity, warmth are some traits that have a way of coming into view. This is especially true of the kind of dance that, instead of representing specific characters, features dancing itself.

Because the body does not lie, people remark on the friendliness of Elizabeth Walton's dancing. She IS friendly. Her warmth, the way she goes out to people, spills over into the way she dances. Her body does not lie. With a little prompting she can reveal qualities of a different nature. For one dance, she needed only to hear about the female preying mantis to understand what a predatory nature looks and feels like. Or take, for instance, *Aureole*. Her hips speak truly. They are the hips of an innocent satyress.

These eight dancers are not exactly like tubes of paint with which to cover the canvas of space. Not exactly. They have character and personality, which they ASSERT. They have individual traits, and just when you think you know how to handle them they CHANGE. Not like canvas that stays stretched once and for all. They sometimes get fat or discouraged or both. They acquire feelings of inadequacy. They have birthdays. On the other hand, they develop surprising and unexpected resources in their range.

An admirable and fairly unique quality of Dan Wagoner is his weight. Not in poundage so much, although he is no mosquito, — but in the way his movements are weighted. It looks as if he were pressing against heavy water rather than air. The effect is quite different from the kind of dancing that gives the illusion of flitting or floating. The viewer is involved in seeing the energy that presses into the floor or lifts out of it. This is a quality of his that shows consistently, whether he is moving slowly or quickly, in the air or on all fours. You see him and are glad that gravity can be a dancer's partner.

His is not the kind of body that will twist into a pretzel or bend double and inside out. It is a typically masculine body — solid and a bit tight in the hips. There is no use trying to make him into a twisting

mosquito. Who wants to see one, anyway? Solidity can be a limitation that works as an asset.

Because of the way I work, Dan Wagoner has another asset, which is his patience or understanding or whatever you call it when a dancer is willing to go through an unusually long and involved process of making a dance. When I start a dance, I rarely know how it is going to turn out. I just start and work in an impermanent, unorganized way. Then I go back to clarify a line that may have come to the surface. I have no qualms about changing music or dancers or throwing the whole thing out entirely. As you may guess, this routine can become disappointing to a dancer, who has worked hard and long on something that later gets erased. Especially if he feels comfortable in it. Dan is usually magnanimous in these matters. He is remarkably fast to learn anything new, which is fortunate because he may go through twenty or thirty different arrangements before we arrive at the performance one. Part of his quickness to memorize long sequences may be due to his analytical mind and part, perhaps, to the training he had in medical science before he became a dancer. If it looks as if he knows what he is doing on stage, it is because he does.

Anything Bettie de Jong may do, no matter how trivial, is usually accompanied by one of the other dancer's explaining to the rest: "Bettie is different; she is Dutch." Actually, she is from reed-land. She happens to be taller than the other girls, but even if she were the same height, she would look taller. In dance formations on stage, when you do not want her to look the tallest, you put her upstage of the others because being in the distance will make her appear shorter. Or you put her downstage so the audience will assume she just looks the tallest because she is the closest. No problem.

Blond and slender, she creates a sensation whether she dances at the Bellas Artes in Mexico City or in Paris. Evidently, she does not need her looks to be effective, though, as she proved in *Insects and Heroes* and in *Three Epitaphs* in which — unpardonably — she was entirely covered, face and all. Surprisingly (but then, she is Dutch), she can do comedy. It has nothing at all to do with her "sense of hu-

mor." She understands the absurd, and her body can translate it.

In spite of all these bonus qualities, she is a slow learner. My own particular dances never come naturally to her. Rehearsals become a siege of endurance for both of us. It does not matter, because her interest in dancing never lags, and she is always ready to try the most unlikely of arrangements. So, come performance time, she blossoms forth.

Fairly regularly, Bettie de Jong will speak of something she calls "organic dance." The rest of us always laugh and tease her about this phrase, but we know what she means, and it is worth mentioning. This "organic" has nothing to do with health food. She is referring to body logic or the way movements are put together so that they are joined functionally. Theoretically, almost any sequence of movements is possible to dance, but there are those that will feel better (though not necessarily easier) to a dancer because of their peculiar kind of muscle logic. An "un-organic" dance phrase would be one containing an extraneous movement, a foreign insertion, which prevents the body from following its natural muscular path. This insertion may seem an appropriate idea for what the choreographer is trying to say, but it remains only an idea if it does not fit into the physical logic of the phrase. It will stop the dancing. It will look false and it will usually feel false to the dancer. It is like those real plants at florists that have convincing plastic blossoms wired on. You sense there is something wrong, somewhere.

There are some dancers who achieve a kind of crystal clarity in their dancing. Perhaps it is because of clean line and precise timing. It is not usually a natural quality, but comes after years of exactitude and self-discipline. This crystal quality can often dazzle an audience with its beauty, but it is often coupled with a certain iciness. Though Sharon Kinney has the clarity, what makes her remarkable is that she also has warmth. She is a kind of heart-shaped crystal.

She is appealing in the way the look of a small child astonishes and touches us with its fragile innocence. But Sharon Kinney, in private life, is Mrs. John Binder, and though she may have small bones and enormous eyes and a child's lightness, these disarming

Tracer: Paul Taylor, Bettie de Jong

features only mask prodigious strength and maturity.

I have to curb a natural tendency to make bird dances for her, or at least curb calling them bird dances in front of her, because she has a curious dislike for anything feathered.

Her speedy grasp of new combinations, which rivals Dan Wagoner's, is something she came into the company with. The happiest satisfaction for the other dancers and me and for Helen Alkire, her teacher at Ohio State University, has been watching her develop from the company "baby" into the old pro she is now after four United States and five foreign tours.

Danny Williams, Molly Moore, Karen Brooke, and Carolyn Adams are the newer members of my company, and for that reason, rather than their considerable innate talents, they have been eased into dance roles as gently, under the circumstances, as possible. At first they had to learn several dances at once — dances that were not choreographed on them. This is a harder task in many ways than being in on the initial working out of a piece. They were thrown together with people whose quirks and working habits were unfamiliar to them and vice versa. It always takes a while for dancers to become used to each others' timings, dancewise and emotionally. For all new members, there is a difficult spell when they are not sure if they will be able to manage and are not sure what the others think of them. This time has its double insecurities, as the choreographer — in turn — is trying to find the best way to bring out the new dancers' best qualities and is trying to discover the points at which criticism will help or hinder. Depending on the individual dancer, it seems best sometimes not to criticize very much rather than risk destroying the dancer's belief in himself. Other dancers seem to ask for an iron hand and may even perform at their best if you get them angry enough. However, there is a point of no return between dancer and director. In the touring concert field, where holding a company together depends on things besides unemotional cash, there is a very fine balance to be attained concerning mutual respect between working cohorts. A lot depends on all parties' abilities to cope with one another in difficult situations. A quick calm-down after a flare-up is

96

most helpful. For the record — but without going into details — let me say that these four dancers possess superbly controlled danders. We cope.

Martha Graham was once talking to a cab-driver, who said that he liked dancing fine; what he could not stand was choreography. That seems sensible. Some dances look like "choreography," because the dancers are not allowed to become their most interesting stage selves. I like to think of a dance as a vehicle, not necessarily for one star, but for everybody. You try to find aspects in individual dancers that can be exploited. That is what people are for — to be used. They like it. Merce Cunningham manages to do this by manipulating his dancers to move through space in a fairly democratic way. Not all lined up in a circle with a big cheese in the middle. Martha Graham does it by spookily knowing what kind of dramatic projection is the bailiwick of each of her dancers. This is what I call a group vehicle. Up with dancers; down with choreography.

II

How would I describe a dance that I had been commissioned to produce with unlimited funds — providing I used the theme of the Prodigal Son?

Although I like the idea, especially the part about the unlimited funds, I am not sure how I would plan it. Maybe I would not plan it at all. All the ideas I have for dances, carefully written down when I wake up at night thinking of things like that, seem awful in the morning.

I think the father and son characters would present a problem right off if one did not depend on program notes. George Balanchine once remarked on the impossibility of showing who is the mother-in-law in a dance. Fathers and sons are hard, too.

As for costumes and scenery and lights, I like to leave them to the designers. It seems a good idea, and a more productive one, to leave the designers alone. Just let them see the dance as many times as they like, answer their questions, and leave them to work it out in their own way. The trick is to select the right designer for the right

dance. If the results do not seem suitable, do not force the designer to do something he does not believe in. Just try another designer. The same for composers. This is where those unlimited funds come in handy.

As for the style of this imaginary project, to me, it would depend on what style I had been working in previously. It is not such a problem to gravitate into a style and continue to do dances in that style. It is harder to keep up a continuous change from one work to another. I like the idea of change, not entirely for variety's sake, but for the sake of the people in the concert audience, who may have to sit through a whole evening of one choreographer's work. If one dance is presented in a particular style and that is developed fully, it is not so interesting to reiterate. A painter is looked on suspiciously if he changes styles too often, but a choreographer is working in the theatre. The time element is different. I would like to change styles for each dance, but that is difficult. If you try to change style completely, often as not, it turns out a LITTLE different. That is something, anyway.

But "style" is a word that has several meanings, and perhaps I had better explain specifically what it means to me. Some styles, or areas, I have worked in and which I would probably not use for the Prodigal Son are:

The archaic flat style. The body is seen either flat front or flat sideways or both at the same time. In a way, the dancer is seen two-dimensionally, like a shadow puppet. My *Three Epitaphs* and *Tablet* are in the flat style. It is a paradox that some painters try to make two-dimensional paintings look like three, and some dance-makers try to make three-dimensional dancers look like two. I have been trying to get out of that style. It is too flat.

Another style I tried (in *Rebus* and *Junction* and the plague section of *Insects and Heroes*) could be related to action painting. I call it dance scribbling. The idea is to see action rather than shape or line. It works best for fast movement. It is very difficult to get the dancers to do it, because the movements must first be broken down into positions in order to be taught. Then the dancers have to get rid of the

99

Insects and Heroes: Paul Taylor Dance Company

positions and just throw themselves into the movement. If they are doing it right, the viewer says: "This is something! But what is it?" It looks anything but two-dimensional. But it can be a terrific mess.

After that scribbling style, I thought perhaps it was clean-up time, and I worked on *Tracer* and *Aureole.* Their style is more lyric and acceptable. Everybody knows what "lyric" means — long arms. It was interesting for me, because most of my dancers have short arms. Now they looked very lyric and long and lovely. So it seemed to be time to do an ugly dance.

Scudorama is less concerned with style than with a slightly vulgar look. The nasty things the dancers do are related, in my mind at least, to Dante's *Inferno,* which he wrote in the coarse vernacular, rather than his *Paradiso,* which he wrote in a loftier manner. It is a dance that includes uncouth gesture in its movement vocabulary, and its style is intentionally unstylish.

I would not like to say if my Prodigal Son project would be serious or comic. It would depend on many things. I like to work on a piece with an open mind — or call it a full palette. You leave as many possibilities open as you can, such as:

MOVEMENT. A range from complete stillness through the kind of exaggerated slow movement one sees in the hand of a clock, on through the fastest steps the body is capable of doing.

LINE. A range from the kind of body line that goes out through the limbs in a direct, long line toward the audience, through the kind of line that is distorted and connected with what is called "in-dancing."

SPACE. Used by inches or used infinitely. A dance can seem to be happening out in the wings as well as on the part of the stage the audience can see.

This full palette includes possibilities of stage design, titles, and everything else that can be part of a dance. Once the mind is open to this idea, the really helpful part is the restrictions. You decide what not to do. You eliminate. You try everything you can and then you eliminate. As in one section of *Ivesiana,* George Balanchine eliminated the idea of having the girl soloist ever touch the floor.

I might start with some kind of idea about the Prodigal Son, but I would not guarantee how it would turn out, because I would have to see what happened on the way. Start with too rigid an idea, stick to it, and there is a good chance the dance will become forced and lifeless. I would rather follow up an aspect that I came across in the actual rehearsals — something I did not think of originally. The aim is to do the most magical work you can — to permit the chain reaction of movement ideas, which spring from the original concept. The mind tends to think in a logical way, but magic is not logical. If dance is too logical, it becomes expected and predictable; then it can lose its life.

On the other hand, it might be interesting to start with the idea of making a lifeless, predictable dance and see where that takes you. There are no rules; just decisions. It is even possible, they say, to eliminate decisions if you adhere to the idea of making dances entirely by chance. Speaking of chance, it would seem that it is one of the most misunderstood of working methods. To those who make use of it, it has nothing to do with improvisation and is simply a way of broadening one's palette. Each person's working methods are his own business, and it is a mistake to evaluate a dance by the choreographer's way of arriving at it. Personally, I like what Edwin Denby said Lou Harrison said about chance: "I'd rather chance a choice than choose a chance."

To be free to choose from a full palette, no matter how unusual the results, has always been the prerogative of the modern dance. Modern dance? To me modern dance is a license to do what I feel is worth doing, without somebody saying that I can't do it because it does not fit into a category.

But back to the Prodigal Son and his father. I would start out with some wishy-washily formed idea, give it up if a better one appeared, perhaps attempt to break out of a previous style. I would try to broaden one part of the palette while allowing another part to drop off, and hope to find a compatible composer, designer, and lighter, who would add their own dimensions. I would try not to forget the individual dancers and their importance to my group vehicle.

101

One idea that I would start with and attempt to achieve, no matter how ruthlessly, is the idea that the stage should become a magic place and unbelievably beautiful in a curious new way that cannot be described, but would cause the viewer to say Yes, uh-huh, yes!

CONTRIBUTORS

CONTRIBUTORS

JOSÉ LIMÓN
"A man of dignity," said his citation for the Capezio Award in 1964, "whose years of intense struggle have culminated in his position as indisputably the foremost male dancer in the field of the American modern dance." Born in Mexico, José Limón knew many years of struggle before he became a leading dancer for Doris Humphrey and eventually had his own company, with Miss Humphrey as artistic director. With his group, he has toured Europe, South America, and the Orient under the auspices of the United States State Department. For many years Mr. Limón has headed the faculty of the Connecticut College School of Dance. He holds an honorary doctorate from Wesleyan University. In 1964 he was named artistic director of the American Dance Theatre, a company sponsored by the New York State Council on the Arts to serve as a repository for the repertory of the American modern dance.

ANNA SOKOLOW
Known as one of the most dynamic and uncompromising of the modern dance choreographers, Anna Sokolow began her career as a member of the Martha Graham company, forming her own group in 1937. She has worked in Mexico for the government's Ministry of Fine Arts, and in Israel, both with the Yemenite company Imbal and with her own ensemble of actor-dancers. In addition to choreographing for her New York company, Miss Sokolow has created dances for the Broadway theatre and for the Robert Joffrey Ballet. She has been in charge of training in movement for actors for the

Lincoln Center Repertory Theatre since its inception. In 1962 she received the Dance Magazine Award for a career "distinguished by integrity and creative boldness" and for her recent works, which "have opened the road to a penetratingly human approach to the jazz idiom."

ERICK HAWKINS

A graduate of Harvard (Greek literature and art), Erick Hawkins was a member of the American Ballet before 1938, when he joined the Martha Graham company and became its leading male dancer. Since 1957 he has had his own group, for which he creates dances in close collaboration with musician Lucia Dlugoszewski and designer Ralph Dorazio. The company has toured extensively in the United States and has appeared in Paris. The philosopher F. S. C. Northrop has described the dances of Erick Hawkins as evoking "the proud pleasure of being splendidly justified in living." The dancing of them he calls "unique butterfly poetry."

DONALD McKAYLE

In 1963 the Capezio Award cited Donald McKayle "for his translation of deeply rooted American folk materials . . . into theatre dances of interracial cast which faithfully reflect life in our land." A student of Martha Graham, he danced also in the companies of Anna Sokolow and Merce Cunningham. Since 1951 he has created works for his own company, as well as for television and the Broadway stage. His most recent contribution to the latter was *Golden Boy*.

ALWIN NIKOLAIS

The Director of the Henry Street Playhouse Dance Company not only choreographs his own theatre pieces but composes their musical (usually electronic) scores as well. In addition to showing his company on their own stage at the Playhouse, Mr. Nikolais has presented them at festivals in Montreal and Spoleto. His works have been seen on television films made in Canada, England, and Italy, and are known to a large public (tremendous for modern dance) through

seven appearances on the Steve Allen Show. Mr. Nikolais has received commissions for new theatre works from the University of Illinois, the American Dance Festival, and the Montreal Arts Festival. In 1964 he held a Guggenheim Fellowship, and in 1965 he was commissioned by the Walker Art Foundation to create a new piece for the Tyrone Guthrie Theatre in Minneapolis.

PAULINE KONER

When she was thirteen, Michel Fokine said, "In her, the soul dances." Her career has ever since inspired similar phrases. At first a concert soloist, Miss Koner joined the company of José Limón in 1946, creating leading roles in many of the finest works of Limón and of Doris Humphrey. She has choreographed for her own group since 1949, and has become known also as a teacher, especially for her course in the art of performing, which she has given at Jacob's Pillow as well as at the Connecticut College School of Dance. In 1965 Pauline Koner spent six months in Japan, teaching and performing, as the recipient of a Fulbright-Hayes Lecturers' Grant. She is now on the faculty of the newly formed North Carolina School of the Arts.

PAUL TAYLOR

In 1957 Paul Taylor's New York concert received a review consisting of a blank white space, signed at the bottom with the critic's initials. In one dance Mr. Taylor just stood still from the time the curtain rose until it fell. It was, another critic later remarked, "something he had to get out of his system." Since then, both he and his dancers have moved a great deal — on stages throughout the United States and Europe. Mr. Taylor had first planned to be a painter. When he changed arts, he danced first with Merce Cunningham and then with Martha Graham. He has been the recipient of a Guggenheim Fellowship in choreography and of a number of commissions, including one from Spoleto's Festival of Two Worlds.

theatre pieces, but I don't like at all any implication that the substance of dance rests wholly in this area. It does not.)

One could attack Scene One by slanting it toward the psychological implications. A relatively few years ago, it would have been expected to have the symbolism of the umbilical cord. Such a scene would likely start with the mother doing a sort of rocking dance, while knitting a thing from an endless, thick strand of cord. The finished end of the knitting could trail offstage. There it is pulled and caused to unravel as fast as the mother knits. It is the son who does the pulling, and in this act he is drawn onstage, revealing himself as the culprit. Then the brothers come in, getting enmeshed in the cord; whereupon there could be a sort of cat's cradle or even a maypole dance. The son continues to be engaged more in unraveling than constructing. The whole thing comes to a climax in a tug-of-war dance with the same cord. Obviously, it eventually breaks, catapulting the son out of the family orbit.

In all this, the father could be busily engaged with some sort of phallic symbolism, if he cannot manage being the symbol himself.

Some would think that, because of the cord-prop involvement, this would be my cup of tea. It isn't! Even if they put the scene on Mars.

There is another way I would not do *The Prodigal Son,* even though it approaches the abstract-expressionist point of view. The son would be in a bulk of bright yellow material against a panel of lavender. The mother would be in a huge, amorphous swath of purple; the father on stilts in an elongated blue. The brothers are bound together in a single large sack of rust-colored stuff, with their heads almost buried in it. Their background is bright green and chartreuse with streaks of sea blue, pale blue, and fiery red. The brothers manipulate this stuff in jagged, spastic gestures. The mother undulates; the father rises and sinks. The son makes clear, clean sculptural gestures, occasionally dashing into mother's swath of lavender — and brothers' rust. There are mixtures of all these stuffs, but the yellow is always more active and precise until an actual separation happens. The motion of all this color would furnish the detail of

Alwin Nikolais
NO MAN FROM MARS

71

Vaudeville of the Elements: choreography, Alwin Nikolais (photo: Eric Sutherland: Walker Art Center)